SOCIETY FOR NEW TESTAMENT STUDIES
MONOGRAPH SERIES

GENERAL EDITOR
MATTHEW BLACK, D.D., F.B.A.

8

THE PURPOSE OF THE BIBLICAL GENEALOGIES WITH SPECIAL REFERENCE TO THE SETTING OF THE GENEALOGIES OF JESUS

THE PURPOSE OF THE BIBLICAL GENEALOGIES

WITH SPECIAL REFERENCE TO THE SETTING OF THE GENEALOGIES OF JESUS

MARSHALL D. JOHNSON
Department of Religion, Wartburg College
Waverly, Iowa

CAMBRIDGE
AT THE UNIVERSITY PRESS
1969

Published by the Syndics of the Cambridge University Press
Bentley House, 200 Euston Road, London N.W.1
American Branch: 32 East 57th Street, New York, N.Y.10022

Library of Congress Catalogue Card Number: 69-10429
Standard Book Number: 521 07317 0

Printed in Great Britain
at the University Printing House, Cambridge
(Brooke Crutchley, University Printer)

CONTENTS

Preface *page* vii

Abbreviations ix

PART I: THE PURPOSE OF THE OLD TESTAMENT GENEALOGIES

1 Genealogies in the Pentateuch 3

A *The older sources: J, E, D* 3

B *The Priestly Narrative* 14

2 Genealogies in Ezra-Nehemiah and Chronicles 37

A *The relation between Ezra-Nehemiah and Chronicles* 37

B *The purpose of the genealogies of Ezra-Nehemiah* 42

C *The relation between I Chron. 1–9 and the narrative* 44

D *The three types of material in I Chron. 1–9* 55

E *The genealogies of Judah and Levi* 69

F *A Note on I Chron. 1* 73

G *Summary* 74

3 Summary: The Purpose of the Old Testament Genealogies 77

PART II: LATER JEWISH GENEALOGIES AND THE GENEALOGIES OF JESUS

4 The Narrowing of Genealogical Interest in Later Judaism 85

A *The concern for genealogical purity* 87

B *Genealogical speculation on the ancestry of the Messiah* 115

5 The Genealogy of Jesus in Matthew *page* 139

A *The question of methodology* 139

B *The setting of Matt. 1: 1–17 and its purpose* 146

1 *Evidence from details of the text* 146
The four women

2 *Evidence from the structure of Matt. 1: 2–17* 189

3 *Summary and conclusion: the Midrashic character of the Matthean genealogy* 209

C *The relation between the Matthean genealogy and the gospel of Matthew* 210

6 The Genealogy of Jesus in Luke 229

A *Jesus as Son of God* 235

B *Jesus as Prophet* 240

7 Summary and Conclusion 253

APPENDIXES

1 Methodology in the Study of Old Testament Chronology 259

2 The Chronology of the Priestly Narrative in Tabular Form 262

3 The Ancestry of Elijah in Later Jewish Sources 266

4 The Ancestry of Tamar in Later Jewish Tradition 270

5 A Neglected Manuscript Bearing on the Genealogies of Jesus 273

Bibliography 276

Index of passages cited 289

Index of authors 307

PREFACE

A comprehensive survey of the purpose of the biblical genealogies has hitherto never been written. This categorical statement holds true in spite of the scholarly studies on various aspects of genealogical interest in the Old and New Testaments which have been appearing with increasing frequency in recent years. The present work is intended to offer a synoptic view of the purpose of the biblical genealogies from the earliest occurrences of the form in the J-strand of the Pentateuch through the genealogies of Jesus in Matthew and Luke. It seemed necessary also, especially as a means of setting the stage for a discussion of the New Testament genealogies, to give an account of genealogical interest in late Judaism (chapter 4) in which most of the relevant sources are identified. In this and the following sections, I have relied strongly on the *Kommentar* of Strack–Billerbeck. This statement of my objective, however, does limit the scope to some extent: I have only briefly alluded to genealogical interest in Graeco-Roman sources and have referred to the early Christian interpretations of the genealogies of Jesus only when such information seemed to illumine the purpose of these genealogies themselves (a study of the Christian interpretation of Mt. 1 and Lk. 3 in the second to fourth centuries A.D. would seem to be especially rewarding). Finally, I have not commented on the references to genealogies in the Pastoral Epistles (I Tim. 1: 4; Tit. 3: 9) or Heb. 7: 6.[1]

It is our special concern in the present study to determine the purpose of the biblical genealogies within their literary contexts, that is, to ascertain the extent to which the genealogical form was utilized by the author of the particular book or source to communicate his characteristic theological convictions. This has necessitated a considerable reliance on the method of editorial criticism, especially in dealing with Chronicles and the New Testament. In general, I have attempted to demonstrate

[1] I would endorse the view of G. Kittel ("Die γενεαλογίαι der Pastoralbriefe", *ZNW*, xx (1921), 49–69) that 1 Tim. 1:4 and Tit. 3:9 are references to midrashic genealogical discussion in Judaism such as is described below in chapters 4 and 5.

that the hand of the respective editor/redactor can be traced in the genealogical sections of both the Old and New Testaments. With regard to the genealogies of Matthew and Luke, the method of editorial criticism can illumine the setting of the genealogies of Jesus in the early Christological traditions.

The generally accepted conclusions of literary criticism have been presupposed (the four-source theory of the composition of the Pentateuch and the four-source theory regarding the writing of the Gospels), even though some recent scholarship has challenged a too facile acceptance of such hypotheses in detail.

Again, it has been my intention to study the relevant material inductively, that is, to allow the conclusions to arise from the exegesis rather than to bring to the evidence a theory to be tested. Even if at times the material has only reluctantly and partially yielded new hypotheses, it is hoped that the following chapters will serve to bring into focus this most neglected of biblical subjects and even possibly to afford fresh insight into certain aspects of the biblical text.

Throughout the course of this study, the patient counsel of Professor W. D. Davies, my adviser for the doctoral dissertation, has left me with a heavy debt of appreciation. His learned guidance has had its effect on various stages of this work, although any weaknesses remaining in the perspectives and interpretations offered are my own. Similarly, Professor Samuel Terrien has offered his suggestive criticism, especially in regard to Part I, as have also Professors John Knox and J. Louis Martyn. To these men, to my secretarial assistants at Wartburg College, to the readers and printers of Cambridge University Press whose expertise and accuracy are a source of amazement, and especially to my wife, I offer hearty thanks.

M.D.J.

September 1968
Waverly, Iowa

ABBREVIATIONS

A & P	*The Apocrypha and Pseudepigrapha of the Old Testament*, ed. R. H. Charles.
AJSLL	*The American Journal of Semitic Languages and Literature.*
A.M.	*Anno Mundi* (in reckoning dates from the time of creation).
ARN	Aboth of Rabbi Nathan.
b	*The Babylonian Talmud* (before references).
BJRL	*Bulletin of the John Rylands Library.*
BZ	*Biblische Zeitschrift.*
CBQ	*Catholic Biblical Quarterly.*
CD	The Zadokite Fragment (Damascus Document).
CPJ	*Corpus Papyrorum Judaicarum*, ed. V. A. Tcherikover and A. Fuks.
CQR	*Church Quarterly Review.*
DSS	Dead Sea Scrolls.
ET	English translation (of a work originally published in another language).
ET	*The Expository Times.*
ETL	*Ephemerides Theologicae Lovanienses.*
EV	English version (used where the English versification of OT passages differs from the Hebrew).
HAT	*Handbuch zum Alten Testament.*
HDB	*Hastings' Dictionary of the Bible.*
HNT	*Handbuch zum Neuen Testament.*
HTR	*Harvard Theological Review.*
HUCA	*Hebrew Union College Annual.*
IB	*The Interpreter's Bible.*
ICC	*The International Critical Commentary.*
IDB	*The Interpreter's Dictionary of the Bible.*
IQS (DSD)	The Manual of Discipline (DSS).
JBL	*Journal of Biblical Literature.*
JBR	*Journal of Bible and Religion.*
JE	*The Jewish Encyclopedia.*
JJS	*Journal of Jewish Studies.*

JNES	*Journal of Near Eastern Studies.*
JTS	*Journal of Theological Studies.*
m	*The Mishnah* (before references).
MGWJ	*Monatsschrift für Geschichte und Wissenschaft des Judentums.*
NTD	*Das Neue Testament Deutsch.*
NTS	*New Testament Studies.*
OTS	*Oudtestamentische Studiën.*
p	*The Palestinian Talmud* (before references).
RB	*Revue Biblique.*
RÉJ	*Revue des Études Juives.*
RQ	*Revue de Qumrân.*
RSR	*Recherches de Sciences Religieuses.*
S–B	Strack–Billerbeck, *Kommentar zum Neuen Testament aus Talmud und Midrasch.*
TDNT	*Theological Dictionary of the New Testament* (trans. of *TWNT*).
TU	*Texte und Untersuchungen.*
TWNT	*Theologisches Wörterbuch zum Neuen Testament.*
VT	*Vetus Testamentum.*
ZAW	*Zeitschrift für die alttestamentliche Wissenschaft.*
ZNW	*Zeitschrift für neutestamentliche Wissenschaft.*
ZTK	*Zeitschrift für Theologie und Kirche.*
ZWT	*Zeitschrift für wissenschaftliche Theologie.*

Other abbreviations are customary or self-explanatory.

PART I

THE PURPOSE OF THE OLD TESTAMENT GENEALOGIES

CHAPTER I

GENEALOGIES IN THE PENTATEUCH

A. THE OLDER SOURCES: J, E, D

Apart from the Yahwistic and Priestly sections of the Pentateuch and the works of the Chronicler, there are only scattered occurrences in the OT of genealogical material. These are most often brief lists or allusions to parentage that serve mainly to identify an individual in a narrative or the author of a prophetic book.[1] At times, to be sure, this genealogical identification also may indicate the individual's status among the nobility. Thus, in Zeph. 1: 1 the prophet's ancestry is traced to a certain Hezekiah who may be identified in the mind of the author with the Judean king.[2] Similarly, Zechariah's lineage is traced to Iddo, who is probably the prominent figure of exilic times mentioned in Neh. 12: 4, 16. Thus it is possible that the keeping of genealogies and pedigrees was of especial importance for the nobility. As a general rule, however, allusions to parentage of OT figures are more brief than these two examples and, in isolation, can provide little information on the character of genealogical records in Israel. For this we must turn to the literary use of genealogies in the great Pentateuchal records of Israel's prehistory and to the work of the Chronicler.

Among the Pentateuchal sources, the lack of genealogical material in D is easily attributed to the nature of that source as primarily a law code to which is prefixed a historical overview of the exodus wanderings.[3] In the E-strand we might expect the

[1] Among such shorter genealogies are I Sam. 1: 1; II Sam. 20: 1; Zeph. 1: 1; and Zech. 1: 1.

[2] Cf. J. P. Hyatt in *Peake's Commentary on the Bible*, rev. ed. by M. Black and H. H. Rowley (1962), p. 640 (561*a*).

[3] Yet there are indications in Deuteronomy of genealogical interest. Cf. the 'third and fourth generation' of Deut. 5: 9 and especially Deut. 23: 3, 4, 9 (ET, 23: 2, 3, 8), where it is said that Ammonites and Moabites are to be excluded from 'the assembly of Yahweh' for a period of ten generations. That this is intended at least to some degree in a literal fashion is indicated by the *positive* sense of *v.* 9 (8): children of the third generation of the Edomite may enter the assembly. It is also noteworthy that in all such

matter to be different, since it is a more extended narrative, reaching back in our composite Pentateuch to the patriarchal stories. However, unless we accept the possibility that traces of an Elohist primeval history are to be found in Gen. 1–11[1] we are able to identify nothing at all in E that can be called genealogical in the proper sense. This leaves to be considered what are probably the earliest and the latest traditions of the Pentateuch, J and P, as the only sources in which actual genealogies have been preserved.

The Yahwistic source

(*a*) *Tribal genealogies.* In the J-strand, leaving aside for the moment the genealogy of Cain in Gen. 4: 17–22, the genealogical material appears to be simply a classification of Semitic tribes around Palestine as descendants or kinsmen of Abraham, the Semite *par excellence*. In addition to considering Moab and the Ammonites as sons of Lot,[2] we find a list of the sons of Nahor

passages only here is the term דור used of personal generations. That this legislation in Deut. 23 implies the keeping of genealogical records is suggested also by the fact that the passage is interpreted genealogically in Neh. 13: 1 ff., where the allusion reveals a use of the combined sources of the Pentateuch.

[1] A forceful argument for the representation of E in the primeval history of Gen. 1–11 has been adduced by S. Mowinckel in *The Two Sources of the Predeuteronomic History (JE) in Gen. 1–11* (1937), pp. 44–61 *et passim*. Together with various bits of narrative material, he considers the genealogical fragments in Gen. 4: 25–6; 5: 28*b*–29; 9: 18–19; 10: 8–14, 24–30; 24: 10; and 31: 53 to be remnants of a genealogical system that extended from creation to Abraham. These fragments, he contends, were derived from the original source used by P (pp. 69–72). Since only snatches of this hypothetical Elohistic genealogy remain, he does not elaborate on its function by a comparison with the parallel genealogies of J and P. Mowinckel, from the references listed above, traced only the following remains: Adam—Seth—Enosh— . . . —Lamech—Noah—Shem, Ham, Japheth. Against the assigning of these elements to E is the fact that in the undoubted E sections of Genesis—where the genealogical form might have been used—E prefers extended narration (e.g. Gen. 30: 1–3, 6, 17–20, 21). We may conclude that Mowinckel has further demonstrated the complexity of the J material in the primeval history, even showing the diversity of genealogical material, but he has not proved that this is to be accounted for by finding E in Gen. 1–11. See further W. F. Albright's reviews of Mowinckel's study in *JBL*, LVII (1938), 230–1; LVIII (1939), 91–103.

[2] Gen. 19: 36–8.

as a group of twelve Aramaic tribes situated in the territory northeast and east of Palestine (Gen. 22: 20–4). Similarly, descendants of Abraham by his second wife, Keturah, are actually the eponyms of a group of northwest Arabian tribes (Gen. 25: 1–6). A comparison of these J passages with the names in the Table of Nations (Gen. 10) reveals the fact that several attempts at a genealogical classification of the same tribes were made in the earliest sources that make up the present text of the Pentateuch: (1) Aram, according to J, is a grandson of Nahor; in Gen. 10: 22, however, he is the fifth and youngest son of Shem. (The subordinate position of the Arameans in both genealogies may be an indication of the Palestinian orientation of the lists.) (2) Uz, the first-born son of Nahor in J, hence a principal Nahorite tribe, is a son of Aram, thus a grandson of Shem, in P. So also there are names in the Keturah list (Gen. 25: 1–6) that are suspiciously similar to those in Gen. 10. (3) It is striking that יקשן, second son of Abraham and Keturah in 25: 2 f., and יקטן in 10: 25 f., both occupy prominent places in these genealogies in terms of the number of their descendants that is traced.[1] Moreover, neither is first-born and Joktan is four generations removed from Shem. It seems probable, therefore, that these two names are variants of one. (4) Most interesting is the parallel grouping of Dedan and Sheba as sons of Jokshan, thus grandsons of Abraham, in 25: 3, but as sons of Raamah, great-grandsons of Ham, in 10: 7.[2] (5) Finally, there is the similarity between אשורם in 25: 3 and אשור in 10: 11 where it is intended as a place-name, and the אשור of 10: 22, a son of Shem.[3] This evidence indicates that several attempts at classifying neighboring Semitic tribes by means of genealogies were made in ancient Israel. Not only did the Priestly section of the Table of Nations overlap with the

[1] Cf. J. Simons, 'The Table of Nations (Gen. 10): Its General Structure and Meaning', *OTS*, x (1954), 168 f.

[2] Cf. Ezek. 38: 13; in Isa. 21: 13 f., Jer. 25: 23, and perhaps Ezek. 25: 18, Dedan is linked with Tema, a location in northwest Arabia. Cf. also Job 6: 19; Gen. 25: 3 (LXX); 36: 11, 15; Ezek. 27: 20, 22 (the latter presupposes the Table of Nations in Gen. 10).

[3] Cf. John Skinner, *A Critical and Exegetical Commentary on Genesis* (ICC), rev. ed. (1925), pp. 350 f., who sees no relation between these two forms; however the identification is accepted by Eduard Meyer, *Die Israeliten und ihre Nachbarstämme* (1906), pp. 320 ff.

Yahwistic Nahorite and Keturite genealogies, but also the triple occurrence of Sheba[1] and perhaps אשור,[2] and the duplication of Jokshan (Joktan) within supposedly J material[3] suggests that a third genealogy, partly preserved as fragments in the Table of Nations, was intended to account for the same tribes. These overlapping genealogical schemes indicate the flexibility—and perhaps apologetic purpose—of the genealogical form. In J (25: 1–6) Sheba and Dedan are grandsons of Abraham; in P (10: 7) they are non-Semitic. This apparent arbitrariness demonstrates that the OT genealogies, at least in dealing with peoples somewhat removed from the time or place of composition, were neither based on definite, precise historical tradition nor basically 'the expression in quasi-historical form of an old mythology'.[4] If they were, such classifications would not have been so variegated. Rather, this type of genealogy is based on strong sense of blood-kinship, both within the tribe and among related tribes.[5] If the tribe is all of one blood, according to this reasoning, then the son is of the blood and thus of the tribe of the father. In a patriarchal society one could, therefore, by using the logical process in reverse, describe the existing closeness of tribes by assuming a common patronymic ancestor, regardless of what might have been the actual historical origin of the groups involved. A feeling of blood brotherhood which actually existed between two or more tribes or clans was thus traced back by means of genealogies to a common eponym as an expression of existing community. Examples of the actual relationship between tribes or clans determining their genealogical classification are not wanting: Although the clan of Caleb was originally probably non-Israelitic[6] it was incorporated into the tribe of Judah in the Priestly narrative[7] and in the Chronicler's

[1] Gen. 10: 7*b*, 28; 25: 3.

[2] Gen. 10: 11, 22; 25: 3.

[3] Gen. 10: 25 f.; 25: 2.

[4] This is demonstrated by W. Robertson Smith, *Kinship and Marriage in Early Arabia* (new ed. 1903), pp. 24 f.

[5] Smith, *Kinship*, pp. 27 f.; see also Julian Obermann, 'Early Islam', in *The Idea of History in the Ancient Near East*, ed. Robert C. Dentan (1955), pp. 244–7, 253 ff., 290–2 *et passim*; also Roland de Vaux, *Ancient Israel: Its Life and Institutions*, tr. John McHugh (1961), p. 6.

[6] Cf. Num. 32: 13; Josh. 15: 17; Judg. 1: 13; Gen. 36: 11.

[7] Num. 13: 6; 34: 19.

genealogical prologue.[1] Genealogies of the surrounding peoples were used in the same way. A radical change in the pedigree of the Caisite and Kalbite tribes was made as late as the time of the genealogist Abu Jáfen Mohammed ibn Habib (d. A.D. 867) when, as a result of their feud with the Caisites, the Kalbites claimed kinship with the Himyar tribe.[2] Josephus provides similar examples from the Samaritans;[3] others could be adduced from Persian genealogical constructions.[4] We conclude, therefore, that the tribal genealogies of J reflect the degree of closeness felt by various elements within Israelitic tribes to their neighbors at different periods in history. Although the compilers may have considered their constructions to be accurate descriptions of tribal origins, the underlying aim of these genealogies is at once political and apologetic. Also, their literary function in the context of J seems to consist in supplementing and tying together the narrative elements.

(*b*) *The Cainite genealogy*. We have singled out the Cainite list as a special case in J mainly because it is distinguished from the loosely formed tribal genealogies by its linear form; that is, it traces a single line of descent through several generations, rather than purporting to record the various branches of descent as in a genealogical tree. But it is possible also to consider this distinctive genealogy of Gen. 4: 17–22 as a tribal genealogy, i.e. a glorification of the tribe by the tracing of its origins to a primeval father from whom, it may have been believed, sprang all civilization.

The facts which must serve as our point of departure in an attempt to understand the purpose of the Cainite genealogy can be summarized briefly. It is well known that the Sethite

[1] I Chron. 2: 9, 18 ff.; see also R. F. Johnson, 'Caleb', *IDB*, I, 482–3; and de Vaux, *Ancient Israel*, p. 6. Numerous similar examples could be drawn from the Chronicler, e.g. the inclusion of Samuel in the genealogy of the Levites I (Chron. 6: 7–15 [ET, 6: 16–28]) while in the earlier sources (I Sam. 1: 1) he is considered an Ephraimite.

[2] Smith, *Kinship*, pp. 8 f. Examples of manipulating Arabic genealogies to claim closer relationship with Mohammed in early Islam are provided by Obermann, 'Early Islam', pp. 290–305.

[3] See below, p. 108.

[4] Ignaz Goldziher, *Mythology Among the Hebrews*, tr. Russell Martineu (1877), excursus N, pp. 357–9; Obermann, pp. 301 f.

genealogy of Gen. 5 and the Cainite genealogy make use of the same names, or at least are drawn from the same tradition.[1] This can be seen by listing the names in parallel columns:

Gen. 4: 17–22 (Cainite)	Gen. 5 (Sethite)
אדם	אדם
	שת
	אנוש
קין	קינן
חנוך	מהללאל
עירד	ירד
מחויאל	חנוך
מתושאל	מתושלח
למך	למך
	נח
יבל יובל תובל-קין	שמ חם יפת

Apparently, the Mahalalel and Enoch of the Sethite list have been transposed.

There is also the problem of the relation of 4: 25–6, usually considered Yahwistic, to the two longer genealogies. Here the first three names of the Sethite genealogy are given as a kind of anticipation of the Priestly narrative of chapter 5, and the passage serves as a transition between the Cain narrative and the Sethite genealogy.[2] We might, on the basis of form and

[1] Cf. S. H. Hooke, *Middle Eastern Mythology* (1963), p. 127; B. Jacob, *Das erste Buch der Tora* (1934), pp. 167 f.; Mowinckel, *Two Sources*, pp. 10, 14; Skinner, *Genesis*, pp. 138 ff.; U. Cassuto, *A Commentary on the Book of Genesis*, tr. Grace Abrahams (2 vols. 1961–4); Hebrew original (1944), *ad rem.*

[2] Jacob, *Das erste Buch der Tora*, p. 150. The notice in 4: 26*b*, 'at that time men began to call upon the name of Yahweh', indicates that some misplacement has taken place here since already in 4:1–16 the name Yahweh is used, in contrast to the double form, Yahweh-Elohim, in 2: 4*b*–3: 24. Simpson, *The Book of Genesis*, IB, 1 (1952), p. 526, explains this double form as being due to some redactor consistently adding the name Yahweh to the original occurrence of Elohim alone. Others (H. Gunkel, *Genesis* (Göttingen Handkommentar, 5th ed. 1922), pp. 1–4; Mowinckel, *Two Sources*, pp. 44–61) trace the double name to two sources which have been conflated. Jacob, pp. 151 ff., mentions but rejects the old Jewish explanation of Gen. 4: 26*b* as referring to the beginning of idolatry, based on a translation of אז הוחל

literary criticism, postulate the following stages of development in the present text of chapters 4–5:

(1) The earliest was the existence in somewhat independent form of various traditions such as the paradise–creation narrative, the flood legend, the tradition of a tripartite origin of civilization, and various accounts of tribal origins. Among the latter was the Cainite genealogy in much the same form as we have it. In itself, it accounted for the origins of nomadic life—probably the only known civilization among the circles in which the genealogy first circulated. Several such units formed the nucleus of a Judean body of tradition concerning origins—a kind of 'Ur-J', but probably not in written form.

(2) An editor, whom we designate Jr, related the Cainite genealogy to the paradise–creation and fall legends by interpolating the story of the fratricide of Cain, which was possibly at first a personalization of a tribal feud,[1] or, better, an etiological explanation for the worship of Yahweh by the Kenites.[2] At any

as 'damals wurde Entweihung (viz. of the Tetragrammaton) getrieben'. This would fit its context—between the fratricide and the fall—and would accord with the negative connotations of חלל in the OT ('to pierce', 'to undo', 'to desecrate', 'to profane', 'to defile oneself'; cf. Brown–Driver–Briggs, *A Hebrew and English Lexicon of the Old Testament* (1907), pp. 319–21). However, the confusion of the text at this point must be considered; the LXX presupposes זה החל, i.e. 'Enoch began to call on the name of Yahweh'.

[1] This would explain the crude song of Lamech, *vv.* 23–4, which is so similar to the tales and verse of pre-Islamic Arabian story-tellers who 'speak of a past in which terror and violence had reigned supreme, and they speak of this aspect of their past to the exclusion of everything else. They tell of incessant blood feuds and tribal wars, of perpetual deadly struggles between brother tribes, kindred clans, and close neighbors, without ever reflecting upon guilt and merit, right and wrong. In verse, too, the past is spoken of exclusively in its sanguinary, warlike, fratricidal aspect' (Obermann, 'Early Islam', pp. 242 f.; see also his discussion of blood revenge among the Arabs, pp. 253–64).

[2] It is significant that, with one doubtful exception (Num. 24: 21–2), the Kenites are favorably referred to in the OT, and are in I Chron. 2: 55 related to the Rechabites, who were overzealous devotees of Yahweh (Jer. 35). Moreover, from a comparison of Judg. 4: 11 with Num. 10: 29 and Exod. 2: 18, we may deduce that Moses' father-in-law was, according to early traditions, a Kenite and that the Kenites were a clan of the Midianites. If, on the basis of the references cited, we may identify Hobab with the Jethro of Exod. 18: 1–12, we have strong evidence that the Kenites were worshipers of Yahweh from an early period. This, together with the eponymous function of Cain, strongly suggests the original etiological character of the

rate, the fratricide story, like the Cainite genealogy, originally had a function different from that which it is given in the present context. The purpose of the fratricide in Jr was to illustrate the effects of the first sin (Gen. 3) and the genealogy, in turn, took on a pessimistic tone from its context.[1]

Next, Jr made a transition to the flood narrative by means of a genealogy extending to Noah, remnants of which appear in 4: 25–6 and 5: 29. It is of course impossible to postulate with any certainty how Jr traced the line from Enosh to Noah; the Priestly tradition has replaced this part of his work.

(3) P recast the work of Jr, incorporating the Cainite genealogy into the list of the descendants of Seth, possibly in imitation of the stereotyped formula of other sources such as the Babylonian (Sumerian) antediluvian king list.[2] The absence of a fall narrative in P left little purpose for another account of the Cainite traditions. Moreover, in the P narrative Seth could be considered the first-born of Adam, as also in I Chron. 1: 1, Luke 3: 38.[3]

From all this we are led to conclude that the Cainite genealogy in its original form was a more or less self-contained unit and that the attempt to find its original purpose must begin with that recognition.[4] This means, above all, that it must first be

narrative of the fratricide of Cain, which occurs in connection with the cultic worship of Yahweh. Note that this theory of the original purpose of Gen. 4: 1–16 is not dependent on the Kenite hypothesis concerning the origin of the Hebrew worship of Yahweh associated with Gilhany and Budde.

[1] Cf. Charles Hauret, 'Réflexions pessimistes et optimistes sur Gen. 4: 17–24', in *Sacra Pagina*, ed. J. Coppens (1959), pp. 358–65.

[2] On the Sumerian king list see Hooke, *Mythology*, pp. 130 ff.; Thorkild Jacobsen, *The Sumerian King List* (1939), pp. 1–4, 69 ff.; Sidney Smith, *Early History of Assyria* (1928), pp. 17–25; Mowinckel, *Two Sources*, pp. 72–84; Mowinckel, *JBL*, LVIII (1939), 87–91; Albright, *JBL*, LVII (1938), 230–1 and LVIII (1939), 91–103; James Pritchard, ed., *Ancient Near Eastern Texts* (1955), pp. 265 f.

[3] Cf. Sirach 49: 16.

[4] For a similar conclusion reached by an interpretation of the Cainite genealogy itself, see Hauret, 'Réflexions', pp. 348–65; see also Gerhard von Rad, *Genesis*, tr. John H. Marks (1961), pp. 106 ff. A different conclusion is reached by Martin Noth, *Überlieferungsgeschichte des Pentateuch* (1948), pp. 236 f., who considers this a 'secondary' genealogy built around the traditional figures of Cain, Lamech, and perhaps Enoch, rounded off with certain empty (*blosse, künstliche*) names. While Noth's criterion of

considered without regard to its purpose in the present context of chapter 4.

We note first that Cain (קן) is in some way related to the tribe of the Kenites (קיני) who occupied an area in the south of Judah, at least until the time of David and probably later.[1] The name Cain itself is generally taken to mean 'smith', and the Kenite clan is supposed to have been a clan of smiths.[2] Two OT passages provide strong evidence for the assumption that Cain is really the eponymous ancestor of the Kenites:[3] In the oracle of the Kenites in Balaam's prophecy (Num. 24: 21–2) the two terms stand in parallel position and are used as synonyms:

And he looked on the Kenite (הקיני), and took up his discourse, and said 'Enduring is your dwelling place, and your nest is set in the rock; nevertheless Kain (קין) shall be wasted. How long shall Asshur take you away captive?'

And again, in Judg. 4: 11,

וחבר הקיני נפרד מקין מבני חבב חתן משה

And Heber the Kenite had separated from Kain, from the sons of Hobab, father-in-law of Moses.

Here also it is evident that הקיני had described Heber as a member of קין and that בני חבב is in apposition to קין, thus indicating the tribal character of the latter.

Assuming then the eponymous character of קין we are prepared to consider the Cainite genealogy of Gen. 4: 17–22 as a unit of tradition from the Kenites, with which the Judaean Yahwistic editor was acquainted. The body of the genealogy, verse 18, tersely comprehends five generations, the names being derived from traditional sources. Attention is focused on the

determining the 'proper' (*eigentlich*) or 'secondary' character of genealogies (on the basis of whether or not the individual names in the genealogy have their own development in the narrative tradition) may be a working hypothesis for the genealogies of later times, it does not fit the Cainite list. The proof of this is that, according to Noth's theory, a secondary list, being a more or less artificial construction, should have a theological or nationalistic purpose for its compiler. The Cainite genealogy, however, appears originally to have had such a purpose only for the Kenite clans.

[1] Gen. 15: 18–19; Josh. 15: 56–7; Judg. 1: 16; 4: 11; I Sam. 15: 6; 27: 10; 30: 29; I Chron. 2: 55.

[2] See, e.g., S. H. Hooke in *Peake's Commentary on the Bible* (1962), p. 181.

[3] See von Rad, *Genesis*, p. 104; E. Meyer, *Die Israeliten*, p. 219.

first and last members of the list, namely Cain and Lamech. It has been argued that the allusion to Cain building a city (verse 17) is incompatible with the actual nomadic life of the tribe. But there is really no need to excise the reference from the genealogy[1] since Kenite cities are mentioned in I Sam. 30: 29, a passage of early date. There is no reason to suppose that a tribe living on the fringe of a desert could not have developed semi-permanent settlements.[2]

The weight of the genealogy, however, is directed toward its culmination in the three sons of Lamech who are represented as the founders of the various aspects of nomadic civilization, as is indicated by the text itself in stating the significance of Jabal and Jubal:[3] הוא היה אבי. Hence, Lamech's sons represent three 'classes' or callings among the inhabitants of the steppe—sheep-breeders, musicians, and smiths.[4] Moreover, in the limited horizon of the tribe, the narrator could envisage all of civilization under the categories of 'city' dwellers, shepherds, musicians, and metalworkers.[5] This view of the purpose of the genealogy, of course, precludes the notion of a subsequent flood, since it purports to explain the origins of an existing culture. Yet it was probably this tripartite view of the origins of human

[1] So Simpson, *Genesis*, pp. 521 f. It is actually anachronistic to consider this an intrusion into the original text on the basis that 'J would never have represented city life as anterior to the rise of nomadism' (*loc. cit.*). The fact is that at some point in the history of the J-strand it was so considered.

[2] Other evidence for this is given by Hauret in *Sacra Pagina* (1959), p. 361; cf. also Judg. 1: 16–17 and perhaps Josh. 15: 56–7 which can be emended to read 'Zanoah, city of the Kenites'.

[3] Cf. Gunkel, *Genesis*, p. 53.

[4] The terms are those of Mowinckel, *Two Sources*, pp. 11, 21. See also Armin Ehrenzweig, 'Kain und Lamech', *ZAW*, xxxv (1915), 1–11.

[5] See Julius Wellhausen, *Prolegomena to the History of Ancient Israel*, tr. Menzies and Black (Germ. or. 1883) (1957), p. 316. Cf. also George M. Landes, 'Kenites', *IDB*, III, 6–7: 'It is probable that they [the Kenites] bore some resemblance to the modern Arab tribe, the Sleib, who ply their trade ...as traveling smiths or tinkers, more or less following regular trade routes with their asses and tools, and who support themselves by means of their craftsmanship, supplemented by music and divination...Nomadic tribes of metalworkers in the ancient Near East are known from the early second millennium B.C., at least if the famous party of Asiatics depicted on a tomb at Benihasan (nineteenth century B.C.) represents such a group, as their portrayal would seem to indicate...' First-hand accounts of the Solubby (Sleib) are given by Charles M. Doughty, *Travels in Arabia Deserta* (n.d.), I, 324–7.

civilization that prompted the Priestly writer, who represented a much broader view of civilization than did the circles from which the Cainite genealogy emanated,[1] to trace all human life back to Shem, Ham, and Japheth.[2] The genealogy begins with Cain, and culminates with Tubal-Cain,[3] and so takes the form of a great tribal legend. What is most significant for our purpose is that it was precisely the genealogical form which was used to describe the pre-history of the Kenite (Cainite) tribe. And, by incorporating this list into his narrative, the Yahwistic editor was simply following a pattern that was common to the mentality of the ancient world:

> It is...self-evident for the ancient world-view—and this applies as much to other near-eastern peoples and also to the Greeks—that the founders lived in primeval history. And this is quite fitting. For, according to ancient thought, this time determined the existence of the whole world, the essence of all things. God created prototypes for each kind and as a result of the divine promise the species is reborn in ever new individuals. Such as were then created continue as long as the world continues...This involves not only interesting stories about the first ages of man, but also explanations. That which was done in primeval times recurs throughout time; it is basic for all succeeding existence and history.[4]

By way of summary of our discussion thus far, we may note that, in contrast to the lack of interest in genealogies in D and E, J reveals considerable interest. Yet this concern is expressed mainly in the sporadic interpolation into his epic of isolated tribal lists which fit the context of his narrative materials. The

[1] The author of the Cainite genealogy attempted to account for human civilization under the three nomadic callings mentioned above; the Priestly author seems rather to reflect a more sedentary—and therefore more comprehensive—view of existence.

[2] Gen. 5: 32; ch. 10. The culmination of genealogies in a threefold division appears to be characteristic also of the Priestly Toledoth book; see below, pp. 22 ff. In the Priestly genealogical scheme, Terah, who probably is intended to mark the conclusion of an era, has three sons who are later considered to be the ancestors of related Semitic and Aramean tribes (Gen. 11: 27–32; see also Gen. 22: 20–4; Josh. 24: 2).

[3] But note the curious LXX reading at 4: 22, Σελλα δὲ ἔτεκεν καὶ αὐτὴ τὸν Θοβελ, καὶ ἦν σφυροκόπος. This is probably the result of a copyist who heard the verbal translation of the scholar, writing καὶ ἦν for an original קין.

[4] Olof Linton, *Synopsis Historiae Universalis* (Festskrift udgivet af Københavns Universitet) (1957), pp. 21 f. (my trans.).

clearest example of this is the Cainite genealogy, the import of which has been changed from an original glorification of the Kenite tribe to, in the present context, an elaboration of the corrupting effects of the fall—which was recounted immediately before the Cainite material. Other examples of this use of isolated genealogies are the Nahorite list (Gen. 22: 20–4) and that of Keturah (Gen. 25: 1–6). We conclude that behind the genealogical material in J there can be discovered no general system or scheme—in short, no broad *literary* purpose that was utilized for the theology of the Yahwist. Rather, the Yahwist was content simply to record occasional lists which showed the interrelation of a certain number of tribes. A full-blown genealogical system delineating the degrees of relationship obtaining among the individuals in the historical tradition of Israel in which the genealogical form was used for literary purposes was first accomplished by the Priestly historians.

B. THE PRIESTLY NARRATIVE

1. *The Toledoth book*

We turn next to the use of genealogies in the Priestly narrative in the Pentateuch, the source which reveals the most complex and comprehensive genealogical speculation. It begins with the first chapter of the Bible, relating how God created the cosmos in six days. At the close of this account we read the words, אלה תולדות השמים והארץ בהבראם,[1] the first two words of which are repeated several times in Genesis, Exodus, and Numbers to introduce a list of names beginning with a patriarch or tribal father.[2]

The term תולדות itself is the feminine plural noun derived from ילד, 'to bear, bring forth, beget', and as such its most literal translation would be 'begettings'. Most often it occurs in the context of formal genealogies as denoting an account of a man and his descendants or of genealogical calculations for such purposes as that of a military census.[3] The noun is probably closest to the Hithpael of the verb, a *hapax legomenon*, occurring only in Num. 1: 18, where it may be translated, 'to get one's

[1] Gen. 2: 4*a*. [2] See the list of references on pp. 15 f.

[3] E.g. Num. 1: 20–42; I Chron. 1: 29; 5: 7; 7: 9, etc.

descent acknowledged'.[1] The common LXX translation of the term γενέσεις is also noteworthy. The latter is used in classical Greek as the antonym of φθορά, which denotes destruction, ruin, perdition, mortality, the decay of matter, and the like.[2] Thus the connotations of γενέσεις are positive; yet its meaning is elusive, as is to be expected from the varied uses of γίγνομαι, the verb from which it is derived. One would have expected the LXX rather to have used γεννήσεις (from γεννάω) which, even though it appears to have been a less common term in classical Greek, is an almost exact translation of תולדות (from ילד). That γενέσεις instead is the more frequent translation of תולדות[3] may indicate a broader understanding of the latter term than that communicated by our word 'begettings'. Thus the knotty problem of the occurrence of the Toledoth formula in a non-genealogical context at the close of the Priestly creation narrative (Gen. 2: 4*a*) may be mitigated by some such translation as, 'This is the sequence of the origins of the heavens and the earth when they were created'.[4] And yet we must allow for the possibility that in all such places the LXX *intentionally* broadens the connotation of the Hebrew and that therefore γενέσεις in the LXX affords only meager aid in an understanding of תולדות.

As the Priestly source now stands, the formula אלה תולדות is applied to the following persons:

Adam	Gen. 5: 1–32
Noah	6: 9–10
'The sons of Noah'	10
Shem	11: 10–26

[1] L. Koehler and W. Baumgartner, *Lexicon in Veteris Testamenti* (1958), *ad rem.*

[2] Liddell and Scott, *Greek–English Lexicon*, abridged from the 7th ed. (1895), *ad rem.*

[3] The only other translations of תולדות are γενεά in Gen. 25: 13 and συγγένεια in Exod. 6: 19 and Num. 1: 20–42; but here the context easily explains the departure from γενέσεις.

[4] The problem of the discrepancy between the MT and LXX arising from the phrase ἡ βίβλος γενέσεως in 2: 4*a*, which is not based on the MT, remains. The most probable explanation is that accepted by von Rad (*Die Priesterschrift im Hexateuch*, Beiträge zur Wissenschaft vom Alten und Neuen Testament, 1934, p. 38): the Priestly editor has introduced the Toledoth phrase into the creation narrative after the pattern of 5: 1, the only occurrence of ספר תולדות in the MT.

Terah	Gen.	11: 27
Ishmael		25: 12–16
Isaac		25: 19–20
Esau		36: 1–6
Esau		36: 9–43
Jacob		37: 1–2
Aaron and Moses	Num.	3: 1–3
[Perez	Ruth	4: 18–22]

(*a*) *Relation to the Priestly narrative.* The first question we must raise is the relation of these Toledoth passages to the rest of P.[1] Von Rad has shown[2] that at several points information given in a Toledoth passage is not compatible with statements made in other Priestly contexts. Thus in Gen. 11: 10, a Toledoth passage, Arpachshad is Shem's first-born son, but according to Gen. 10: 22 he is Shem's third son. Similarly, as wives of Esau, P names Judith, Basemath, and Mahalath;[3] the Toledoth list Adah, Oholibamath, and Basemath.[4] Again, there is a different use of אדם in the Toledoth list of Gen. 5: 1 *a*, where Adam is the *Urmensch*, from that in 1: 27 f., where the term is used collectively of the creation of the species man. In the former passage Adam is a proper name; in the latter it is not.[5]

From these and other observations, it is clear that a distinction must be drawn between the Toledoth-source and the remaining Priestly material in the Pentateuch; that is to say, the two represent different sources or at least different levels or stages of tradition.[6] A possible clue to the relation between P and the Toledoth scheme is found in Gen. 5: 1 *a*, זה ספר תולדות אדם, a phrase that can be understood only as referring to an independently existing compilation of Toledoth. Moreover, the

[1] For a summary of the earlier discussion on the Toledoth passages, cf. K. Budde, 'Ella Toledoth', *ZAW*, XXXIV (1914), 241–53 and his sequel in *ZAW*, XXXVI (1916), 1–7.

[2] *Priesterschrift*, p. 34.

[3] Gen. 26: 34; 28: 9.

[4] Gen. 36: 2.

[5] It will be readily admitted that in 5: 1 *b*–2 אדם is used collectively; but this is generally held to be an interpolation based on 1: 27 f. That it disrupts the stereotyped pattern of the chapter is obvious. This distinction between 1: 27 and 5: 1 *a* cannot, however, be drawn from the LXX where אדם in 5: 1 *a* is translated ἀνθρώπων and denotes, as in 1: 27 f., the species man.

[6] Cf. Noth, *Überlieferungsgeschichte des Pentateuch* (1948), p. 254.

phrase reads as a title to a 'book'[1] and its frequent recurrence (without the word ספר) suggests that the 'book' was an arrangement of genealogies containing little narrative material. Considering the scope of the Toledoth book, and the present placing of its fragments, it is entirely possible that it served as the skeleton for the Priestly history up to the exodus, rather than as a subsidiary source incorporated by P.[2]

Our point of departure in the attempt to ascertain the original purpose of the Toledoth book is to determine its scope. It is only to be expected that the mixing of the Toledoth book with other Priestly material—narrative, cultic, and legal—would result in misplacements, interpolations, and perhaps even duplication of material. So it is not to be assumed that the occurrence of the term Toledoth in P always points to an origin in the Toledoth book. This caveat probably applies, for example, to Num. 1: 20–40, the census of the twelve tribes.

The Toledoth book, so far as it can be reconstructed from the extant text, began with the 'begettings' of Adam and traced his descendants through ten antediluvian patriarchs down to Noah, ending with Noah's three sons (Gen. 5). A stereotyped formula is followed throughout this chapter: the age of the patriarch at the birth of his first-born (which permits the dating of the flood *Anno Mundi*); the number of his remaining years; a reference to his 'other sons and daughters'; the patriarch's age at the time of his death. Typical is the mention of Seth (Gen. 5: 6–8):

When Seth had lived a hundred and five years, he became the father of Enosh. Seth lived after the birth of Enosh eight hundred and seven years, and had other sons and daughters. Thus all the days of Seth were nine hundred and twelve years; and he died.

Deviations from this formula occur only in the case of Adam, Enoch, and Noah. Theological differences are clearly seen in the case of Adam (verses 1–3), where the list has been altered according to the theology of the Priestly creation story in the attempt to show that the image of God was not only the privileged status of the first man but was passed on also to his descendants: God had created Adam בצלמנו כדמותנו (Gen. 1:

[1] Von Rad, *Priesterschrift*, pp. 34 ff.; O. Procksch, *Die Genesis* (3rd ed. 1924), p. 459.

[2] This is the thesis advanced by von Rad, *Priesterschrift*, pp. 33–40.

26 f.; 5: 1*b*) and of Adam, in turn, it is said ויולד בדמותו כצלמו (5: 3). Thus we may assume that 5: 1–6, the link from Adam to Seth, originally followed the stereotyped pattern, and that verses 1*b*–2, 3*b* did not originally stand in the Toledoth of Adam. This implies that for the Priestly editor the fall narrative had no decisive theological import. Similarly, the saying of Lamech at Noah's birth in verse 29 depends for its meaning on the fall legend, especially 3: 17–19, where the ground is cursed, and so may be considered to be an interpolation from J. The remaining narrative fragment concerning Enoch, 5: 22–4, is probably to be explained as a reflection or anticipation of the abundant esoteric speculations concerning the seventh member from the created man.[1] Twice it is said of Enoch ויתהלך את־האלהים, a phrase denoting intimate companionship with God. Further, we read, in place of the expected notice of his death, the words ויאנני כי־לקח אתו אלהים, which could be used as a springboard for speculations on immortality and apocalyptic 'translation'. Finally, the 365 years of Enoch's life may be connected to the number of days in the solar year, another sign of speculative interest at work.[2] The section as a whole leaves the impression of understatement. Is it possible that it reflects *current* speculation[3] rather than served as the origin of *later* developments?

It remains to be discussed whether the form of this chapter, which strikes us as being so stereotyped, was actually taken from the Toledoth book.[4] To be sure, it is followed throughout the Toledoth of Shem (Gen. 11: 10–26) with the exception that here the concluding statement for each is omitted, namely, 'Thus all the days of [name] were [number] years; and he died'. This rigid scheme is to be found in no other Toledoth passage. Possibly this uniqueness is to be accounted for by recognizing

[1] The Enoch legend is reflected in Sirach 44: 16; Jub. 4: 17 ff.; Heb. 11: 5; Jude 14; and, above all, I, II Enoch. A more extreme form is to be seen in the so-called III Enoch (ed. H. Odeberg) in which 'the deified Patriarch was, in fact, the centre of a cult, where he actually appears to have been worshipped (his worship is forbidden in the Talmud), and to have become a divine–human mediator between God and man' (Matthew Black, 'The "Son of Man" in the Old Biblical Literature', *ET*, LX (1948), 13).

[2] Skinner, *Genesis*, p. 132.

[3] See below, pp. 29 f., for parallels with Sumerian mythology.

[4] So von Rad, *Priesterschrift*, p. 35.

the function of the first two Toledoth lists as bridging the gap between the primeval history and the earliest specifically Israelite traditions. This use of genealogies is identical with that of the Greeks, where artificial genealogical constructions are used to connect the Homeric age with the period of the dawn of historical consciousness several centuries later.[1] Such are the character and function of the books of γενεαλογίαι written by Hecataeus, Pherecydes of Leros, and Acusilaus of Argos:[2] 'The interest in genealogies linking actual families with legendary heroes was closely allied to the interest in "origins" connecting the foundations of cities with the heroic age... '[3] Among the Sumerians, the king list accomplished the same purpose by the same means.[4]

In other Toledoth passages we find a variety of formulae used to designate one's descendants. Thus, while the imperfect Hiphil of ילד is characteristic of the Toledoth of Adam and the sons of Noah, the Hiphil perfect (הוליד) is used in Gen. 11: 26, 27; 25: 19; Ruth 4: 18–22; the Niphal imperfect (יולדו) in Gen. 10: 1*b*; the Qal perfect (ילדה) in Gen. 10: 8, 13, 15, 24, 26; 25: 12; the Qal imperfect (תלד) in 36: 4, 12, 14; the Pual perfect (ילד) in 10: 21, 25.

Moreover, in the Table of Nations (Gen. 10) we find that the simple forms of ילד are used in the sections which were obviously incorporated later, namely verses 5*a*, 8–19, 21, 24–30, while the blunt introduction of names of descendants by means of the simple *bene*-formula is preferred in the core of chapter 10

[1] Cf. Linton, *Synopsis*, pp. 43, 57 *et passim*.

[2] Texts and fragments in F. Jacoby, *Fragmente der griechischen Historiker*, I, 'Die alte Genealogie'; cf. also *ibid.* 'Über die Entwicklung der griechischen Historiographie', *Klio*, IX (1909), 80–123; also J. B. Bury, *The Ancient Greek Historians* (1909), pp. 5–35. A penetrating analysis of this mode of Greek thought is provided by Paula Philippson, 'Genealogie als mythische Form: Studien zur Theologie des Hesiod', *Symbolae Osloenses*, Fasc. Suppl. VII (1936), pp. 3–37. For a discussion of such concepts in later Greek sources, cf. van Groningen, *In the Grip of the Past* (1953), esp. pp. 59 ff.

[3] Bury, *Ancient Greek Historians*, pp. 5 f.

[4] Cf. below, pp. 28 ff. An interesting alternative view, suggested in private communication by Professor James A. Sanders of Union Theological Seminary, that the names in the first Toledoth list are variations of ancient deities whose mortality—and therefore falsity—is underlined by the phrase 'and he died', fails to convince because the names are based on an earlier source represented by the Cainite genealogy in which there is no emphasis on their transitoriness or any hint of their divinity.

(namely verses 2–4, 6–7, 20, 22–3, 31, 32). Literary analysis of the chapter must, indeed, begin with the recognition of the alternation of the *bene* and *yalad* formulae.[1]

Exod. 6: 14–25 is probably by the same hand as the core of Gen. 10. This is proved by the identical, blunt introductory *bene*-formula, and by the same technical use of the progression from בני־שם (10: 31; cf. 10: 20; Exod. 6: 16) to משפחת בני־נח (10: 32; Exod. 6: 19); the next stage, as we can deduce from Exod. 6: 25, would be ראשי אבות בני נח.[2]

There are more peculiarities. In the Toledoth of Ishmael (Gen. 25: 12, 16), in the second Toledoth of Esau (Gen. 36: 9 ff.), and in that of Aaron ('and Moses', Num. 3: 1–3) there is a double introductory formula, the following sequence being followed in each case: first the words ואלה תלדת ישמעאל (אהרן עשו); second, a historical note;[3] third, the pleonastic ואלה שמות בני ישמאל (עשו, אהרן). This redundancy of the introductory formula is explained by von Rad as a mild departure from the usual Toledoth scheme,[4] but there is no sound basis for such an assumption. It seems, rather, that the triple duplication of this three-part sequence could be used as evidence for its authenticity, that is, for the supposition that it originally belonged to the Toledoth scheme. This would involve accepting the priority of the second Esau Toledoth (Gen. 36: 9 ff.), it being parallel in form to the Toledoth of Ishmael and Aaron, over the first (Gen. 36: 1–6). Von Rad comes to the same conclusion concerning the relative priority of the two by assuming that the original Toledoth book was composed entirely of names, and that, since 36: 9 ff. is a dry list of names rather than including various kinds of historical notes as 36: 1–6, it was probably a part of the Toledoth book.

[1] See J. Simons, *OTS*, x (1954), 155–84; Jacob, *Das erste Buch der Tora*, pp. 274–6.

[2] For a discussion of these terms as relating to the divisions of the tribe, see Bernhard Luther, 'Die Israelitischen Stämme', *ZAW*, xxi (1901), pp. 1–76; cf. also the use of משפחה in Gen. 8: 19; Josh. 15: 1 with בת אב in Gen. 24: 38.

[3] Gen. 25: 12, '...of Ishmael, Abraham's son, whom Hagar the Egyptian, Sarah's maid, bore to Abraham...'; Gen. 36: 9*b*, '...of Esau the father of the Edomites in the hill country of Seir'; Num. 3: 1, '...of Aaron and Moses at the time when the Lord spoke with Moses on Mount Sinai'.

[4] *Priesterschrift*, p. 36. Von Rad, however, does not include Num. 3: 1–3 in this judgment.

Three Toledoth (of Noah, Gen. 6: 9–10; of Terah, 11: 27, and of Isaac, 25: 19–20) are preserved only in fragmentary form and consequently it is difficult even to postulate their original form. We note only that the Hiphil is used in each case, e.g. ויולד נח שלשה בנים (Gen. 5: 10).

So also, in view of its being preserved only as a fragment and out of context, the problem of the original form of the Jacob Toledoth (Gen. 37: 1–2) cannot be solved. This is, however, the only genuine Toledoth which has lost all allusion to descendants or ancestors. Considering the detail of the Jacob and Joseph stories in the present text of Genesis and also the occurrence of several lists of Jacob's sons[1] it is probable that the Toledoth of Jacob has suffered displacement at some point in the development of the Pentateuch. The actual Toledoth of Jacob may be preserved in Gen. 35: 22*b*–26 or possibly in 46: 8–27[2] although the introductory formula in each of these is not characteristic of other Toledoth passages. Hence, if either of these lists does preserve the Jacob Toledoth, it has been displaced by a later redactor.

Finally, the difficult Toledoth formula at the close of the Priestly creation narrative (אלה תולדות השמים והארץ; Gen. 2: 4*a*) must be considered an interpolation,[3] although it would be difficult to assign it to the redactor of P because in that case the Toledoth formula of 5: 1 would immediately follow that of 2: 4*a*. The best hypothesis is to consider 2: 4*a* to be the interpolation of the redactor who combined J E D with P, desiring to give the opening section of his work the dignity and importance associated with the formula and yet being reluctant to tamper with the traditional ברשית of Gen. 1: 1.[4]

This array of variety leads to the conclusion that in all likelihood there was no one stereotyped editorial introduction consistently used in the Toledoth book, the compilation itself possibly repeating the variety of its own sources. We have found the following formulae to recur.

[1] Gen. 29: 31—30: 24; 35: 22*b*–26; 46: 8–27; 49: 1–28*a*; Exod. 1: 1–5; and other lists of the twelve tribes, e.g. Num. 1: 5–15; 1: 20–42; 2: 1–31; 7: 12–78; 10: 14–27; 13: 1–16; 26: 5–57.

[2] So Simpson, *Genesis*, p. 743.

[3] The LXX reading obviously presumes the MT of 5: 1.

[4] Skinner, *Genesis*, p. 41, following Holzinger: '...The formula in this place owes its origin to a mechanical imitation of the manner of P by a later hand'; cf. also Noth, *Überlieferungsgeschichte*, p. 17 n. 41.

(1) A list of nine or ten descendants—all apparently first-born—characterized by the consistent use of the Hiphil imperfect of ילד and above all by a detailed chronological scheme (Gen. 5; 11: 10–27).

(2) An introduction using the Hiphil of ילד with only a brief list of immediate descendants (Gen. 6: 9–10; 11: 21; 25: 19–20).

(3) The double introductory formula: ...אלה תולדות and ...אלה שמות (Gen. 25: 12–17; 36: 9–14; Num. 3: 1–3).

(4) The simple בני־ formula with no form of ילד (Gen. 10: 2–4, 6–7, 20, 22–3, 31–2; Ex. 6: 16–19).

There is no real reason to think that any of these was foreign to the Toledoth book, unless it be the last. The fact that in Gen. 10: 22, a 'core' section of the chapter, Arpachshad is listed as the third son of Shem, while in the Toledoth of Shem (Gen. 11: 10) he is apparently the first-born, indicates at the least that different editors have been at work on the two lists. Also, in Exod. 6: 14–25 the characteristic אלה תולדות is wanting. On the other hand the latter passage clearly interrupts the narrative into which it was placed. Its position was probably determined by the reference to the 'people of Israel' in verse 13, and, as we would expect, the genealogical material begins as if it would enumerate the families of all twelve tribes. We find, however, that the list ends with Levi, the third son of Jacob, and in fact concentrates its attention on the Levites, especially the sons of Kohath, and of these the sons of Aaron are prominent. Our conclusion, based on the clear signs of two levels of tradition in the Table of Nations (one of which closely approximates Exod. 6: 14–25) and on the necessity of a bridge between Jacob and Aaron in the Toledoth book, is that the two passages in the fourth group are remnants of the Toledoth book whose form has been slightly altered in the process of development of the Priestly tradition.

(*b*) *The plan of the Toledoth book.* We are thus left with a genealogical system in which the individual lists must have run in sequence; that is, the first name in each list would be the last of the preceding Toledoth. This may be tabulated as follows (occurrences of the Toledoth formula are capitalized).

ADAM
Seth
Enosh
Kenan
Mahalalel
Jared
Enoch
Methuselah
Lamech
NOAH

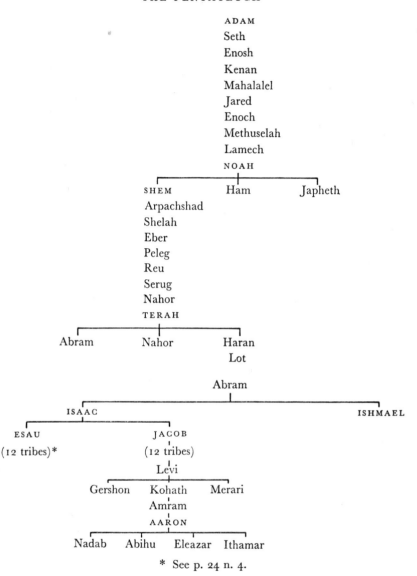

SHEM | Ham | Japheth

SHEM
Arpachshad
Shelah
Eber
Peleg
Reu
Serug
Nahor
TERAH

Abram | Nahor | Haran

Haran
Lot

Abram

ISAAC | ISHMAEL

ISAAC

ESAU | JACOB

ESAU
(12 tribes)*

JACOB
(12 tribes)
Levi

Gershon | Kohath | Merari

Kohath
Amram
AARON

Nadab | Abihu | Eleazar | Ithamar

* See p. 24 n. 4.

The Toledoth ran in an unbroken line from Adam to the three sons of Noah; from there the line of the Shemites is traced up to the three sons of Terah, who is himself probably viewed as the direct ancestor of the Semitic peoples.

The surprising lack of a Toledoth of Abraham may thus be due to an original emphasis on Terah,[1] although it is significant that the Toledoth passages as they now stand[2] trace confederacies of twelve tribes[3] each to Ishmael, Esau,[4] and Jacob, all immediate descendants of Abraham. Indeed, Wellhausen, on the basis of a comparison of the patriarchal stories, considered Abraham to be subordinate to both Isaac and Jacob in the earliest Hebrew tradition: 'He is perhaps the youngest figure in the company, and it was probably at a comparatively late period that he was put before his son Isaac.'[5] Thus, accepting the prior existence of the Toledoth book as such, the omission of Abraham may have been due to his relative unimportance in the narrative tradition. It is more probable, however, that the converse instead is true, namely that originally the emphasis in the Toledoth book was placed on the role of Abraham but that, as with Jacob, the great amount of narrative material dealing

[1] Significantly, it is only in P that Terah begins the migration 'to the land of Canaan' which is completed by Abraham (Gen. 11: 31 ff.); cf. Budde, *ZAW*, XXXIV (1914), 249. It is also noteworthy that in the chronological scheme of the LXX the birth of Terah (A.M. 3242) occurs exactly 1,000 years after the flood (A.M. 2242) and, moreover, that Terah is the ninth from Noah, thus completing a possible 9-1-9 genealogical scheme. These observations lead F. Bork ('Zur Chronologie der biblischen Urgeschichte', *ZAW*, XLVII [1929], 209) to conclude 'dass man in der Geburt Terahs den Beginn eines neuen Weltalters, das der Erzväter, gesehen hat'. The complexity of the interrelation of the divergent chronologies in the MT, Samaritan Pentateuch, LXX, Josephus, and the Book of Jubilees, however, precludes dogmatic assertions regarding the value of such reconstructions in the interpretation of the place of Terah in the Toledoth book; see Appendix 2.

[2] The link between Terah and the descendants of Ishmael, Esau, and Jacob depends, in the Toledoth passages as we have them, solely on the phrase בן־אברהם applied to Ishmael (Gen. 25: 12) and Isaac (25: 19) and to a brief historical note which in the case of Ishmael may be an interpolation.

[3] Note also the twelve sons of Nahor (Gen. 22: 20–4), and the six of Keturah (25: 2) and Seir (36: 20, with emendation). Martin Noth, *Das System der zwölf Stämme Israels* (Beiträge zur Wissenschaft vom Alten und Neuen Testament, IV, 1), pp. 43 ff., alludes to the importance of the six- or twelve-part divisions of tribal amphictyonies among ancient near-eastern peoples in general.

[4] The twelve-tribe confederacy is traced only in the second Esau Toledoth, and in this by reckoning the sons of Oholibamah on a level with the grandsons of Adah and Basemath, and excluding the illegitimate Amalek; cf. Skinner, *Genesis*, p. 431.

[5] *Prolegomena*, p. 320.

with Abraham made his Toledoth seem superfluous to the redactor.[1] However, as can be seen from the tabulation of the first Toledoth passages, the position of Terah is in several ways parallel to that of Noah. Both Noah and Terah end a list of Toledoth[2] and yet have a Toledoth applied to them in another context. Similarly, with each, the Toledoth ends with three sons and this fact is repeated in the Toledoth passage named for them. To be sure, there is also a similarity between Shem and Abram: each is the first-born of the three sons and is the ancestor of that line of descent which is the most important for the compiler. But Abraham does not begin a new series of names as does Shem: instead he is taken to be the direct ancestor of three confederacies of Semitic tribes, namely those traced to Ishmael, Esau, and Jacob.[3]

The fact that the Toledoth of Aaron (Num. 3: 1–3) is identical in form with the Toledoth of Ishmael (Gen. 25: 12–16) and of Esau (Gen. 36: 9–14) leads to the assumption that a connection was made between Jacob and Aaron. Of the extant Levitical genealogies in the Pentateuch, that which is best suited for this purpose is Exod. 6: 16–25. Although there is no Toledoth formula used to introduce the list, yet the phrase אלה שמות used to introduce the sons of Levi is unlike the framework of the Table of Nations and is rather reminiscent of genuine Toledoth passages, for example Gen. 25: 12 and 36: 9, lacking only the 'normal' Toledoth introduction, אלה תולדות. Moreover, the Levitical list is in this passage distinguished by its listing the length of life only of Levi, Kohath, and Amram, emphasizing a progression from Jacob to Aaron. The fact that this list overlaps with the Toledoth of Aaron in Num. 3: 1–3 does not suggest an origin apart from the Toledoth book since a similar duplication occurs also in the case of Noah[4] and Terah.[5]

[1] For other solutions to this problem, see Budde, *ZAW*, XXXIV (1914), 248 ff.

[2] The LXX interpolates Cainan between Arpachshad and Shelah (Gen. 11: 13*b*), making the parallel between the two lists more obvious.

[3] Two problems emerge from this consideration: the omission of the list of Keturites and also the slight treatment given to the figure of Isaac, who serves only as 'the genealogical link between the Abraham and Jacob cycles' of the narrative (see L. Hicks, *IDB*, III, 728–31).

[4] Cf. Gen. 6: 9, 10; 10: 1, 32.

[5] Cf. Gen. 11: 26; 11: 27. If some prototype of the Table of Nations was included in the Toledoth book, there is also the duplication of Shem.

We may assume, at least, that this list or one like it is presupposed by the undoubted Toledoth passages.

(*c*) *The symmetry and purpose of the Toledoth book.* We are now in a position to see the symmetry of plan of the Toledoth compilation and its overall purpose. The plan hinges on certain pivotal figures, each having three sons or divisions of descendants: Noah, Terah,[1] Abraham,[2] and Levi. To these we may possibly add Esau with descendants from three wives, and probably also Jacob, whose twelve sons are traditionally traced to Leah, Rachel, and the two concubines.[3] It is indeed striking that the Toledoth system sets in relief a series of names comprising three great tribal confederacies (Esau, Jacob, and Ishmael), two of which (Esau and Jacob) are again divided into three groups—a sort of Abrahamitic Table of Nations.

All of this does not support the common view that the Priestly genealogies 'lead from the general to the particular, from the human race to the children of Israel, becoming ever narrower until they finally culminate in Moses and Aaron... '.[4] Rather, the peculiar form of the pre-Abrahamitic genealogies indicates that they serve—just as the tribal lists of J—to set the stage for the enumeration and categorization of those tribes most closely related to the Israelites. But in doing so there is a double advance over the methodology of J: (1) the gap between the primeval (paradise) age and the time of the patriarchs is bridged over (Gen. 5, 11) and (2) the great narrative figures of

[1] Noth, *Überlieferungsgeschichte*, p. 235, traces the tradition of the fraternal relationship of Abraham, Nahor, and Haran to the result of the combination of tribal traditions from various localities; the weakness of this section of Noth's work (pp. 232–7), however, is that he does not consider the possibility of the independent existence of a compilation of actual genealogies and, moreover, that he assumes that, except for certain 'proper' (*eigentlich*) genealogies, the majority of genealogical constructions dealing with the beginnings of Israel's history are later than, and derived from, the narrative material with which they are now associated. On this view it is difficult to account for the present form of the Toledoth introductions, the divergence of which indicates that the genealogical material has been worked into the context of the Priestly narrative.

[2] Reckoning Ishmael and the two sons of Isaac as parallel.

[3] In J E, Gen. 29–30; in P, Gen. 35: 22*b*–26; 46: 8–27.

[4] Curt Kuhl, *The Old Testament: Its Origins and Composition*, tr. C. M. Herriott (1961), p. 56.

the patriarchal age are systematized by being cast in their family relationships, and, thereby a greater degree of coherence is given to the materials of the tradition. Thus, the Toledoth book consisted of the two types of genealogies distinguished by Noth, namely lists having bare names with no independent position in the narrative tradition (here we include Gen. 5 and 11) and names derived from the tradition that are set into a connected genealogical system (here may be included the remaining Toledoth passages). By utilizing both types of genealogical material, the Toledoth book accomplished the first overall classification of previously existing lists in the Pentateuch; in short, it is a real family tree and, as such, can be contrasted with the more or less isolated genealogical lists of J, which lack any discernible systematization in the present text.

But the compiler of the Toledoth book had a purpose beyond this. Once the stage had been set with its great tribal confederacies, the line did indeed narrow until it reached Aaron, the seventh from Abraham,[1] who was for the Priestly tradition the focal point in the establishment of the cultus. Traditional lists were used in order to set the establishment of the cultus within the context of the origins of the Semites and, in turn, of all mankind. Moreover, the narrative fragment in Num. 3: 1, 'These are the Toledoth of Aaron and Moses in that day when Yahweh spoke with Moses on Mount Sinai', specifically links the culmination of the Toledoth book with the core event of the exodus, emphasizing the uniqueness of the Israelitic cultus and also implicitly hinting at the concept of divine election. Thus, in its overall design, the Toledoth book led from Adam to Aaron, from the Creation of the world to the Creation of the cultus. This centrality of the Sinai events in the Priestly *narrative* is noted by Wellhausen, who remarks that the three covenants (in P) of God with Adam, Noah, and Abraham and the periods they initiate 'are preliminaries to the fourth period and the fourth covenant. The narrator everywhere has an eye to the

[1] Cf. Lev. R. 29: 11 (377 f.): 'All sevenths are favourites in the world... Thus: Adam, Seth, Enosh, Kenan, Mahalalel, Jared, Enoch, and of him it is said, "And Enoch walked with God" (Gen. 5: 22). Among the patriarchs the seventh was the favourite. Thus: Abraham, Isaac, Jacob, Levi, Kohath, Amram, and Moses, of whom it is written, "And Moses went up to God" (Exod. 19: 3).' David is given similar treatment in the same context.

Mosaic law, and the thought of it determined the *plan* which comes so prominently into view in his representation of the origins of human history.'[1] But here we may be able to trace a distinctive emphasis of the Toledoth book as compared with P: While in the Priestly narrative Moses and the institutions established through him (the Torah) stand at the center, in the Toledoth book it is Aaron who marks the culmination of pre-history and the founding of the cultus. In this respect the plan of the Toledoth book has close affinities with the theology of the Chronicler, for whom Moses the Lawgiver receives much less attention than Aaron, founder of the cultus.[2]

This utilization of genealogical materials for lofty theological sentiments was no mean accomplishment:

Die Verbindung der Einzeltraditionen und die Zusammenfassung aller Stämme und Völker zu einem wohlgeordneten Ganzen ist das Produkt individueller Tätigkeit, die wir ihrer Tendenz nach bereits als gelehrte Arbeit bezeichnen müssen, ganz derselben Art wie die, wodurch Hesiod und die übrigen genealogischen Dichtungen der Griechen die Hellenen und die übrigen ihnen bekannten Völker systematisch in Stammbäumen geordnet haben.[3]

2. *The chronology of the Priestly narrative*[4]

Linked to the genealogies of Adam (Gen. 5) and of Shem (Gen. 11: 10–26) is a chronology of the primeval period that shows signs of careful calculation. The fact that such chronological speculation is limited to these two lists is added evidence not only for the necessity of distinguishing these from the later lists[5] but also for the supposition that at this point extra-Israelitic influences are to be seen. Parallels between the various forms of the Sumerian king lists and the antediluvian genealogy of P (Gen. 5) have often been drawn. It is usually noted, for example, that the Berosus list[6] and one of the Larsa king lists have ten names before the flood, the last being the hero of the

[1] *Prolegomena*, pp. 339–40.
[2] See below, pp. 54 f.
[3] Meyer, *Die Israeliten*, p. 231.
[4] On the methodology followed in this section, see Appendix 1.
[5] See above, pp. 26 ff.
[6] The source for excerpts from Berosus used here is Paul Schnabel, *Berossos und die Babylonisch-Hellenistische Literatur* (1923), esp. pp. 261 ff.; see also Smith, *Assyria*, pp. 17–25.

flood, and that in both Gen. 5 and the Sumerian lists the age of life (or reign) is given in fantastic figures, especially the Sumerian tradition, where the range of length of reign varies from 10,800 to 64,800 years according to Berosus[1] to 18,000 to 43,000 years in the most ancient list.[2] Moreover, it is striking that the seventh figure in the Sumerian lists—here the same name is given by Berosus and the older lists (En-men-dur-Anna = Εὐεδώραγχον = Enmeduranki)—is regarded as possessing special wisdom concerning the gods and as being the first man to practice divination.[3] Similarly, the seventh name in Gen. 5 is Enoch, around whom grew up a speculative tradition concerning the heavenly secrets.[4]

In evaluating the extent of Babylonian influence in Gen. 5 we must first recognize that there is no borrowing of actual names or even translation of names involved. Attempts to explain אנוש (Gen. 5: 3) and קינן (5: 4) as translations of Ἀμήλων and Ἀμμένων in the Berosus list[5] are, in the light of discoveries of the more original form of the Sumerian names involved, no longer convincing. The names in Gen. 5 are obviously based on the Cainite list in 4: 17–24, which shows no signs of Babylonian influence. Similarly, in view of the numerous discrepancies in the various sources for the chronological calculation, it is highly questionable to assert that the actual figures, or the total of the figures given in Gen. 5, are to be explained as being directly derived from the numbers in the king list.[6]

Nonetheless, there are similarities between Gen. 5 and the king list which have not generally been noted. First, there is the descending range of the length of life of the primeval individuals in Genesis: from Adam to Noah the normal length of life appears to be 750–1,000 (with the exception of Enoch); from Noah to Abraham, 148–600; then, among the Israelite patriarchs the

[1] Schnabel, *Berossos*, p. 262.

[2] Jacobsen, *King List*, pp. 70–7.

[3] Hooke, *Mythology*, p. 130.

[4] It is striking also that, according to a ritual tablet from the library of Asshurbanipal, Enmeduranki is king of Sippar, city of Samas, the sun god; to this may be compared the 365 years of Gen. 5: 23; cf. Skinner, *Genesis*, p. 132.

[5] Skinner, p. 137.

[6] As, for example, Oppert (cited by Skinner, p. 135) suggests that the year of the flood (A.M. 1656) in the MT is related to the total figure for antediluvian history in Berosus (432,000) in the ratio of five solar years to one week.

life-span is 100–200 years and, subsequently, seventy to eighty years. This descending scale may serve partially to take the place of the fall legend in P, or at least to indicate a 'deterioration of man's vital energy, but without seeing his sinfulness as the cause'.[1] Strikingly, we also find a descending order of length of reign (and, by implication, life-span) in the king list: the antediluvian kings reigned from 18,600 to 43,200 years; of the next dynasty, at Kish, the longest reign of the twenty-three kings is 1,560 years; in the following dynasty, at Eama, the range is from 6 years to 1,200. However, direct borrowing of method from the Babylonian tradition seems somewhat improbable in view of the fact that such ideas, based on a cyclical view of history, were common to various cultures in the ancient world. Indian speculation conceived of existence as governed by the regular rise and fall of cycles, the *Mahayuga*, each composed of four ages of unequal duration, the *Yuga*. The first yuga lasts 4,800 years; the second 3,600; the third 2,400; and the last 1,200. 'To the progressive decrease in duration of each new yuga, there corresponds, on the human plane, a decrease in the length of life, accompanied by a corruption in morals and a decline in intelligence.'[2] Close parallels to this system could be adduced also from Buddhist and Iranian traditions;[3] the similarities to the OT antediluvian and patriarchal lists is self-evident.

Perhaps a more meaningful similarity between the king list and Gen. 5 is the fact that, in both, the introductory formulae are highly stereotyped and serve the sole purpose of *establishing a line of succession*. The fact that only one descendant of each figure is named in Gen. 5 proves that this list is no more a 'family tree' than the Sumerian king list. Moreover, an examination of Josephus' treatment of the Gen. 5 list[4] reveals a very probable conscious imitation of Berosus (whom Josephus mentions in *Ant.* I. 3. 6). The transition from one antediluvian figure to his successor is made by some such statement as 'N delivered the government (τὴν ἀρχὴν παρέδωκεν) to N his son, whom he begat in his [number] year'. That the number given

[1] Kuhl, *Old Testament*, p. 62.

[2] Mircea Eliade, *Cosmos and History: The Myth of the Eternal Return*, tr. Willard R. Trask (1959), p. 113.

[3] Eliade, p. 116.

[4] *Ant.* I. 3. 4 (Loeb, *Ant.* I, 86).

for the total age of the figures in Gen. 5 is here taken to be the *length of reign* is also to be understood in the warning to the reader which Josephus affixes to this paragraph: '... but let no one inquire into the deaths of these men, for they extended their lives along with their children and grandchildren; but let him have regard to their births only'.[1] So also in the king list the formulae characteristic of the antediluvian section differ from those of the main body of the text,[2] just as the lists of Adam and Shem must be distinguished from the later lists.

All this leads us to suspect that the Priestly narrator was familiar with traditions of the *Urzeit* in surrounding cultures including a list of names with extraordinary numbers for the antediluvian period. The exact purpose of the numbers in the king list is obscure; they may reflect astrological speculation[3] or, more probably, each figure may have its own hidden meaning.[4] The Priestly author used the framework of the king list (or a similar tradition) as the structure of his first genealogy, imposing upon it the Priestly chronological calculations which aimed at determining the year *Anno Mundi* of several pivotal events, including the flood, Abraham's migration, the exodus, and the founding of the sacrificial cultus in Solomon's temple.

When we proceed to an interpretation of the purpose of the numerical system itself, we face a host of difficulties. There are, first of all, several varying traditions presenting chronologies that diverge widely from each other, namely the MT, the Samaritan Pentateuch, the LXX, Josephus, the Book of Jubilees, and the Assumption of Moses—to mention only the most important early sources.[5] Moreover, at some crucial points the text of any one tradition is itself difficult to reconstruct or to

[1] *Loc. cit.*; it may also be true that this caveat is issued in recognition of certain difficulties that arise from a comparison of the total ages of the figures and the year of the flood.

[2] This leads Jacobsen to ascribe the former to a different author; *King List*, pp. 61–8.

[3] Smith, *Assyria*, p. 21.

[4] The numbers are given in Berosus in terms of the *Sar* (3,600 years), the *Ner* (600 years), and the *Soss* (60 years); cf. Schnabel, *Berossos*, p. 261. These periods obviously were related to the Babylonian idea of the 'Great Year' or world cycle; cf. Eliade, *Cosmos and History*, pp. 87, 107. The idea of the Great Year is shared also by Josephus (*Ant.* I. 3. 9) and may be, in fact, the basis of the numerical calculations in Gen. 5 and 11.

[5] See the tabulations in Appendix 2.

interpret.[1] Hence, from the start, any dogmatic assertions regarding the original form and purpose of the chronological speculations or the point of culmination of the scheme are excluded. All that can be done is to examine the extant sources and to postulate the pivotal events on which such reckoning centers.

Perhaps the most widely accepted hypothesis regarding the chronology of the MT in its present condition is that the year A.M. 2666 for the exodus represents $26\frac{2}{3}$ generations of 100 years[2] or two-thirds of a world cycle (Great Year) of 4,000 years. This would correspond to the fact that Aaron is the 26th from Adam while the last two-thirds of a generation is probably represented by Eleazar.[3] There are signs that the remaining one-third of the supposed Great Year is also accounted for in the dating of the beginning of the building of Solomon's temple 480 years after the exodus,[4] that is, A.M. 3146. Then, according to the historical books, the total length of the reign of the kings of Judah from that point to the fall of Jerusalem was 430 years[5] which, if we add the fifty years of the exile, results in the symmetrical number 480 and places the edict of Cyrus—itself celebrated as a 'messianic' event[6]—in the year A.M. 3626. Assuming that the post-exilic Jerusalem community in all probability kept historical records of some accuracy, it is curious to note that from 538 B.C., the usual reckoning of Cyrus' edict, to 164 B.C., the rededication of the temple by the Maccabees, 374 years elapsed, which, when added to the year A.M. of Cyrus' edict, results in a complete Great Year of 4,000 years.[7] If this reconstruction is considered to be due to anything more than pure chance or manipulation, we must assume that the

[1] The 430-year Egyptian sojourn is not provided with a *terminus a quo*; LXX and Sam. Pent. include Canaan as part of the sojourn.

[2] Wellhausen, *Prolegomena*, pp. 308–9, following Buttmann.

[3] Wellhausen, pp. 308–9; Gen. 15: 13–16 reckons 100 years to a generation.

[4] I Kings 6: 1.

[5] The biblical figures are tabulated by E. L. Curtis, 'Chronology of the OT', *HDB*, I, 401–3, where the artificial symmetry of length of reigns of kings of both Judah and Israel is alluded to.

[6] Cf. Isa. 45: 1.

[7] Cf. Kuhl, *Old Testament*, p. 62; however, if the text of Gen. 11: 24 is emended to read 79 years instead of 29, as Kuhl suggests, this reconstruction would fail.

biblical chronology was revised at a quite late date, for example sometime during the Maccabean period soon after the independence of the Judean state was achieved.

The divergence of the various traditions can be taken as support of this hypothesis in so far as it reveals uncertainty not only with regard to the lists of numbers in Gen. 5 and 11, but especially in calculating the intervals separating the pivotal events. A glance at the figures for the ages of the primeval ancestors in the five traditions shows that all systems are somehow related, that is, dependent on the same basic tradition. But it is scarcely possible to determine with certainty which is nearest the original or to postulate that from which the others could have arisen.[1] Moreover, the entire chronology has been manipulated in the other passages that bear on chronology. The date A.M. of the exodus depends entirely on the note in Exod. 12: 40 where the MT gives the duration of the Egyptian sojourn as 430 years, implying the *terminus a quo* in the removal of Jacob and his family to Egypt.[2] On the other hand, the best textual tradition of both the LXX and the Samaritan Pentateuch gives the same total for a combined sojourn in Canaan and Egypt,

[1] Kuenen's summary of the status of the problem has frequently been quoted and it cannot be said that more recent research—for all its painstaking creativity—has rendered it out of date: 'Die Frage, die uns durch die drei Textgestalten von Gen. 5 und 11: 10–26 vorgelegt wird, harrt noch der Lösung. Eine Lösung wie sie hier gemeint ist, besässen wir, wenn evident bewiesen wäre, dass und wie aus einer der drei Recensionen die beiden andern, oder aus einem hypothetischen Grundtext die drei Recensionen entstanden seien, und wenn ferner noch die Wahrheit oder Richtigkeit des chronologischen Systems dieser ältesten Recension über allen Zweifel erhoben werden könnte. Unter Wahrheit und Richtigkeit verstehe ich natürlich nicht Übereinstimmung mit der historischen Wirklichkeit. Meine Meinung ist, dass das als ursprünglich angenommene *chronologische System* sich deutlich als das des (priesterlichen) Redactors der "Bücher Mosis" erweisen muss. So aufgefasst sind die von mir gestellten Anforderungen nicht übertrieben zu nennen' (Dutch or., 1873, trans. K. Budde, *Gesammelte Abhandlungen zur biblischen Wissenschaft von Dr. Abraham Kuenen* (1894), p. 119; quoted by D. W. Bousset, 'Das chronologische System der biblischen Geschichtsbücher', *ZAW*, XX (1900), 136; Alfred Jepsen, 'Zur Chronologie des Priesterkodex', *ZAW*, XLVII (1929), 251).

[2] Gen. 47: 9, 28. Gen. 15: 12–16 need not be interpreted as referring to a 400 year sojourn in Egypt. Note that the descendants (זרע) of Abraham are to be 'sojourners in a land that is not theirs', a saying strikingly similar to Gen. 23: 4, where Abraham describes himself as a 'stranger, a sojourner' in Canaan; see Linton, *Synopsis*, pp. 14 ff., *et passim*.

assuming a calculation based on the year of the migration of Abraham from Haran to Canaan.[1] The reading of the LXX and the Samaritan Pentateuch is clearly known to Paul when he dates the coming of the law 430 years after Abraham.[2] That such a calculation was the more original of the two may be indicated also by the symmetrical division of the sojourn into two equal parts of 215 years each for Canaan and Egypt which is still preserved in the MT, the LXX, and the Samaritan Pentateuch.[3] Moreover, in the chronological calculations of Josephus the removal of Jacob and his family to Egypt is only incidentally mentioned, while the migration of Abraham is considered a pivotal event.[4]

Finally, that the MT of Exod. 12: 40 has been manipulated is proved by the fact that, figuring the 430 years sojourn from the migration of Abraham, the date of the exodus is A.M. 2451, exactly the figure given twice by Josephus[5] and identical with the date for the crossing of the Jordan by Joshua in the Book of

[1] Gen. 12: 4.

[2] Gal. 3: 17; the 400 years of Acts 7: 6 is based on Gen. 15: 13.

[3] In Jubilees these periods have been slightly stretched in order to allow the year of the Exodus in the MT (A.M. 2451, reckoning from Abraham's migration) to represent the beginning of the conquest of Canaan (Jub. 50: 9), which for the author was the beginning of the actual history of his people. 'Die bemerkenswerteste Zahl des Jubiläenbuches scheint mir die letzte zu sein, das nämlich Israel 50 Jubiläen nach Erschaffung der Welt in Palästina einzieht. Die Chronologie sieht also die mythische Urzeit seines Volkes erst in dem Augenblick als beendet an, da Israel im Besitze des gelobten Landes ist. Sein chronologisches System ist also politisch-religiös orientiert. Für ihn beginnt also die wirkliche Geschichte seines Volkes erst auf dem Boden Palaistinas', Bork, *ZAW*, XLVII (1929), 206–22.

[4] *Ant.* II. 15. 2; in *Ant.* VIII. 3. 1, five central events are dated: creation, flood, migration of Abraham, exodus, and the beginning of Solomon's temple; cf. *Ant.* x. 8. 4–5.

[5] *Ant.* I. 6. 5 and II. 15. 2; x. 8. 4–5; the 59-year difference in *Ant.* VIII. 3. 1 is difficult. The fact that Josephus' date for the exodus is identical with this interpretation of an 'earlier' chronology in the MT must be taken into account in any hypothesis concerning the question as to whether Josephus used a Greek OT with its larger numbers in the chronological calculations. Thus, for example, while Linton is no doubt correct in his statement that Josephus 'staar i en anden situation end rabbinerne', he cannot adduce as evidence the statement that 'han lever i den hellenistiske jødedoms skole-tradition, hvor man benyttede den graekske bibel med dens høje tal og hvor intentionen netop er den at bevise den jødiske histories og den jødiske "filosofis" høje alder' (p. 79).

Jubilees.[1] According to this calculation of the year of the exodus —a calculation which must antedate that of the present MT— the beginnings of Solomon's temple would fall in A.M. 2931 and the institution of the cultus twenty years later, 2951.[2] The somewhat longer interval between the exodus and the temple given in Josephus (592 years rather than 480 in the MT, both numbers being derived from the figures given in the book of Judges, the difference being that the MT reckons only the duration of the activity of the Judges while Josephus includes also the periods of foreign domination)[3] results in dating the beginning of the temple in A.M. 3043.[4] This view that approximately 3,000 years elapsed from creation to the founding of the temple cultus is reflected also in II Esdras:

This woman whom you saw, whom you now behold as an established city, is Zion. And as for her telling you that she was barren for thirty years, it is because there were three thousand years in the world before any offering was offered in it. And after three thousand years Solomon built the city, and offered offerings; then it was that the barren woman bore a son...[5]

We may therefore assume that a chronological system, perhaps prior to the scheme of the present MT, fixed the exodus at around 2500 and the founding of the temple approximately

[1] I.e. 50 Jubilees (according to the author one Jubilee is 49 rather than 50 years) which are 2,450 years; cf. Jub. 50: 4. This statement is fully compatible with the statement in Ass. Moses 1: 1 f. that Moses was 120 years old at the time of his death and that this occurred about the year A.M. 2500.

In a recent study, Ernst Wiesenberg ('The Jubilee of Jubilees', *RQ*, III (1961), 3–40) has examined the importance of the number 2,451 as being the 50th jubilee year (49 × 50), a 'kind of *annus mirabilis*, the year chosen by divine design to be marked by the most momentous event in the national epic of Israel...' (p. 17). Wiesenberg points out that this number is of central importance not only in Jubilees and the Assumption of Moses but also in Pseudo-Jonathan, where the exodus is dated in A.M. 2451, and in the chronological calculations in Talmudic literature where the exodus occurs in the year A.M. 2448 (pp. 20 ff., Talmudic references, p. 21 n. 92).

[2] I Kings 6: 1; 7: 1; 8; it is also possible that the age of Nahor at the time of Terah's birth should be lengthened in accordance with the LXX and Sam. Pent. from 29 to 70, with the result that the founding of the cultus would fall in A.M. 3001.

[3] Linton, *Synopsis*, pp. 32 ff., 80.

[4] *Ant.* X. 8. 4–5; but cf. the dating in *Ant.* VIII. 3. 1.

[5] II Esd. 10: 45 f., RSV.

500 years later; yet we must acknowledge that all attempts to ascertain the total scope of the system remain tenuous.[1]

What has been adduced above, however, is sufficient to prove that a great interest was taken by the ancient scribes in numerical calculation of epochs. That this interest was not confined to the Hebrews is made abundantly clear by Albiruni,[2] who refers to concepts of world cycles among Persians, Greeks, Egyptians, and Arabs as well as among Jews and Christians. But it is especially noteworthy that this speculation in the OT has been linked to genealogies by *Priestly* circles[3] and that subsequently, in the Apocrypha and Pseudepigrapha, the apocalyptic aspect of chronological speculations comes to the fore.[4]

[1] For other theories, see Linton, *Synopsis*, pp. 23–41 *et passim*; Bousset, *ZAW*, XX (1900), 136–47; Jepsen, *ZAW*, XLVII (1929), 251–5; Curtis, *HDB*, I, 401–3; Skinner, *Genesis*, pp. 134 ff., 233 ff.; Bork, *ZAW*, XLVII (1929), 206–22; L. J. Delaporte, *Chronographie de Mar Elie Bar Sinaya* (1910), pp. 6, 12; A. Bosse, *MVAG* (1908), p. 2; Merx, *BZAW*, XVII, 23; Cassuto, I, 249–90; II, 250–87.

[2] The Islamic scholar whose major work, written *c.* A.D. 1000, has been translated by C. Edward Sachau, *The Chronology of Ancient Nations* (1879), see especially ch. 3.

[3] Chronological speculation also determined the genealogy of the High Priest in I Chron. 5: 27–41 [EV, 6: 1–15]; see below, pp. 40 f.

[4] Cf. II Esdras 10: 45 ff. *et passim*; Jubilees; Ass. Moses; I Enoch 91, 93. After completing this section I have found that similar conclusions were reached by A. Murtonen, 'On the Chronology of the OT', *Studia Theologica*, VIII (1955), 133–7. Murtonen provides additional evidence for the schematization of OT chronology and writes: 'The date of the creation is based on eschatological calculations. But it seems to the present writer that not only this, but all of the chronological data given in the OT bear an eschatological character—at least in a certain sense of the word.'

CHAPTER 2

GENEALOGIES IN EZRA-NEHEMIAH AND CHRONICLES

We have seen that in the earlier historical sources genealogies either do not occur (in E or D) or they occur simply as groups of tribal names linked to a common ancestor, with no continuing line of descent being traced (in J). In contrast to this, the Priestly sections of the Pentateuch reveal a genealogical speculation that knits together all of the important figures of the Israelitic traditions of the primeval and patriarchal periods by means of a continuous genealogical tree, the culmination of which was probably the inauguration of the cultus with its Aaronic priesthood and also an enumeration of the main clans that constituted the people of Israel.[1]

A. THE RELATION BETWEEN EZRA-NEHEMIAH AND CHRONICLES

In turning to the genealogies in the writings usually attributed to the Chronicler (here used as a designation for I and II Chronicles only), we must first deal with the preliminary question of the relation between the genealogies in Ezra-Nehemiah and those of Chronicles. A study of the genealogical material common to both suggests that that of Ezra-Nehemiah is probably the earlier and that either it or the sources from which it was fashioned was used as the basis for the parallels in I Chronicles. There are three relevant passages that lead to this conclusion.

(1) The first purports to be a list of the inhabitants of restoration Jerusalem (Neh. 11: 3–24; I Chron. 9: 2–34). It is not practicable here to examine the numerous differences of detail between these two lists[2] but rather to allude to parallels

[1] E.g. the list in Num. 26: 5–51, taken by Noth, *System*, pp. 14 ff., as the prototype for further genealogical speculation in the OT.

[2] For this see Edward Lewis Curtis and A. A. Madsen, *A Critical and Exegetical Commentary on the Books of Chronicles*, ICC (1910), pp. 168 ff. and Loring W. Batten, *A Critical and Exegetical Commentary on the Books of Ezra and Nehemiah*, ICC (1913), pp. 266 ff.

that point to the priority of Neh. 11.[1] The introductory statement in Neh. 11: 3–4*a* prepared the way for a list of the '*chiefs* [ראשי] of the province who lived in Jerusalem', while the parallel statement in I Chron. 9: 2 refers to 'the *first* [הראשנים reminiscent of Neh. 7: 5] to dwell again in their possessions in their cities' in spite of the fact that the following names are taken as the leading citizens—the 'chiefs'—of the restoration. In the same verse the hand of the Chronicler can be seen in his interpolating of Ephraim and Manasseh so that they are represented among the dwellers in Jerusalem, a slip that shows the desire to represent 'all Israel' in the reconstituted Davidic theocracy.[2] Again, in the lists of the priests (which are in both sources sharply distinguished from the Levites)[3] the Chronicler has conflated the genealogies of Adaiah (Neh. 11: 12*b*) and Amashai (verse 13*b*) so as to give a genealogy of Adaiah only. Moreover, the numbers given in the two sources support a later date for I Chron. 9. In Neh. 11 the total laity in Jerusalem is given as 1,396; clergy 1,648. In I Chron. 9 the laity is 1,646 while the priests alone (the figures for the Levites and all other clerical officials except 'the gatekeepers of the thresholds' are missing) amount to 1,760. The larger numbers probably can be attributed to the Chronicler's tendency to numerical exaggeration rather than to the changing conditions of a later time.[4]

(2) The second group consists of several fragments intended to give the genealogy of the high priest, namely Neh. 11: 11 (=I Chron. 9: 11); Ezra 7: 1–5; I Chron. 5: 27–41 (EV 6: 1–15); and a few shorter notes. That these are intended as high-priestly genealogies can be seen by the terms used to designate their office: נגד בית האלהים (I Chron. 9: 11; Neh. 11: 11) and

[1] Dogmatic statements are by the nature of the sources excluded; cf. Noth, *Überlieferungsgeschichtliche Studien* (2nd ed. 1957), pp. 130 f.: 'Sich eine Abhängigkeit der einen von der anderen Liste nicht erweisen lässt...' Yet Rudolph's conclusion seems to be justified: 'Es ist eine alte Streitfrage, wie sich dieser Abschnitt zu Neh. 11: 3 ff. verhält, aber es lässt sich, wie ich glaube, mit genügender Sicherheit nachweisen, das Neh. 11: 3 ff. die Grundstelle ist, die der Verfasser von I Chr. 9 an ihrem jetzigen Ort vorgefunden und ausgehoben hat' (Wilhelm Rudolph, *Chronikbücher*, HAT [1955], p. 83).

[2] The Chronicler assumes that after the fall of Samaria a remnant of the north adhered to Judah; cf. II Chron. 28: 7; 30: 11, 18; 34: 9.

[3] See de Vaux, *Ancient Israel*, pp. 364 ff.

[4] *Contra* Curtis and Madsen, *Chronicles*, p. 170.

הכהן הראש (of Aaron; Ezra 7: 15). The relationship obtaining among these lists can be most easily seen when they are set in parallel columns:

A	B	C	D	E
Neh. 11: 11	I Chron. 9: 11	Ezra 7: 1–5	I Chron. 5: 27–41	I Chron. 6: 35–8
			Levi	
			Kohath	
			Amram	
		Aaron	Aaron	Aaron
		Eleazar	Eleazar	Eleazar
		Phinehas	Phinehas	Phinehas
		Abishua	Abishua	Abishua
		Bukki	Bukki	Bukki
		Uzzi	Uzzi	Uzzi
		Zerahiah	Zerahiah	Zerahiah
		Meraioth	Meraioth	Meraioth
			Amariah	Amariah
			Ahitub	Ahitub
			Zadok	Zadok
			Ahimaaz	Ahimaaz
			Azariah	
			Johanan	
		Azariah	Azariah	
		Amariah	Amariah	
Ahitub	Ahitub	Ahitub	Ahitub	
Meraioth	Meraioth	Zadok	Zadok	
Zadok	Zadok	Shallum	Shallum	
Meshullam	Meshullam	Hilkiah	Hilkiah	
Hilkiah	Hilkiah	Azariah	Azariah	
Seraiah	Azariah	Seraiah	Seraiah	
		Ezra	Jehozadak	
			Jeshua [Joshua][1]	
			Joiakim	
			Eliashib	
			Joiada[2]	
			Jonathan [Johanan]	
			Jaddua	

It will be seen that A and B serve as the core of the two longer lists, and thus may be prior to them, even though none is probably pre-exilic in its present form. All the variations between A-B and C-D can be easily attributed to transcriptional

[1] From this point names are from Neh. 12: 10; continuity from Haggai 1: 1.

[2] For the last three names, cf. I Chron. 2: 32 (MT); Neh. 12: 23.

errors or traditional variations in spelling—with one exception: in A-B Meraioth is inserted between Ahitub and Zadok while in C-D Zadok is the son of Ahitub. This can be explained as the result of the desire to provide Zadok with a genealogy worthy of that of Abiathar, whom he gradually replaced in the tradition as the chief priest of David and Solomon.[1] Abiathar, however, was the grandson of Ahitub (I Sam. 22: 9, 20; cf. 14: 3) and—so the genealogist insists—was Zadok. List C, followed by D, made Zadok the son of Ahitub, probably due to the influence of II Sam. 8: 17,[2] and also conflated the variants Seriah שריה and Azariah עזריה,[3] making the former the son of the latter. Hence A and B are both earlier than either C or D and all reveal the mark of different hands.

In a comparison of lists C and D the supposition that the shorter of the two is prior is borne out by further details. The seventeen names of C are lengthened in D by the addition of six others, Amariah through Johanan, each of which is somewhat suspicious. The first three, Amariah, Ahitub, Zadok, are simply a repetition in direct order of names from a later part of the list; Ahimaaz in Kings is a brother of Azariah rather than his father;[4] Johanan is mentioned in the list of restoration high priests in Ezra 3: 2—a predecessor of Jaddua, who was, according to Josephus, a contemporary of Alexander the Great.[5] That these six names have been added to list D rather than subtracted from list C is supported also by the probability that D reveals the influence of chronological speculation. From Aaron to Jehozadak, that is, from the exodus to the exile, are twenty-three priests. As we have seen, OT chronological speculation allotted

[1] On Abiathar and Zadok see E. Auerbach, 'Die Herkunft der Sadokien', *ZAW*, XLIX (1931), 327–38.

[2] The peculiar statement of II Sam. 8: 17, 'Zadok the son of Ahitub and Ahimelech the son of Abiathar were priests...' is due to disorder; on this the analysis of de Vaux (*Ancient Israel*, p. 373) is surely right. But the probable purpose of the disorder is to demonstrate a closer relationship between Zadok and Ahitub than between Abiathar and Ahitub.

[3] Note the possibility of reading the two letters עז as ש; Seraiah is probably the older form since II Kings 25: 18 and Jer. 52: 24 allude to a Seraiah who was high priest when Nebuchadnezzar took Jerusalem. Here again is support for the priority of Nehemiah (11: 11) as compared with I Chron. 9: 11.

[4] I Kings 4: 2; II Sam. 15: 36; cf. Wellhausen, *Prolegomena*, pp. 221 ff.

[5] *Ant.* XI. 8. 5.

480 years from the exodus to the building of the temple,[1] and the same number of years from the building of the temple to the establishment of the restoration community.[2] Significantly, the historical notes in the list divide the names into two groups—those before the building of Solomon's temple and those who served in the temple until the exile (I Kings 4: 2 indicates that I Chron. 5: 36*b* [ET, 6: 10*b*] originally was intended to apply to the Azariah of *v.* 35 [ET, *v.* 9], thus dividing the list evenly, twelve from the exodus (Aaron) up to the temple (Ahimaaz), and twelve from the founding of the temple cultus (Azariah) through the exile, the priest of the exile not being named). Thus forty years are allotted to each generation.[3]

Parenthetically, and to anticipate a later chapter, we may note that this genealogy bears a similarity to that of Jesus in Matt. 1: 1–17 in two important respects: the number of members in the chain has a special significance; also, the names are divided into epochs by certain pivotal events. For our immediate purpose this schematization is an indication of a theological—and, considered in the perspective of 'objective' history, an artificial—use of genealogical data.

We can best account for list E by considering it as a simple representation of the first half of list D, that is, as a list of high priests who held office up to the beginning of the cultus of Solomon's temple. As such, list E is also an indication of the misplacement of 5: 36*b* [ET, 6: 10*b*].

(3) The third relevant detail in assessing the relation between Chronicles and Ezra-Nehemiah is a comparison of passages specifying the minimum age for Levitical service. In Ezra 3: 8*b* it is said that 'Zerubbabel and Joshua' appointed the Levites, from twenty years old and upward, 'to have the oversight of the work of the house of Yahweh'. This same figure is given in II Chron. 31: 17, a narrative context dealing with Hezekiah, and again in I Chron. 23: 24, 27, a genealogical (or rather cultic, non-narrative) section. The latter passage, especially verse 27, in its over-insistence on the change of age by David himself, reads strangely when compared with the thirty-year

[1] I Kings 6: 1; in list C, Zadok is the twelfth from Aaron; cf. I Kings. 4: 1–4.

[2] See above, p. 32.

[3] See Wellhausen, *Prolegomena*, pp. 221–2; Rudolph, *Chronikbücher*, p. 51.

figure given earlier in the chapter (verse 3); verse 3, in turn, is based on Num. 4: 3.[1] It would seem most probable that Ezra 3: 8 reflects the existing regulations of the restoration cultus and that II Chron. 31: 17 is an attempt to pre-date this innovation to Hezekiah's religious reform. Since I Chron. 23: 3 conflicts with both Ezra and the narrative section of Chronicles, it must be considered an interpolation, itself possibly containing also the incongruous verse 24. Verse 27 would then be a harmonizing attempt by a later editor. In any case Ezra 3: 8 must be prior to the Chronicler's passages with their insistence on tracing post-exilic customs to the Davidic monarchy.

B. THE PURPOSE OF THE GENEALOGIES OF EZRA-NEHEMIAH

As for the purpose of the genealogies in Ezra-Nehemiah, a duplicated note[2] in a genealogical context leaves us in no doubt that the question of legitimacy and continuity was of utmost importance for membership not only in the priesthood but also in the theocracy itself. At the end of a lengthy list of names of clans who returned from Babylon are six clans, three of them priestly, who 'could not prove their fathers' houses nor their descent, whether they belonged to Israel'.[3] The term Israel here, as in the rest of Ezra-Nehemiah, denotes the entire body of Jews—returning or indigent—who were faithful to the cultus and government of the restoration community.[4] The judgment in the case of the non-priestly clans is not stated; but of the priests it is said, 'These sought their registration among those enrolled by genealogies, but it was not found there, so they were excluded [lit. "exiled"] from the priesthood [ויגאלו מן־הכהנה]

[1] Num. 8: 24, however, gives the age as 25.

[2] Ezra 2: 1–63; Neh. 7: 6–65.

[3] Ezra 2: 59 ff.; Neh. 7: 61 ff.

[4] E. Meyer's view that the term in Ezra-Nehemiah designates only the returned exiles (cited by Curtis and Madsen, *Chronicles*, p. 73) fails to convince since both David and Solomon are called 'kings of Israel' (Ezra 3: 10; 5: 11) and the repeatedly occurring phrase 'the children of Israel, the priests and the Levites' (e.g. Ezra 6: 16) is intended to include the entire province of Judea, although it is true that the two lists of returning exiles are organized in this tripartite form. Curtis's view that the term denotes 'all the Israelites [i.e. northerners] in Judah' (*loc. cit.*) does even more violence to such passages as Ezra 4: 3; Neh. 1: 6; 2: 10.

as unclean; the governor told them that they were not to partake of the most holy food until a priest with Urim and Thummim should arise'.[1]

The clear implication of this passage is that anyone who could not provide evidence of the בת־אב of his ancestry in the tribe of Levi could not be installed for service in the temple, but was considered ritually unclean. We must thus assume that the chief priests had access to an authoritative and contemporary list of בת־אבות to which every authorized priest and Levite must be able to connect himself. Indeed, such a purpose could be attributed to lists like that of the 'heads of fathers' houses' in Neh. 12: 12–23, where the clan name is followed by the name of the individual who is its representative. This particular list is apparently the result of the attempt to bring the roster of 'heads of fathers' houses' up to date soon after the return, 'in the days of Joiakim', who was the first high priest to serve in the restored temple.[2] The author notes that the records were then kept current by listing the priestly heads of fathers' houses 'until the reign of Darius the Persian'[3] and the Levitical lists 'until the days of Johanan the son of Eliashib',[4] that is, two generations after Joiakim. Implicit in all this is the assumption that the head of the father's house was a hereditary office.[5]

The books of Ezra and Nehemiah as a whole present the idea of genealogical purity more explicitly than any other OT material. The author is concerned lest 'the holy seed' (זרע הקדש) mix itself with the peoples of the lands.[6] So also the genealogical material is here used to safeguard the purity of the nation—a function not explicit in other genealogical sections of the OT. Jeremias has pointed to the possibility that Talmudic classifications of degrees of racial purity were based on the organization of lists similar to Ezra 2 and Neh. 7.[7] But underneath the notion of legitimacy and racial purity is the desire to express the continuity of the people of God, that is to say, the identity of the

[1] Ezra 2: 62–3; Neh. 7: 64–5.

[2] Cf. I Chron. 5: 41; Haggai 1: 1; Neh. 12: 10.

[3] Neh. 12: 22.

[4] Neh. 12: 23.

[5] Neh. 10: 34 indicates that this office served also as the basis for the rotation of service periods at the temple.

[6] Ezra 9: 2; cf. 9: 8, 11; 10: 10; Neh. 9: 2; 13: 1–3.

[7] Joachim Jeremias, *Jerusalem zur Zeit Jesu* (3rd ed. 1962), pp. 304–17; see below, ch. 4.

new Israel of the restoration with the old Israel of the monarchy. This continuity, which must be demonstrated genealogically, applies as thoroughly to the remnants of Israel left in the land (as is proved by the question of mixed marriages)[1] as to the returned exiles who were asked to produce their genealogical connections to the Israel of the monarchy.

Thus, in essence, this use of the genealogical form is comparable to the previous attempts to maintain a kind of continuity between the patriarchal period and the emergence of Israel as a nation during the exodus and conquest. The 'census' list of Num. 26, taken by Moses and Eleazar, purports to show the identity of the people of the exodus with the families of the patriarchs enumerated in Gen. 46, thus affirming the status of the Israelites in Palestine as 'sons of Abraham' and therefore the true heirs of God's promises to the patriarchs.

C. THE RELATION BETWEEN I CHRON. 1–9 AND THE NARRATIVE

Proceeding to the genealogies in Chronicles, we face the crucial problem of the relation of the genealogical prologue to the narrative body of the books, since, if it is an original part of the Chronicler's work, we would assume that some of the characteristic ideas and themes in the narrative section would be reflected in the genealogical prologue.

1. *Evidence against common authorship*

The evidence concerning the relation of I Chron. 1–9 to the narrative sections seems at first glance somewhat ambivalent. On the one hand, there are indications that chapters 1–9 are incompatible with the narrative both in point of detail and also in matters of general perspective.[2] The following points are most frequently adduced to demonstrate this tension:

(*a*) In the list of high priests (I Chron. 5: 27–41 [6: 1–15]) which we may assume to have been intended to be inclusive, several high priests mentioned in the narrative section are

[1] Ezra 9–10; cf. also Neh. 13: 1–3.

[2] But in details of terminology and style no great variety can be discerned; cf. Curtis and Madsen, *Chronicles*, pp. 27–36.

omitted, namely the Jehoiada of II. 22: 11, the Azariah of II. 26: 17, 20 under King Uzziah, the Azariah of II. 31: 10 under Hezekiah, and possibly the Amariah of II. 19: 11 under Jehoshaphat, although the last-named may be identified as the Amariah of I. 5: 37 [6: 11]. The objection that the intentional artificiality of the scheme of I. 5: 27–41 may have led the Chronicler deliberately to omit names fails to convince in view of the fact that this list itself appears to be a somewhat crude lengthening of earlier forms of the high-priestly genealogy.

(*b*) The genealogy of Saul (I. 8: 33–40; 9: 39–44) indicates an interest in the family of Saul during post-exilic times (the list runs ten or twelve generations beyond Saul); yet in the narrative material Saul is either ignored or depreciated—he serves merely as the point of departure for the career of David. While all details of the darker side of David's life are studiously overlooked by the Chronicler, the ignominious end of Saul is recounted and, as an ironic epitaph, the Chronicler adds, 'Yahweh slew him...'[1] It is difficult not to feel some tension between these two texts.

(*c*) The sons of David born in Jerusalem are listed in I. 14: 4–7 and so it is not clear what purpose the Chronicler could have had in anticipating the same list in I. 3: 5–7. Yet the fact that both lists are identical in contrast to the list on which both are dependent[2] could indicate that they are in some way related.

(*d*) 'In the introduction [I. 1–9] the Galilean tribes have no prominent place, but in the rest of the book they make a favourable appearance (see especially I Chron. 12: 32–4, 40, and II Chron. 30: 10, 11, 18).'[3] Wellhausen's note is certainly true of the text as it now stands; in the material given to record genealogies of the twelve tribes (I. 2–8), only some 16 verses out of over 300 are given to the five 'Galilean' tribes: Issachar (7: 1–5), Naphtali (7: 13), Zebulon (missing), Dan (a possible remnant in 7: 12*b*), and Asher (7: 30–40). On the other hand, in the genealogical introduction Issachar is said to have had 87,000 warriors[4] and out of Zebulon and Naphtali the same number, 87,000, came to David at Hebron.[5] Moreover, dis-

[1] I. 10: 14.
[2] II Sam. 5: 14–16.
[3] Wellhausen, *Prolegomena*, p. 214.
[4] I. 7: 5.
[5] I. 12: 33–4.

turbances in the text certainly account for much of this supposed imbalance, especially in 7: 6–14.[1] It is also true that precisely these tribes were geographically most distant from Jerusalem, and we may assume that their traditions were less accessible to a scribe at Jerusalem than traditions even of the indistinct or extinct clans of the Transjordan.

(*e*) Welch's main argument against considering chapters 1–9 as a *Vorhalle* to the narrative body of Chronicles[2] is the fact that chapters 1–9 actually do not serve the only purpose which he feels the Chronicler could have had in writing them, namely to link David with the past of the nation.[3] He points to those fragments of genealogies which trace descendants down to exilic or post-exilic times, for example chapters 3; 5: 27–41; 9 (=Neh. 11); 5: 22. But these fragments may be later interpolations and the Chronicler may actually have written the genealogies with a broader purpose in view than Welch envisages—such as providing an idealistic summary of the constituents of the Davidic theocracy.

(*f*) In I. 3: 15–16, the genealogy of David's descendants, two Zedekiahs are mentioned, one the uncle and the other the brother of Jeconiah. This conflicts with the relationship described in Kings (where only one Davidic Zedekiah, the uncle of Jeconiah, is known). A number of difficulties present themselves here but it is relevant for our purpose simply to note that in the narrative section of Chronicles Zedekiah is called the brother of Jehoiachin (=Jeconiah).[4] This is in all likelihood a result of the interpretation of I. 3: 16 where the בנו follows both Jeconiah and Zedekiah, and the two were taken to be brothers. On the other hand the repetition of בנו in lists of names more often denotes a line of descent, as in I. 6: 35–8; and this is the probable explanation for the deviation of 3: 16 from the early

[1] Attempts to reconstruct the text at 7: 6, 13 are summarized by Rudolph, *Chronikbücher*, *ad rem.*

[2] A term used to describe the function of I. 1–9 by Rothstein, von Rad (*Das Geschichtsbild des chronistischen Werkes*, 1930), and (regarding only a core of chs. 1–9) Rudolph (*Chronikbücher*).

[3] Adam C. Welch, *Post-Exilic Judaism* (1935), pp. 185–6.

[4] II. 36: 10; the LXX reading of this verse, Σεδεκιαν ἀδελφὸν τοῦ πατρὸς αὐτοῦ (i.e. brother of Jehoiakim), presumes the Hebrew אחי אביו rather than the MT צדקיהו אחיו; but this is most probably a harmonizing attempt.

tradition in II Kings, where only one Davidic Zedekiah is known. The genealogist in I Chron. 3 knew the tradition of Zedekiah being the brother of Jeconiah[1] but he was also working from a list of kings of Judah and here Zedekiah followed Jeconiah. This accounts for the apparent rupture between verse 16 and verse 17. Hence, according to this reconstruction, I Chron. 3: 15–16 is from a different hand, though not a different school, from II Chron. 36: 10.

(*g*) We have already alluded to the conflict between the figures given for the age at which Levites begin their service. In II. 31: 17 it is 20; in I. 23: 3 it is 30; I. 23: 24–7 corrects this to 20. This can be explained only as a conflict between a narrative section (II. 31) and a 'genealogical' section (I. 23–7). In this case I. 23 must be considered an interpolation and verses 24, 27 (or at least verse 27) an interpolation within an interpolation.

For these and other reasons several scholars including Welch,[2] de Vaux,[3] and Elmslie[4] have concluded that all of chapters 1–9 and possibly also I. 23–7 are later additions to the work of the Chronicler.

2. *Themes common to both sections*

Yet we must take account of the fact that at several points there seems to be a close relationship—possibly a literary interdependence—between the genealogical sections and the narrative. Since this is a matter of theological perspective for the most part, it can perhaps best be presented as a summary of the author's attitude at several key points.

(*a*) *Leading motifs of the narrative section.* In the narrative section of Chronicles there is, both implicitly and explicitly, a concern for all twelve tribes of Israel. A favorite phrase of the Chronicler is 'all Israel', apparently used to designate the whole people of God, the twelve tribes, rather than the tribes of the southern kingdom or northern kingdom only. This phrase כל־ישראל occurs thirty-four times absolutely and about half so frequently in construct forms such as 'all the elders of Israel', 'all the

[1] II Kings 24: 17; I Chron. 3: 15.
[2] *Post-Exilic Judaism, ad rem.*
[3] *Ancient Israel*, p. 390.
[4] W. A. L. Elmslie, *Chronicles* (IB, III) (1952), pp. 349 ff.

congregations of Israel', 'all the tribes of Israel', 'all lands of Israel', 'all princes of Israel', 'every man of Israel', 'all thy people Israel', 'all who were in Israel', 'all the kings of Israel'. That this term had a special significance for the Chronicler is indicated by the fact that it occurs almost as frequently in the chapters dealing with the divided monarchy and even after the fall of the northern kingdom as it does in the chapters recounting the history of the monarchy.

This feeling of the necessity of including the northern tribes as part of 'all Israel' is hinted at throughout the narrative. 'All Israel' and 'all the elders of Israel' came to make David king at Hebron[1] (nothing is said of a prior anointing of David as king only of Judah);[2] great numbers of men from all twelve tribes are said to have come for this purpose,[3] and it is emphasized that they 'were of a single mind to make David king'.[4] Even during the time of the divided kingdom, in the Chronicler's view, 'great numbers' from Ephraim, Manasseh, and Simeon were included in the people of God,[5] which meant for our author that they deserted to Judah and its king Asa 'when they saw that Yahweh his God was with him'; moreover, 'the Levites left their common lands and their holdings [in Israel] and came to Judah and Jerusalem, because Jeroboam and his sons cast them out from serving as priests of Yahweh'.[6] Jehoshaphat, also, gathered the schismatics 'from Beersheba to the hill country of Ephraim, and brought them back to Yahweh, the God of their fathers'.[7] Shortly after the fall of Samaria[8] Hezekiah invited 'all Israel', including Ephraim and Manasseh, to keep a passover at Jerusalem,[9] after which those who had kept the passover carried out a Yahwistic reform in 'all Judah and Benjamin, and in Ephraim and Manasseh',[10] since Jerusalem was to serve as the focus of the cultus for all the tribes of Israel.[11] Josiah's reform similarly extended, according to the Chronicler, to 'the cities of Manasseh, Ephraim, and Simeon, and as far as Naphtali',[12] and subsequently the temple in Jerusalem was repaired with money 'collected from Manasseh and Ephraim

[1] I. 11: 1, 3, 4, 10.
[2] As in II Sam. 2: 1–4.
[3] I. 12: 23–7.
[4] I. 12: 38.
[5] II. 15: 8–9.
[6] II. 11: 13–14.
[7] II. 19: 4 ff.
[8] II. 30: 1, 6.
[9] II. 30: 1, 6, 10 ff., 18.
[10] II. 31: 1.
[11] II. 33: 7–8.
[12] II. 34: 6 ff.

and from all the remnant of Israel and from all Judah and Benjamin and from the inhabitants of Jerusalem'.[1]

A paradoxical attitude toward the northern kingdom is to be seen in such contexts as these: on the one hand the people of God must be complete; the ancient covenants between Yahweh and his people were made with all twelve tribes;[2] the covenant had been renewed with David, the man of the covenant *par excellence*,[3] and this Davidic covenant was itself renewed to the righteous Davidic kings.[4] The Davidic kingdom embraced the twelve tribes; hence the breach between Rehoboam and Jeroboam was a sundering of the people of God. Because of this the Chronicler speaks of 'all the remnant of Israel', that is, those of the northern tribes who were loyal to the Davidic ruler and to the Jerusalem cultus both during the divided kingdom and even after the population had become mixed with foreign elements by the king of Assyria. Extinct tribes are brought back to life in order to complete what was lacking among the people of Yahweh.[5] And yet, on the other hand, there is the conviction that Jerusalem, the center of the kingdom of Judah, is in a unique sense the dwelling-place of Yahweh[6] and the sole legitimate place of his cultus[7] where the priests and Levites, special servants of Yahweh, dwell.[8] The cultus begun by Jeroboam I is not valid worship of Yahweh but rather is a meaningless invocation of 'what are no gods'.[9] Only by a return to Jerusalem and the true worship of Yahweh can Israel claim its rightful place in the Davidic theocracy. Until that happens, however, the Chronicler does not hesitate to say, 'Yahweh is not with Israel, with all these Ephraimites'.[10]

(*b*) *Leading motifs of the genealogical section.* Is this double attitude toward Israel reflected also in the genealogical introduction to Chronicles? In general it appears that the same overall view of

[1] I. 16: 14–18. [2] *Ibid.*

[3] I. 11:3; II. 21: 7; cf. Adrien-M. Brunet, 'La théologie du Chroniste: Théocratie et messianisme', in *Sacra Pagina*, ed. J. Coppens (1959), esp. p. 391.

[4] II. 13: 4–5; to Hezekiah, II. 29: 10; to Josiah, II. 34: 29–31.

[5] Cf. Wellhausen, *Prolegomena*, p. 212.

[6] I. 23: 25. [7] II. 6: 6; 30: 3, 11; 33: 7; 36: 14.

[8] II. 19: 8. [9] II. 13: 8–9; cf. 11: 14–15.

[10] II. 25: 7; cf. II. 35: 18.

the relation between north and south does indeed prevail in I. 1–9, where, after the opening introductory chapter, the author gives a genealogical sketch of 'all Israel'.[1] In the text as we have it, some disturbances, especially in the first half of chapter 7, have marred this intention but the following outline still obtains:

Judah	2: 3—4: 23
Simeon	4: 24–43
Transjordanian tribes	5: 1–26
Reuben	5: 1–10
Gad	5: 11–17
Half Manasseh	5: 23–6
Levi	5: 27—6: 66 (6: 1–81)
Issachar	7: 1–5
Benjamin	7: 6–12; 8: 1–40 (=9: 35–44)
Naphtali	7: 13
Manasseh	7: 14–19
Ephraim	7: 20–9
Asher	7: 30–40

The only tribes omitted from the traditional lists are Zebulon and Dan. It may be that the first Benjaminite list, I. 7: 6–11, was originally that of Zebulon;[2] certainly a remnant of the Danite genealogy is preserved in verse 12.[3] Before textual distortions, then, the introductory part of Chronicles was intended to present the genealogies of the twelve tribes.

This conclusion is further strengthened by an examination of the use of the more ancient lists of tribal subdivisions, especially Num. 26 and Gen. 46, by the genealogist of Chronicles. Noth's hypothesis[4] that these two lists, especially Num. 26, represent the starting-point for most of the later OT genealogical speculation concerning the twelve tribes is widely accepted, at least in its broad lines, and they certainly form the core of the tribal lists in I. 1–9. The Chronicler apparently intended to assimilate most of the names in these lists. In comparing the Numbers list, which gives only the immediate descendants of

[1] I. 9: 1*a*.

[2] So Curtis and Madsen, *Chronicles*, pp. 147–9, followed by Adrien-M. Brunet, 'Le Chroniste et ses Sources', *RB*, LX (1953), 485 ff.; but contrast Rudolph, *Chronikbücher*, p. 65.

[3] Noth, *System*, pp. 14 f., 17 f., 121–32 *et passim*.

[4] *System*, pp. 14 f., 17 f., 121–32 *et passim*.

each patriarch, with the genealogies of I Chron. 1–9 we are able to classify the Chronicles lists according to the degree to which they reproduce the names of the earlier lists:

(1) Some of the lists in Chronicles almost exactly reproduce the names of Num. 26,[1] considering in each case only the immediate descendants mentioned in Chronicles. Among these are Judah, Simeon, Reuben, Levi, Issachar, Naphtali, and Asher.

(2) Three tribes, Manasseh, Ephraim, and Benjamin, show a mixed relationship; that is, certain names from Numbers recur but sometimes in a different sequence or relationship. For example, in Num. 26: 29 ff. Asriel is the grandson of Machir; in I Chron. 7: 14 he is the father of Machir. Other names out of place in the Manasseh list of I Chron. 7: 14–19 are Mahiah, Shechem, and probably Shemida. In the Ephraimitic list, I Chron. 7: 20–9, we have two linear lists of names, each name being followed by בנו, leaving a confusion as to whether the series is to be a line of descent or a group of siblings. But verses 25–7 are apparently intended as a pedigree[2] and thus probably also verses 20–1. As such, it departs from the scheme of Num. 26; there is also the changing of Becher to Bered and the omission of Eran (Num. 26: 36). As for the Benjaminite lists, we are able to identify only the first name of the first list,[3] while in the second[4] the genealogist apparently conflated the diverging lists of Gen. 46 and Num. 26 (one of the few points of variance between these two). Certain names are common to Gen. 46, Num. 26, and I Chron. 8 (Bela, Ashbel, Naaman); others are common to Genesis and Chronicles (e.g. Gera); others to Numbers and Chronicles (e.g. Shephupham, Ahiram = Aharah); others to Numbers and Genesis (e.g. Ard, Huppim). Attempts to apply the principles of literary criticism to these Benjaminite lists have resulted only in a further demonstration of the impossibility of doing so.[5]

[1] Slight deviations can usually be explained as due to transcription.

[2] Of Joshua; it is strange that Joshua is placed in the tenth (possibly eleventh) generation from Ephraim while Moses in the traditional lists is only three generations removed from Levi.

[3] I. 7: 6.

[4] Ch. 8.

[5] Cf. Hope W. Hogg, 'The Genealogy of Benjamin, A Criticism of I Chronicles VIII', *JQR*, XI (1899), 102–14; J. Marquart, 'The Genealogies of Benjamin', *JQR*, XIV (1901–2), 343–51.

(3) Of the remaining tribes, Zebulon and Dan are not represented in I Chron. 1–8 and the Gadite list (5: 11 ff.) bears no relationship whatever to the lists in Genesis and Numbers.

In the second group, leaving aside the lists of Benjamin, which probably were in a state of confusion before the activity of the Chronicler, we find that only the genealogies of Ephraim and Manasseh, the heart of the northern kingdom, show signs of having been altered from the form of the earlier lists. Names in lists of other northern tribes—Issachar, Asher, and Naphtali—are almost exactly repeated from Num. 26. This leads us to concur with the opinion of Wellhausen, who worked from the nature of the two lists themselves: 'The proper kernel of Israel, Ephraim and Manasseh, is, in comparison with Simeon, Reuben, Gad, Issachar, treated with very scant kindness (7: 14–29)—a suspicious sign. The list of the families of Manasseh is an artificial *réchauffé* of elements gleaned anywhere... In the case of Ephraim a long and meagre genealogy only is given, which... constantly repeats the same names.'[1]

This lack of 'kindness' on the part of the genealogist bears a certain resemblance to the paradoxical attitude toward the northern kingdom in the narrative sections of Chronicles mentioned above. Ephraim and Manasseh stand in a problematic relation to 'all Israel';[2] again, Ephraim is isolated as the center of opposition to the true cultus.[3] At this point, the narrative is consistent with the genealogies.

We have seen that the narrative sections of Chronicles assume the centrality of Judah and Jerusalem among the people of Israel, even though to be complete the kingdom must embrace 'all Israel'. This, too, is what we find in the genealogies. Of the more than three hundred verses given to the genealogies of the twelve tribes, Judah occupies one-third of the total, followed in order by Levi with eighty-one verses, Benjamin with forty-seven, and Simeon with twenty. Surprisingly the Transjordanian tribes—which in the Chronicler's day had been long extinct—are given more than double the space[4] occupied by Ephraim and Manasseh together.[5] The position of Ephraim and Manasseh in the order of the twelve tribes is itself somewhat

[1] *Prolegomena*, p. 214.
[2] Esp. II. 30: 1.
[3] II. 25: 7; II. 30: 11.
[4] I. 5: 1–26.
[5] I. 7: 14–29.

curious considering the fact that in no other list of the twelve tribes is this exact sequence found, even allowing for textual corruption in 7: 6, 12 f. Probably the first names are listed in a geographical order,[1] the underlying purpose of which is to show the centrality of Judah. But the purpose of the order of the northern tribes is unclear; it may well be that before the additions of 7: 30—8: 40 Ephraim and Manasseh were in last place. At any rate, these details point to the Chronicler's anti-Samaritan feeling.[2] The centrality of Jerusalem in the narrative is explicit: Yahweh has chosen Jerusalem that his name might be there;[3] so in the genealogical sections Jerusalem is the focus of the cultus; the house of Yahweh is there.[4] For the genealogist of Chronicles, the whole Levitical cultus is bound inextricably to Jerusalem:

> For David said, 'Yahweh, the God of Israel, has given peace to his people; and he dwells in Jerusalem for ever, And so the Levites no longer need to carry the tabernacle or any of the things for its service'.[5]

Here again the genealogist and the Chronicler are in close agreement.

Again, it should be noted that a favorite doctrine of the Chronicler, the idea of short-ranged retribution,[6] finds expression in a casual remark within a genealogy, namely that 'Achar, the troubler of Israel, transgressed in the matter of the herem', referring to the story narrated in Josh. 7: 1, 24–6. So also the half-tribe of Manasseh is carried into exile by 'Pul' of Assyria because 'they transgressed against the God of their fathers, and played the harlot after the gods of the peoples of the land, whom God had destroyed before them'.[7] If the hand of the Chronicler is not to be discerned here, certainly his doctrine is.

As a minor point, but one that demonstrates the integrity of a passage usually considered a later interpolation, we note that

[1] Noth, *System*, p. 21.

[2] Rudolph (*Chronikbücher*, p. ix) views the whole of the Chronicler's work as largely an anti-Samaritan polemic; cf. also Robert North, 'Theology of the Chronicler', *JBL*, LXXXII (1963), esp. 377.

[3] II. 6: 6.

[4] I. 6: 10, 32.

[5] I. 23: 25–6, in a genealogical context.

[6] Cf. North, pp. 372–4.

[7] I. 5: 25 ff.; cf. 5: 19–20.

the Hur–Uri–Bezalel genealogy of I. 2: 20, derived from Exod. 31: 2; 35: 30, is repeated in II. 1: 5.[1]

An important phenomenon, although admittedly an argument from silence, is the Chronicler's scanty mention of Moses or the exodus events in the narrative, and, indeed, his removal of references to the exodus which appeared in his source material.[2] Several attempts to explain this neglect have been made,[3] ranging from, on the one hand, Noth's view that the Chronicler's silence shows his support for the Mosaic covenant as something to be taken for granted to, on the other, North's view that the Chronicler attempted to show that David, not Moses, was the 'primary vehicle' in Israel's *Heilsgeschichte*.[4] But, whatever his intention, it is clear that the same neglect of Moses and the exodus is to be seen in the genealogical sections. In the Levitical genealogies of I. 5: 27—6, Moses is but mentioned;[5] in the other genealogical sections he fares scarcely better. Although in I. 23: 12–23 he is called 'the man of God', in I. 26: 24 ff. his descendants are described as being in charge of the dedicated gifts (הקדשים) during the reign of David; that is, they were to distribute the spoils of battle for the upkeep of the temple—hardly a position of great prestige in comparison with David and his descendants.[6] This subordination of the exodus and Moses is entirely consistent with what we find in the narrative.

Finally, a striking set of parallels has to be noted which surprisingly has missed the attention of the commentators. This has to do with the military terminology that is used in the same way in both narrative and in the genealogies. Among these is the technical use of ראשי בית־האבות to designate captains of subdivisions (גדודים) of the army,[7] which represents a depar-

[1] Cf. Brunet, 'Le Chroniste', p. 494.

[2] The allusion to the exodus in I Kings 8: 20*b*–21 is omitted in the parallel account of II. 6: 10*b*–11; I Kings 8: 51 is suppressed by the Chronicler; and for I Kings 8: 53 the Chronicler in II. 6: 41–2 has substituted Ps. 132: 8–11; see Brunet, 'La Théologie', pp. 389–90.

[3] Several are mentioned by North, *JBL*, LXXXII (1963), 376–8.

[4] North, pp. 377–8.

[5] I. 5: 29 [6: 3]; 6: 34 [6: 49].

[6] These two passages, together with the notes in Exod. 2: 22; 18: 3–4, are the only references to descendants of Moses in the OT, unless Judges 18: 30 should be emended from מנשה to משה, as seems probable.

[7] Compare I. 7: 40; 5: 24; 7: 2, 4, 6, 9, 11; 8: 6, 13, 28 with I. 27: 1; II. 17: 14–19; 25: 5; 26: 11–12.

ture from the previous use of the same term in the Priestly source of the Pentateuch. The frequently occurring 'mighty warriors' used in apposition to 'heads of fathers' houses' or to the men under their command is to be found in both genealogies and narrative[1], as is also the phrase אנשי שמות לבית אבותם.[2] As we shall see,[3] these military allusions can illumine several sections of I Chron. 2–9 where the Chronicler's sources have been in doubt.

3. *Conclusion*

We are now ready to summarize the results of our discussion of the relation of the genealogical portions of Chronicles to the narrative body. Although there are a few points of detail where a common authorship seems to be excluded,[4] these can be accounted for by recognizing the ease with which genealogical material can be added to and subtracted from. The result to which we are led is to consider chapters 1–9 of I Chronicles an integral part of the Chronicler's work, although the hand of later editors is to be admitted at several points. At the least, the weight of the evidence puts the burden of proof on those who would consider the entire genealogical introduction to Chronicles a later addition. But, what is more, the evidence renders the attempt to minimize the Chronicler's hand in this material difficult and tenuous. This judgment must apply in some degree to the detailed analysis of Rudolph, who classifies each pericope in Chronicles as either 'das ursprüngliche chronistische Werk' or as 'Zutaten'.[5]

D. THE THREE TYPES OF MATERIAL IN I CHRON. 1–9

Rudolph's analysis does, however, have the merit of isolating what is here designated as the 'core' material of each tribal genealogy[6] that appears to be the common denominator of each,

[1] Compare I. 5: 24; 7: 2, 7, 9, 11, 40; 8: 40 with I. 12: 28; 26: 6 (of gate-keepers!); II. 26: 12.

[2] Compare I. 5: 24 with I. 12: 31 [30]. [3] See below, pp. 62–8.

[4] Duplication of names, exceedingly numerous, is not valid evidence for or against the Chronicler's hand, since in a work of this sort the utilization of various sources must be assumed.

[5] *Chronikbücher*, pp. 1–5 *et passim*.

[6] Designated by him as 'Das ursprüngliche chronistische Werk'.

largely derived from the Pentateuch.[1] The remaining material—Rudolph's 'Zutaten'—is quite variegated. But in general this additional material is of two sorts: a description of the dwelling-places of the clans based on tribal allotments in the book of Joshua and an assortment of disconnected historical notes. The clearest example of this structure of a tribal genealogy is that of Simeon, I. 4: 24–43. First is the 'core' (verses 24–7) based on Num. 26: 12–14; then a description of the dwelling-places of the tribe (verses 28–33) based on Josh. 19: 1–9; finally some miscellaneous names and historical notes giving the impression of being derived from a variety of sources.[2] The extent to which these three categories apply to each of the tribes can be seen in the following table, which of necessity is somewhat arbitrary:

Tribe	Core	Geographical data	Other notes
Judah	2: 3–17, 25–33, 42–50*a* (3: 1–24)	2: 22*b*–23, 50*b*–55	2: 18–22, 24, 34–40 (3: 1–24) 4: 1–23
Simeon	4: 24–7	4: 28–33	4: 34–43
Transjordanian tribes	5: 1–3	5: 8*b*–9*a*, 11–17, 23–6	5: 4–8*a*, 9*b*–10, 18–22
Levi	5: 27—6: 38	6: 39–66	(?)
Issachar	7: 1–2*a*, 3	—	7: 2*b*, 4–5
Benjamin	7: 6	8: 28*b*, 31*b* (=9)	7: 7–11; 8: 1–28*a*, 29–31*a*, 32–40
Naphtali	7: 13	—	—
Manasseh	7: 14–19	—	—
Ephraim	7: 20–1*a*, 25–7	7: 28–9	7: 21*b*–24
Asher	7: 30–7	—	7: 38–40
Jerusalem	9: 1*b*–3	9: 4–34	*passim*

Because this tripartite division of the genealogies seems to apply to several of the tribes we may raise the question of the purpose of each in turn.

1. *The purpose of the 'core' material*

This has already been discussed to some extent above. Essentially this is a slight elaboration of Pentateuchal data where the subdivisions of the tribes were listed. The result is announced in

[1] The one exception is Gad (I. 5: 11–17), where the names apparently bear no relation to Pentateuchal sources.

[2] Cf. Brunet, 'Le Chroniste', p. 486.

9: 1 *a*: 'And all Israel was enrolled in genealogies; and these are written in the Book of the Kings of Israel.' This verse forms a conclusion to the genealogies of the preceding chapters[1] and actually is a statement of the Chronicler's purpose: to present a summary of the members of 'all Israel', that is, of the true Davidic theocracy; in short, to give a picture of the complete kingdom of God.

2. *The purpose of the geographical data*

Just as the Chronicler was concerned with the inclusion of the members of all tribes in the Davidic theocracy, so too he is anxious that the territory occupied by Israel under the united monarchy be retained. This is for him the will of God who gave the land to the patriarchs and to their descendants as an inheritance forever.[2] Only willful rebellion against Yahweh can invalidate this promise,[3] but even then national repentance will lead to its restoration.[4] That the Chronicler took this promise quite literally is indicated by his use of the concrete expression אדמה in four of the relevant passages; the more fluid ארץ only once. This view of the Chronicler is close to S. A. Cook's reconstruction of the OT concept of the relationship between people and land:[5]

> People and land are essentially one (cf. Hos. 1: 2), each is Yahweh's inheritance (I Sam. 26: 19; cf. Zech. 2: 16) and Israel is sown or planted (Hos. 2: 23; Amos 9: 15) in a land which Yahweh gave his servant Jacob (Ezek. 28: 25)...There is a strong sense of soil (Prov. 10: 30): the land is inalienably Israel's (Lev. 25: 23)...Naaman must take away with him Israelitic soil in order to worship Yahweh fitly in his own land (II Kings 5: 17) and strangers entering the sacred land must learn the cult of the God of the land.

[1] That 9: 1 *a* has been viewed rather as an introduction to ch. 9 by several scholars (among them Bertheau, Benzinger, Curtis, Noordtzij [cited by Rudolph, *Chronikbücher*, p. 83]) is surprising; much more natural is the opinion of Rudolph (following Keil, Oettli, Rothstein, van Selms, and Goettsberger [Rudolph, *loc. cit.*]) that 'es wäre schwer zu sagen, was die Erwähnung der Registrierung von ganz Israel in der Einleitung zu einer auf Jerusalem beschränkten nachexilischen Einwohnerliste bedeuten solle' (*loc. cit.*) and that 9: 1 *a* serves as the concluding formula relative to the introductory formula of 2: 1 *a*.

[2] I. 28: 8; II. 6: 25 *b*, 31; 7: 20; 33: 8. [3] II. 7: 19–20. [4] II. 6: 24–5.

[5] *The Old Testament: a Reinterpretation*, pp. 119 f., cited by W. D. Davies, *Paul and Rabbinic Judaism* (2nd ed. 1955), p. 77 n. 2.

The אדמה included in Yahweh's promise, according to the Chronicler, is 'all the land of Israel',[1] which includes 'Judah and Jerusalem... the cities of Manasseh, Ephraim, and Simeon as far as Naphtali'.[2] In short, it is the approximate extent of the Davidic kingdom, 'from Beersheba to Dan'.[3] So also in the genealogical introduction, the Chronicler is concerned that all the land of Israel should be populated with Israelites or allotted to them. This concern is expressed in several ways, among them the use of place-names as eponyms;[4] the assigning of a tribe to the territory allotted to it in the book of Joshua;[5] and the assigning of clans to a general area.[6]

Of special interest is the attention given to the inhabitants of Jerusalem in the narrative of Chronicles. But, contrary to what we would expect, no list of inhabitants of Jerusalem occurs in the extensive genealogy of Judah; rather it occurs after the formal conclusion of the genealogies of 'all Israel' (9: 1*a*) and forms the body of chapter 9.[7] This is the only post-exilic set of names presented as such in Chronicles (9: 2), apart from a hint in the list of David's descendants in 3: 17 ff. ('Jeconiah, the captive'). One of the curiosities here is that the author relates that 'some of the people of Judah... dwelt in Jerusalem'. These

[1] I. 13: 2; II. 34: 7.

[2] II. 34: 5–7; significantly, Josiah's reform is said to have reached into these areas—another indication of the Chronicler's view that Jerusalem rightfully should have authority over the northern areas in cultic matters.

[3] I. 21: 2; II. 30: 5; cf. II. 19: 4, where the region 'from Beersheba to the hill country of Ephraim' is taken as the extent of the northern kingdom.

[4] Especially in the genealogy of Judah; cf. 2: 23, 50–1; that the Chronicler is fully aware of the eponymous character of these names and does not attempt to conceal this fact is evident from 2: 52, 54, where among the 'sons' of Shobab are 'half of the Menuhoth', the other half being a 'son' of Salma. See M. Noth, 'Eine siedlungsgeographische Liste in I Chr. 2 und 4', *Zeitschrift des Deutschen Palästina-Vereins*, LV (1962), 97–124. Cf. also the genealogy of Manasseh, I. 7: 14–19.

[5] Esp. Simeon, I. 4: 28–33 (cf. Josh. 19: 2–8) and Levi, I. 6: 39–66 (cf. Josh. 21: 1–42).

[6] Of the Transjordanian tribes Reuben is located in Gilead (I. 5: 9), Gad in Bashan (5: 11), and the half tribe of Manasseh in the region from Bashan to Mt Hermon (5: 23).

[7] The phrase in 8: 28, 'These dwelt in Jerusalem', may be due to the influence of 9: 34*b*, the passage which follows being identical in both cases; 8: 31*b* may indicate that some post-exilic Jerusalemite names are preserved here also.

observations are entirely consistent with the relation between Judah and Jerusalem that obtains in the narrative body of Chronicles. The phrase 'Judah and Jerusalem', when used to designate the southern kingdom, occurs only once in the history of the united monarchy,[1] but after the division of the kingdom it becomes a stereotyped designation which seems to supplant the earlier 'Judah and Benjamin'. Clearly we have here a sign of the conditions in the province of Judea in the Chronicler's day when it was apparently possible to distinguish between the returned exiles—who were designated 'Jerusalem'—and the population who had not been removed by Nebuchadnezzar, that is, 'Judah'.[2] This identification of 'Judah and Jerusalem' could possibly explain the enigmatic oracle in the book of Zechariah (12: 1—13: 9). The context is a warning of imminent battle and the resultant mourning; but exactly who is waging the war or its precise outcome remains nebulous. What is most relevant for our purpose, however, is the fact that in this passage the 'clans of Judah' (or simply 'Judah' or 'the tents of Judah') are set in antithetical parallelism to 'Jerusalem' no less than five times (verses 2, 3–4, 5, 6, 7). The catastrophe 'will be against Judah also in the siege of Jerusalem'; the 'clans of Judah shall say to themselves, "The inhabitants of Jerusalem have strength through the Lord of hosts, their God"'. But there is hope for victory in 12: 7–9, where it is said that 'Yahweh will give victory to the tents of Judah first, that the glory of the house of David and the glory of the inhabitants of Jerusalem may not be exalted over that of Judah'. This part of the oracle reveals that some fear of oppression by Jerusalem was being felt among 'the clans of Judah'. Such passages as these can best be set over against the conflict between the indigenous clans of Judah—occupying mainly the villages around Jerusalem—and the post-exilic leadership in Jerusalem proper, stemming from the returned exiles.[3]

[1] II. 2: 7.

[2] Cf. Welch, *Post-Exilic Judaism*, pp. 64–8; de Vaux, *Ancient Israel*, likewise alludes to the preservation of the Judean clan system during the exile (p. 68).

[3] The 'house of David' (Zech. 12: 7, 12), the 'house of Nathan' (12: 12), that of Levi (12: 13), and the 'family of the Shimeites' (12: 13) are apparently the prominent families of 'the inhabitants of Jerusalem', the first two political (cf. II Sam. 5: 14; I Chron. 3: 5); the latter two priestly (cf. Num. 3: 18; I Chron. 6: 17).

If such a distinction between Judah and Jerusalem can be attributed to the Chronicler,[1] then the necessity of considering 9: 1*b*–34 a later addition to the Chronicler's work[2] does not seem so urgent. The plan adopted in chapters 2–9 would then appear to be first to list the dwelling-places of the twelve tribes in order to specify the rightful heirs of the land and then to list as a summary the core population of the heart of the restoration community, the political and religious leaders of post-exilic Jerusalem.[3]

3. *The purpose of the miscellaneous data*

Interspersed among the core material and the geographical data of the genealogies in I Chron. 2–8 are notes which are more than a supplementary collection of names—they give historical or quasi-factual information about the tribe and its clans. We learn, for example, that certain members of the tribe of Simeon 'journeyed to the entrance of Gedor, to the east side of the valley, to seek pasture for their flocks, where they found rich, good pasture, and the land was very broad, quiet, and peaceful...' and that these same persons 'in the days of Hezekiah, king of Judah... destroyed their [the former inhabitants'] tents and the Menunim who were found there, and exterminated them to this day, and settled in their place, because there was pasture there for their flocks'.[4] We learn also that the Reubenites 'in the days of Saul... made war on the Hagrites, who fell by their hand; and they dwelt in their tents throughout all the region east of Gilead',[5] and that 'the men of Gath slew [certain Ephraimites] because they came down to raid their cattle. And Ephraim their father mourned many days, and his brothers came to comfort him.'[6]

[1] It is readily admitted that the identification of 'Jerusalem' with the returned exiles and of 'Judah' with the indigenous population cannot be described as characterizing the books of Ezra and Nehemiah; cf., for example, Ezra 2: 1; 2: 70; Neh. 7: 6.

[2] Cf. Rudolph, *Chronikbücher*, p. 85.

[3] A.-M. Brunet has hinted at the importance of these geographical data for the Chronicler but only in a brief and general statement: 'I Chron. II–VIII s'efforcent en effet de replacer la descendance d'Israël dans le cadre géographique de la Terre Sainte. C'est même cette division du pays entre les tribus qui commande la disposition des généalogies' ('La Théologie', esp. p. 490).

[4] I. 4: 39–41. [5] I. 5: 10. [6] I. 7: 21–2.

Such notes as these seem quite out of place in a genealogical survey and the commentators usually regard them as being derived from 'some old source'[1] or as subsequent interpolations into the Chronicler's core of genealogies.[2] Are they indeed out of place in a genealogy? The publication in recent years of the Safaitic inscriptions (which were found in a basaltic area south-east of Damascus and date from the first centuries B.C. and A.D.) sheds light on the use and character of genealogies in the ancient east.[3] These graffiti constitute for the most part names of the ancestors of the author, encompassing up to twelve generations. Sometimes the names are isolated, sometimes they are followed by an invocation of a deity, by a brief allusion to the reasons for travelling through the area, by laments over the deceased, by the mention of a funeral memorial, and sometimes by alluding to a historical event of significance to the particular tribe. These crude etchings provide additional evidence for the universality of genealogies in the intertestamental and NT period and demonstrate that even a simple Bedouin might be aware of his ancestors for as far back as ten generations.[4] The fact that they were written down is itself significant, and this desire to record one's ancestors is further shown by placing a curse on anyone who would dare to efface it.[5] But most important for our purposes are those fragments which are similar to the miscellaneous notes in I Chron. 2–8. In these inscriptions also we read of tribal battles: 'By 'Awidh Saniy ben Bikhaliah ben Zannel ben Sur. And he was present in the year in which the tribe of Kumair did injury to the tribe of Humaiy. And he

[1] E.g. Curtis and Madsen, *Chronicles*, p. 116.

[2] Rudolph, *Chronikbücher, ad rem.*

[3] See G. Ryckmans, 'Les Noms de Parenté en Safaitique', *RB*, LVIII (1951), 377–92; here pp. 377 f. Safaitic inscriptions have been published by Enno Littmann, *Safaitic Inscriptions* (Publications of the Princeton University Archaeological Expeditions to Syria in 1904–5 and 1909, Division IV, 'Semitic Inscriptions', Section C, 1943), and by G. Ryckmans, *Inscriptiones Safaiticae* (Corpus Inscriptionum Semiticarum, Pars Quinta, 'Inscriptiones Saracenicae', Sectio Prima, 1950); a full bibliography will be found in the latter, pp. xi–xiii.

[4] Littmann, for example, no. 244, p. 59; no. 87, p. 19; no. 18, p. 6; no. 233, p. 53 *et passim*. The average length of pedigree, however, is about four or five generations.

[5] Typical is the hex in no. 308, p. 76 (Littmann): 'O Allat, dumbness to him who destroys the inscription and grief to him.'

laid a stone on the tomb of Ghauth, striken with grief in spite of him.'[1] Here also there is a concern for the pasturing of cattle in a genealogical context[2] and in one inscription a tribal war is connected with the loss of a watering-place for camels.[3] To be sure, these inscriptions are much more crude than the passages from Chronicles, but this simply reflects the relative sophistication and literary aims of the writers. The salient point is that in this genealogical material the same kind of historical notes are included. The individual inscription is thus intended as a history of the writer; the genealogies in Chronicles, on the other hand, were histories of the various tribes with a particular event that was in some way of importance for it.

Yet to admit the analogy of the Safaitic genealogies to parts of the genealogies of Chronicles does not fully account for the miscellaneous notes referred to above. The question remains: if we have pedigrees of individuals in the Safaitic inscriptions, what do we have in tribal genealogies? Are we to understand these names entirely as eponyms, a mixture of historical persons and place-names, or as leading representatives of the tribes? The clue which leads to a satisfactory answer to this question and indeed which points toward an explanation of the derivation of much of this material is the recognition of the importance of allusions to the military in both the genealogies and the narrative of Chronicles. This importance can be seen by a study of the frequently occurring phrase, ראשי בית אבות (or a variation) used in apposition to a series of names.[4] This phrase is also characteristic of the Priestly section of the Pentateuch, where it denotes the leaders of a section of the tribe who represented the tribe in cultic ceremonies,[5] divided the spoils of war,[6] who were commanders in war,[7] acted as a judicial body,[8] or who helped divide the land of Canaan among the tribes during the conquest.[9] Occasionally the 'head of the father's house' is the sole representative of the tribe[10] and

[1] Littmann, no. 254, p. 61; cf. no. 360, p. 95; no. 435, p. 116.

[2] Littmann, no. 406, p. 107, no. 407, p. 107.

[3] Littmann, no. 435, p. 116; cf. I Chron. 4: 41.

[4] I. 5: 13, 15, 24; 7: 2, 4, 7, 9, 11, 40; 8: 6, 10, 13, 28; cf. I. 4: 38; 9: 9, 13, 19.

[5] Num. 7: 2.

[6] Num. 31: 25 ff.

[7] Num. 1: 3*b*–4; 32: 28 ff.

[8] Num. 36: 1 ff.; Josh. 22: 13 ff.

[9] Josh. 14: 1; 19: 51; 21: 10 ff.

[10] Num. 17: 17 [17: 1 ff.].

at times the term is also applied to non-Israelite tribal organizations.[1]

But in Chronicles, and especially in the genealogies, the 'heads of the fathers' houses' are given one main characteristic: they are military commanders. This fact is proved by the phrases used in apposition to 'heads of fathers' houses'; they are throughout 'mighty warriors' (גבורי חיל),[2] 'men of repute' (אנשי שמות)[3] who led units of the army for war (גדודי צבא מלחמה)[4] and were themselves 'ready for service in war' (יצאי צבא למלחמה[5] or בצבא במלחמה מספרם).[6] The heads of fathers' houses commanded 'thousands and hundreds'[7] who were arranged in divisions 'according to the numbers in the muster [במספר פקדתם] made by Jeiel the secretary [הסופר] and Maaseiah the officer, under the direction of Hananiah, one of the king's commanders'.[8] This sheds light on the purpose of various other census lists in the OT. In Num. 1 Moses takes a census of every tribe 'by families, by fathers' houses'[9] in order to number 'all in Israel who are able to go forth to war'.[10] Similarly the great list of tribal divisions in Num. 26—the very list that is used as the core of I Chron. 2–8—is taken to number 'all in Israel who are able to go forth to war' (verse 2). A typical use of the verb פקד is also I Sam. 11: 8, where it denotes a taking count of the soldiers before battle, and thus appears to be a technical term for 'counting off' both before and after battle.[11] That the census taken by David (II Sam. 24) also falls into this category is

[1] Num. 25: 15.

[2] I. 5: 24; 7: 2, 7, 9, 11, 40; 12: 30; II. 17: 14; 26: 12.

[3] I. 5: 24; 12: 30.

[4] I. 7: 4; cf. II. 26: 11–12; the term גדוד is used in the War Scroll (I. 1 *et passim*) to denote troops of 'the sons of darkness'. Much else in the War Scroll is closely parallel to the military terms of the Chronicler.

[5] I. 7: 11; II. 26: 11.

[6] I. 7: 40.

[7] I. 27: 1; II. 1: 2; 17: 14–19; 25: 5; II. 26: 12–13 shows that the average size of the גדוד was around one hundred men, a figure sometimes identical with the size of the 'company' (ראש) mentioned in Judg. 7: 16, although the latter unit seems to have usually denoted one-third of the available troops, whether of the Israelites (Judg. 9: 43 f.; I Sam. 11: 11; II Sam. 18: 1–2) or of the enemy (I Sam. 13: 17 f.; Job 1: 17). Cf. George E. Mendenhall, 'The Census Lists of Numbers 1 and 26', *JBL*, LXXVII (1958), esp. p. 58 n. 32.

[8] II. 26: 11.

[9] 1: 2.

[10] Num. 1: 3; cf. 1: 20*b*, 22*b*, 24*b*, etc.

[11] Cf. I Sam. 14: 17; II Sam. 15: 4–5; 18: 1–2; I Kings 20: 15, 26; II Kings 3: 6 ff.; I Sam. 13: 15 ff.

demonstrated by the fact that it is undertaken by 'Joab and the commanders of the army' (verse 2) and by the results of the census that are stated: 'In Israel there were 800,000 valiant men (איש־חיל) who drew the sword, and the men of Judah were 500,000.'[1] This militaristic use of פקד is characteristic of the earlier historical sources[2] and its occurrence in Chronicles may be a conscious archaism.[3] But the passages cited are clear in this important respect: they explicitly state that lists of names of leaders of 'families' (משפחת) were drawn up according to the larger subdivisions of the tribe, the 'fathers' houses' (בית אבות) and this for military purposes, tribe by tribe.[4] When certain of the tribal genealogies of I Chron. 2–8 are examined in this light, the conclusion is inescapable that these names and notes are remnants from a military census. This is especially clear in the case of Issachar (7: 1–5), Benjamin (7: 6–11), and Asher (7: 30–40) in which all of the persons named are said to be 'heads of fathers' houses', men fit for war. Moreover, their total number is given and in each case it is based on 'their enrollment'[5] (התיחשם) which, as is evident from I. 4: 41 ('These, written by name [הכתובים בשמות] came in the days of Hezekiah, king of Judah, and destroyed their tents and the Menunim who were found there... '), was a written military record.[6] The men of Asher were 'enrolled for service in war' (התיחשם בצבא במלחמה).[7] The root יחש in these and other occurrences in the OT[8] appears to be closely synonymous with the use of פקד to denote a numbering or mustering of troops. This is borne out by the LXX rendering of the word by καταλοχισμός, 'distribution into military companies or bands'.[9]

Examined in the light of this evidence, other tribal genealogies in the Chronicler's prologue reveal similar militaristic interests. The tribe of Reuben, which, according to the tradition, should have been enrolled first in the military census, gives way to Joseph and especially Judah, who 'became strong among his

[1] Cf. Mendenhall, *JBL*, LXXVII (1958), 52–66.

[2] Judges, Samuel, Kings.

[3] Cf. II. 25: 5; 26: 11.

[4] Num. 1: 2.

[5] I. 7: 5, 7, 9, 40.

[6] The meaning of the root יחש (or יחס) is unknown.

[7] I. 7: 40.

[8] The term is used only in Chronicles, Ezra, Nehemiah.

[9] An alternative translation of התיחשם as simply ὁ ἀριθμὸς αὐτῶν can be viewed as support for its similarity to פקד.

brothers'.[1] In the genealogy of Reuben itself (I. 5: 1–10), the individuals named engage in military campaigns either defending themselves against Tiglath-Pilezer (verse 6) or making war 'on the Hagrites' (verse 10). The Gadites (5: 11–17) are listed 'according to their fathers' houses' (verse 13) and 'all of these were enrolled [התיחשו] in the days of Jotham king of Judah, and in the days of Jeroboam king of Israel'. The half-tribe of Manasseh (5: 23–6) is also listed by heads of fathers' houses, 'mighty warriors, famous men' (verse 24). In the genealogy of the Simeonites (4: 24–43) the continuity breaks down after the Num. 26 list and instead there is only a list of disconnected names described as 'princes in their families'. These were 'registered by name in the days of Hezekiah' (verse 41) and carried out military expeditions (verses 41, 43). Finally, the supplementary genealogy of Benjamin (8: 1–28) describes its men as 'heads of fathers' houses' (verses 6*b*, 10, 13*b*, 28*a*) in different geographical areas.

The weight of evidence thus inclines us to consider the genealogies of Issachar, Benjamin, Asher and the Transjordanian tribes as being at least in part based on actual lists of military leaders and war heroes.[2]

[1] I. 5: 1–2.

[2] The results of the discussion of the threefold interest of the genealogist in pedigrees, geographical data, and military information should be compared with the curious passage in the *Iliad* (II. 487–760 [Richmond Lattimore, trans., *The Iliad of Homer* (1951), pp. 89–96]) which purports to be a list of 'the chief men and lords of the Danaans' (cf. II. 487, 760), that is, military leaders of the Achaians and Argives. At first glance the similarity between Chronicles and these 'catalogs' is striking: the author of the latter lists a geographical area of Achaia and the names of the leaders of the contingent from that area, along with the names of their immediate ancestors; interspersed among these are various miscellaneous notes which usually describe the physical features or military prowess of the men and give the total number of ships in their part of the fleet. Thus the tripartite interest of the genealogies of Chronicles seems to be shared by the author of this section of the *Iliad*. Perhaps this similarity should be qualified by the fact that in the *Iliad* genealogical relationships are stated for the purpose of showing the nobility and aristocratic status of the leaders, most often by tracing the individual to a god two or three generations back (cf. II. 653, 731, 740–1, 746, 763 ff., 818 ff., 822, etc.), while in Chronicles it seems that the genealogical relationship (in military contexts) is used as a basis for dividing the military forces along tribal lines. But it is entirely possible that such lists in Israel also preserved the status of a military aristocracy.

The question raised by this conclusion must now be faced, namely, why a list of military commanders should be drawn up in genealogical form. It is perhaps too hasty to assume that the Chronicler simply found in these lists a convenient set of names from which artificially to reconstruct a genealogical survey of extinct tribes—for whatever his purpose might be. If this were the case we could find no reason for the crude lack of continuity within the genealogies (which contrasts so sharply with the highly artificial and sophisticated Levitical genealogies), nor could we account for the retaining of apparently irrelevant military allusions.

One other alternative must be considered, namely the possibility that the military 'census' lists were themselves organized in a genealogical form. Even a cursory reading of the census list of Num. 26 demonstrates that this is actually the case. Not only are the immediate 'sons' of the tribal patronym listed as clans, but sometimes also more remote descendants are mentioned, as when the descendants of Reuben are traced to the third generation (26: 5–11) and those of Joseph (through Manasseh) to the sixth (26: 28–34). All the while each 'descendant' is considered the representative of a clan.[1] The unchanging introductory formula of the list of Num. 1, which gives only the tribal names, proves that this list also was organized in the same way: 'their generations, by their families, by their fathers' houses, according to the number of names' (תולדת למשפחתם לבית אמותם במספר שמות). So when the 'heads of fathers' houses' are alluded to in genealogical fashion[2] it may indicate that such a military office was, at least in some cases, hereditary and thus amenable to genealogical treatment.

This conclusion is supported by what is said of the military aristocracy in the Alalakh texts, where frequent reference is made to 'a social rank in the state of Mitanni' denoted by the term *mariannu*.[3] This word 'is, in formation, a Hurrian word

[1] This is shown by the stereotyped formulae which allude to the מִשְׁפָּחָה being named from the sons of the patriarch.

[2] E.g. I. 5: 13–15; 7: 2–3, 30–7; 8: 1–40.

[3] Sidney Smith, 'A Preliminary Account of the Tablets from Atchana', *Antiquities Journal*, XIX (1939), 38–48; cf. pp. 43 f. For texts see D. J. Wiseman, *The Alalakh Tablets* (1953).

and appears to mean something like "charioteer"...'.[1] Document ATT. 8/49 is translated by Smith as follows:[2]

> Seal of Niqmepa, the king. As from this day forth, Miqmepa, the king, son of Idrimi, has released Qabia to (be a) *mariannu*. As the sons of *mariannu*-men of the city-state of Alalakh (are), so also are Qabia and his grandsons in perpetuity, and priests of Enlil...[3]

This text reveals that the *mariannu* status was conferred by the king, had some religious significance, and—most importantly for our purpose—was hereditary. According to Mendenhall,[4] the *mariannu* status is similar to the 'freeing' of the father's house alluded to in I Sam. 17: 25 and also illuminates such passages as I Sam. 22: 7. In any case we have here a reference to a tradition which recognized a military aristocracy that was, at least in part, hereditary.

So also the personal names which are designated 'heads of fathers' houses' in I Chron. 2–8 are to be understood. This would explain the phenomenon in which some names are linked genealogically and others are not. Thus, in 4: 34–7, where a 'prince' of the family inherited his position, his ancestors who held the same office are mentioned; where this information is lacking the name is given by itself.

As an illustration of the application of this conclusion to the text we may consider the genealogy of Issachar (7: 1–5)

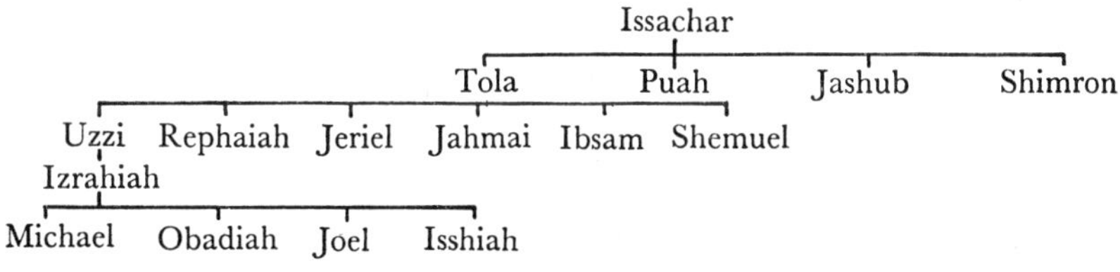

The second generation denotes the tribal clans derived from some such list as Num. 26; the third generation are military leaders of the one clan, Tola ('heads of their fathers' houses, namely of Tola, mighty warriors of their generations', appointed 'in the days of David').[5] The fourth generation is represented

[1] Smith, pp. 43 f.
[2] Cf. also Wiseman, no. 15, p. 39.
[3] Smith, p. 43.
[4] *JBL*, LXXVII (1958), 59 n. 35.
[5] I. 7: 2*b*.

by a military commander, a more or less close descendant of Uzzi; the fifth generation represents Tola's military leaders at a later time, traced through the line of Uzzi. The numbers allotted to the troops commanded by the warriors of Tola is consistent with this understanding since they increase from 22,600 'in the days of David' to 36,000 at a later time. The figure 87,000 is intended to include troops from all clans of Issachar.

Whether or not the Chronicler has preserved these overtly military allusions for a specific purpose can be answered only by conjecture. One could argue that the similarity of these notes to the military terminology of the narrative sections indicates that he had more than an antiquarian interest in the armies of Israel. But does the evidence allow for a further possibility, for example that he intended to sketch a blueprint for a holy war such as that planned in detail by the author of the well-known Qumran scroll? It seems more probable that the Chronicler, in his attempt to construct a genealogical survey of all Israel, found little source material for the extinct tribes (beyond the names in Num. 26) other than these military lists which were already in genealogical form. His faithfulness to the details of his sources where he had no theological reason to change them, a procedure seen in his treatment of the biblical texts available to him,[1] is sufficient to explain his inclusion of the military and historical notes.[2]

[1] Cf. Brunet, 'Le Chroniste', pp. 486–90.

[2] After working with the details of the argument presented above, I was encouraged to note a hint towards the same general conclusion in Yigael Yadin's comprehensive and detailed study, *The Scroll of the War of the Sons of Light Against the Sons of Darkness*, tr. Batya and Chaim Rabim (1962), p. 53 n. 1. Yadin maintains that the military information in the War Scroll make possible an explanation of a number of apparently unintelligible passages, 'in particular I Chron. 5: 23–6; 7; 11. These lists enumerate the tribes and families according to households, and include the census lists for mobilization purposes. In them the title "mighty men of valor" is given to the chiefs of the households, the highest rank in the tribal division, who often served *ex officio* as commanders of the thousands.'

E. THE GENEALOGIES OF JUDAH AND LEVI

It is significant that in only four genealogies of I Chron. 2–9 are there no military allusions: Judah, Levi, Manasseh, and Ephraim,[1] that is, the core tribes of Israel, both south and north. This singling out of Ephraim and Manasseh may indicate that the Chronicler considered these two as the core of the northern kingdom. But, more probably, the richer genealogical material available to him in the biblical tradition made any dependence on military census lists unnecessary for these four tribes.[2]

As for the two lengthiest tribal genealogies, those of Judah and Levi, the general purpose of the Chronicler is clear. These two tribes not only constituted the bulk of the restoration community but it is from these two that the political and religious leadership of that community must be derived.[3] Thus, of the leaders of the restoration, two pairs, each consisting of a priest and a lay 'governor', are prominent, namely Jeshua and Zerubbabel[4] and subsequently Ezra and Nehemiah.[5] These facts are sufficient to account for the detailed attention given Judah and Levi in the Chronicler's genealogical prologue.

But certain differences in approach to the composition of these two tribal genealogies should be noted. The great list of Judahites is a highly composite structure, incorporating with

[1] The quasi-militaristic note in I. 7: 21 *b* has the function of introducing the purported ancestry of Joshua (constructed from unrelated materials in the Pentateuch); it may, however, have the same origin as I. 5: 9*b*–10.

[2] Cf. Wellhausen, *Prolegomena*, p. 214.

[3] The fact that in Ezra-Nehemiah there is no mention of any of the twelve tribes except Judah, Benjamin, and Levi is somewhat curious in face of the obvious concern of the author of I, II Chronicles for 'all Israel'. This contrast is especially noteworthy in those passages in Chronicles that are derived from Ezra-Nehemiah; cf., for example, the mention of Ephraim and Manasseh in I. 9: 3, lacking in Neh. 11: 4.

[4] Cf. Ezra 2: 2; 3: 2; 5: 2.

[5] Cf. Neh. 12: 26. Perhaps we have here an explanation of the relative chronology of the men Ezra and Nehemiah. The Chronicler assumes the necessity of priest and governor working hand in hand to establish the new theocracy; this tendency resulted in making contemporary the work of Ezra and Nehemiah in contrast to the sources the Chronicler had before him which dated the work of Nehemiah prior to the ministry of Ezra. The recognition of this tendency would support the general conclusions of H. H. Rowley's study, 'Nehemiah's Mission and its Background', *BJRL*, XXXVII (1954–5), 528–61.

some ingenuity[1] as much genealogical information contained in the earlier historical books as possible and, indeed, perhaps more than was appropriate. The fragmentary nature of the sources used partly obscures the underlying structural design of the list, which follows the Chronicler's method in chapter 1. After enumerating the sons of Judah (2: 3–4) the Chronicler gives the names of the sons of Perez (verse 3) and of Zerah (verse 6). Then, in inverse order, he gives what are considered to be the descendants of Zerah (verses 7–8), those of Perez (2: 9—4: 20) and finally those of Shelah (4: 21–3). The descendants of Perez are organized under the three sons of Hezron: of Ram (2: 10–17), of Caleb (2: 18–24) and of Jerahmeel (2: 25–33). To these are then added, once again in inverse order, the completions: to Jerahmeel (2: 34–41), to Caleb (2: 42–55), to Ram (3: 1–24) and finally a general Hezronite supplement (4: 1–20).[2]

1. *Judah*

The bulk of the genealogy of Judah is given over to the descendants of Hezron (2: 9—4: 20); indeed, the remaining elements of this genealogy are roughly equivalent in scope to that devoted to each of the northern tribes. And the fact that two of the three Hezronite branches are traced to individuals who were probably originally non-Israelites[3] illustrates the degree of artificiality in the construction and thus the determined interest of the Chronicler in the Hezronites. This interest is, of course, to be explained as due to the concern to enumerate the ancestors (2: 10–17), descendants (chapter 3), and kinsmen of David, the theocratic king *par excellence*. In all this there is perhaps the desire to demonstrate—or reflect—the probability that a large part of the restoration community was Davidic.

[1] To provide one of Judah's 'sons', Zerah, with posterity, the Chronicler drew on two narrative episodes in the historical books, the story of Achan's transgression in Josh. 7 and from I Kings 4: 31, where it is related that Solomon 'was wiser than all other wise men, wiser than Ethan the Ezrahite, and Heman, Calcol and Darda, the sons of Mahol'. Like the one, the other three are Ezrahites (אזרחי) and thus sons of Zerah (זרח). Cf. Brunet, 'Le Chroniste', pp. 492–3, and on the Chronicler's sources for chs. 1–9, pp. 481 ff.

[2] Curtis and Madsen, *Chronicles*, pp. 82–4; Brunet, 'Le Chroniste', p. 491.

[3] Caleb was originally connected with the Kenites (Num. 32: 12; Josh. 15: 13; I Sam. 30: 14), cf. I Sam. 27: 10; 30: 29 for the phrases 'Negeb of the Kenites' and 'Negeb of the Jerahmeelites' as hostile territory.

Of particular interest is the form of the list of ancestors of David (2: 10–17)—a linear pedigree tracing only one line of descent (characteristic also of the Levitical genealogies) rather than a list enumerating various branches of descent, which is the pattern in the rest of the Hezronite genealogy.[1] Where a single line of descent is traced in any given genealogy, one can find one of two purposes: either to enumerate the names of those who held an office of importance (e.g. the Judean kings, I. 3: 10–16; the priests and Levites, I. 5: 27–38 [6: 1–53]) or to provide a prominent individual with a pedigree (e.g. David, I. 2: 10–17; the two lists comprising the Ephraimite genealogy, I. 7: 20–1, 25–7; Ezra, Ezra 7: 1–5).

2. *Levi*

It is in the Levitical genealogies that we can most easily come to understand something of the genealogical procedure of the Chronicler's day since, in view of the special importance attached to the purity of descent among the priests and Levites, especially in post-exilic times,[2] these groups came to be the special object of the genealogist's art. It is not our intention here to analyze the *Gattungen* of the various Levitical genealogies —this has been done previously in sufficient detail[3]—but rather to adduce one example of the artificial construction of genealogies suggested by André Lefèvre.[4] It is well known that the genealogy of the Kohathite singer, Heman (I. 6: 18–23 [6: 32–8]), is the same list of names as the Kohathite list of I. 6: 7–13 [6: 22–7]. There are three problems that such a recognition raises in dealing with I. 6: 7–13: (1) Verses 10 and 13 do not follow the linear scheme but represent the formula of a genealogy that branches out; (2) the name of Elkanah occurs no less than five times and at the beginning of verse 11 it is doubled (MT); (3) even apart from verses 10 and 13 the linear form is troubled four times by the intrusion of the conjunction 'and' (verse 8 twice, verse 9, verse 11). These difficulties are best explained by assuming that the author of 6: 18–23 (the Heman list) read the

[1] The list of Judean kings (3: 10–16) is, of course, also linear.

[2] Cf. Num. 3: 5–13; 8: 14; Deut. 10: 8–9; Ezra 2: 62; Neh. 7: 64.

[3] See esp. the works of Noth and also de Vaux, *Ancient Israel*, pp. 345–405.

[4] 'Note d'Exégèse sur les Généalogies des Qehatites', *RSR*, XXXVII (1950), 287–92; parts of this article are paraphrased in translation in the immediately following remarks.

earlier list as a linear genealogy rather than one that named branches of descendants. In this way, the seemingly superfluous use of *waw* is explained: the first (verse 8*a*) indicates that Assir, Elkanah, and Ebiasaph are siblings, as in the earlier sources;[1] the second (verse 8*b*) prepares for the list of descendants of Assir; and the third (9*b*) marks Shaul as the last of Assir's descendants; the *waw* in verse 10*b* makes Amasai and Ahimoth brothers. We are thus left with the following reconstructed genealogy, to which is appended the pedigree of Samuel:

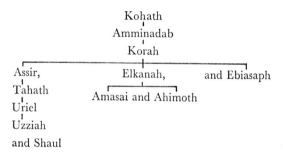

Kohath
- Amminadab
  - Korah
    - Assir,
      - Tahath
        - Uriel
          - Uzziah
          - and Shaul
    - Elkanah,
      - Amasai and Ahimoth
    - and Ebiasaph

When this arrangement is compared with the pedigree of Heman, the differences in names in the two lists[2] appear much less significant than the change from the 'family tree' form to the linear form.

It is clear that the compiler of the second—and later—list has used the material of the first and arranged it in his own way. Again we are faced with what seems, from our perspective, to be an illegitimate literary artifice. But perhaps there is a better perspective: 'Cet auteur connaissait mieux que nous les procédés des généalogistes, et s'il nous a transmis une liste ainsi manipulée, c'est qu'il ne l'estimait pas mensongère; le procédé lui paraissait légitime. Pourquoi alors ne l'emploierait-il pas

[1] Cf. Exod. 6: 24.

[2] All differences are easily explained except Ishar–Amminadab and Zephaniah–Uriel (cf. Lefèvre, pp. 289–90). But, if a suggestion is to be offered, the first may be an attempt to make Amminadab, who in the earlier tradition was a leader of Judah, and father-in-law of Aaron himself (cf. Num. 1: 7; Exod. 6: 23), a good Levite. The second defies solution unless one is bold enough to see some significance in the change of name from 'Light of God' (Uriel) to, perhaps, 'Hiddenness [darkness?] of Yah' (Zephaniah).

lui-même? La 'généalogie' était une œuvre d'art, autant qu'une pièce juridique, et bien plus qu'un document biologique; c'est nous qui sommes dans l'erreur, quand nous exigeons du généalogiste une exactitude matérielle qu'il ne prétend pas donner et qui était pour lui d'importance très secondaire.'[1] In short, this kind of genealogical construction can be considered the product of a kind of midrashic activity.

F. A NOTE ON I CHRON. I

The first chapter of Chronicles is usually considered to serve the purpose of setting the stage for the story of David by presenting the OT *Heilsgeschichte* in a nutshell,[2] a sort of tracing the 'superior strain of line through which the Biblical way of life was transmitted from generation to generation'.[3] This general statement would seem ill-suited to the lists of the sons of Ishmael (1: 29 ff.), Keturah (1: 32 ff.), Esau (1: 35 ff.), Seir (1: 38 ff.) and especially the Edomite king list (1: 43–51). Hence it is not sufficient to point out that in chapter 1 these 'extraneous' elements are introduced only in order to be finished with so that the 'superior strain of line' could be continued.[4] Moreover, the more common solution to account for these non-Israelite lists, namely theories of interpolation into an 'original', are not really solutions since (1) the critics have not been able to excise all these extraneous elements[5] and (2) one would then have to

[1] Lefèvre, *RSR*, XXXVII (1950), 291. [2] See the commentaries, *ad rem.*

[3] E. A. Speiser, 'The Wife–Sister Motif in the Patriarchal Narratives', *Biblical and Other Studies*, ed. Alexander Altmann (1963), p. 28; this quotation is taken to describe 'the ultimate purpose of the biblical genealogies'.

[4] It is, however, true that the author's sequence in dealing with the central figures is significant; usually among a list of siblings, the one who will lead to the twelve tribes of Israel is dealt with last: for example, although Noah's sons are first mentioned in the order Shem, Ham, Japheth (1: 4), this order is reversed in listing their sons (1: 5–23); similarly, Ishmael's genealogy is given before that of Isaac (1: 28–31, 34); finally, the descendants of Esau (1: 35–54) are listed before the central interest of the Chronicler—the twelve tribes of Israel—is reached (chs. 2–9).

[5] The usual source-criticism of the chapter results in retaining 1: 1–4*a*, 24–31, 34*b*–42 as primary; 1: 4*b*–23, 32–4*a*, 43–54 as secondary. Yet the evidence for considering verses 17–24*a* as an interpolation is a case of homoeoteleuton in the LXX where the copyist omitted all names between the Arpachshad of *v.* 17 and that of *v.* 24.

postulate the purpose of later editors in introducing them—plainly a task as difficult as the former.

Much more in harmony with the evidence is E. Podechard's theory[1] that the goal of the Chronicler in chapter 1 is not only to attach Israel to the origins of mankind but to incorporate in his work all the genealogical data contained in Genesis. Thus all theories of interpolation are superfluous and the chapter in its wholeness may be assigned to the author of the narrative.[2] The author abridged the material of Genesis but preserved the details of the introductory formulae. This chapter, then, is the result of the interest of a genealogist in an 'art for art's sake' approach to genealogies.[3]

G. SUMMARY

We have now to summarize the results of our analysis of the genealogies in Chronicles by making more explicit what has implicitly emerged from our study.

The Chronicler, drawing from all the sources at his disposal—biblical, military, folk-traditional, cultic—has expressed in genealogical form many of the theological and nationalistic concepts that are so prominent in his narrative. He has, in I. 2–9, painted a genealogical picture of 'all Israel', the Israel of the Davidic theocracy, preceded by a sketch of the antecedents of this theocracy. Within this sketch (1–9) he brought into emphasis the pre-eminence of Judah, the tribe which above all others remained loyal to the Davidic line and which constituted a large part of the post-exilic community. Placed in prominence also is Levi, from whose members came the cultic leaders as well as the great number of lesser officiants who were, in the mind of the author, chosen by David to serve Yahweh at his dwelling-place, Jerusalem. Also within this survey can be seen in the geographical notes an interest in the land of Israel—but this not so much because of the promise of God to Abraham or Moses as

[1] 'Le premier Chapitre des Paralipomènes', *RB*, XIII (1916), 363–86.

[2] Podechard has some doubts about the authenticity of 1: 32–3.

[3] The only genealogy in Genesis that is omitted by the Chronicler (Haran and Nahor do not really have proper genealogies) is that of Cain; the reason is probably that Cain is not the ancestor of any people, since, according to the present text, his line perished with the flood.

the conviction that the land over which David ruled—from Beersheba to Dan—was to be the inheritance of David's sons forever. In short, it is a picture of the ideal theocracy of Israel. This general statement, of course, raises the question of the Chronicler's view of the Davidic theocracy and especially its future. Did the Chronicler intend this picture, both the genealogical *Vorhalle* and the narrative body, to be simply a reminiscence—idealistically framed—of the high point of all previous Israelite history, the organization of the cultus by David?[1] Or did he believe that the actual Jewish community of Neh. 12: 44—13: 3 was so perfectly the realization of the theocratic ideal that it was for him no longer an eschatological hope?[2] Or, quite the opposite, did he intend to show that the ideal of the theocracy had not been attained even during the reigns of David and his descendants and was not to be attained in the missions of Ezra and Nehemiah but would reach its fulfillment only in the future realization of the prophetic promises?[3] Or is the truth once more to be found in the golden mean—that the Chronicler remains faithful to his conviction that an intimate bond unites the perfect theocracy and the Davidic dynasty but that the post-exilic community is a restoration of the theocracy which slowly approaches its goal, as yet not reached?[4] Or is what the Chronicler has written about David the expression of an eschatological hope for the perfect kingdom of God on earth?[5]

Fortunately, it is not necessary for our purpose to examine in detail the various answers given to the question. It is enough to admit that the genealogical introduction is presented as a picture of the theocracy *par excellence*, that of David and a few of his more worthy successors.

In concluding this summary we may allude to a favorite term used to define the Chronicler's purpose, namely the 'concern for legitimacy'[6] which is purportedly based on the assumption

[1] So David Noel Freedman, 'The Chronicler's Purpose', *CBQ*, XXIII (1961), 436–42.

[2] So Rudolph, *Chronikbücher*, cf. p. xxiii.

[3] So A. Noordtzij, 'Les intentions du Chroniste', *RB*, XLIX (1940), 161–8, esp. pp. 167–8.

[4] So Brunet, 'La théologie', pp. 384–97, esp. pp. 395–7.

[5] Cf. Millar Burrows, 'Ancient Israel', in Robert C. Dentan, ed., *The Idea of History in the Ancient Near East* (1955), p. 125.

[6] Freedman, *CBQ*, XXIII (1961), 437 ff.

that '"family trees" were necessary to authenticate the nation and the leader...'.[1] North argues that, since the Chronicler often includes in his lines of descent individuals or groups who were not biologically and historically related to the chain, the Chronicler therefore intended to trace succession of a certain office or type of work—a 'genealogical attestation of the passing down of skills from father to son, a juridical rather than biological framework'.[2] In Ezra and Nehemiah 'we can detect the same concern for safeguarding God's will by legitimating the title of every *member* of the community to be in the position he is occupying'.[3] This theme of 'legitimating' is probably an apt one in interpreting the few lists in Ezra-Nehemiah, but concerning I Chron. 1–9 it raises more problems than it solves. Who is being 'legitimated' in I Chronicles, where the bulk of the material is placed in pre-exilic times and where are found lists of nine or ten tribes which were extinct in the Chronicler's day? Probably only the leaders of the post-exilic cultus in the Levitical genealogies and possibly also the list of Davidic descendants (3: 10–24). But the whole is intended as a panegyric on David, whose ancestors and kinsmen—Hezronites—outshone all others in number, whose descendants sat on the throne of Judah, and, above all else in the Chronicler's view, who was even more than Moses responsible for the divinely ordained temple cultus. One gains the impression from these genealogies that things will never be quite the same again as they were in the days of David when the people of God were complete, dwelling in 'all the land of Israel', being ruled over by David, the servant of Yahweh.

[1] W. F. Stinespring, 'Eschatology in Chronicles', *JBL*, LXXX (1961), 210.
[2] *JBL*, LXXXII (1963), 369.
[3] Pp. 371 f.

CHAPTER 3

SUMMARY: THE PURPOSE OF THE OLD TESTAMENT GENEALOGIES

In the course of our study we have had occasion to mention several functions of genealogies in the OT, among which are the following:

(1) The demonstration of existing relations between Israel and neighboring tribes by tracing them back to common patronyms, thus establishing a degree of kinship and at the same time a degree of distinction between Israel and her neighbors. This use of genealogies is characteristic of the Yahwistic source in the Pentateuch, and is illustrated by the lists of the descendants of Lot (Gen. 19: 36–8), of Nahor (Gen. 22: 20–4), and of Keturah (Gen. 25: 1–6). Parts of the 'Toledoth book' must also be included here, namely the sons of Ishmael (Gen. 25: 12–16) and of Esau (Gen. 36). The form of these genealogies is simply that of a group of tribal names attached to the ancestor with little linear or 'family tree' elaboration. Moreover, this kind of tribal classification was accomplished with no comprehensive scheme to knit together the various clusters.

The 'Table of Nations' of Gen. 10 has a similar, although more comprehensive, purpose: it intends simply to show how 'the whole earth was peopled' from the three sons of Noah;[1] to show, in sum, the relative kinship of all the known nations of the world and the position of Israel in relation to them. The fact that exactly seventy nations are listed in Gen. 10[2] was also taken by the Rabbis to mean that this was the total number of peoples in the world,[3] and may have signified as much for the final redactor of the chapter.[4]

[1] Gen. 9: 19.

[2] Japheth, 14; Ham, 30; Shem, 26.

[3] Cf. George Foot Moore, *Judaism in the First Centuries of the Christian Era* (3 vols. 1927), I, 226 ff., 278.

[4] Since the figure seventy is the total of the MT as it now stands and the text itself is composite, we must assume that this speculative figure is the result of the work of a redactor rather than that of the sources he used.

(2) The interrelating of the previously isolated traditional elements concerning Israelite origins by the creation of a coherent and inclusive genealogical system. The priestly Toledoth book is the first clear attempt in the OT to elaborate systematically such a scheme; it accomplished the possibility of setting in relief all of the Israelite traditions of the pre-conquest times. Whether or not this book of genealogies served as the basis for the priestly narrative or was subsequently incorporated into the latter cannot be ascertained.

(3) Related to the previous point is the use of genealogies to establish continuity over those periods of time not covered by material in the tradition. The most conspicuous example of such use is the bridging of the gap between the creation–paradise legends and the narratives of the patriarchal age by two lists, both linear in form (Gen. 5; 11). The Toledoth of Perez appended to the book of Ruth (4: 18–22) may similarly be intended to establish continuity during the time of the judges, that is, from the conquest to the beginning of the Davidic monarchy. This use of the genealogical form is found also in the early Greek historians who bridged the gap between the age of Homer and their own age with more or less fabricated genealogies (see above, p. 19).

(4) Genealogies also served as the vehicle for chronological speculation concerning the 'Great Year' or world cycles. The numbers in Gen. 5 establish a date for the flood; those in Gen. 11 the birth of Abraham; other notes are intended to date the exodus. Speculative influence is to be seen in the dating of the establishment of the temple cultus by Solomon and in the reigns of the kings of both north and south. Finally, the list of high priests in I Chron. 5: 27–41 (6: 1–15) divided the pre-exilic history of Israel into two equal periods by assigning twelve priests from the Exodus to Solomon's temple and the same number from there to the exile. The problem of ascertaining the purpose of the chronological speculation is made extremely difficult by the many divergences of textual traditions.

(5) Several genealogies of tribes in I Chron. 2–8 no longer in existence in the Chronicler's day show signs of being constructed of material from lists of military leaders. Census lists preserved in the OT, which are all military in content and purpose, show that such material as was used by the Chronicler for these tribes

was genealogical in form prior to his use of it. This, together with evidence from extra-biblical sources, leads to the conclusion that the military leadership of the tribal subdivisions was probably hereditary. Whether this hereditary aspect was biological, that is, passed from father to son, or was understood more loosely as the continuity of succession of office, cannot be determined.

(6) Genealogies were also used to demonstrate the legitimacy of an individual in his office or to provide an individual of rank with connections to a worthy family or individual of the past. The legitimacy principle—perhaps given too high an importance by the commentators—appears to have been crucial only with regard to cultic functions and this above all with regard to the priesthood. Although the Chronicler goes to great lengths to trace the pedigree of even minor officiants in the Jerusalem cultus, it is perhaps as much for the purpose of demonstrating the Davidic institution of the temple worship as the legitimizing of contemporary officiants. The author(s) of Ezra-Nehemiah, however, indicates that those who could not trace their descent from pre-exilic priests were 'excluded from the priesthood as unclean'.

Apart from the priesthood we find numerous political and religious leaders provided with a pedigree. In the early historical sources this appears to signify not so much the principle of legitimacy—since no line of hereditary political succession was evolved until the Davidic monarchy—but rather the attempt to show the relationship of the individual to the tribe and nation as a whole by tracing his family and its connection with the tribe. In the later historical sources the Chronicler provides an elaborate genealogy of the ancestry and descendants of David but, even here, the question of legitimacy is not primary, since the fact of David's non-royal ancestry is recognized by pointing to the natural priority of Reuben among the sons of Jacob as 'first-born' (I. 5: 1 ff.). Rather, the Chronicler used the genealogical form to express his conviction that God had chosen David by an act of grace to become prince among the tribes of Israel (I. 5: 2; 17: 7). And in the list of the descendants of David we find no assurances of the blessing of God on a ruler simply because he was Davidic. The list of I. 3: 10–24 itself reads as a kind of anticlimax to the genealogical treatment of David. In short, apart from the lists in Ezra-Nehemiah, isolated individual genealogies serve more to identify and enhance the stature of the individual than to legitimize him. Other examples of this function are the genealogies of Samuel (I Sam. 1: 1), Saul (I Sam. 9: 1), Sheba (II Sam. 20: 1), Zephaniah (Zeph. 1: 1) and Zechariah (Zech. 1: 1). Akin to these, but on a non-literary level, are the genealogical graffiti of ancient nomads which are preserved in the Safaitic inscriptions.

(7) Related to what we have said about Ezra-Nehemiah in the above section, it must be admitted that in these two books (and only in these) genealogies are important for establishing and preserving the homogeneity of the race. This concern for the purity of 'the holy seed' (Ezra 9: 2) was taken up and strengthened in the Rabbinic tradition (chapter 4).

(8) Taken as a whole, the Chronicler's genealogical survey of 'all Israel' and the lists of returned exiles in Ezra-Nehemiah may be viewed as the attempt to assert the importance of the principle of the continuity of the people of God through a period of national disruption. The post-exilic Israel of the restoration is identical with the Israel of the monarchy, sharing its promises and its cultus. For this the genealogical form was especially suited. Similarly, it is possible to consider the great tribal lists of Gen. 46 and Num. 26 as serving to show the continuity of the Exodus community with the patriarchal family. The Exodus clans of Num. 26 are the same as the sons of the patriarch Jacob whose names are listed in Gen. 46.

(9) Finally, attention must be drawn to the curious fact that in the OT the most frequent use of the genealogical form is to be found in those writings which emanate from priestly circles, and that this use has a primarily literary function. In the Pentateuch it is especially the Priestly source which is organized around a tightly knit genealogical scheme, drawn in all probability from a previously existing compilation of genealogies, the Toledoth book. This was organized around a group of pivotal figures culminating in Aaron, thus exhibiting a sense of movement within history toward a divine goal. This conviction is manifested also in a chronological scheme embedded within the priestly narrative and closely attached to the genealogical system. Here the major events of pre-Israelitic

tradition—flood, call of Abraham, exodus—are used at once to divide history into epochs and also to demonstrate the outworking of the divine plan for history. The predetermined character of the course of history is to be inferred especially from the symmetrical arrangement of epochs in the priestly chronology. Finally, in the post-exilic histories of Chronicles-Ezra-Nehemiah, we have noted the strong emphasis on establishing the continuity of pre-exilic Israel and the post-exilic Judean community. Here also is to be found the priestly concern for demonstrating the meaningfulness of history under the guidance of God. And the special concern to reveal the continuity of the cultus through the period of disruption is in harmony with the desire of the priestly narrative of the Pentateuch to trace the origins of the sacerdotal cultus to Aaron and, in turn, to reveal Aaron as the culmination of a long genealogical process. Thus the genealogical form was well adapted to express the priestly concern for order and arrangement; for a genealogy is, by its very nature, entwined in history and the order of history. Beyond this, however, the priestly genealogies reveal the conviction that the course of history is governed and ordered according to a pre-arranged plan. The generations come and pass; epochs begin and end. But the worship of God through the cultus ordained by him in previous epochs continues.

So it becomes clear that in the OT the genealogical form was used in a variety of ways, but above all for apologetic purposes, both nationalistic and theological. As such, a kind of midrashic exegesis could be utilized to construct genealogies that communicated the convictions of the author. This is more true of the later literary sources, in which genealogies are used as a flexible form adapted to theological speculation, than of the earlier historical sources, where the apologetic element was not yet so highly developed. Of course, the early tribal genealogies are in one sense highly speculative and apologetic; yet it is only in the P-strand that the traditions of Israelite origins are united in a genealogical system extending from creation to the institution of the Aaronic cultus. Later, in the work of the Chronicler, we have a mass of genealogical material, the purpose of which is to center attention on the institution of the temple cultus by David as well as on the loyalty of all Israel to the Davidic theocracy. For the Chronicler, above all, 'la généalogie était une œuvre d'art'.[1] This means, in essence, that the genealogical form could be used as an alternative to narrative or poetic forms of expression, that is, as one of several methods of writing history and of expressing the theological and nationalistic concerns of a people.

[1] A. Lefèvre, *RSR*, XXXVII (1950), 291 f.

PART II

LATER JEWISH GENEALOGIES AND THE GENEALOGIES OF JESUS

CHAPTER 4

THE NARROWING OF GENEALOGICAL INTEREST IN LATER JUDAISM

It was our contention in chapter 1 that the interest in genealogies in the OT is broad-based and variegated to such an extent that the genealogical form can be said to have become one of the available forms for writing—and re-writing—history, and thus for expressing the nationalistic and religious hopes and beliefs of the people. When we move from the biblical materials to the even more varied sources of later Judaism it becomes clear that a narrowing or specialization of genealogical interest has taken place. The OT genealogical data are by and large accepted as authoritative by all Jewish sources of the period, whether apocalyptic, historical, or Rabbinic. Consequently, the construction of genealogies for most of the purposes mentioned in the previous chapters was superfluous. We see in the genealogical interest of later Judaism the effects of the political situation within which it emerged, especially the subservient political status of the Jewish state. There are also the problems caused by the mixing of cultures on a large scale and increasing tendencies toward syncretism in religion. The results of these conditions which specifically concern us are twofold: (1) Genealogical interest becomes closely connected with the concern for preserving the purity of the nation, that is, the identity of the Jewish people; and (2) messianic speculation achieves a place of prominence, including discussions of the ancestry of the Messiah. In so far as there are any traces of genealogical interest in the post-OT Jewish literature, it can generally be associated with either of these concerns. Hence our use of the phrase, the 'narrowing of genealogical interest'.

At the outset two preliminary points should be made clear. It is our contention that there is a high degree of uniformity of interest in genealogical purity in the Rabbinic writings which for our purposes mitigates the knotty problem of dating the particular sayings and texts. The same general attitude toward genealogical questions prevails in those sayings attributed to the earliest Tannaim as we find, for example, in the Amoraim.

Indeed, on this point there seems to be a tradition of consistency beginning with Ezra-Nehemiah and continuing into talmudic times.[1] In view of this general perspective, we have not attempted to examine the Rabbinic interest in genealogies in terms of an exclusively chronological methodology, although the citations are dated wherever possible. This is done with full knowledge that many of the Rabbinic citations date from a period considerably later than the NT. Our plan is somewhat systematic: to summarize the nature and characteristics of this Rabbinic interest in general and under specific topics, such as the interest in priestly genealogies and the question of the existence of genealogical records. It is our conviction that this general description of Rabbinic genealogical interest will provide a better insight into the Rabbinic tradition itself than would a study limited to a few of the very earliest extracts.

Secondly, the reference to 'narrowing' does not suggest a decreasing interest in genealogies, either quantitatively or qualitatively, but rather a narrowing of the purpose for which the genealogical form was used. It is not difficult to demonstrate the fact that this interest was at a peak even during first-century Judaism.[2] That the lists of I Chron. 1–9 were the object of special speculation which, in turn, itself reveals the sometimes pedantic nature of genealogical interest, is shown by a well-known saying in the Talmud which looks back upon a long Rabbinic tradition of exegesis:[3]

Mar Zutra [fourth century] said, Between Azel and Azel [I Chron. 8: 38 and 9: 44] they were laden with four hundred camels of exegetical interpretations!

A reference to the genealogies of Chronicles probably also occurs in this somewhat nebulous passage:[4]

Since the days when the Book of Genealogies (ספר יוחסין) was hidden (נגנז) the power of the wise was weakened, and the light of their eyes dimmed.

[1] See pp. 87–95 below.

[2] The information provided by Josephus is especially relevant here; see below, pp. 97 f.

[3] bPes. 62*b* (314). Unless otherwise noted, references to the Babylonian Talmud will be from the translation edited by I. Epstein (1938), the section number followed by the page number in parentheses. Citations from the Midrash Rabbah will follow the translation edited by H. Freedman (1939), again with page numbers in parentheses.

[4] bPes. 62*b* (314).

What is meant by the 'hiding' of the 'Book of Genealogies' is by no means clear,[1] but the saying does show that genealogical speculation was high among the concerns of the scribes. This is further demonstrated by another incident reported in the same context:[2]

R. Simlai came before R. Johanan [d. 279] and requested him, Let the Master teach me the Book of Genealogies [ספר יוחסין]. Said he to him, Whence are you? He replied, From Lod [Lydda]. And where is your dwelling? In Nehardea. Said he to him, We do not discuss it either with the Lodians or with the Nehardeans, and how much more so you, who are from Lod, and live in Nehardea! But he urged him, and he consented.

A. THE CONCERN FOR GENEALOGICAL PURITY

Even a casual reading of the Rabbinic literature reveals that uppermost in the scribal concern for genealogies was the question of preservation of one's full standing within the nation. According to a well-attested saying, the context of which has to do with genealogical purity, 'R. Ḥama b. R. Ḥanina [first half of third century] said: When the Holy One, blessed be He, causes his Shekinah to rest, it is only upon the families of pure birth in Israel...'.[3] Those who could demonstrate pure and noble ancestry were refined and purified as silver,[4] and like 'a rope which is all intertwined, since they could all trace their descent back to their ancestors, and no strange offspring broke

[1] The attempt of G. Kittel ('Die γενεαλογίαι der Pastoralbriefe', *ZNW*, XX (1921), 51 ff.) and others to connect this reference to the supposed destruction of genealogical records by Herod, reported by Africanus (Eus. *H.E.* I. 7. 13), is not convincing (see below, pp. 103 f.). It is more probable that the reference is to some Rabbinic decree that forbade or limited discussion on I Chron. 1–9, which was considered potentially dangerous. Rashi (on Pes. 62 *b*) understood the 'Book of Genealogies' to be the biblical Chronicles (see Jeremias, *Jerusalem zur Zeit Jesu* (3rd ed. 1962), pp. 315, 324: 'Entschloss man sich—wann, wissen wir nicht; sicher vor der Zeit R. Johanan (*ca.* 199–279)—die öffentliche Auslegung des I Chronikbuches zu verbieten und dieses dem esoterischen Überlieferungsstoff zuzuweisen'; this statement of Jeremias appears to be deduced from bPes. 62 *b*). Whether there actually was such a decree cannot be determined, although other Rabbinic passages indicate that the discussion of genealogies in general was a delicate matter; see below, pp. 106 f., and the citation from bPes. 62 *b* on p. 86.

[2] bPes. 62 *b* (313).

[3] bKid. 70 *b* (358); Num. R. 12: 4 (459).

[4] Num. R. 12: 4 (459).

their continuity, for they all guarded themselves from adultery'.[1] While admission to the priesthood and the marriage of priests was of especial concern, the question of the legitimacy of one's descent—however this was to be ascertained—was not necessarily limited to the priesthood since the determination of various 'stocks' within Judaism and their mutual relationships came to include not only full Israelites of both priesthood and laity, but also those who were 'tainted', that is, Israelites only in part. That complications would arise was inevitable. Indeed, the straightening out of genealogical relationships came to be considered a matter that had 'to wait for Elijah', that is, that was beyond settlement by the Rabbis.[2]

1. *Degrees of legitimacy*

We noted earlier that it is only in the explicitly post-exilic writings, and in those of a 'proto-Rabbinic' character, that the interest in maintaining the homogeneity of the nation by means of genealogical purity appears in the OT. Thus, in Ezra-Nehemiah the attempt is made to establish a genealogical connection between the Israel of the monarchy and the post-exilic community; there we have the fragments of lists of full Israelites ('heads of fathers' houses') with whom one could prove genealogical relationship and thus legitimacy. Indeed, the later Rabbinic materials clearly show that the element of national identity, and especially continuity, lies behind the emphasis on the purity of one's descent. In the Midrashic literature the exile is seen as a time of crisis, when the reality of national identity was threatened:

What, then, is meant by 'Glorious things are spoken of Thee' (Ps. 87: 3)? It means that the men of all the nations will bring the children of Israel in honor, and that as these men take leave to depart from the King Messiah, they will speak of the glorious ancestry of the children of Israel, saying, 'This one is a priest, and that one is a Levite, and that other one is an Israelite commoner'. Why will they speak so? Because the children of Israel, having been sold

[1] Num. R. 9: 7 (246). The severe strictures against adultery are usually accompanied by a warning against confusion of descent; cf. Num. R. 12: 4 (459).

[2] See esp. mEd. 8: 7 (436); also bKid. 71 *a* (360 f.), below, p. 106; cf. also W. D. Davies, *The Setting of the Sermon on the Mount* (1964), pp. 158 ff.

as slaves, had under the oppression of exile lost trace of their ancestry, had forgotten their identity, and under duress became gentiles.[1]

Although this extract is anonymous, the names mentioned in the context support a date in the third century (R. Judah, *c.* 165–200; R. Berechiah, fourth century; R. Eleazar, third century; R. Phinehas the Priest b. Ḥama, third century). The importance of the exile as the starting-point for later genealogical classification is seen also in the fact that 'the Exile' (Babylon) became a symbol for genealogical purity: according to R. Jose b. R. Ḥanina (*c.* 240), 'Between the rivers is as the Exile in respect of genealogy'.[2] In the immediately following passage a similar statement is attributed to Rab (d. 299). The fact that the picture of the messianic blessings cited from Mid. Ps. includes the praise of Israel's genealogical purity indicates the seriousness with which the matter was viewed by the Rabbis. More particularly, we see in this passage the threefold structure of society that was determinative from the days of Ezra-Nehemiah to the late Rabbinic period. This threefold structure—priests, Levites, Israelites—is here related to the loss of national identity during the exile. That this stereotyped formula is a reflection of an old tradition is proved by the fact that it occurs in the lists of returned exiles in Ezra 2 (par. Neh. 7) which are arranged according to the following order:[3]

A. Families of pure descent:	Israelites	Ezra 2: 2–35 (Neh. 7: 7–38)
	Priests	Ezra 2: 36–9 (Neh. 7: 39–42)
	Levites	Ezra 2: 40–2 (Neh. 7: 43–5)
B. Temple servants		Ezra 2: 43–54 (Neh. 7: 46–56)
King's servants		Ezra 2: 55–8 (Neh. 7: 57–60)
C. Israelites and priests without genealogies		Ezra 2: 59–63 (Neh. 7: 57–65)

[1] Mid. Ps. 87: 6 (78); cf. Num. R. 8: 8 (519), where the same concern is expressed for national continuity during the sojourn in Egypt: 'R. Judah says that the reason why Scripture enumerates Reuben, Simeon, and Levi separately [in Ex. 6: 14] is that all the other tribes did not preserve their genealogical purity in Egypt while Reuben, Simeon, and Levi did, and that accordingly Scripture recounts their genealogies.'

[2] bKid. 72*a* (367).

[3] Cf. Jeremias, *Jerusalem*, p. 306.

These same three classes are preserved in Ezra 10 in the enumeration of those who had defiled their genealogical purity by marrying 'foreign women'.[1] Thus Ezra-Nehemiah provided the basis for all later categorizations of degrees of genealogical purity.

Long before the compilation of the Mishnah, the classification of degrees of genealogical purity had extended beyond a distinction among full Israelites to a division of degrees of legitimacy also among those who were not considered full Israelites. Once again this distinction is traced back to the situation obtaining among the exiles who returned from Babylon:

> Ten family stocks came up from Babylon: the priestly (כהני), levitic (לויי), and Israelitish (ישראלי) stocks, the impaired priestly stocks (חללי), the proselyte (גרי), freedman (חרורי), bastard (ממזרי) and *Nathin* (נתיני) [temple-servants] stocks, and the *shetuki* (שתוקי) [those unable to show their origin, 'fatherless'], and *asufi* (אסופי) [foundlings] stocks. The priestly, levitic, and Israelitish stocks may intermarry; the levitic, Israelitish, impaired priestly stocks, proselyte, and freedman stocks may intermarry; the proselyte, freedman, bastard, *Nathin*, *shetuki*, and *asufi* stocks may all intermarry.[2]

Although anonymous in the Mishnah, this list is attributed to Hillel in bKid. 75*a* (383) and there is no reason to doubt its pre-Christian origin. As the passages indicate, among these ten stocks are three groups within which intermarriage is permitted: families of legitimate descent (priests, Levites, full Israelites) from whom the priests must choose their wives; families of illegitimate descent, yet with only a slight taint (these could marry Levites or full Israelites but not priests); families of illegitimate descent with serious taint.

[1] Ezra 10: 18–22, priests; 10: 23–4, Levites; 10: 25–43, Israelites.

[2] mKid. 4: 1 (327). References from the Mishnah will follow the translation of Herbert Danby, *The Mishnah* (1933), and will be cited by tractate, chapter, and paragraph followed by the page number in Danby.

This list (mKid. 4: 1) is repeated exactly in bYeb. 37*a* (233), where it is also attributed to Hillel by Samuel. Here, however, after the enumeration of the ten stocks it is said, 'all these may intermarry'. Another occurrence of this list is in bYeb. 85*a* (573), where the Mishnaic passage is quoted verbatim in answer to a query concerning the legality of a woman of legitimate birth marrying a man of tainted descent.

A parallel classification of degrees presents some variation in rank:

A priest precedes a levite, a levite an Israelite, an Israelite a bastard, a bastard a *Nathin*, a *Nathin* a proselyte, and a proselyte a freed slave.[1]

When these two lists are considered together with a third, Tos. Meg. 2: 7,[2] we have the following tabular comparison:[3]

I. mKid. 4: 1 (par.)	II. mHor. 3: 8 (par.)	III. Tos. Meg. 2: 7 (par.)
1. Priests	1. Priests	1. Priests
2. Levites	2. Levites	2. Levites
3. Full Israelites	3. Full Israelites	3. Full Israelites
4. Impaired priests	4. Bastards	4. Proselytes
5. Proselytes	5. Temple servants	5. Freed slaves
6. Freed slaves		
7. Bastards	6. Proselytes	6. Impaired priests
8. Temple servants	7. Freed slaves	7. Temple servants
9. Fatherless		8. Bastards
10. Foundlings		
		9. Castrates
		10. טומטום[4]
		11. Hermaphrodites

This detailed classification reflects the concern for the separation of true Israelites from those who had become mixed with alien blood, a concern expressed in early post-exilic times.[5] Implicit in this concern is the assumption that only families of pure descent belong to and constitute the true Israel.[6] This assumption was implemented in the daily life of the Jews in several ways: aspirants to public office were assumed to be able to prove legitimacy;[7] a priest who would marry a priest's daughter had to trace her family back four generations or, if the woman were of levitical or Israelite stock, through five generations;[8] the privilege of bringing wood for the temple on feast

[1] mHor. 3: 8 (446).
[2] Par.: Tos. Ber. 5: 14; Tos. Rosh. H. 4: 1 (text: M. S. Zuckermandel, *Tosephta* (1881), p. 223).
[3] Jeremias, *Jerusalem*, p. 305.
[4] A man with abnormal genitals.
[5] Cf. Ezra 9: 1—10: 44; in bKet. 5*a* (23) the ideal of genealogical purity is based on Ezek. 44: 9.
[6] Cf. bKid. 70*b* (358), cited above, p. 87 (par. Num. R. 12: 4 (459)).
[7] mKid. 4: 5 (328); par. Num. R. 9: 7 (249 f.).
[8] mKid. 4: 4 (327).

days belonged to the recognized families of the noble laity.[1] Family lineage was considered an important factor in the appointment to the presidency of the academy, as is evident from the fact that R. Eleazar b. Azariah was named to the presidency of Jamnia's academy rather than R. Akiba because he was considered a tenth-generation descendant from Ezra.[2] Also, the Seder Olam Rabba was re-edited to establish the link of the Babylonian exiliarch with the Davidic line. In sum, the entire question of civil liberties and social position was connected with genealogical status.[3]

The categorization of degrees of legitimacy was of particular importance for the regulation of marriages—which was the one essential element for the preservation of the degree system itself. Thus, in what is probably the earliest form of such a classification in the Mishnah (mKid. 4 : 1 (327), see above, pp. 90, 91) the stating of ranks between which marriage is permitted follows immediately the list of ranks; the succeeding paragraphs record Rabbinic discussion of some of the more debated questions which are not settled in the Mishnah.[4] The implications of this concern can be illustrated by two later incidents recorded in the Talmud:

Ulla [*c.* 250] visited Rab Judah [*c.* 200–20] in Pumbeditha. Seeing that R. Isaac [*c.* 250], the son of Rab Judah, was grown up, yet unmarried, he asked him, 'Why have you not taken a wife for your son?' 'Do I know whence we are descended?' he retorted. 'Perhaps from those of whom it is written, "They ravished the women in Zion, the maidens in the cities of Judah"' [Lam. 5: 11].[5]

Ulla's somewhat jestful rebuke to Rab Judah's pedantic concern for the genealogical purity of his son's future wife can be taken

[1] Cf. Jeremias, pp. 308, 319 f.; also mKid. 4: 5 (328), cited below.

[2] bBer. 27*b*; cf. Asher Finkel, *The Pharisees and the Teacher of Nazareth* (Arbeiten zur Geschichte des Spätjudentums und Urchristentums) (1964), pp. 49, 103; see also below.

[3] On the social position of the various ranks, see Jeremias, *Jerusalem*, pp. 166–394.

[4] mKid. 4: 3–7; cf. mYeb. 2: 4; 6: 2.

[5] bKid. 71*b* (363 f.). The danger of defilement during war is often expressed in connection with genealogical purity; cf. Josephus, *Ant.* XIII. 14. 5, where the Maccabean Alexander Jannaeus is reviled as being descended from a captive, hence of doubtful descent. The same slander was earlier levelled at John Hyrcanus (*Ant.* XII. 10. 5; cf. bKid. 66*a*; mKet. 2: 9; *Ant.* III. 12. 2; *Cont. Ap.* I. 7).

as a mild qualification of the rigor of the genealogical purists. It shows also that questions of genealogical status were not easily solved, perhaps indicating the lack of adequate records.

In another incident[1] there are probably traces of a genealogical polemic:[2]

Rabbi [*c.* 200–20] was engaged in the arrangements for the marriage of his son into the family of R. Ḥiyya [*c.* 200–20], but when the *kethubah* was about to be written the bride passed away. 'Is there, God forbid, any taint?' said Rabbi. An inquiry was instituted into [the genealogy of the two] families [and it was discovered that] Rabbi descended from Shephataiah the son of Abital while R. Ḥiyya descended from Shimei a brother of David.

Abital was one of David's wives and thus Shephatiah was a son of David (II Sam. 3: 4). The implication may be that one whose descent was from a non-royal line could not marry into the royal family. But it is more probable that the account indicates the relative status of the two Rabbis: Rabbi was directly a descendant of David and consequently his authority was superior to that of R. Ḥiyya, who descended from a collateral line.

In spite of the well-attested concern for preserving the different ranks of racial purity in tannaitic Judaism, however, there does emerge in the Mishnah, but more especially in the later writings, a reaction against the pedantic and exclusivistic attitude of determining the ultimate worth of an individual and his social position by examining the genealogical traditions of his family. It is striking to find an expression of this reaction in the context of one of the three classifications of legitimacy alluded to above (the date of this passage is doubtful; yet, in view of the parallels listed above, a date within the first century is not unreasonable):

A priest precedes a levite, a levite an Israelite, an Israelite a bastard, a bastard a Nathin; a Nathin a proselyte, and a proselyte a freed slave. This applies when they all are [otherwise] equal; but if a

[1] bKet. 62*b* (376).

[2] Cf. Jeremias, *Jerusalem*, pp. 321–2, where the Rabbinic references to the ancestry of R. Judah I are analyzed; see also Jacob Liver, 'The Problem of the Davidic family after the Biblical Period', *Tarbiz*, XXVI (1957), i–iii (English summary).

bastard is learned in the Law and a High Priest is ignorant of the Law [Heb. *Am-haaretz*], the bastard that is learned in the Law precedes the High Priest that is ignorant of the Law.[1]

And again:

Our Rabbis taught [an indication of an old source]:[2] It happened with a High Priest that as he came forth from the sanctuary, all the people followed him, but when they saw Shemaiah and Abtalion,[3] they forsook him and went after Shemaiah and Abtalion. Eventually Shemaiah and Abtalion visited him, to take their leave of the High Priest. He said to them: May the descendants of the heathen come in peace!—They answered him: May the descendants of the heathen, who do the work of Aaron, arrive in peace, but the descendant of Aaron, who does not do the work of Aaron, he shall not come in peace![4]

One Rabbinic tradition in the Mishnah[5] affirms that only one man, Adam, was created, 'for the sake of peace among mankind, that none should say to his fellows, "My father is greater than thy father..."'. This saying is a reflection on such pride of ancestry as is reproached in pTaan. 76*d*:

R. Akiba [d. A.D. 132] was troubled [that R. Eleazar b. Azariah had been chosen] and said: It is not that he is a greater scholar than I, but rather that he is the son of more distinguished ancestors than I. Blessed is he whose father has acquired merit. Blessed is he who has a peg in which he can be proud. And what was the superiority of R. Eleazar b. Azariah? That he was the tenth member [in descent] from Ezra.

Examples of such a reaction against the mechanical value of descent are found also in the Talmud. The following passage may be compared with mHor. 3: 8 (cited above), since both

[1] mHor. 3: 8 (466), cf. bHor. 13*a*.

[2] See W. D. Davies, *Paul and Rabbinic Judaism* (2nd ed. 1955), p. 277, citing E. H. King, *Yalkut on Zechariah*, pp. 107–8; '...The formula ת/ר "our Rabbis have taught"...according to Dr. Schiller-Szinessy, is only used in the Talmud of the very oldest traditions, such, indeed, as by reason of their age, are unable to be traced to any known Rabbi.'

[3] According to one tradition, they were descendants of non-Jews.

[4] bYom. 71*b* (339–40).

[5] mSan. 4: 5 (388). Davies, *Paul*, pp. 53–5, has shown that Rabbis of the first half of the second century derived the unity of mankind from haggadic interpretations of Adam.

hold study of the Torah as a higher measure of value than genealogical ancestry:

The Rabbis said to R. Perida, 'R. Ezra, the grandson of R. Abtolas, who is the tenth generation from R. Eleazar b. Azariah, who is the tenth generation from Ezra, is standing at the door.' Said he to them, 'Why all this [pedigree]? For if he is a learned man, it is well; if he is a learned man and also a scion of noble ancestors, it is all the better; but if he is a scion of noble ancestors and not a learned man may fire consume him.'[1]

Finally, we cite a passage from the Talmud which indicates that there was no unanimity even in Rabbinic circles regarding the importance of the long Midrashic discussion on genealogies, especially the somewhat artificial exegesis of genealogical passages in the OT.[2] The introductory formula favors an early date. Although the critical remarks are here put on the lips of the 'heretic' Manasseh, yet the tradition here preserved obviously reflects Rabbinic discussions:

Our Rabbis taught: 'But the soul that doeth aught presumptuously' (Num. 15: 30): this refers to Manasseh the son of Hezekiah, who examined [Biblical] narratives to prove them worthless. Thus, he jeered, had Moses nothing to write but, 'And Lotan's sister was Timna, And Timna was concubine to Eliphaz, and Reuben went in the days of the wheat harvest and found mandrakes in the field' [Gen. 36: 22, 12; 30: 14]. Thereupon a Heavenly Voice cried out: 'Thou sittest and speakest against thy brother; thou slanderest thine own mother's son...' [Ps. 50: 20].[3]

Although they are generally haggadic in character, these attempts to mitigate the rigidity of the genealogical classification of the nation must be given their due weight. They are, for the most part, early (first and second centuries A.D.). But they can probably not be taken as typical. Genealogical purity was a prized possession and most of the discussion seems to have had the goal of determining the degree of legitimacy, rather than to question the merits of the system itself. How this determination of rank was made we will discuss below.

[1] bMen. 53*a* (319).

[2] Examples of such exegesis are provided by Kittel, *ZNW*, xx (1921), 59–65; see also below, pp. 108 ff.

[3] bSan. 99*b*, par. Mid. Sifre on Num. 15: 30.

2. *Priestly genealogies*

We now briefly summarize the evidence that points to the special concern for genealogical purity in connection with the priesthood,[1] and also to the supposition that, since the priests were permitted to choose a wife from the priesthood or from those families that were considered full Israelites,[2] it might be expected that genealogical traditions of some historical reliability would be preserved even among the laity.[3] On these matters the various sources—Josephus, Philo, and the Rabbis—are in remarkable agreement, no doubt because the specifications of the Pentateuch, especially Lev. 21–2, were detailed enough to become normative. Thus, both Josephus[4] and Philo[5] in their accounts of the laws governing priestly marriages paraphrase Leviticus and at the same time reflect the language of the Mishnah.[6]

The concern for purity of the priestly stock is already manifest in post-exilic biblical material. Those priests who returned to Jerusalem from Babylon and yet could not prove their descent 'were excluded from the priesthood as unclean' (Ezra 2: 61–3; par. Neh. 7: 63–5), and were forbidden from eating 'the most holy food[7] until there should be a priest to consult Urim and Thummim', that is, when a reconsideration of the case could be undertaken. Besides this dread of losing one's genealogical connections is a matter considered even more grievous, the

[1] 'As nobility among several peoples is of different origin, so with us to be of the sacerdotal dignity is an indication of the splendour of the family' (Josephus, *Vita*, 1).

[2] Philo, *On Monarchy*, II. 11, seems to contradict the other sources when he affirms that the high priest was allowed to marry only within the priestly families.

[3] Most of the pertinent sources from later Judaism are given by E. Schürer, *Geschichte des jüdischen Volkes im Zeitalter Jesu Christi* (5th ed. 1920), section 24. 1 (vol. 2, pp. 277–96); also Hermann L. Strack and Paul Billerbeck, *Kommentar zum Neuen Testament aus Talmud und Midrasch* (1922–8), I, 1–6 (hereafter cited as S–B); and by Jeremias, *Jerusalem*, pp. 166–251 *et passim*.

[4] *Ant*. III. 12. 2.

[5] *On Monarchy*, II. 8–11.

[6] Ezek. 44: 15–31 also seems to reflect the Pentateuchal data although what is applied to the high priest in Lev. 22: 13 ff. is there applied to the priesthood in general.

[7] Is this the *Terumah*, to eat which was the prerogative of the priests? Cf. mYeb. 7–8 and Danby, *Mishnah*, p. 797.

transgression of the laws of marriage. According to Ezra 9–10, Ezra appointed a committee from the approved 'heads of fathers' houses' to examine the accusations of mixed marriages. The results are given in Ezra 10: 18–44, a lengthy list of guilty individuals including sons of the high priest (10: 18)! The book of Nehemiah similarly ends on a pessimistic note—with lamentation over the defilement of the priesthood by one whose father was high priest.[1]

As a summary of the later Jewish attitude concerning marriage of priests, the above-mentioned passage in Josephus is typical:

As for the priests, he prescribed to them a double degree of purity: for he restrained them in the instances above [laws against incest, etc.] and moreover forbade them to marry harlots. He also forbade them to marry a slave, or a captive, and such as got their living by cheating trades, and by keeping inns; as also a woman parted from her husband, on any account whatsoever. Nay, he did not think it proper for the high priest to marry even the widow of one that was dead, though he allowed that to the priests; but he permitted him only to marry a virgin, and to retain her.[2]

It is to be noted that the priests were not required to marry only within priestly families. Hence, the primary purpose of such strictures as are enumerated by Josephus is not primarily to preserve a closed priestly aristocracy but rather to assure an untainted ministry for the cultus. And yet it is clear that such a priestly aristocracy did, in fact, develop even in pre-Maccabean times. The supposition that there was a considerable extent of intermarriage within priestly circles is borne out by the Mishnaic list of physical defects which render one unfit for service in the temple, a considerable number of which are genetic in nature and possibly the result of in-breeding.[3] Among such defects are listed total baldness, abnormalities in eyes or legs, and having six fingers or toes on each hand or foot. In any case, the halakoth which regulated priestly marriages served the purpose of defining ever more precisely the somewhat nebulous boundaries among the various stocks.[4]

[1] Neh. 13: 23–31, esp. *v.* 28.

[2] *Ant.* III. 12. 2.

[3] mBek. 7 (538–9).

[4] This is the function of such contexts as mBik. 1: 5 (94): the daughter of a proselyte and a full Israelite woman may marry into the priestly stock; also mYeb. 5: 2 (227); mYeb. 9 (230–2); mSot. 4: 1 (297); mSot. 8: 3 (302); mKid. 4: 1–7 (327–8); cf. also Num. R. 9: 7 and bMak. 3: 1 (405).

The regulations for the marriage of the high priest were, as Josephus suggests (see above), even more stringent; the most detailed rules are found in mYeb. 6: 4:

A high priest may not marry a widow whether she had become a widow after betrothal or after wedlock; and he may not marry one that is past her girlhood. But R. Eliezer [*c.* A.D. 80–120] and R. Simeon [second century] declare one that is past her girlhood eligible. He may not marry one that is not *virgo intacta*. If he had betrothed a widow and was afterward appointed high priest, he may consummate the union...If a woman awaited levirate marriage with a common priest and he was appointed high priest, although he had bespoken her he may not consummate the union. If the brother of the high priest died, the high priest must submit to *halitzah* and may not contract levirate marriage.

In view of this meticulous concern for an unblemished priesthood, it was only natural that a prospective wife's pedigree should be examined with the greatest care, as is revealed by a typical halakah:

If a man [i.e. priest] would marry a woman of priestly stock, he must trace her family back through four mothers, which are, indeed, eight: her mother, mother's mother, and mother's father's mother, and this one's mother; also her father's mother and this one's mother, her father's father's mother, and this one's mother. [If he would marry] a woman of levitic or Israelitish stock, he must trace the descent back to one mother more.[1]

The passage shows that, in general, greater probability was given to the purity of descent of the priests than to that of full lay Israelites. Immediately following this section is a list of cases in which genealogical purity can be assumed by the nature of the office held, the occupants of which were apparently scrutinized as to pedigree:[2]

They need not trace descent beyond the altar[3] or beyond the Platform[4] or beyond the Sanhedrin;[5] and all whose fathers are

[1] mKid. 4: 4 (327).

[2] mKid. 4: 5 (328); this is repeated verbatim in Num. Rab. 9: 7 (249 f.).

[3] 'If he found that her father ministered as a priest in the temple he need not trace her descent further' (Danby, *Mishnah*, p. 328 n. 1).

[4] 'Where the levites sang in the temple...If he found that her father sang as a levite in the temple, that suffices' (Danby, p. 328 n. 2).

[5] 'In Jerusalem, membership of which provides valid proof of unimpaired stock' (Danby, p. 328 n. 3).

known to have held office as public officials or almoners may marry into the priestly stock and none need trace their descent. R. Jose [second century] says: Also any whose name was signed as a witness in the old archives[1] at Sepphoris. R. Hananiah b. Antigonus says: Also any whose name was recorded in the king's army.[2]

3. *The existence of genealogical records*

The Rabbinic references to the necessity of tracing one's descent (צריך לנדוק) raise the question of the methodology by which this was accomplished. Was it a matter of preserving the names of one's ancestors of several generations back as a part of a family's oral traditions?[3] Or were actual written records of family genealogies available and, if so, among which stocks, and to what extent?

With regard to *the priesthood*, it seems clear that if we are to trust Josephus—and at this point there seems to be no good reason against his evidence—rather careful and formal genealogical records were kept in Jerusalem, and that some records of priestly marriages were kept even in the larger Jewish communities of the diaspora, such as those in Egypt and Babylon. This latter fact suggests that the status and regulations belonging to priestly stock were observed even where there was no possibility of service in the temple at Jerusalem. Whether this was true also in Palestine after the destruction of the temple (as at the time of Josephus' writing) remains somewhat problematical. The passage to which we refer is somewhat unusual in its detail and deserves to be quoted at length:

For our forefathers did not only appoint the best of these priests... but made profession that the stock of priests should continue unmixed and pure; for he who is partaker of the priesthood must

[1] 'Those inscribed in the court's records as eligible to be judges and witnesses...' (Danby, p. 328 n. 4).

[2] Possibly a reference to lists of military commanders in I Chron. 4–8; see above, pp. 60–8.

[3] This seems to be implied (in the case of a priestly descent!) by a curious passage in the Mishnah (Ket. 2: 7–8 (247)), where the question debated is whether 'they may not admit any to the standing of a priest on the evidence of a single witness...'. The 'witness' in this case, however, may be one who offers evidence that a certain man is a close relative of a priest who served at the altar, thus doing away with the need for 'documentary' proof.

propagate of a wife of the same nation,[1] without having any regard to money, or any other dignities; but he is to make a scrutiny and take his wife's genealogy from the ancient tables (ἐκ τῶν ἀρχαίων),[2] and procure many witnesses to it; and this is our practice, not only in Judah, but wheresoever any body of men of our nation do live; and even there, an exact catalogue of our priests' marriages is kept: I mean at Egypt and at Babylon, or in any other place of the rest of the habitable earth, whithersoever our priests are scattered; for they send to Jerusalem the ancient names of their parents in writing, as well as those of their remoter ancestors,[3] and signify who are the witnesses also; but if any war falls out, such as have fallen out a great many of them already, when Antiochus Epiphanes made an invasion upon our country, as also when Pompey the Great and Quintilius Varus did so also, and principally in the wars that have happened in our own times, those priests that survive them compose new tables of genealogy out of the old records, and examine the circumstances of the women that remain, for they still do not admit of those that have been captives, as suspecting that they had conversation with some foreigners; but what is the strongest argument of our exact management in this matter is what I am now going to say, that we have the names of our high priests, from father to son, set down in our records, for the interval of two thousand years; and if anyone of these have [*sic*] been transgressors of these rules, they are prohibited to present themselves at the altar...[4]

Among the points of interest here is the reference to examination of the wife's pedigree, which is to be attested by 'many witnesses'. This datum could be taken as evidence that records of genealogies were available among the non-priestly stocks,[5]

[1] Cf. Lev. 21: 14; Philo, from the LXX of this verse, concludes that the high priest could marry only within the priesthood.

[2] Another reading, ἐκ τῶν ἀρχείων, would possibly suggest 'archives'; ἀρχαίων is the reading of Codex Laurentianus (eleventh century), which appears to be the source for all other Greek manuscripts of *Cont. Ap.*; the reading ἀρχείων is based on the Latin. But, in either case, the meaning is not clear.

[3] A reference to a statement of connection to a name mentioned in Chronicles, Ezra, or Nehemiah?

[4] *Cont. Ap.* I. 7.

[5] Jeremias, *Jerusalem*, p. 317, assumes that *Cont. Ap.* I. 7 suggests that some records of lay genealogies would be included; also Schürer, *Geschichte*, II, 282 n. 14. The reference to the 'public records' of genealogies in which Josephus found his own pedigree does not add anything to the discussion of lay genealogies since he was 'from a sacerdotal family' (*Vita*, I).

although it is possible that Josephus is here drawing on the old halakah which occurs also in mKid. 4: 4 (327):

If a man would marry a woman of priestly stock, he must trace her family back through four mothers, which are, indeed, eight: her mother, mother's mother, and mother's father's mother, and this one's mother; also her father's mother and this one's mother, her father's father's mother, and this one's mother. [If he would marry] a woman of levitic or Israelitish stock, he must trace the descent back to one mother more.

Nonetheless, there is no mention in this halakah of genealogical tables and this investigation of pedigree could have been made without written records. The beginning of the Gemara on this passage (which is anonymous) suggests that the investigation was indeed a questioning of the persons involved, since, if there were official records, one's genealogical status would not become the object of a quarrel:

Why are women investigated but not the men?—When women quarrel among themselves, they quarrel [only] about immorality, so that if there is anything [objectionable in their pedigree], it is not generally known. But when men quarrel among themselves, they quarrel over birth; if there is anything, it is generally known.[1]

Moreover, it is not clear that the halakah is a regulation of priestly marriages as such ('If a man would marry a woman of priestly stock'—הנושא אשה כהנת). Thus Josephus' reference to taking 'his wife's genealogy from the ancient tables' would apply especially to cases in which a priest marries into another priestly family. In addition to this, it should be remembered that Josephus refers rather vaguely to genealogical records in other passages, as of the Samaritans.[2] In sum, while *Cont. Ap.* I. 7 might support an inference concerning the existence of genealogical records among the non-priestly Israelites, it is not in itself decisive and must be considered in the light of other evidence. The Gemara on mKid. 4: 5 (382) also points to a

[1] bKid. 76*a* (389); cf. bKid. 79*a* (406): 'A man is well-informed in matters of genealogy...a woman is not well-informed.'

[2] *Ant.* XI. 8. 6; see below, p. 108.

separation of the priests and Levites from the rest of the nation in the matter of genealogical purity:

'They need not trace descent...beyond the Platform.' What is the reason?—Because a Master said: For there sat those who certified the genealogies of the priestly and the Levitical families.[1]

What, then, is the evidence for the existence of accurate historical genealogical records among *non-priestly families* during NT times? On this question Jeremias has supplied a detailed and exhaustive analysis of the evidence which leads him to conclude that (1) there were in many cases written records of genealogical descent among lay families and (2) often these records were historically accurate.[2] Before offering an evaluation of Jeremias' conclusions, we summarize the evidence. This falls into two categories:

(*a*) *Individuals traced to tribes other than Levi.* Reference to tribal ancestry of individuals in Jewish and Christian sources later than the Old Testament are not frequent. Jeremias adduces the following:

(1) Traced to Judah (most often to the family of David): most of the families appointed to bring the wood-offering to the temple (mTaan. 4: 5 (200)); relatives of Jesus persecuted as descendants of David;[3] R. Hiyya the elder (A.D. 200; pKil. 9:4); and Rabbi Huna.

(2) Traced to Benjamin: Mordecai (Esther 2:5); Paul (Rom. 11: 1; Phil. 3: 4); R. Gamaliel;[4] and the family of Senaah (mTaan. 4: 5 (200)).

(3) Traced to Naphtali: Tobit (Tobit 1: 1–2).

(4) Traced to Simeon: Judith (Jud. 8: 1; 9: 2).

(5) Traced to Asher: Anna the prophetess (Luke 2: 36).

(6) Several references to descendants of the Rechabites.[5]

The preponderance of the references to Judah and Benjamin is explained by Jeremias as being due to the fact that these two tribes (with Levi) constituted the kernel of post-exilic Judaism.

[1] bKid. 76*b* (390).

[2] *Jerusalem*, pp. 304–24.

[3] Eusebius, *H.E.* III. 12; III. 19–20; III. 32. 3–4.

[4] Gamaliel is the ancestor of R. Judah, whose Benjaminite ancestry is proved from pKil. 9: 4; pKeth. 12: 3; Gen. R. 33: 3 (on Gen. 8: 1); see Jeremias, p. 311 n. 29.

[5] Jeremias, p. 311.

But as a list of individuals attached with some historical probability to a specific tribe, it may be regarded as fairly comprehensive. The relative brevity of such information should be noted.

(*b*) *References to genealogical records.* Jeremias alludes to the following:

(1) The two genealogies of Jesus (Matt. 1: 1–17; Luke 3: 23–38).

(2) mYeb. 4: 13 (225): 'R. Simeon b. Azzai (*c.* 120–40) said: I found a family register (מגילת יוחסין) in Jerusalem and in it was written, "Such-a-one is a bastard through [a transgression of the law of] thy neighbor's wife"...'

(3) The report of J. Africanus (*c.* A.D. 160–240)[1] that Herod 'burned the records of their families' (ἐνέπρησεν αὐτῶν τὰς ἀναγραφὰς τῶν γενῶν, that is, of 'the Hebrew families and those traceable to proselytes, such as Achior the Ammonite, and Ruth the Moabitess, and the mixed families which had come out of Egypt'. This report is the basis of a similar statement in a later Syrian text,[2] but its historicity is made questionable by the silence of other historians on the matter, especially Josephus, as well as by its somewhat legendary coloring.

In the same context Africanus relates that 'a few careful people', among them the relatives of Jesus, were able to preserve the record of their descent, 'either remembering the names or otherwise deriving them from copies...'[3] It will be admitted, however, that Africanus introduces these references in order to support his attempt to show that the NT genealogies of Jesus are accurate and historically trustworthy. The reference to Herod's burning the genealogical records would explain why, in Africanus' day, Jewish lay families would not generally have family records of considerable length. The allusion to some people preserving their records would explain how it was that accurate pedigrees of Jesus were available. Africanus himself had hoped for more convincing evidence: 'Whether this [the account of the family of Jesus preserving their ancestral records and expounding their genealogies among the Jewish villages] be

[1] Eus. *H.E.* I. 7. 13–15 (Loeb, p. 63).

[2] C. Bezold, *Die syrische Schatzhöhle*, p. 53 (cited by Jeremias, pp. 314 f.).

[3] *H.E.* I. 7. 14.

so or not no one could give a clearer account...and it may suffice us, even though it is not corroborated, since we have nothing better or truer to say: in any case the gospel speaks the truth.'[1]

Thus, even though Africanus usually displays an acutely critical mind,[2] it is difficult to avoid the conclusion that his reference to the burning of Jewish genealogical records by Herod is occasioned, and partly determined, by his efforts to harmonize the two genealogies of Jesus in Matthew and Luke. This does not exclude the possibility that Africanus found some such reference to Herod in previous Christian tradition.

(4) In bKet. 62*b* (376)[3] it is related how R. Judah and R. Ḥiyya 'instituted an inquiry' into their descent in connection with a proposed marriage of their son and daughter. Whether or not this involved written records is, however, problematical.

(5) In the Damascus Document provision is made for 'the order of the session of the camps: they shall all be enrolled by their names; the priests first, the Levites second, the sons of Israel third, and the proselyte fourth...'[4] Here again, even though we find the order of rank reminiscent of the Mishnah (both being based on Ezra-Nehemiah), we cannot be certain that this 'enrollment' was in any sense genealogical. The context points rather to the opposite, namely that it was a list of rank in the Qumran community ('so shall they sit, and so shall they ask concerning anything').

(6) The references of Josephus to genealogical records in the temple has been alluded to above. The relevant passages do not prove decisively that any records of lay genealogies were kept there except possibly in cases of a priest taking a wife from a lay family.

Some additional remarks by way of an evaluation of this evidence would seem to be in order. With regard to the data which link individuals to various tribes, the relative paucity of information appears to be equally as significant as the references that are extant. One might surmise that feelings of attachment to individual tribes, again with the exception of the priests and

[1] *H.E.* I. 7. 15.

[2] This perceptive critical faculty is best evidenced in his letter to Origen contesting the genuineness of the story of Susanna on linguistic and literary grounds.

[3] See above, p. 93.

[4] CDC 17: 1 ff. (translation by Millar Burrows, *Dead Sea Scrolls* (1955), p. 362).

Levites, were not strong in post-biblical Judaism, although, as in the case of Paul, there are exceptions to this generalization. But it is especially relevant to point out that in none of the sources mentioned by Jeremias are the traditions of tribal membership explicitly based on written genealogical records. In every case the relation to the tribe could have been derived from non-literary tradition.

Our conclusions regarding the references to genealogical records of the laity must also be somewhat negative. We have noted the apologetic character of the report of Africanus and have shown that Josephus refers especially to the purity of the priesthood. The genealogies of Jesus would seem to require special treatment as Toledoth of the Messiah. Again, the phrase, 'a genealogical scroll (מגילת יוחסין) was found in Jerusalem...' proves little, since in pTaan. 4: 2[1] it is used to introduce an artificial connection of Rabbis with prominent figures of the past.[2] Similarly, the reference in mYeb. 4: 13 (225), cited above, may reflect an anti-Christian polemic.[3] In both cases the attempt

[1] Par. Gen. R. 98: 8 (956).

[2] This tradition traces the descent of Hillel from David, the house of Yazath from Asaph, the house of Zizith Haleseth from Abner, the house of Kobshin from Abah, the house of Kalba Shabua from Caleb, the house of Jannai from Eli, the house of Jehus from Sepphoris, R. Ḥiyya the Elder from Shephatiah the son of Abital, R. Jose b. R. Halafta from Jonadab the son of Rechab, and R. Nehemiah from Nehemiah the Tirshathite. Although the Midrash ascribes this information to 'a genealogical scroll...found in Jerusalem', it is clear that similarity or identity of name has played a role in the formation of the list. Jeremias alludes to this account as an example of Rabbinic handling of 'pretended' genealogical tradition which is based on 'völlig wertlose Wortspielerei, die aus volksetymologischer Namensdeutung genealogische Schlüsse zieht, zu Worte kommt' (p. 318). He further designates it as a 'Phantasieprodukt' (pp. 318–19; following Lévi, *RÉJ* (1895), pp. 209 ff.) and assigns its provenance to the town of Sepphoris. This passage is cited below, pp. 110f.

[3] This view goes back at least to Joseph Derenbourg (1881), who thought that these words 'se rapportent sans doute à Jésus' (cited by H. L. Strack, *Jesus: die Häretiker und die Christen nach den ältesten jüdischen Angaben* (1910), p. 27* n. a. 4); Strack himself is dubious since the point of b. Azzai's information is to confirm the opinion of R. Joshua (*loc. cit.*). However, E. Stauffer (cited by Davies, *Setting*, p. 287 n. 5) holds that the genealogy of Matthew is designated 'to counteract such calumny as lies behind Mishnah Yebamoth IV. 13'. So also Kittel, *ZNW*, xx (1921), 54. For the view that this is not an allusion to Jesus, see Morris Goldstein, *Jesus in the Jewish Tradition* (1950), pp. 67–8.

to find authority for a particular tradition by tracing it to Jerusalem before the destruction of the temple throws considerable suspicion on the use of such passages to demonstrate the existence of written lay genealogies. Again, the references to the 'Book of Genealogies' (ספר יוחסין) in bPes. 62*b* and elsewhere[1] are most convincingly interpreted as denoting the canonical Chronicles, as was suggested as early as Rashi, rather than as a later collection of pedigrees.

Beyond this evidence adduced by Jeremias, there are several passages in which reference is made to an examination or a tracing of one's descent and which, therefore, are relevant to a discussion of the nature of the preservation of genealogical tradition. The most interesting and perhaps enigmatic example is preserved in bKid. 71*a* (360):

In the days of R. Phineas [*c.* 165–200, a contemporary of Rabbi Judah, A.D. 135–220] it was desired to declare Babylon as dough *vis-à-vis* Palestine. Said he to his slaves, 'When I have made two statements in the Beth haMidrash, take me up in my litter and flee'. When he entered he said to them, 'A fowl does not require slaughter by Biblical law'. Whilst they were sitting and meditating thereon, he said to them, 'All countries are as dough in comparison with Palestine, and Palestine is dough relative to Babylon'. [Thereupon] they [his slaves] took him up in his litter and fled. They ran after him, but could not overtake him. Then they sat and examined [their genealogies], until they came to danger, so they refrained.

The framework of this story indicates that the two statements made by R. Phineas dealt with highly controversial matters. In the second, the symbol 'dough' can be interpreted only as designating genealogical impurity:[2] this statement provoked the students to an examination of their own ancestry. In light of the context, we must assume that they had no recourse at the moment to written records but rather shared their knowledge of ancestry as transmitted orally.

The immediate continuation of this passage sheds more light on the inadequacy of genealogical information, the possibility of distorting such data, and the handing down of certain kinds

[1] See above, p. 87 n. 1.

[2] Cf. Freedman, *Kiddushin* (Bab. Tal.), p. 350 n. 5: 'Dough is a mixture of flour and water. I.e. the Jews there [in Babylon] have not such a pure descent as those in Palestine.' The reference to dough in genealogical contexts occurs several times in the Babylonian Gemara on Kid. 4.

of genealogical information by means of oral tradition within the Rabbinic schools themselves:

R. Johanan [A.D. 75][1] said: By the Temple! It is in our power [to reveal the families of impure birth in Palestine]; but what shall I do, seeing that the greatest men of our time are mixed up therein. [Thus] he holds with R. Isaac, who said: Once a family becomes mixed up, it remains so.[2] Abaye [d. 339] said, We have learnt likewise: There was a family, Beth haZerifa, in Transjordania, which Ben Zion forcibly expelled [i.e. declared impure by manipulation]. There was another which Ben Zion forcibly admitted. Such as these Elijah will come to declare unclean or clean, to expel and to admit. [Hence, only] such as these who are known; but once a family becomes mixed up, it remains so. It was taught: there was yet another, which the Sages declined to reveal, but the Sages confided it to their children and disciples once a septennate...[3]

This Gemara, which is only a slightly fuller version of a Mishnaic passage,[4] clearly alludes to the fabrication of genealogical relationships by a certain Ben Zion or, as a more probable variant has it, Bene Zion, that is, the scribes of Jerusalem. The concluding remark refers to the existence of an oral genealogical tradition within Rabbinic schools. In any case, the problematic nature of questions of genealogical purity is underlined here; the least one can say is that, even if there existed written records of ancestry of some non-priestly families, they were not available for all. This inadequacy of records is tersely expressed by those Rabbis who declared that such problems were beyond settlement by the scribes and would have to wait for the appearance of Elijah, who would 'restore all things':[5] 'The like of these Elijah will come to declare unclean or clean, to remove afar or to bring nigh.'[6]

[1] See below, n. 4.

[2] I.e. a family declared to be full Israelite by error cannot be declared impure later.

[3] bKid. 71*a* (360 f.).

[4] mEd. 8: 7 (436); this latter reference is attributed to R. Johanan b. Zakkai and may indicate that the R. Johanan in bKid. 71*a* is the same; this would trace the existence of such discussion to the first century A.D. In any case mEd. 8: 7 indicates that the matter was discussed by the Tannaim.

[5] Cf. Mark 9: 12 and par.

[6] mEd. 8: 7, attributed to Johanan b. Zakkai (*c.* 75). Cf. also V. Aptowitzer, *Parteipolitik der Hasmonaerzeit im Rabbinischen und Pseudoepigraphischen Schrifttum* (1927), p. 102 n. 66; and Davis, *Setting*, pp. 159, 160, 172. According to bKid. 70*a* (354), Elijah punishes those who choose a wife from forbidden ranks; this is an old tradition, attributed to 'a Tanna' or to Rabbah b. R. Adda (date unknown) or R. Salla (date unknown).

What we know of the customs of other ancient Semitic peoples supports this general conclusion. As we pointed out in Part I, the Safaitic graffiti prove that even a simple Bedouin might be aware of his ancestry as far back as ten or twelve generations. But these crude inscriptions tell us nothing about the existence of written family pedigrees. The genealogical information recorded by the Bedouin was apparently the result of oral family traditions. Josephus indicates that the Samaritans, likewise, used genealogies for apologetic purposes:

> ...For such is the disposition of the Samaritans...that when the Jews are in adversity they deny that they are of kin to them, and then they confess the truth; but when they perceive that some good fortune hath befallen them, they immediately pretend to have communion with them, saying, that they belong to them, and derive their genealogy from the posterity of Joseph, Ephraim, and Manasseh.[1]

At the time of Antiochus Epiphanes, during the persecution of the Jews, the Samaritans 'said they were a colony of Medes and Persians' and were 'originally Sidonians, as is evident from the public records [ἐκ τῶν πολιτικῶν ἀναγραφῶν]'.[2] In this context the historical value of the records must remain insignificant.

Thus the evidence for the existence of genealogical records of the laity in post-biblical Judaism is somewhat ambivalent; yet the lack of explicit and unquestioned references to written genealogies, apart from those of the priests, points to the probability that the genealogical traditions were usually transmitted orally, and that one without written records might be aware of his male ancestors for several generations and probably also of his membership in a tribe or clan.[3]

4. *Genealogical speculation and Midrashic exegesis*

This somewhat negative conclusion raises a perplexing problem: how could the concept of a true Judaism be main-

[1] *Ant.* XI. 8. 6; so also *Ant.* IX. 14. 3.

[2] *Ant.* XII. 5; it is noteworthy that Josephus here uses a phrase similar to that of the source of his own pedigree: 'Thus I have set down the genealogy of my family as I have found it described in the public records [ἐν ταῖς δημοσίαις δέλτοις]' (*Vita*, 1).

[3] These conclusions are in substantial agreement with the views of Jacob Liver, *Tarbiz*, XXVI (1957), 229–54 (Hebrew); pp. i–iii (English summary).

tained along lines of ancestry in view of the lack of generally available genealogical records? In a word, how could the degree of legitimacy of individuals within the nation be established without access to historically reliable genealogical records? We submit that this difficulty was often faced and 'solved' by midrashic exegesis of genealogical data in the OT. This was especially true, as is indicated by bKid. 71*a* (360 f.),[1] with respect to individuals of rank in society whose ancestry would be traced to biblical names by midrashic exegesis. The nature of this biblical interpretation has been summarized by G. Kittel,[2] who describes the methods used to deduce information regarding the ancestry of OT figures beyond that which is supplied by the biblical text. Kittel adduces a passage from Gen. R. 71 where the descent of Elijah is established by word-plays[3] and a similar discussion of Jonah, which we cite as a typical example:

R. Judah b. Naḥman [*c.* 280] and R. Levi [*c.* 300] each received two selas per week to keep R. Johanan's congregation together. [One Sabbath] R. Levi entered and lectured: Jonah was descended from Zebulun, as it is written, 'And the third lot came up for the children of Zebulun...and from thence it passed along eastward to Gath-hepher' [Josh. 19: 10–13]; while it is also written, 'According to the word of the Lord, the God of Israel, which he spoke by the hand of his servant Jonah the son of Amittai, the prophet, who was of Gath-hepher' [II Kings 14: 25]. Gath-hepher is Gobebatha of Sepphoris. Then R. Johanan entered and lectured: Jonah was descended from Asher, for it is written, 'Asher drove not out the inhabitants of Acco, nor the inhabitants of Zidon' [Judg. 1: 31]; while it is written, 'Arise, get thee to Zarephath, which belongeth to Zidon, and dwell there; behold I have commanded a widow there to sustain thee' [I Kings 17: 9].[4] [The following Sabbath] R. Levi said to R. Judah b. Naḥman: Though it is your Sabbath, take the two *selas* and permit me to lecture. R. Levi then entered and said: Although R. Johanan taught us last Sunday that Jonah was from Asher, in truth his father was from Zebulun while his mother was from Asher, for the verse, 'And his flank (*Yarkatho*) shall be upon Zidon' [Gen. 49: 13] means, the thigh (*Yerek*) whence he was

[1] Cited above, p. 107.
[2] *ZNW*, xx (1921), 49–69.
[3] P. 60; see also Appendix 3, on the ancestry of Elijah.
[4] A tradition in Pirke R. Eliezer 33 identifies the widow as the mother of Jonah.

sprung was from Zidon. Said R. Johanan to him: You have taught this standing; may you be privileged to teach it sitting; and he functioned as a preacher for twenty-two years.[1]

Kittel finds in such passages some general exegetical methods:

Das Bestreben ist—eine Eigentümlichkeit des menschlichen Geistes zu aller Zeit—vor allem das der Kombination. Man hat das Bedürfnis, möglichst viele Identifikationen und Beziehungen innerhalb des AT herzustellen. Die leichteste Möglichkeit aber, zu verknüpfen, ergibt sich durch genealogische Spekulation. Besonders beliebt sind die Versuche, Unbekanntes mit Bekanntem in Verbindung zu bringen.[2]

Ein weiterer methodischer Grundsatz ist, Näheres über unbekannte Persönlichkeiten von den mit ihnen in Verbindung gebrachten Personen aus zu erschliessen.[3]

All this, we might add, is in harmony with the methods of haggadic exegesis as set forth by the Rabbis themselves: 'R. Simon said in the name of R. Joshua b. Levi [mid second century], and R. Ḥama, the father of R. Hoshea, in the name of Rab [*c.* 200–20]: The book of Chronicles was given only to be expounded midrashically.'[4] One might also compare the several lists of hermeneutical *Middoth* which allowed for various combinations of scriptural data in the exegetical process.

But, so far as genealogical interest is concerned, was this type of exegesis, as Kittel suggests, limited to a filling out of the data concerning OT personalities, and thus, more or less, simply an antiquarian endeavor? There is good reason to think otherwise. A list preserved in pTaan. 4: 2 (par. Gen. R. 98: 8 (956)) traces ten prominent Rabbinic figures to OT personalities:

R. Levi [*c.* A.D. 300] said: A genealogical scroll was found in Jerusalem, in which it was written:
Hillel [*c.* A.D. 20] descended from David,
the house of Yazath from Asaph,
the house of Zizith Hakeseth [*c.* A.D. 70] from Abner,
the house of Kobshin from Ahab,
the house of Kalba Shabua [*c.* A.D. 70] from Caleb,
the house of Jannai [*c.* A.D. 225] from Eli,

[1] Gen. R. 98: 11 (959–60).
[2] P. 62.
[3] P. 63.
[4] Lev. R. 1: 3 (4); par. Ruth R. 2: 1 (23).

the house of Jehu from Sepphoris,
R. Ḥiyya the Elder [*c.* A.D. 200] from Shephatiah the son of Abital [II Sam. 3: 4),
R. Jose b. R. Ḥalafta from Jonadab the son of Rechab,
R. Nehemiah [*c.* A.D. 150] from Nehemiah the Tirshathite [Neh. 8: 9].[1]

Jeremias' evaluation of this passage has been alluded to above: 'Das angeblich in Jerusalem gefundene Geschlechtsregister ist ein um 250 p. in Sepphoris entstandenes Phantasieprodukt...'[2] Since the list is recorded in answer to the question of Hillel's descent, we may consider it as evidence for the interest taken in the ancestry of several Rabbis of the past who were remembered with admiration. The conclusions on the ancestry of these Rabbis are reached by 'Wortspielerei' which is closely akin to the kind of exegesis surveyed by Kittel in passages dealing with OT personalities. The second derivation in the above list is based on a pun on the names יצאה and אסף; the fifth is based on the identity of the name כלב, just as the last draws a significance from the name נחמיה. Finally, the Davidic ancestry of Hillel is proven by Jeremias[3] to be a *Geschichtsfälschung*. Hence we conclude that Rabbis did attempt to exalt the memory of admired predecessors by providing them with honorable ancestry but that such attempts were not always based on genealogical records.

As for the intertestamental literature, we shall presently see that the question of the ancestry of the Messiah came to be a subject of discussion. Essentially the same exegetical method was applied here as throughout the Rabbinic texts: We find, especially in Jubilees, a similar interest in etymologies (cf. 4: 15) and names of kinsmen not given in the OT; we discover, for example, the name of the daughter of Eve (4: 1) who became the wife of Cain (4: 9), the names of the wives of the antediluvian patriarchs (chapter 4), including the pedigree of Noah's wife (4: 33). The genealogical activity to be found in both Jubilees and the Rabbinic sources may therefore be described as midrashic in method. This means that the primary

[1] Order of names from pTaan.; transliteration from Gen. R. 98: 8; dates of Rabbis from Jeremias, *Jerusalem*, p. 318.

[2] P. 319, following Lévi, *RÉJ* (1895), pp. 209 ff.; see above, p. 105 n. 2.

[3] *Jerusalem*, pp. 320 ff.

concern is very different from critical historical research into family lines. But some caution is required in using the term 'midrash'; to designate a text as showing 'midrashic tendencies' is not to deny the possibility that it contains valid historical information. On the contrary, there was in the nature of midrashic exegesis itself a regulative factor: the emphasis on the letter of Scripture:

Il importe de donner à ce terme son sens véritable. On le prend en effet souvent pour synonyme de fable, d'affabulation légendaire. En réalité, il désigne un genre édifiant et explicatif étroitement rattaché a l'Écriture, dans lequel la part de l'amplification est réelle mais secondaire et reste toujours subordonnée à la fin religieuse essentielle, qui est de mettre en valeur plus pleinement l'œuvre de Dieu, la Parole de Dieu.[1]

It is this religious concern and emphasis on the letter of authoritative Scripture that distinguishes Jewish and Christian midrashic discussion of genealogies from the use of the genealogical form in contemporary Graeco-Roman culture. It is interesting to note what connotations the word γενεαλογία had for Polybius; in his discussion of historical methodology he writes:

For nearly all other writers, or at least most of them, by dealing with every branch of history, attract many kinds of people to the perusal of their works. The genealogical side [ὁ γενεαλογικὸς τρόπος] appeals to those who are fond of a story, and the account of colonies, the foundations of cities, and their ties of kindred, such as we find, for instance, in Ephorus, attracts the curious and lovers of recondite lore, while the student of politics is interested in the doings of nations, cities, and monarchs...[2]

My aim, therefore, being not so much to entertain readers as to benefit those who pay careful attention, I disregarded other matters and was led to write this kind of history...[3]

Since genealogies, myths [τά τε περὶ τὰς γενεαλογίας καὶ μύθους], the planting of colonies, the foundations of cities, and their ties of kinship have been recounted by many writers and in many different styles...I decided on writing a history of actual events...[4]

[1] Renée Bloch, art. 'Midrash', *Dictionnaire de la Bible, Suppl. V* (1955), p. 1263; on the historical value of midrash as it applies to Matt. 1–2, see M. M. Bourke, 'The Literary Genius of Matthew 1–2', *CBQ*, XXII (1960), 160–75.

[2] IX. 1. 3.

[3] IX. 1. 6.

[4] IX. 2. 1.

Polybius considered the genealogical form especially adapted for legends and myths of the origin of cities and families, and distinct in method from the utilization of records of historical events.[1]

As early as Theophrastus (*c.* 370–287 B.C.) 'the genealogists' were satirized: ask a backbiter who a person is and he will reply in the manner of the genealogists, by noting his lowly parentage and debased stock.[2] In the *Rhetoric to Alexander* (*c.* 300 B.C.?) the author proposes the method for 'the oratory of eulogy and vituperation':

...We shall place first after the introduction the genealogy of the person we are speaking of, as that is the fundamental ground of reputation or discredit for human beings, and also for animals...The proper way to employ genealogy is this. If the ancestors are men of merit, you must enumerate them all from the beginning (ἐξ ἀρχῆς) down to the person you are eulogizing, and at each of the ancestors summarily mention something to his credit. If the first ones are men of merit but the rest do not happen to have done anything remarkable, you must go through the first ones in the same way but omit the inferior ones, explaining that because of the number of the ancestors you do not wish to make a long story by mentioning them all, and moreover that it is patent to everybody that the scions of a worthy stock naturally resemble their ancestors...If he has no ancestral distinction in his favour, say that he himself is a fine fellow, suggesting that all men by nature well-endowed with virtue are 'well-born'. Also rebuke all the other people who praise their ancestors by saying that many men who have had distinguished ancestors have been unworthy of them...Similarly in vituperation use must be made of genealogy in a case of bad ancestry.[3]

The Roman satirists are more explicit in their handling of the concern for noble ancestry. So Juvenal (*c.* A.D. 60–140):

What avail your pedigrees? What boots it, Ponticus, to be valued for one's ancient blood...Of what profit is it to boast a Flavius on your ample family chart, and thereafter to trace kinship through many a branch with grimy Dictators and Masters of the Horse, if in the presence of the Lepidi you live an evil life?...[4]

[1] The attitude of Dionysius of Halicarnassus (d. 7 B.C.?) is more positive. He refers (I. 11. 1) to the Roman historian, 'Porcius Cato, who compiled with the greatest care the "origins" (τὰς γενεαλογίας) of the Italian cities...'.

[2] *Character* 28 (Loeb).

[3] *Character* 35 (Loeb).

[4] Satire VIII, 'Stemmata quid faciunt?' (Loeb).

And Persius (b. *c.* A.D. 34):

Or are you to puff out your lungs with pride because you come from Tuscan stock, yourself the thousandth in the line?[1] So did Ennius speak his mind [lit., heart] when he had given up dreaming that he was Maeon's son, fifth in descent from the peacock of Pythagoras.[2]

The lofty genealogical claims of the Roman emperors are noted by the Roman historian Suetonius (b. *c.* A.D. 69–77), who records the 'customary orations' of Julius in praise of his deceased aunt, Julia, and his wife:

And in the eulogy of his aunt he spoke in the following terms of her parental and maternal ancestry and that of his own father: 'The family of my aunt Julia is descended by her mother from the kings, and her father's side is akin to the immortal gods; for the Marcii Reges [her mother's family name] go back to Ancus Marcius, and the Julii, the family of which ours is a branch, to Venus. Our stock therefore has at once the sanctity of kings, whose power is supreme among mortal men, and the claim to reverence which attaches to the gods, who hold sway over kings themselves.'[3]

And, finally, Suetonius on Galba:

Nero was succeeded by Galba, who was related in no degree to the house of the Caesars, although unquestionably of noble origin and of an old and powerful family; for he always added to the inscription on his statues that he was the great-grandson of Quintus Catulus Capitolinus, and when he became emperor he even displayed a family tree in his hall in which he carried back his ancestry on his father's side to Jupiter and on his mother's to Pasiphae, the wife of Minos.[4]

The concern over ancestry in these sources is no less strong than that which we find in the Jewish sources; nonetheless there appears to be a wide difference between the panegyrics of the Graeco-Roman 'genealogists' and the midrashic methods of the Rabbis. To be sure, Hellenistic authors could look back to their earliest 'histories', such as the books of 'Genealogia' written by Acusilaus of Argos (*c.* 500 B.C.)[5] and Hecataeus of Miletus (*c.* 500 B.C.), and perhaps even give credence to the subdivisions of Greek clans in the epics of Homer (*c.* tenth

[1] Satire 3. 27–9 (Loeb).
[2] Satire 6. 10–11 (Loeb).
[3] *The Deified Julius* 6. 1 (Loeb).
[4] *Galba* 2 (Loeb).
[5] Cf. Josephus, *Ant.* I. 2.

century B.C.). But the Rabbinic attitude toward the text of the OT is a different matter, and the essentially religious character of the Midrashic genealogical interest in Judaism and Christianity is to be distinguished from the Graeco-Roman genealogies, which can be described either as mythical in the classical sense or as specimens of panegyric.

5. *Summary*

Our study of the Rabbinic tradition relating to genealogical interest has attempted to show that this interest is concerned largely with the question of genealogical purity. This question became acute in post-biblical Judaism when the nation was threatened on the one hand by an increasing religious syncretism and, on the other, by long periods of political subservience. But, in spite of the seriousness of the concern for purity of descent, the evidence indicates that genealogical records were not available for all, especially non-priestly families. In the attempt to ascertain the genealogical status of individuals or families oral tradition was relied upon. In other cases, especially among prominent citizens, recourse was had to a relating of individuals to biblical families by means of Midrashic exegesis of the text.

B. GENEALOGICAL SPECULATION ON THE ANCESTRY OF THE MESSIAH

It is not our intention in this section to provide anything approaching a rounded survey of Messianic passages in the extant literature; this has been done in detail by others.[1] Nor is it intended to trace the origins and development of the Messianic idea, as has been done by Klausner, Mowinckel, Bentzen, and Ringgren. It is rather our purpose here (1) to demonstrate the importance of the ancestry of the Messiah in the sources concerned, and (2) to outline the varying conceptions of Messianic descent which prevailed around the beginning of the Christian era. It is, of course, superfluous to point out that, whatever the ultimate antecedents of the Messianic concept might be, specula-

[1] A fairly recent and comprehensive bibliography of the Messianic expectations in Judaism will be found in the article, 'Messiah, Jewish', by E. Jenni in *IDB*, III, 365.

tion on the role and nature of the eschatological Messiah reached its height in the post-biblical writings of Judaism. As we have mentioned, the political insecurity of the Judean state gave impetus to the utilization of genealogical ranks for the preservation of the national identity. We have now to examine another concomitant of this instability which can be traced, namely discussion of the ancestry of the Messiah.

We find in the post-biblical Jewish writings three main views of the ancestry of the Messiah which seem not to have been mutually exclusive: a Messiah (or Messianic figure) might be expected from Judah (David), from Levi (Aaron), and from Ephraim (Joseph).

1. *The Messiah ben David*

Although in the OT there is a variety of conceptions of future messianic deliverance (the collective house of David in Amos, Ezekiel, Obadiah; an ideal, human Messiah in Hosea, I Isaiah, Micah, Jeremiah, and II Zechariah; the whole people of Israel in II Isaiah and Daniel 7),[1] and, even though it is difficult to determine the significance of the term משיח in its varied usages, it can be emphasized that never in the OT is the future Messianic deliverance to come from any tribe but that of Judah and within that tribe from the house of David.[2] The wellspring of much of the later emphasis on the Davidic descent of the Messiah is undoubtedly to be located in the promise of God to David in II Sam. 7: 11–16:

Moreover the Lord declares to you that the Lord will make you a house. When your days are fulfilled and you lie down with your fathers, I will raise up your son after you, who shall come forth from your body, and I will establish his kingdom. He shall build a house for my name, and I will establish the throne of his kingdom for ever. I will be his father, and he shall be my son. When he

[1] Klausner, *The Messianic Idea in Israel*, tr. A. J. Mattill (1966), pp. 241–2.

[2] Throughout this section it is the future eschatological Messiah that is our concern; hence the application of the term to Cyrus (Isa. 45: 1) and a similar expression in Zech. 4: 14 applied to Joshua and Zerubbabel as well as the common application to priests and kings is not our immediate concern. The term 'Messiah' as referring exclusively to a future deliverer is actually an anachronism when dealing with the biblical texts, since it was not commonly used as such until late Hasmonean times.

commits iniquity, I will chasten him with the rod of men, with the stripes of the sons of men; but I will not take my steadfast love from him, as I took it from Saul, whom I put away from before you. And your house and your kingdom shall be made sure for ever before me; your throne shall be established for ever.

The Davidic king is here the son of Yahweh and the Davidic line is guaranteed perpetuity. In the early prophets David is seldom mentioned although in both Amos and Hosea we have clear indications of the expectation of a renewed Davidic ruler in Israel in an eschatological context.[1] Similarly, I Isaiah speaks of 'a shoot from the stump of Jesse, and a branch...out of his roots'; he looks forward to the final victory of Yahweh over all the forces of evil when 'the root of Jesse shall stand as an ensign to the peoples...'[2] And Jeremiah, who is not beyond warning the house of David of approaching doom brought about by its own waywardness,[3] holds the perpetuity of the Davidic line[4] as well as the expectation of a 'righteous Branch to spring forth for David'[5] and in a striking passage seems to expect a David *redivivus*: 'But [in that day] they shall serve the Lord their God and David their king, whom I will raise up for them.'[6] In Ezekiel we have the idea of David as the eschatological shepherd[7] who is also prince[8] and king[9] over Israel. Finally, as we noted above,[10] the work of the Chronicler has as one of its major themes the exaltation of David and may reflect eschatological hopes for a renewal of the Davidic line. In a word, wherever in the OT a future 'Messianic' deliverer is expected and his tribal origin stated, he is to come from Judah, from the house of David.

This emphasis on the Davidic descent of the Messiah also dominates the later Jewish literature. In the books of the Apocrypha, although there is no individual Messiah, the perpetuity of the house of David is alluded to in Sirach 47: 22:

> But the Lord will never give up his mercy,
>   nor cause any of his works to perish;

[1] Amos 9: 11; Hos. 3: 5; but contrast the allusion to David in Amos 6: 5.
[2] Isa. 11: 1, 10.
[3] Jer. 21: 11–14; 22: 1–5, 24–30 *et passim*.
[4] 33: 17.
[5] 33: 15; 23: 5–6.
[6] 30: 9.
[7] 34: 23.
[8] 34: 24; 37: 25.
[9] 37: 24.
[10] Ch. 1, pp. 48 f., 74–6.

He will never blot out the descendants of his chosen one,
nor destroy the posterity of him who loved him;
So he gave a remnant to Jacob
and to David a root of his stock.[1]

Significantly, however, Ben Sira also holds forth the perpetuity of the priesthood of Aaron in the line of Phinehas ben Eleazar and Simon ben Onias.[2] The author holds belief in the perpetuity of the throne of David and the priesthood of Aaron to be of equally great importance. In a noteworthy passage Phinehas and David appear side by side:

Therefore a covenant of peace was established with him
[Phinehas], that he should be leader of the sanctuary
and of his people, that he and his descendants should
have the dignity of the priesthood for ever.
A covenant was also established with David, the son of Jesse,
of the tribe of Judah:
The heritage of the king is from son to son only;
so the heritage of Aaron is for his descendants.[3]

Reminiscences of the Chronicler's exaltation of David and the priestly cultus are probably to be seen here.

A hint of a similar point of view is to be found in a book which is otherwise lacking in Messianic interest, I Macc. 2: 54–7. There, in a list of heroes of the OT, we read concerning Phinehas and David the following:

Phinehas, our father, because he was deeply zealous,
received the covenant of an eternal priesthood.
David, because he was merciful, inherited the throne of
his kingdom for ever.

Most probably, such an elevation of the priestly office to the level of the house of David, so that both are eternal, is to be explained as arising out of the traditional prestige of the two offices, and their combination in the person of the later Macca-

[1] Cf. also Sirach 47: 11.

[2] 45: 6–7, 13; 50: 1 ff. On the expectation of two Messiahs, see below, pp. 120 ff.

[3] Sirach 45: 24–5; cf. Klausner, *Messianic Idea*, pp. 255 f.; the significance of the inclusion of David in this passage, an inclusion which breaks the historical sequence of the context, is pointed out by John Priest, 'Ben Sira 45: 25 in the Light of the Qumran Literature', *RQ*, 17. 5 (October 1964), pp. 111–18.

bean rulers, who were of priestly descent.[1] Such concepts as these are hints of the idea of the two Messiahs which emerges explicitly in the Testaments and the Dead Sea Scrolls.[2]

As for the pseudepigraphal books, we find the expectation of the exclusively Davidic Messiah in a most emphatic form in IV Ezra and the Psalms of Solomon:

This is the Messiah whom the Most High has kept until the end of days, who will arise from the posterity of David...[3]

In the strongly eschatological chapter 17 of the Psalms of Solomon the future, eschatological Messiah is linked to the Davidic line:

> Thou, O Lord, didst choose David (to be) king over Israel,
> And swearedst to him touching his seed that never should his kingdom fail before Thee. (verse 4)
> Behold, O Lord, and raise up unto them their king, the son of David,
> At the time in which Thou seest, O God, that he may reign over Israel thy servant. (verse 21)

Ps. Sol. 17: 36 is the oldest source in which the expected royal deliverer is designated as 'Messiah'; here, and in 18: 5, this son of David is called 'the anointed of the Lord' (χριστὸς κυρίου = משיח יהוה = 'The Lord's Messiah'). This is the development which brings us to the common Messianic designation in the NT and the Talmud.

The NT evidence for the ancestry of Jesus the Messiah is unanimous: 'For it is evident that our Lord was descended from Judah...'[4] of the line of David;[5] indeed Jesus is addressed as 'Son of David', an especially common title in Matthew.[6]

So also in the Talmud and Midrash the most frequently used Messianic designation is 'Son of David'[7] in such phrases as 'the

[1] I Macc. 2: 1; cf. I Chron. 9: 10; Neh. 11: 10.

[2] On the Messianism of the Testaments and the Scrolls, see below.

[3] IV Ezra 12: 32.

[4] Heb. 7: 14.

[5] Rom. 1: 3; II Tim. 2: 8; Matt. 1: 1–17, 30; Luke 1: 27, 32; 2: 4; 3: 23–8; Acts 2: 25–31; 13: 23, 34–7; 15: 16; Rev. 5: 5; 22: 16; cf. 3: 7.

[6] Mark 10: 47 f. par.; Matt. 9: 27; 15: 22; 21: 8, 15; cf. Mark 11: 10; Matt. 12: 23; see below, pp. 217 f., 224 ff.

[7] Jastrow, *Dictionary of the Targumin, the Talmud Babli and Yerushalmi and the Midrashic Literature*, 2 vols. 1903 (reprinted 1950), I, 283.

Son of David will not come until...'[1] The importance and early date of the title in the Jewish tradition is seen in its inclusion in both the Palestinian and Babylonian recensions of the *Shemoneh Esreh* (benedictions 15 and 14, respectively).[2] This view of the ancestry of the Messiah is held without regard to the particular conception of the office of the Messiahship involved. Thus, although the Son of David in the earlier literature is 'a man born of men',[3] in the 'Revelation of R. Joshua b. Levi' and in the Midrash Konen the pre-existent Messiah is also called 'Messiah ben David'.[4] In sum, we may assert that for both the Christian and Jewish traditions the expectation that the Messiah would be Davidic was the prevailing view.

2. *Varieties in Messianic speculation: the Messiah ben Aaron*

To maintain the priority of the Davidic ancestry of the Messiah in Judaism, however, is not to suggest that there was universal agreement on the subject. There is evidence from Judaism roughly contemporary with the NT to show that significant debate on the ancestry of the Messiah was carried out on two fronts: there is, on the one hand, the suggestion that the Messiah, or a second Messianic figure, would stem from a tribe other than Judah; and, on the other hand, the variety in the genealogical relation of the Messiah to David.

The most explicitly attested view of a non-Davidic ancestry of a Messianic figure is the conception of a priestly Messiah or a Messianic priest. It is possible to find traces of this idea in the OT itself,[5] and we have seen above that Ben Sira as well as I Maccabees place belief in the perpetuity of the throne of David and the priesthood of Aaron in juxtaposition. Yet it is true that the idea of a priestly *Messianic figure* occurs explicitly only in the Testaments of the Twelve Patriarchs, the Dead Sea Scrolls, and a few Rabbinic sources. At the risk of appearing

[1] bSan. 97*a*, 98*a*; bAbod. Z. 5*a*; cf. Klausner, *Messianic Idea*, p. 332; Drummond, *The Jewish Messiah* (1877), p. 282.

[2] *JE*, VIII, 510 f., 508*a*.

[3] Cf. Trypho in Justin, *Dial.* 49 (beginning).

[4] *JE*, VIII, 511*a*.

[5] Cf. I Sam. 2: 35; Jer. 33: 17–22; Ezek. 44–6; Zech. 4: 14; Haggai 1: 1. Also, as G. Friedrich ('Messianische Hohepriestererwartung in den Synoptikern', *ZTK*, LIII, 273) points out, the juxtaposition of king, priest, and prophet is found in Jer. 8: 1; 13: 13; 2: 26; 4: 9.

overly dogmatic in my general view of this material, I mention a few of the most important passages first, and then survey the modern critical stance.

Regarding the Testaments, I would accept the views of those who maintain that in the original strata there was the expectation of two Messianic figures, one royal and the other priestly. In T. Reub. 6: 5–12 Levi is 'until the consummation of the times...the anointed high priest' (ἀρχιερέως χριστοῦ) while Judah is 'chosen to be king over all the nation'. From Levi and Judah 'shall arise unto you the salvation of God. For the Lord shall raise up from Levi as it were a high priest, and from Judah as it were a King...' (T. Sim. 7: 1 f.). In T. Levi 18 we have the most explicit description of the role of this future priestly figure:

Καὶ μετὰ τὸ γενέσθαι τὴν ἐκδίκησιν αὐτῶν παρὰ Κυρίου, τῇ ἱερατείᾳ τότε ἐγερεῖ Κύριος ἱερέα καινόν, ᾧ πάντες οἱ λόγοι Κυρίου ἀποκαλυφθήσονται· καὶ αὐτὸς ποιήσει κρίσιν ἀληθείας ἐπὶ τῆς γῆς ἐν πλήθει ἡμερῶν. Καὶ ἀνατελεῖ ἄστρον αὐτοῦ ἐν οὐρανῷ, ὡς βασιλεύς, φωτίζων φῶς γνώσεως ἐν ἡλίῳ ἡμέρας.[1]

The priestly Messiah is the eschatological 'new priest' who will 'execute a righteous judgment upon the earth for a multitude of days. And his star shall arise in heaven as of a king' (verses 2–3). These words are an obvious allusion to Num. 24: 17 ('A star shall come forth out of Jacob, and a scepter shall rise out of Israel'), one of the favorite proof-texts in all Jewish and Christian Messianism, and clearly reveals the Messianic character of this 'new priest'.[2] He not only marks the renewal of the priesthood, but seems to combine that with the functions of royalty (ὡς βασιλεύς). Yet is seems clear that this cannot be a Christian interpolation since it is included within the Testament of *Levi*, not Judah, and the tradition of Jesus' Davidic descent seems to have been almost universal within the early church. At any rate the role of this 'new priest' is Messianic in the later traditional sense: 'In his priesthood shall sin come to an end...and Beliar shall be bound by him, and he

[1] Text, M. de Jonge, *Testamenta XII Patriarcharum* (1964), p. 21.

[2] Only one other reference to a 'new priest' or 'new priesthood' occurs in the Testaments, namely T. Levi 8: 14, 'A king...from Judah will establish a new priesthood'. This latter reference, however, reads much like a Christian interpolation. Translated passages follow Charles, *A & P*.

shall give power to his children to tread upon the evil spirits...' (verses 9, 12). The kingship proper, however, belongs to Judah:

And now, my children, I command you, love Levi, that ye may abide, and exalt not yourselves against him, lest ye be utterly destroyed. For to me the Lord gave the kingdom, and to him the priesthood, and He set the kingdom beneath the priesthood.[1]

The giving of the priesthood to Levi and the kingdom of Judah, with the superiority of Levi ('as the heaven is higher than the earth')[2] is a common theme in the Testaments.[3] The result would seem to be a unified picture: The Testaments hold forth the expectation of a new priest at the end of days,[4] and also a Messianic king at the end of days;[5] in several passages they are mentioned together as the source of Israel's salvation[6] although Levi is consistently placed in a position superior to that of Judah.[7]

It must be admitted, however, that the interpretation of the Testaments is still in a state of flux and the conclusions stated above, while representing the most commonly held views, have been seriously challenged. In 1953 M. de Jonge published his book, *The Testaments of the Twelve Patriarchs: A Study of their Text, Composition, and Origin*,[8] in which he set forth the thesis that the Testaments as we have them, while incorporating earlier Jewish materials, are basically Christian in origin. Thus, according to de Jonge, one must speak not merely of 'Christian interpolations' within the Testaments but rather think of them as a thorough re-working of Jewish materials. In many of the passages cited above from the Testaments, therefore, de Jonge

[1] T. Jud. 21: 1–2; cf. 1: 6; 15: 2; 17: 5–6; 22: 3.

[2] T. Jud. 21: 4.

[3] T. Is. 5: 7; T. Dan 5: 4, 10; T. Naph. 5: 31; 8: 2; T. Gad 8: 1; T. Jos. 19: 11.

[4] T. Reub. 6: 8; T. Sim. 7: 2; T. Levi 18: 1 ff.; T. Jud. 24: 1–2.

[5] T. Reub. 6: 12; T. Sim. 7: 2; T. Jud. 22: 2–3; 24: 5–6.

[6] T. Reub. 6: 8, 10; T. Sim. 7: 1–2; T. Levi 8: 11–12; T. Is. 5: 7; T. Dan 4: 7; T. Naph. 8: 2–3; T. Gad 8: 1; T. Jos. 19: 11.

[7] T. Reub. 6: 7, 11; T. Jud. 21: 1–2; 25: 1, 2; T. Naph. 5: 3–4.

[8] De Jonge has elaborated and defended this thesis in his more recent study, 'Christian Influences in the Testaments of the Twelve Patriarchs', *Nov. Test.* IV (1960), 182–235.

would insist that it is impossible to reconstruct the original Jewish material and use it as evidence for Jewish Messianic expectation.[1]

In a recent article,[2] Higgins accepts the thesis of a Christian origin of the Testaments, while believing it possible 'at certain points to discern earlier Jewish ideas which have been adapted'. But, even in the earlier Jewish strata, Higgins does not find unequivocal evidence in the Testaments for the expectation of a priestly Messiah: 'A possible exception is Test. Simeon 7: 2, where perhaps the older form of the now Christianized statement spoke of an eschatological high priest from Levi alongside the Messiah from Judah. Such a high priest, however, is not necessarily a Messiah. The figure would bear a certain resemblance to the high priest who, it was believed, would be the head of the Qumran community when the Messiah appeared... Most significant...is the absence in both [the Testaments and the Qumran literature] of the notion of a priestly Messiah, coupled with the importance attached to the priesthood and its superiority to the secular power...'[3] One of the difficulties which characterizes Higgins' study, however, should be noted: he seems to posit some sharp distinction between *The* Messiah and any other eschatological figures, without carefully defining what is meant by the term 'Messiah'. This tendency comes to a focus when Higgins deals with a crucial passage in the Qumran Manual of Discipline (IQS 9: 10 f.) in which both the priestly figure and the kingly figure are designated 'Messiahs' or 'anointed', and yet only the kingly figure is denoted as 'Messiah' by Higgins (see below).

Earlier scholars had at one time concluded that in the original strata of the Testaments there was the expectation only of one Messiah. R. H. Charles claimed that this was the Levitical

[1] The Christian origin of the Testaments appears correct also to F. M. Cross, *The Ancient Library of Qumran and Modern Biblical Studies* (1958), p. 149 n. 6. De Jonge's hypothesis has been rejected by A. S. van der Woude, *Die messianischen Vorstellungen der Gemeinde von Qumran* (1957), and by M. Philonenko (cf. A. J. B. Higgins, 'The Priestly Messiah', *NTS*, XIII (1967), 220 n. 6).

[2] Higgins, pp. 211–39.

[3] *NTS*, XIII (1967), 229 f. In an earlier study (*VT*, III (1953), 323 f.) Higgins suggested that in the Testaments there was to be one Messiah, descended from both Levi and Judah.

Messiah,[1] while K. Kohler[2] and L. Ginzberg[3] held that only the Messiah from Judah belongs to the original stratum.

We may conclude that, while the interpretation of the messianism of the Testaments is in a state of flux, the earlier judgment of Beasley-Murray has not been disproved: 'The juxtaposition of the Messiah from Judah and the Messiah from Levi is too deeply rooted in the fabric of the book for either element to be discarded...'[4] Since the statement was written, moreover, the data of the Qumran material must be taken into account in any discussion of the question whether there was a variety of messianic speculation in Judaism of the NT period.

Did the community at Qumran at any time hold the expectation of a priestly Messianic figure? This question is still answered in the affirmative perhaps by most interpreters on the basis of the following evidence:

(1) The clearest passage supporting the contention that the Dead Sea community expected at least two Messianic figures occurs in the Manual of Discipline (IQS 9: 10 f.), where we read:

> They shall not depart from any counsel of the law, walking in all the stubbornness of their hearts; but they shall be judged by the first judgments by which the men of the community began to be disciplined, until there shall come a prophet and the Messiahs of Aaron and Israel.[5]

While this plural (מישיחי) is commonly taken as a reference to two eschatological 'Messiahs', Higgins is led by the paucity of such references in Jewish Messianism generally and at Qumran in particular to state the matter in what appears to me to be an extreme fashion:

> [In IQS 9: 10 f.] the *mešîḥîm* of Aaron and Israel are less probably 'the Messiahs' than 'the anointed ones'. The term has a wider sense, including both the (Davidic) Messiah proper and the ruling High Priest at the time of his coming. Both could appropriately be called 'anointed ones of Aaron and Israel' after the name of the community. The conclusion suggests itself, therefore, that at

[1] *A & P*, II, 294.   [2] *JE*, XII, 113 f.

[3] 'Eine unbekannte jüdische Sekte', *Monatsschrift zu Geschichte und Wissenschaft des Judenthums*, LVIII (1914), 403–11.

[4] 'The Two Messiahs in the Testaments of the Twelve Patriarchs', *JTS*, XLVIII (1947), 1 ff.

[5] Burrows' trans., *The Dead Sea Scrolls*, p. 383.

Qumran there was not a belief in a secular and a priestly Messiah, but only in a messianic Davidic prince and deliverer. Of course, the possibility of variety or of development of messianic belief among the men of Qumran must be recognized.[1]

It is not clear to me how one can make a sharp distinction here between the translation 'the Messiahs' and 'the anointed ones', or how one can distinguish between the status of 'the anointed of Aaron' and that of 'the anointed of Israel'. Those who would deny the pre-Christian existence in Judaism of the concept of a priestly Messianic figure have yet to provide an adequate explanation of this passage.

(2) In IQSa 2: 18 ff., in a description of what is probably the eschatological banquet, there is the priest who 'shall bless the first of the bread and the wine, and he shall put forth his hand on the bread first; and next the Messiah of Israel shall put forth his hand on the bread...'[2] Again, Higgins states:

> The High Priest is as such also an anointed one, but not a messianic figure in the full sense. He is the future religious head at the time when the Messiah is to appear, just as the community has a priest as its superior. It is because of his position as the religious head that even the Messiah will be subordinate to him.[3]

The interpretation of this passage, of course, hinges on the prior question whether or not this meal was considered to be a Messianic banquet. Again scholarly opinion is divided. Driver[4] thinks that the meal described in IQSa 2: 11–22 is not a messianic banquet, though it is envisaged as taking place with the Messiah present and is a solemn meal. M. Black, however, writes in response to Driver: 'There seems little doubt... that the meal here described is a messianic banquet of some kind, possibly that of Ezekiel's vision in chapter 44.'[5] I am inclined to believe that the Messiah referred to in this passage is identical with the Messiah of Israel alluded to above in IQS 9: 11, while 'the priest' stands for the eschatological high priest, the 'Messiah of Aaron'.[6] It might be pertinent to suggest that the

[1] *NTS*, XIII (1967), 218 f.

[2] Burrows' trans. *More Light on the Dead Sea Scrolls* (1958), p. 395.

[3] *NTS*, XIII, 218.

[4] *The Judaean Scrolls* (1965), p. 468; cited by M. Black in a review article in *NTS*, XIII (1966), 84.

[5] *NTS*, XIII, 84.

[6] Cf. Kuhn, 'The Two Messiahs of Aaron and Israel', in *The Scrolls and the New Testament*, ed. K. Stendahl (1957), p. 55.

term 'the priest' here appears to be used in a way corresponding closely to the 'new priest' of the Testaments, since the context in which each is introduced is eschatological.

(3) The Damascus Document (CD) contains several references to 'the Messiah of Aaron and Israel' (12: 23; 14: 18; 19: 10) and similar phrases. The problem occasioned by the similarity of this expression to the plural form in IQS 9: 10 f. has been much discussed. It seems that the older theory that an original plural (משיחי) in CD was changed to a singular by the medieval copyists of this document is no longer tenable because of the discovery at Qumran of this phrase in the singular in an incomplete manuscript of CD.[1] The question which emerges is whether the CD should be interpreted in light of the plural form in the Manual of Discipline or the reverse. Another possibility is that the sect believed at one time in two messianic figures, a priestly Messiah and a lay Messiah (reflected in IQS), and at other times in one Messiah, a lay ruler of the lineage of David.[2] Certainly it is a striking fact that, in the passages alluded to above, David is not mentioned as an ancestor of the Messiah. This becomes more puzzling in light of the fact that we have several other texts from Qumran which do specifically name David in Messianic contexts. There are three relevant passages, each from Cave 4:

(1) 'A ruler shall not depart from the tribe of Judah' [Gen. 49: 10] while Israel has dominion, nor shall one who sits on the throne for David be cut off. For the staff is the covenant of kingship; the thousands of Israel are the feet, until the coming of the Messiah of righteousness, the branch of David, for to him and to his seed is given the covenant of the kingship of his people until the generations of eternity, because he kept the...law with the men of the community. For...that is the synagogue of the men of...[3]

[1] J. T. Milik, *Ten Years of Discovery in the Wilderness of Judaea* (1959), p. 125.

[2] So Driver, *Judaean Scrolls* (cited by M. Black, *NTS*, XIII (1966), 83). The variation in messianic expectation at Qumran is explained as due to the historical development of the theology of the sect also by J. Liver, 'The Doctrine of the Two Messiahs in Sectarian Literature of the Second Commonwealth', *HTR*, LII (1959), 162–3, and in a more detailed fashion by J. Starcky, 'Les quatre étapes du messianisme à Qumrân', *RB*, LXX (1963), 481–505.

[3] 4Q Patr. Bl. (Commentary on Gen. 49); Burrows' trans. as also are the two following (*More Light*, p. 401); cf. J. M. Allegro, 'Further Messianic References in Qumran Literature', *JBL*, LXXV (1956), 174 ff.

(2) [After citing II Sam. 7: 11–14] He is the branch of David, who will arise with the interpreter of the law who...in...in the latter days; as it is written, 'And I will raise up the booth of David that is fallen' [Amos 9: 11]. That is the booth of David that is fallen; but afterward he will arise to save Israel.[1]

(3) [Isa. 11: 1–4 is quoted in fragments]...(The branch) of David who will arise in the latter...And God will sustain him with...Law...a glorious throne, a...wreath, and many-colored robes...in his hand, and over all the nations shall he rule; and Magog...his sword will execute judgment on all the peoples...[2]

In these passages there is only one Messiah, the Davidic warrior and deliverer, and he is not designated the 'Messiah of Israel'. Thus those who argue that there was some historical development of Qumran Messianism do recognize the divergence of views reflected in the texts. These variations could, of course, also be explained as the result of internal differences of belief held simultaneously within the Qumran community.

The strongest denial of variations in Qumran messianism is made by Higgins: the sect expected only one 'Messiah', namely 'a Davidic prince, warrior, and deliverer', while the future priest would be 'an anointed one, but not a messianic figure in the full sense'.[3] But perhaps this whole discussion needs to take into account the nature of the Qumran community as such. Here the words of M. Black deserve to be cited:

So far as the Qumran secular Messiah is concerned, there is little doubt that Driver is right; the messianic ideal is virtually identical with that of the Pharisaic *Psalms of Solomon*—he is the Davidic Warrior Messiah. To reduce the Messianism of Qumran to this simple equation is, however, an over-simplification of the problem. Driver does not, for instance, discuss in the same detail the sacerdotal messianism of the sect; and this seems, in fact, to have been the distinctive form of Qumran or Essene belief (the secular Messiah is largely a Pharisaic ideal). There are now cogent grounds for concluding that this predominantly priestly sect began as a legitimist priestly movement whose earliest aspirations came to be focused on the arising from its midst of a legitimate High Priest who would reinstate the sect as the true priesthood of Israel of the Sons of Zadok

[1] 4Q Florilegium; Burrows, *More Light*, p. 401; cf. Allegro, p. 176.

[2] Fragment of a commentary on Isa. 10–11; Burrows, *More Light*, p. 403.

[3] *NTS*, XIII, 218.

and rule as High Priest in Jerusalem. As the sect's hope of actual restoration receded, however, their aspirations shifted from a historical to a supra-natural plane; the High Priest in the War scroll may still be a man of human kind, but the warfare he solemnly inaugurates is to be waged on a higher than human plane...The sect did have some ideas about resurrection and an after-life...and IQS 4: 1–28, the *Blessings on the Priests*, seems to imply that the High Priest, and probably the messianic High Priest is meant, would share in that future life.[1]

While it may be difficult to demonstrate that the concept of the priestly Messiah was more determinative or more characteristic of the Qumran community than the expectation of a Davidic warrior Messiah, it is nonetheless highly probable that the former was a well-defined part of their eschatology. Thus, our basic question—Was there in pre-Christian Judaism any expectation of a non-Davidic Messianic figure?—can be answered in the affirmative, and the basic views within the *Testaments of the Twelve Patriarchs* can be considered to be represented also by the documents from Qumran.[2]

N. Wieder has shown that the 'Messianic dualism' of Qumran was current also among the Karaites of the ninth century A.D.[3] According to Wieder, 'their Messianic expectations centered around two figures, the Messianic priest and the Davidic Messiah, and, further...the Messianic priest was

[1] *NTS*, XIII, 83.

[2] Among those who hold to the variation of pre-Christian Jewish messianism may be mentioned the following: Aptowitzer, *Parteipolitik*, *passim*; Beasley-Murray, *JTS*, XLVIII (1947), 1–12; K. Schubert, *Judaica*, XI (1955), 216–35; H. L. Silbermann, *VT*, V (1955), 77–82; Friedrich, *ZTK*, LIII (1956), 268–75; Kuhn, in *The Scrolls and the NT*, ed. Stendahl, pp. 54 ff.; Van der Woude, *Die messianischen Vorstellungen* (1957); Liver, *HTR*, LII (1959), 149–85; M. Smith, *JBL*, LXXVIII (1959), 66–72; F. F. Bruce, *Biblical Exegesis in the Qumran Texts* (1960); J. Gnilka, *RQ*, II (1960), 395–426; P. Grelot, in *La Venue du Messie*, ed. E. Massaux *et al.* (1962); Starcky, *RB*, LXX (1963), 481–505; Davies, *Setting*, pp. 147–5; F. Hahn, *Christologische Hoheitstitel* (2nd ed. 1964), pp. 145 ff., 231 f.; D. S. Russell, *The Method and Message of Jewish Apocalyptic* (1964), ch. 12; Driver, *Judaean Scrolls*, pp. 465–7; M. Black, *The Dead Sea Scrolls and Christian Doctrine* (1966), pp. 10 ff.; R. E. Brown, *CBQ*, XXVIII (1966), 51–7; A. R. C. Leaney, *The Rule of Qumran and its Meaning* (1966); O. Cullmann, *Christology of the NT* (2nd ed. 1963), p. 86.

[3] 'The Doctrine of the Two Messiahs among the Karaites', *JJS*, VI (1955), 14–23.

identified by some Karaites with the prophet Elijah'.[1] The Messianic activities of the latter include, together with functions also assigned to him by the Rabbis, the making known of the genealogies [וחן אלדי יערף אליחושים].[2]

This discussion of the second Messiah is found also in scattered sayings within the Rabbinic writings.[3] The earliest explicit evidence is bSuk. 52*b* (251):

> 'And the Lord showed me four craftsmen' [Zech. 2: 3]. Who are these four craftsmen?—R. Hana b. Bizna [end of third century] citing R. Simeon Hasida (the Pious)[4] replied: The Messiah the son of David, the Messiah the son of Joseph, Elijah, and the Righteous Priest [כהן צדק].

The same four figures appear also in the Midrashim: אליהו ומלך המשיח ומלכי צדק ומשיח מלחמה[5] in which the מלכי צדק must be considered to be identical with the כהן צדק of the Talmud. This alternative term is most probably the result of the conjoining of Zech. 4: 14 with Ps. 110: 4:

> Similarly, with the verse, 'These are the two anointed ones, that stand by the Lord of the whole earth' [Zech. 4: 14]. This is a reference to Aaron and the Messiah, but I cannot tell which is the more beloved. However, from the verse, 'The Lord hath sworn and will not repent: thou art a priest for ever after the manner of Melchizedek' [Ps. 110: 4], one can tell that the Messianic king is more beloved than the righteous priest.[6]

[1] P. 14.

[2] MS. British Museum, Or. 2401, fol. 260*a*, cited by Wieder, p. 16; cf. mEd. 8: 7. Significantly, it is only in this MS. that we have a parallel in Jewish sources for the idea, mentioned by Justin in the name of Trypho as Jewish belief (*Dial.* 49), that Elijah will anoint the Messiah.

[3] The Rabbinic evidence for a priestly Messiah is noted by Aptowitzer, *Parteipolitik*, pp. 82–95 (notes, pp. 236–43); Ginzberg, *MGWJ*, LVIII (1914), 395–429 (esp. pp. 418–29); R. Young, *Christology of the Targums*, n.d., *passim*; and Friedrich, *ZTK*, LIII (1956), 274–5.

[4] 'Zeit und Lebensumstände dieses Tanna sind ganz unbekannt, obwohl eine ziemlich grosse Anzahl haggadischer Sätze—beinahe alle verraten eine mystische Tendenz—von ihm überliefert sind...' (Ginzberg, p. 418 n. 1); yet he is earlier than the Amoraic Halakist of the same name; cf. also C. G. Montefiore and H. Loewe, *A Rabbinic Anthology* (1938), p. 703: the date of Simeon the Pious is uncertain, although definitely Tannaitic.

[5] Pesikta 51*a*; Pes. Rab. 15: 75*a*; S. Songs R. on 2: 13 (125) (cited by Ginzberg, p. 419); cf. also *En Ya'aqob* (cited by H. Odeberg, *3 Enoch* (1928), p. 147 n.).

[6] Tr. Judah Goldin, *The Fathers According to Rabbi Nathan* (1955), pp. 137–8. In Gen. R. 43 the 'righteous priest' is identified with Melchizedek; the

One can best understand these data as being remnants or an elaboration of such Messianic speculation as that contained in the Testaments and the Scrolls. The 'righteous priest' is Aaron; the Messiah b. David is the 'King Messiah'. Thus we have here the Messiahs of Israel (David) and Aaron, together with the prophet, and the appearance of one new figure, the Messiah ben Joseph, the 'Messiah of war' who has taken over the militaristic role which was formerly part of the task of the Son of David.[1] The passage cited from ARN, despite the difficulty of following the exegetical argument,[2] also clearly subordinates the priestly Messiah to the Davidic Messiah, a view that is in direct opposition to that in the material from Qumran. The tendency of the Rabbinic writings as a whole to give the king precedence over the high priest[3] could be due to the cessation of the sacrificial cultus with the destruction of Jerusalem in A.D. 70. On the other hand, in one passage,[4] the two Messiahs are seemingly placed in equal positions:

two 'sons of oil' are said to be Aaron and David also in Sifra צו, 18; Sifre zutta (ed. Horowitz), p. 253; Lam. R. on 1:16; and Num. R. on 18:16 (cited by Aptowitzer, *Parteipolitik*, p. 236 n. 1). 'Die Gesamtliteratur der Juden kennt keine andere Deutung "der Olivenbäume" als die, dass sie für das aharonidische Priestertum und das davidische Königstum stehen' (Ginzberg, p. 424).

[1] On the Messiah ben Joseph, see esp. Odeberg, *3 Enoch*, pp. 144–7 (note on 45:5), where the Rabbinic and bibliographical references are collected and various views on the origin of the concept are summarized; cf. also Aptowitzer, pp. 105–13, and Charles C. Torrey, 'The Messiah Son of Ephraim', *JBL*, LXVI (1947), 253–77. Torrey thinks that 'the doctrine antedated the Christian era by several centuries, and was accepted on all hands' (p. 255); yet he completely ignores the idea of the Levitical Messiah in Judaism, and his exaggeration of the importance of the Messiah b. Joseph is no less than amazing when he writes: 'The doctrine of the two Messiahs holds an important place in Jewish theology...It is not a theory imperfectly formulated or only temporarily held, but a standing article of faith, early and firmly established and universally accepted. The doctrine, in substance, is this. There are two eternally appointed Messiahs, divine beings, destined to appear on earth at the end of the present age. The one is the *Son of David*...; the other is the Son of Joseph...' (p. 253). In actuality, the origins of the idea of the Messiah b. Joseph are unknown, and there is no explicit source earlier than bSuk. 52*a*.

[2] Aptowitzer, *Parteipolitik*, pp. 82 f., presents three explanations of this exegetical 'proof'.

[3] Cf. Tos. Hor. 2:9; bHor. 13*a* (cited by Liver, *HTR*, LII (1959), 156 n. 22).

[4] Gen. R. 71:5 (656).

[On Num. 17: 17] R. Levi [third century] said: Out of them [the tribes] two tribes were exalted, the tribe of priesthood and the tribe of royalty. You will find that whatever is written in connection with one is written in connection with the other. Thus, anointing is written in connection with both, a rod [sceptre] in connection with both, a 'covenant of salt' in connection with both, 'time' in connection with both, crown in connection with both, a genealogical tree is given for both, and 'ẓiẓ' [headplate] in connection with both.

As for the Targums, the view is consistent: there is no other eschatological high priest than Elijah,[1] although in the later Targums, those of Pseudo-Jonathan (*c.* A.D. 500) and of R. Joseph the Blind (*c.* A.D. 600), the Messiah ben Joseph frequently appears along with the Messiah ben David.[2]

3. *The origin of the idea of the Levitical Messiah*

(*a*) *Aptowitzer's hypothesis.* How did the conception of the Levitical Messiah arise? V. Aptowitzer, in his *Parteipolitik der Hasmonäerzeit*,[3] suggests that the bulk of the Rabbinic and sectarian references to the priestly Messiah reflects the political struggles of the Hasmonean era, especially under John Hyrcanus and Alexander Jannaeus.[4] The starting-point of the debate, according to this view, was the Haggadic exposition of Ps. 110: 4, as transmitted in ARN, cited above. The Hasmoneans, descendants of the Maccabees who were of priestly stock and could trace their descent to a family of early post-

[1] See Appendix 3.

[2] Cf. Young, *Christology of the Targums, passim.*

One Midrashic passage speaks of a Messiah ben Manasseh, probably a variant of the Messiah ben Joseph, even though the Ephraimite Messiah is mentioned in the same text: '"And Manasseh is mine" alludes to the Messiah who is to spring from the sons of Manasseh, as is borne out by the text, "Before Ephraim and Benjamin, Manasseh, stir up thy might, and come to save us" [Ps. 80: 3 (ET, 80: 2)]. "Ephraim also is the defence of my head" alludes to the Messiah anointed for war who will be descended from Ephraim, as may be inferred from the text, "His firstling bullock, majesty is his" [Deut. 33: 17]. "Judah is my sceptre" alludes to the Great Redeemer who is to be a descendant of the grandchildren of David...' (Num. Rab. 14: 1 [558]).

[3] Pp. 82–94; this position is summarized by Liver, *HTR*, LII (1959), 165 n. 55; by Davies, *Setting*, pp. 110 f. n. 3; and in detail by A. Marmorstein, *MGWJ*, LXXIII (1929), 244–50.

[4] Pp. 34 ff.

exilic times,[1] held forth the expectation that the Messiah would be from the tribe of Levi, that is, a priestly Messiah who would also be king. This idea, according to Aptowitzer, is reflected in the Testament of Levi 29: 10; 8: 11–15; 18. The anti-Hasmoneans also, according to this reconstruction, expected the kingship and priesthood to be united in one Messiah but, again basing their view on Ps. 110: 4, this would be the Davidic Messiah who would also be priest. Later disputes on this question hinged on the expectation of one Messiah who would arise from both Levi and Judah. The Hasmoneans, whose views are found in the Testaments, especially, according to Aptowitzer, in later interpolations contained in the present text, claimed that the sons of Aaron are also sons of Judah.[2] The anti-Hasmonean view, reflected in later Midrashic sources, was that the Messiah ben David could legitimately hold the priesthood since he is a descendant of Miriam, sister of Moses and Aaron.[3] Aptowitzer contends that the anti-Hasmonean view was elevated to a dogma in the Epistle to the Hebrews, where the priestly character of the Messiah from Judah is emphasized.[4]

The ensuing debate between the Hasmoneans and the anti-Hasmoneans, according to Aptowitzer, produced continuing charges and countercharges. The Sadducees (representing the later Hasmonean point of view) held that, because of the illegal

[1] I Macc. 2: 1 ff.

[2] Aptowitzer alludes to T. Jos. 19; T. Sim. 7; T. Levi 2: 11; T. Dan 5: 10; T. Gad 8: 1; and the Damascus Document.

[3] The earliest witness to this idea is found in Sifre on Num. par. 78 (tr. Paul P. Levertoff 1926, pp. 54 ff.), which may be dated at the end of the first century A.D. (see below, p. 163): '"When Solomon built both houses, the house of the Lord and that of the king" [II Kings 9: 10], one knows that "the house of the Lord" is priesthood, and "the house of the king" is kingship: Yohebed had the merit of priesthood, and Miriam of kingship. Miriam married Kaleb, of whom it says [I Chron. 2: 19]: "He took a wife with the name Ephrath". And of David it says [I Sam. 17: 12] "David was the son of that Ephrathite". Thus, David was descended from Miriam. "Lo, he who draws near is being drawn near from heaven."' Aptowitzer (pp. 92 f.) feels that the connection of Caleb and Miriam was a matter of tradition such as is reflected in bYom. 71*b*; bTaan. 17*a*; bB. Bath. 17*a*; bSan. 22*b*; bSheb. 18*b*; bBer. 41*b*; bShab. 55*b*; bSuk. 6*a*; bKer. 13*b*; and bKid. 2*b*. In Josephus (*Ant.* III. 2. 4), however, Caleb's son, Hur, is Miriam's husband. This kind of playful exegesis is frequently found in Midrashic debates on ancestry; cf. also bSot. 11*b*; Ex. R. 1: 17.

[4] P. 94.

aspects of the marriage of Judah and Tamar, both David and his descendants were of tainted descent. Moreover, they pointed to the Gentile ancestry of David in the Moabitess Ruth. Both of these charges are reflected in Ruth Rab. 8: 1 (92):

R. Abba b. Kahana [third century] opened [his exposition with the verse], 'Tremble and sin not' [Ps. 4: 4]. David said to the Holy One, blessed be He, 'How long will they rage against me and say, "Is he not of tainted descent? Is he not a descendant of Ruth the Moabitess?" "Commune with your heart upon your bed" [Ps. 4: 4]. Ye also, are you not descended from two sisters? Look upon your own genealogy "and be still" [Ps. 4: 4]. And Tamar who married your ancestor Judah—is it not a tainted descent? She was but a descendant of Shem the son of Noah. Have you then an honourable descent?'

Another passage reflecting, no doubt, the same polemic is of such obscurity that its significance must also wait for Elijah:

For, said R. Joshua b. Levi [mid third century], the Moabites murdered David's father and mother, and forced Ruth. But, according to R. Judah, the Moabites murdered David's father, mother, and also his brothers, and forced Ruth.[1]

It is possible that Josephus knew of such polemics when he appended to his account of Ruth this explanation: 'I was therefore obliged to relate this history of Ruth, because I had a mind to demonstrate the power of God, who, without difficulty, can raise those that are of ordinary parentage to dignity and splendour, to which he advanced David, though he were born of such mean parents.'[2]

The Rabbis also dwell at some length on David's adultery and his hand in the death of Uriah. These various charges are brought together in the Midrash on Psalms:

'And Shimei went along the rib [צלע] of the hill' [II Sam. 16: 13*b*], the word 'rib' intimating that as Shimei went along, he recalled to David the incident of the rib [creation of Eve], of which David was to say, 'I have been made ready for the rib' [כי־אני לצלע נכון] [Ps. 38: 18]. By this David meant to declare to the Holy One, blessed be He: Master of the universe! It is revealed and known to thee that Bath-sheba was held ready for me from the six days of Creation, yet she was given to me for sorrow: 'My sorrow is continually before me' (Ps. 38: 18). And David was to instruct and

[1] Mid. Ps. 7: 5.

[2] *Ant.* v. 9. 4.

point out to Solomon his son and say to him: 'Shimei...abused me with grievous [נמרצת] abuse in the day when I went to Mahanaim' [I Kings 2: 8*a*]. How is *NMRST* to be understood? As an acrostic [lit. 'notarikon']: The letter N stands for *no'ef*, 'adulterer'; the letter M, for 'Moabite'; the letter R, for *roseah*, 'murderer'; the letter S for *sores*, 'persecutor'; and the letter T for *to'ebah*, 'abomination'. Shimei had previously said to David, 'Behold, thou art taken in thine own mischief' [II Sam. 16: 8]. What was he referring to?... According to R. Abba bar Kahana [*c.* 310], to Bath-sheba's canopied litter which David had along with him.[1]

The anti-Hasmoneans were also faced with the problem presented by the Moabite ancestry of David which put him under the ban of Deut. 23: 3: 'No Ammonite or Moabite shall enter the assembly of the Lord; even to the tenth generation... ' This they solved by the saying, 'Not an Ammonite, but certainly an Ammonitess; not a Moabite, but certainly a Moabitess'.[2]

Similarly, the anti-Hasmoneans, according to Aptowitzer, levelled certain charges against the ruling Hasmoneans: the mother of John Hyrcanus was taken captive in Modiim, thus casting aspersions on the legitimacy of her children.[3] In particular the genealogical purity of Phinehas (who, as we have seen, was an especially important figure in both the apocrypha and in Rabbinic circles) was brought into question: his mother was 'a daughter of Putiel'[4] (=Jethro, an idolater).[5] So also, 'four persons descended (on their mothers' side) from humble families, and thus their ancestry was set aside; therefore the scripture has to emphasize their fathers' pedigree and designate them as priests: Phinehas, Jeremiah, Ezekiel, and Uriah'.[6] The Hasmoneans retorted that Putiel was not Jethro, but Joseph.[7]

There was yet another aspect to this dispute, according to Aptowitzer, which was caused by the double accusation of the Hasmoneans: not only was David of Moabite descent, but the

[1] Mid. Ps. 3: 3 (I, 53).

[2] bYeb. 76*b*–77*a*; pYeb. 8: 3, 9; Ruth R. 4: 1; cf. mYeb. 8: 3.

[3] Josephus, *Ant.* XIII. 10. 5; cf. bKid. 66*a*; see above, p. 92 n. 5.

[4] Aptowitzer, *Parteipolitik*, p. 26; Lev. Rab. 33: 4 (420 f.); cf. Sifre Num. par. 131; bSot. 43*a*; bB. Bath. 109*b*; bSan 82*b*; Pes., ed. Buber, 115*b*; Tan. פנחס par. 1; Num. Rab. 21: 2; Ex. Rab. 7, end.

[5] Targ. Jon. on Ex. 6: 25 (Putiel=Jethro).

[6] Pes., ed. Buber, 115*b*, cited by Aptowitzer, p. 29 n. 42.

[7] Sifre Num. par. 157; bSot. 43*a*; cf. bB. Bath. 110*a*; Gen. Rab. 36: 13.

mother of Rehoboam, son and successor of Solomon, was 'Naamah, the Ammonitess':[1]

Raba [d. 352] made the following exposition [of the saying, 'An Ammonite, but not an Ammonitess; a Moabite, but not a Moabitess']: What was meant by, 'Thou hast loosed my bonds!'? [Ps. 116: 16]. David said to the Holy One, blessed be He, 'O Master of the world! Two bonds were fastened on me, and you loosed them: Ruth the Moabitess and Naamah the Ammonitess.[2]

That a polemic lies behind this saying is obvious. One might compare bYeb. 63*a* (420):

R. Eleazar [third century] further stated: What is meant by the text, 'And in thee shall the families of the earth be blessed?' The Holy One, blessed be He, said to Abraham, 'I have two goodly shoots to engraft on you: Ruth the Moabitess and Naamah the Ammonitess.'

Aptowitzer finds a more explicit counter-argument to the charge of impurity in the royal Davidic line: the Messiah would descend from David through a non-royal line, namely that of Nathan, the immediately elder brother of Solomon.[3] The evidence adduced to support this hypothesis can be summarized briefly:[4] (1) Trypho[5] says that Elijah will anoint the Messiah, although in Pes. R.[6] it is affirmed that the king of a royal dynasty does not need anointing.[7] Therefore, it must be assumed that Trypho is referring to a Messiah from a non-Solomonic line. (2) In Luke's genealogy of Jesus the Messianic line runs through Nathan rather than Solomon (3: 31). (3) The Targum on Zech. 12: 12 refers to 'the family of the house of Nathan, *the prophet, the son of David*. . . '. (4) In the 'late unofficial Haggadic work',[8] The Apocalypse of Zerubbabel, we have a striking juxtaposition of motifs:

Puis il me dit: 'Le Messie de Dieu restera caché ici jusqu'à l'avènement de la fin. C'est le Messie fils de David et son nom est Menahem

[1] I Kings 14: 31, 21; II Chron. 12: 13.

[2] bYeb. 77*a* (519); the whole section (pp. 516–32) seems to be concerned with such polemics.

[3] II Sam. 5: 14; I Chron. 3: 5; 14: 4.

[4] Aptowitzer, pp. 113–16 and notes.

[5] Justin, *Dial.* 49.

[6] Chapter 35, end.

[7] Aptowitzer does not consider Gen. Rab. 71: 5 (656), cited above, (p. 131); an 'anointing' is prescribed for both priesthood and royalty.

[8] Ed. and tr. I. Lévi, 'Apocalypse Serubabel', *RÉJ*, LXVIII (1914), 135–57; the work is dated by Lévi between A.D. 629 and 636 (pp. 135, 142).

fils d'Ammiel. Il est né au temps de David, roi d'Israël, et a été transporté par un vent où il attend la fin.'[1]

More information regarding 'Menahem ben Ammiel' is provided: his mother is Hephzibah,[2] 'the wife of *Nathan the prophet* and mother of Menahem son of Ammiel'.[3] Now, since Nathan is the third son of David from 'Bathsheba, daughter of Ammiel' (II Chron. 3: 5), we must infer that the author of this apocalypse assumed the following relationships:

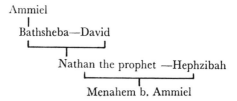

Ammiel
|
Bathsheba—David
|
Nathan the prophet —Hephzibah
|
Menahem b. Ammiel

The non-biblical identification of David's son Nathan with the prophet Nathan—a striking accomplishment even for Midrashic exegesis!—is clearly evidenced by the Targum and the apocalypse. Whether or not we accept Aptowitzer's hypothesis that this identification is to be traced to political debates during Hasmonean times, the contortion of biblical data revealed in this Rabbinic reconstruction points to some kind of polemic regarding the ancestry of the Messiah. Moreover, the divergence of the NT genealogies at precisely this point proves that the debate was carried on also by Christian (or Jewish-Christian) theologians.[4]

(*b*) *Evaluation of Aptowitzer's hypothesis.* In attempting an analysis of Aptowitzer's overall hypothesis, one must acknowledge his mastery of the materials, intertestamental as well as Rabbinic. On questions of Messianism there is little pertinent information he has overlooked. Yet his attempt to trace the origin of all disputes over the ancestry of the Messiah to the political struggles during the reign of the Hasmoneans, especially John Hyrcanus and Alexander Jannaeus, is open to serious qualifica-

[1] Lévi, p. 148. [2] Cf. II Kings 21: 1.

[3] Lévi, p. 151; cf. pp. 150, 157.

[4] The data used in this discussion of Nathan are those adduced by Aptowitzer; for additional Christian sources available, and the bearing on the discussion of the Lukan genealogy, see below, pp. 240 ff.

tions:[1] (1) It does not take into consideration the wide differences in the date of the material; late Haggadic traditions are, for example, taken as representing the anti-Hasmonean position while the Hasmonean view on the same question is culled from the Testaments. The date of sources ranges from the second century B.C. to the early medieval period.[2] (2) A substantial part of Aptowitzer's argument is dependent on finding several strata of sources in the Testaments, including one which contained the expectation of one Messiah descended from both Judah and Levi. But, although there are interpolations in the text, probably from Christian hands, there is considerable agreement that the doctrine of two Messiahs is part of the fabric of the original text. (3) *Explicit* evidence of polemics as such between partisans of a Messiah b. David and a Messiah b. Aaron does not appear in any pre-Christian text, even though in the Testaments and the Scrolls the priestly Messiah is superior to the royal. In the Testaments the two Messiahs are placed harmoniously in juxtaposition. Accusations of taint in the line of David or Aaron are contained entirely in both the 'official' and the 'unofficial' Rabbinic writings. (4) Aptowitzer has put all of the emphasis on one of the crucial events during the period of the second temple but has neglected the possible implications of several others for Messianic speculation, such as the coming to power of the Romans and the end of the line of the Hasmoneans; the rise of Christianity with its claims of a Davidic Messiah; the fall of Jerusalem with the abrogation of the priestly functions and hence of the high status of the priesthood within Judaism; the abortive revolt of Bar-Kokba, who was hailed as Messiah by R. Akiba.[3] Thus, the particular situation that gave rise to the idea of the two Messiahs remains cloudy, although the ascendancy of the Hasmoneans undoubtedly had some effect on the idea.[4] In any case, once the

[1] See the extensive critique of Aptowitzer by A. Marmorstein in *MGWJ*, LXXIII (1929), 244–50; Aptowitzer's reply, pp. 403–14; and a final response by Marmorstein, pp. 478–87.

[2] Cf. Marmorstein, p. 246: 'Wie ist das literarische Verhältnis zwischen Testamentum und Tannaiten denkbar?'

[3] Cf. Kuhn, 'The Two Messiahs of Aaron and Israel', in *The Scrolls and the New Testament*, ed. K. Stendahl (New York, 1957), pp. 60–2.

[4] Marmorstein, p. 247, mentions the devastation of the Marcionite biblical criticism and the anti-Jewish elements of Gnosticism as calling forth

idea of the two Messiahs arose, it was not difficult to find scriptural support for it, as we have suggested above.[1] Indeed, when the idea of the Messianic priest is seen in connection with the traditionally exalted office of the High Priest in Judaism and the great importance attached to the priesthood in much of the OT, it appears to be the logical conclusion of a long development of thought.[2]

On the positive side, however, Aptowitzer has demonstrated that disputes on the descent of the Messiah were carried on within Judaism at least as early as the Tannaim and that the Davidic ancestry of the Messiah was not be to taken for granted within Judaism even in the first century. As we shall attempt to show in the following chapters, it is most probable that the authors of the genealogies of Jesus in Matthew and Luke were acquainted with Jewish discussion on the ancestry of the Messiah, and that this discussion had its effect on the shape of the New Testament genealogies. The evidence for this conclusion and its implications remains to be sketched.

a reaction by both church fathers and Rabbis who attempted to defend biblical heroes such as David from slander.

[1] Pp. 118 ff.

[2] Cf. James Barr, art. 'Messiah', *HDB*, p. 652: 'It now seems probable that, though the Hasmonean dynasty may have had some influence, the idea [of the Levitical Messiah] has its origin in older tradition, in the co-ordination of king and priest, and that the importance of priestly influence in this period, and of the centrality of the temple for atonement and liturgy, was the main influence working for the prominence of Levi.'

CHAPTER 5

THE GENEALOGY OF JESUS IN MATTHEW

A. THE QUESTION OF METHODOLOGY

Although the scope of our first four chapters has required an analysis of what must seem variegated and far-flung sources, one general conclusion can be stated with some assurance: the genealogical form was especially suited for apologetic purposes accomplished by midrashic exegesis. We have noted that in the earliest strata of the Pentateuch, the J-source, the chief function of the genealogies is to express the varying degrees of closeness between Israel and her neighbors. In the Priestly genealogies, which reveal considerable skill in composition, we can trace several concerns: the genealogical classification of the known peoples of the world (Gen. 10); the attempt to create a coherent whole from the various Israelitic traditions of the pre-history; and the heightening of the traditions of the beginnings of the cultus at Sinai. In general, by structuring history into epochs, the priestly genealogies served as a means of imbuing history with meaning and thus served to present the conviction of a divine purpose with and within Israelitic history. The Chronicler, according to our interpretation, expresses his major theological tendencies in the genealogical sections as well as in his narrative. These observations perhaps necessitate a distinction between the *literary* use of genealogies in which the genealogical form serves a definite function within the context of historical writing (P and the Chronicler) and such non-literary use as is exemplified by the Safaitic graffiti and, in part, by J.

In our fourth chapter we traced the continuation of the OT interest in genealogical speculation on two levels: (1) The concern expressed within the Rabbinic writings for individual legitimacy by a genealogical stratification of society, a concern which appears in both the earliest halakoth and the later Midrashim with the same character and intensity. We have shown, however, that the evidence does not allow us to conclude that genealogical records were readily available to individual families within Judaism, with the important exception of the priesthood. This led to the necessity of utilizing oral traditions and also Midrashic exegesis to carry on genealogical investigation and speculation. (2) The rise of Messianic expectations has as one corollary the debates on the ancestry of the Messiah—debates which may reflect the views of different parties within Judaism. Aptowitzer has documented this approach most thoroughly, although he oversimplifies the data by ascribing the bulk of the relevant material to only one crucial aspect of Jewish history, the combination of the offices of priesthood and kingship by the later Hasmoneans. Nonetheless, the expectation of the Messiah ben Aaron was apparently strong in first-century Judaism, along with the more general expectation of a Davidic Messiah. We shall attempt to show, in this and the following chapter, that the two genealogies of Jesus, in different ways, reveal a knowledge of such Rabbinic discussion on the ancestry of the Messiah and are written on the basis of the same Midrashic methodology.

1. *Attempts to harmonize Matthew and Luke*

We are now in a position to raise the question of methodology in approaching the genealogies of Jesus in Matthew and Luke. Traditionally, the plan of approach has assumed that, if the genealogies are to have a legitimate place in the gospel tradition, they must be evaluated from the point of view of historical reliability. Consequently, the points of divergence between Matt. 1: 1–17 and Luke 3: 23–38 have occupied Christian scholars since the early church. There are actually only four problems raised by the assumption that both lists preserve historically accurate information which necessitate rather complicated and creative efforts at harmonization: (1) From David to the exile Matthew traces the line of descent through the royalty of Judah while in Luke the line passes through Nathan, David's son; (2) the two lists meet again in Zerubbabel and Salathiel; (3) from Salathiel to Jesus both lists are composed of unknown names, those in one list differing from those in the other, until the two lines meet again in Joseph; and (4) the number of names from Solomon to the exile in Matthew is fourteen, in Luke twenty (Nathan through Neri, inclusive), while from the exile to Jesus in Matthew there are thirteen, in Luke twenty-one. There are, of course, several other differences, such as the inclusion of the four women and the 3 × 14 scheme in Matthew; Matthew's ascending order in contrast to Luke's descending order; Matthew's omission of the names prior to Abraham; the form of the list (in Matthew, 'N ἐγέννησεν N', in Luke, τοῦ with the genitive); and minor variations in orthography and form of names. The four basic problems, however, have caused a great deal of concern for Christian scholars since the time of Julius Africanus. Briefly stated, the most frequently recurring harmonizing attempts have been the following:

(1) Both genealogies are Joseph's, but Matthew traces the biological ancestry, Luke the legal. Thus Africanus,[1] in the earliest extant harmonizing attempt,[2] proposed the theory of Levirate marriages, the essentials of which may be summarized thus: Matthan, grandfather of Joseph in Matthew's list, married Estha and begat Jacob. After the death of Matthan, Melchi (unrelated to Matthan), grandfather of Joseph in Luke's list, married Estha and begat Eli; hence Jacob and Eli were half-brothers. Eli died without children; Jacob married the widow in a Levirate marriage and begat Joseph. Thus Matthew gives the physical ancestry of Joseph, Luke the legal. In diagram form the relationships are seen more clearly:[3]

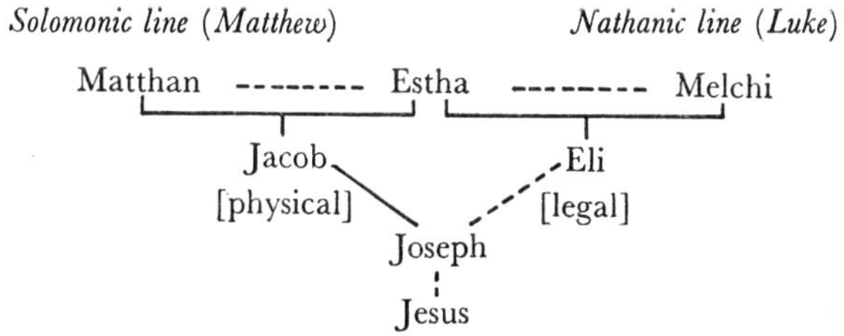

[1] In Eusebius, *H.E.* I. 7.

[2] Dr Robert A. Kraft of the University of Pennsylvania has brought to my attention an anonymous manuscript dated A.D. 1056 in which is preserved a harmonizing attempt that presents a view against which Africanus seems to argue in the section of his letter which immediately precedes the portion cited by Eusebius (the latter is cited below, p. 242); for text, see Appendix 5.

[3] Cf. F. Prat in *Dictionnaire de la Bible*, 3rd ed. III, 169.

In view of the artificial quality of this reconstruction, few modern scholars have considered it to be a convincing explanation.

(2) In modern times this theory has been reversed by several scholars, according to whom Matthew gives the legal line of succession while Luke gives the line of natural descent. This theory has been suggested by A. Hervey,[1] and T. Zahn,[2] and is preferred also by Vincent Taylor[3] (following Westcott, Burkitt, Box, Allen, Barnard, A. J. Maclean, and Moffatt), who contends that 'the verb ἐγέννησεν is used throughout [Matt. 1: 1–17] of legal, not physical descent'. This approach, however, has been propounded in a most acute form by K. Bornhäuser[4] and, most recently, by P. Gaechter.[5] Bornhäuser contends that Matthew gives the legal line of throne succession, explicit prior to the exile, and becoming a 'secret royal line' of descent between Zerubbabel and Joseph, while Luke is said to provide the line of blood-relationship. According to Bornhäuser, at certain points in Matthew's list ἐγέννησεν can mean 'adopted' rather than 'begat'. Thus Jeconiah, who was irrevocably condemned to childlessness in Jer. 22: 24–30, adopted Shealtiel, actual son of Neri, descendant of David through Nathan. Matthew, after Zerubbabel, followed the secret kings' line until it reached Jacob, who was without heir and did precisely what Jeconiah had done, namely 'appointed' Joseph, son of Eli from another Zerubbabel line, as his descendant, communicating to him the tradition of the continuation of the secret royal line from which the Messiah would arise.

This harmonization has the merit of recognizing the evident artificiality of the Matthean genealogy as compared with that of Luke. Yet, especially in the extreme form set forth by Bornhäuser with his assumption of a 'secret royal line', it is no more satisfactory than that of Africanus, and can be safely rejected as a creative conjecture for which any real evidence is lacking.

[1] *The Genealogies of Our Lord and Saviour Jesus Christ* (1853), pp. 14–22.

[2] *Das Evangelium des Matthäus* (2nd ed. 1903), pp. 42 ff.

[3] *The Historical Evidence for the Virgin Birth* (1920), p. 89 and n. 2.

[4] *Die Geburts- und Kindheitsgeschichte Jesu* (1930), pp. 22–36; cf. also F. C. Grant, 'Genealogy of Jesus Christ', *HDB*, p. 321 *a*.

[5] *Das Matthäus Evangelium* (1963), pp. 30–1; Gaechter bases his views on Hervey and Bornhäuser.

(3) Another common solution, first set forth in an explicit way[1] by Annius of Viterbo (*c.* 1490) and Luther, and subsequently adopted by Bengel in his *Gnomon*,[2] F. Godet,[3] B. Weiss,[4] and, most exhaustively, by Joseph M. Heer,[5] is that Matthew gives the ancestry of Joseph while Luke presents the genealogy of Mary.[6] This position is based on a rather forced exegesis of Luke 3: 23. Starting from the observation that the genitive article is attached to each name in the series except that of Joseph, it is suggested that the phrase ὡς ἐνομίζετο is to be applied only to him; hence the punctuation: ὢν υἱός, ὡς ἐνομίζετο Ἰωσήφ, τοῦ Ἡλὶ τοῦ Ματθὰτ τοῦ Λευί, etc., 'being the son, supposedly of Joseph (but actually) of Eli, son of Matthat, son of Levi... '.[7] Eli is then assumed to be the actual grandfather of Mary and the whole list to be her pedigree.[8]

Against this position several points can be made: (*a*) The anarthrous Ἰωσήφ at the beginning of a genealogical chain may be entirely consonant with contemporary style. Moulton gives a close parallel to this verse from a bilingual inscription, Palmyrene-Aramaic and Greek: Ἀαιλάμειν Αἱράνου τοῦ Μοκίμου τοῦ Αἱράνου τοῦ Μαθθᾶ.[9] Moreover, in two of the three places where Jesus is designated 'son of Joseph' in the NT, Ἰωσήφ is anarthrous (Luke 4: 22; John 6: 42).[10] (*b*) A more

[1] M.-J. Lagrange, *Évangile selon Saint Matthieu*, 4th ed. 1927, *ad rem*) suggests that this interpretation goes back to the fifth century.

[2] John Albert Bengel, *Gnomon of the NT*, tr. C. T. Lewis and M. R. Vincent (1860) (or. 1762), I, 406–7.

[3] *A Commentary on the Gospel of St Luke*, 2nd ed. tr. E. W. Shalders and M. D. Cusin (1881), pp. 128–32.

[4] *Das Matthäus-Evangelium* (1890), *ad rem.*

[5] *Die Stammbäume Jesu nach Matthäus und Lukas* (Biblische Studien 15 (1910), pp. 1–224), esp. pp. 32–106.

[6] A. Vezin, *Das Evangelium Jesu Christi* (1938), pp. 9–11, combines elements of our numbers two and three: Matthew presents the legal succession of the royal line as Joseph's ancestry while Luke records the 'natural' succession of the *priestly* line as Mary's ancestors; see above, p. 141 n. 2.

[7] The reading of the Koine group (Koridethi *et al.*) would seem not to affect the exegesis at this point.

[8] Cf. Godet, *Luke*, pp. 127–30.

[9] J. H. Moulton, *A Grammar of NT Greek* (3rd ed., 3 vols. 1908); I, 236, n. on p. 84. Cf. also the total lack of the article in the Jewish papyri collected by V. A. Tcherikover and A. Fuks, *Corpus Papyrorum Judaicarum* (hereafter referred to as *CPJ*) (3 vols. 1957–64), I, 192–3 (no. 47).

[10] Luke 4: 22; John 6: 42; John 1: 45; the Lukan genealogy may be a response to a previous 'Jesus ben Joseph' tradition.

serious objection is the question of syntax. If Luke intended to apply the phrase ὡς ἐνομίζετο only to Joseph it would have been expressed more clearly in some other way, for example, υἱὸς ὤν—ἐνομίζετο μὲν τοῦ 'Ιωσήφ—ἀληθῶς δὲ (or ὀρθῶς δὲ, or ἦν δὲ, or ἀληθείᾳ δὲ, or ἔργῳ δὲ) τοῦ 'Ηλὶ τοῦ πατρὸς τῆς Μαριάμ.[1] (*c*) Again, τοῦ is more naturally taken here in its obvious sense, 'son', not 'grandson'.

(4) Other attempts at harmonizing the two lists have been attempted only sporadically. The view that Matthew presents the genealogy of Mary may be reflected in Tertullian,[2] although this suggestion has few modern supporters.[3] Perhaps the most bizarre attempt has been made by the 'anthroposophist' Rudolph Steiner, whose views are taken up by Emil Bock: the differences between the birth stories of Matthew and Luke, including the divergence between the genealogies, are to be explained by supposing that the two accounts originally concerned two different individuals, born of parents with the same names![4]

2. *Criticism of the harmonizing attempts*

Such are the attempts to preserve full historical authenticity for both of the NT genealogies; each is unconvincing and strained. But the important consideration is one of methodology and purpose. What would be gained if we could demonstrate in a final way the historical accuracy of the two genealogies? It is my contention that such a demonstration would affect neither the existential response to the NT witness to the Messiahship of

[1] Maximilian Lambertz, 'Die Toledoth in Mt. 1: 1–17 und Lc. 3: 23*b* ff.', in *Festschrift Franz Dornseiff*, ed. H. Kusch (1953), esp. pp. 223–4.

[2] Cf. *On the Flesh of Christ*, p. 20.

[3] This theory has been revived by H. A. Blair, 'Mt. 1: 16 and the Matthean Genealogy', *TU*, LXXXVII (1964), 149–54; Blair suggests that Mary is the fourteenth member of Matthew's third group, the original text of *v.* 16 reading: 'Jacob begat Joseph, and Joseph begat Mary, of whom was born Jesus who is called Christ' (p. 153).

[4] Emil Bock, *Kindheit und Jugend Jesu* (Beiträge zur Geistesgeschichte der Menschheit II–2) (1939), esp. pp. 38–41. For Steiner's view, which embraces theories of reincarnations involving the egos of Zarathustra and Buddha in an adoptionistic Christology, see *Von Jesus zu Christus* (Esoterische Betrachtungen) (1933), ch. 8, 'Die beiden Jesus-Knaben...'. The first appearance of this view was in Steiner's essay of 1911, 'Die geistige Führung des Menschen und der Mencheit'.

esus nor our interpretation of NT theology in any material way. A more serious objection to this methodology, however, emerges: the attempt to harmonize the data of Matt. 1 and Luke 3 does not consider the function of the genealogical form in the first-century milieu and, consequently, does not do justice to the function of the lists in the context of the gospels in which they are located. I have presented evidence for the midrashic character of genealogical speculation within Judaism immediately before and after the NT period. But also, as has been pointed out by G. H. Box,[1] W. D. Davies,[2] and others, the immediate context of the Matthean genealogy itself, namely the birth stories of chapters 1–2, can best be considered the product of Jewish-Christian Midrashic activity. Since the function of Jewish midrash was to 'comfort, exhort, and edify',[3] it would be most natural to attempt to discover whether there are certain theological purposes implicit in the genealogy. Once such motifs and purposes are isolated, it should be possible to draw a comparison between such motifs in the genealogy and the theological tendencies of the author of the body of Matthew in an attempt to reach a conclusion concerning the integrity of the genealogy within the Gospel of Matthew. Hence, it will be my purpose within this chapter to suggest that the Matthean genealogy finds its most natural setting in the genealogical and Messianic speculation of Judaism which is preserved in the intertestamental and Rabbinic literature, and that this is to be seen in both the details of the text of Matt. 1: 1–17 and in its overall design. I shall then examine the relation of the genealogy to the gospel as a whole, suggesting that the motifs and function of the genealogy find parallels in the narrative and that, consequently, the conclusions reached regarding the setting of the genealogy may be relevant for an understanding of the general character of the Gospel of Matthew.

[1] *The Virgin Birth of Jesus* (1916), pp. 10–33.

[2] *Setting*, pp. 64 ff.

[3] Cf. H. L. Strack, *Introduction to the Talmud and Midrash* (1931) (tr. from the 5th German ed., 1920), p. 202.

B. THE SETTING OF MATT. 1: 1–17 AND ITS PURPOSE

1. *Evidence from details of the text*

In any attempt to uncover the theological conceptions and tendencies of the compiler of a genealogy, one faces obvious limitations. Where the compiler has faithfully followed his sources it is hazardous to speculate on his exact intention. In the case of the Matthean genealogy, however, the situation is somewhat different. In Matt. 1: 1–17 there are several points of detail which are not precisely determined by the OT sources or which would seem to be superfluous in a consistently linear genealogy. Moreover, it is possible to find theological significance in the arrangement of the genealogy. Any attempt to discover the theology implicit in this genealogy should take into account these apparently superfluous details and also the structure of the genealogy.

The textual details here referred to include the introduction (1: 1) and conclusion (1: 16–17), and several phrases which are not essential to the pedigree of Joseph, namely καὶ τοὺς ἀδελφοὺς αὐτοῦ (verse 2), καὶ τὸν Ζαρὰ ἐκ τῆς Θαμάρ (verse 3), ἐκ τῆς Ῥαχάβ (verse 5), ἐκ τῆς Ῥούθ (verse 5), τὸν βασιλέα (verse 6), ἐκ τῆς τοῦ Οὐρίου (verse 6), and καὶ τοὺς ἀδελφοὺς αὐτοῦ (verse 11).

(*a*) In the first verse of Matthew we read: Βίβλος γενέσεως Ἰησοῦ Χριστοῦ υἱοῦ Δαυὶδ υἱοῦ Ἀβραάμ. The phrase βίβλος γενέσεως could be a translation of either of two Hebrew expressions, ספר תולדות or ספר יוחסין; or it could have been suggested by the LXX rendering of Gen. 2: 4*a* or 5: 1 without an awareness of the Hebrew. If it is a rendering of ספר תולדות, it is then a conscious allusion to the genealogical lists of Genesis, most of which in the priestly narrative, after the ספר תולדות of Gen. 5: 1, begin with אלא תולדות followed by the person whose descendants are enumerated.[1] While it is true that in some such cases there is included non-genealogical information,[2] the term is generally used as a technical formula to introduce genealogical material and would probably carry definite genealogical connotations to the compiler of such a list as Matt. 1: 1–17. This observation applies in spite of the fact that the Toledoth passages

[1] See above, pp. 14–28. [2] E.g. Gen. 37: 2.

of Genesis enumerate descendants of the person named, while in Matthew the toledoth is 'of Jesus Christ', the end-point and goal of the list.

If, however, the Greek phrase in Matt. 1: 1 translates ספר יוחסין as S–B are inclined to think,[1] a somewhat different background must be assumed. The root יחס (יחש) is late Hebrew, OT occurrences of which are found only in Chronicles, Ezra, and Nehemiah. It is used throughout the Rabbinic literature in preference to תולדות. The noun form is used but once in the OT (Neh. 7: 5), and this with the governing noun to introduce a list of exiles returning to Jerusalem from Babylon:[2] ואמצא ספר היחש העולים בראשונה. The two important references in Rabbinic literature that are pertinent here have been alluded to above; they are mYeb. 4: 13 (225)[3] and pTaan. 4: 3 (68*a*). The former reference occurs as one response to the question, 'Who is accounted a bastard?' It reads in full:

Who is accounted a bastard [according to Deut. 23: 2]? [The offspring of] any [union of] near of kin which is forbidden [in the Law]. So R. Akiba [d. A.D. 132]. Simeon of Teman says: [the offspring of any union] for which the partakers are liable to extirpation at the hands of heaven. And the Halakah is according to his words. R. Joshua[4] says: [The offspring of any union] for which the partakers are liable to death at the hands of the court. R. Simeon b. Azzai [*c.* A.D. 110–40][5] said: I found a family register [מגלת יוחסין] in Jerusalem and in it was written, 'Such-a-one is a bastard through [a transgression of the law of] thy neighbor's wife' [איש פלוני ממזר מאשת איש], confirming the words of R. Joshua.

Several scholars, both Jewish and Christian, have considered this statement of Ben Azzai to be an indirect reference to Jesus, among them Levy, Strack, Derenbourg, S. Krauss, Laible, Herford, S–B, and Klausner.[6] This view is rejected by Rengstorf[7]

[1] Vol. 1, p. 1.

[2] The parallel list of names in Ezra 2: 1–70 has no such introduction.

[3] Par., as a baraita, in bYeb. 49*a* and pYeb. 4: 15.

[4] Probably Joshua b. Hananiah, latter part of the first century A.D.; cf. Goldstein, *Jesus*, p. 67.

[5] 'A contemporary of Akiba...a Tanna who lived at the end of the first, and in the first third of the second century C.E.' (Goldstein, p. 67).

[6] Cited by Karl Heinrich Rengstorf, *Jebamot: Text, Übersetzung und Erklärung* (Die Mischna, III. 1) (1929), pp. 67–8; and Goldstein, p. 67.

[7] P. 68.

and Goldstein.[1] Assuming that the reference is to Jesus, what are we to make of it? It has been commonly held that the prologue to Matthew is designed to meet Jewish calumny on the birth of Jesus. Thus McNeile contended that 'Matthew's whole object was to show, in the face of current calumnies, that the Messiah's genealogy was divinely ordered and legally correct', while the story of the Virgin Birth 'is designed to show that there is nothing new or extravagant in the thought of a miraculous birth'.[2] Similar views have been expressed by Box, Wright, Taylor, and Burkitt.[3] But we may well ask if the contrary might not be true, namely that Jewish calumnies on the birth of Jesus were suggested by the Matthean account itself. 'To remind Jewry that there was illegitimacy in their "royal line" was no defence of the "purity" or "legality" of Jesus' birth.'[4] Moreover, the relative dating of the Gospel of Matthew (*c.* 80–100) and the saying of Ben Azzai (*c.* 110–40) support the view that the Rabbi is referring to Matt. 1 in his reference to the 'genealogical scroll'. The ease with which the genealogy and birth story in chapter 1 could be used or misused in polemic fashion is clear: one can imagine that, in a Rabbinic discussion of the technical definition of 'bastard', Simeon b. Azzai refers with polemic irony to Matt. 1 as an example of a birth which, according to R. Joshua, is illegitimate.

The second passage is pTaan. 4: 2 (par. Gen. R. 98): 'R. Levi (*c.* 300) said: A genealogical scroll was found in Jerusalem in which it was written: Hillel descended from the sons of David... ', etc.,[5] which, as we have noted, is of insignificant historical value. In any case, the possibility that βίβλος γενέσεως in Matt. 1: 1 translates מגלת יוחסין or ספר יוחסין and consequently was taken over from contemporary Rabbinic usage is balanced by the further possibility that the Rabbinic phrase was itself a reflection on the opening words of Matthew's gospel. Either possibility, of course, necessitates a relationship or acquaintance between Matthew's gospel and the Rabbis.

Thirdly, the view that βίβλος γενέσεως was suggested by the

[1] P. 67.

[2] Alan H. McNeile, *The Gospel According to St Matthew* (1915), pp. 6, 11; cited by Davies, *Setting*, p. 65.

[3] Cf. Davies, *Setting*, p. 65; see also below, pp. 157 ff.

[4] Davies, *Setting*, pp. 65–6.

[5] See above, pp. 105, 110.

LXX rendering of Gen. 2: 4*a* or 5: 1 faces one difficulty: in no text of the LXX is the phrase connected, as in Matt. 1: 1, with a personal name. In Gen. 2: 4*a* we read: Αὕτη ἡ βίβλος γενέσεως οὐρανοῦ καὶ γῆς... and in 5: 1: Αὕτη ἡ βίβλος γενέσεως ἀνθρώπων where the Hebrew has **זה ספר תולדות אדם**. This would indicate that there is no clear parallel between Adam (understood as an individual) and Jesus implied by the use of the phrase βίβλος γενέσεως in Matt. 1: 1 on the assumption that the author of Matthew drew the phrase from the LXX. Yet the possibility that the phrase in Matt. 1: 1 does hark back to the LXX is strengthened by the probability that the author of the genealogy used the Greek OT (as we shall see below).[1] The use of Greek, however, does not preclude knowledge of Hebrew since there is strong evidence of Rabbinic interest in Greek during the Matthean period.[2]

Thus, while the evidence does not permit any dogmatic conclusions, the phrase can perhaps best be considered as a reflection of the toledoth formula in Genesis, in either the Hebrew or Greek form, or both, and therefore as an indication of a detailed knowledge of the OT text on the part of the author of the genealogy.

(*b*) Abraham and David are in the same verse singled out as pivotal points in the genealogical development of the ancestry of Jesus Christ. A remarkable parallel to this is found in a saying attributed to R. Nehemiah (middle of the second century):

R. Berekiah b. R. Simon said in R. Nehemiah's name: this [Gen. 4: 25] may be illustrated by a king who was passing from place to place, when a gem fell from his head. Whereupon the king halted and stationed his retinue there, gathered the sand in piles, and brought sieves. He sifted the first pile but did not find it; the second but did not find it; but in the third he found it. Said they: 'The king has found his pearl.' Similarly, the Holy One, blessed be He, said to Abraham, 'What need had I to trace the descent of Shem, Arpachshad, Shelah, Eber, Peleg, Reu, Serug, Nahor, and Terah? Was it not on thy account?' Thus it is written, 'And *foundest* his heart [Abraham's] faithful before thee' [Neh. 9: 8]. In like manner, God said to David: 'What need had I to trace the descent of Perez, Hezron, Ram, Amminadab, Nachshon, Shalmon, Boaz, Obed, and

[1] Pp. 181–6.

[2] See below, pp. 186–9.

Jesse? Was it not on thy account?' Hence it is written, 'I have *found* David my servant, with My holy oil have I anointed him' [Ps. 89: 21].[1]

An anonymous passage in the same section of Gen. R. (39: 4 (314)) also shows the pivotal position of Abraham in the chain of genealogy:

'Wisdom maketh a wise man stronger than ten rulers' [Eccl. 7: 19]: this refers to Abraham [whom wisdom made stronger] than the ten generations from Noah to Abraham; out of all of them I spoke to thee alone, as it is written, 'Now the Lord said to Abraham' [Gen. 12: 1].

S–B refer also to an anonymous passage which gives an allegorical interpretation of Nahshon's offering in Num. 7: 15 ff. 'One golden pan of ten shekels was to symbolize the ten generations from Perez to David, as it says, "Now these are the generations of Perez..." [Ruth 4: 18–22 is quoted]; "One young bullock [בן־בקר] symbolizes Abraham who was the root of the genealogical tree" [עיקר חיחס], and of whom it says, "And Abraham ran unto the herd [בקר]" (Gen. 18: 7).'[2] Matthew, too, has placed Abraham in the position of עיקר, the beginning of the genealogy.

David, of course, occupies an especially important position in the Rabbinic literature; an anonymous exposition of Micah 5: 4 in bSan. 52*b* (251) is clear in its significance:

'And this shall be peace: when the Assyrian shall come into our land and when he shall tread in our places, then shall we raise up against him seven shepherds and eight princes among men' [Micah 5: 4]. Who are the 'seven shepherds'?—David is in the middle; Adam, Seth, and Methuselah on his right; and Abraham, Jacob, and Moses on his left. And who are the 'eight princes among men'?—Jesse, Saul, Samuel, Amos, Zephaniah, Zedekiah, the Messiah, and Elijah.

In view of the difficulty of dating these sayings (except for the story of the pearl, middle of the second century), can we legitimately draw a parallel between the *genealogical* importance of Abraham and David here and in Matt. 1? There would seem

[1] Gen. R. 39: 10 (318–19); par. Yalkut Neh. 9: 8 (1071) and Tanch. 42*b*; cited by S–B, I, 13–14.

[2] Num. R. 13: 14 (529–30).

to be no necessity for any direct relationship. Abraham is remembered throughout Jewish literature and especially in the NT[1] as the *father* of the nation and is given a pre-eminent role in the intertestamental literature, notably in Jubilees. In I Macc. 2: 51–60 Abraham begins a summary of *Heilsgeschichte* which is similar in other respects to the more detailed list in Heb. 11. The same emphasis on David can be traced from Chronicles into Talmudic times. Thus υἱοῦ Δαυίδ υἱοῦ ᾿Αβραάμ represents the mainstream of Jewish messianism in both intertestamental and Rabbinic literature as well as Christian messianism.

(*c*) Is there a special significance in Matthew's inclusion of the phrase καὶ τοὺς ἀδελφοὺς αὐτοῦ applied to ᾿Ιούδαν in verse 2? S–B suggest that the brothers of Judah are mentioned in order to express their equality with him, and thereby to honor them.[2] They refer to Tanch B ויחי 17 (111*a*), where it is noted that in Gen. 49: 28 (the conclusion to Jacob's blessings on his sons) the text reads ויברך אותם ('And he blessed *them*'), with a plural object rather than the singular 'him', in order that Judah, who has the strength of a lion, be not favored above his brethren.[3] Others assume that the reference is intended to recall the misdeeds of the sons of Jacob, who did not refrain from selling their brother; or again that there is in the phrase a hint of the divine choosing of Judah as ancestor of King David and the Davidic Messiah even though Reuben, not Judah, was first-born.[4] Allen accounts for the phrase by supposing it to be the compiler's way of summarizing I Chron. 2: 1, which he has before him[5]; but of course the question of the purpose of the inclusion of such a summary remains. We suggest that it is intended to recall the unity of Israel in all twelve tribes,[6] an

[1] Cf. Matt. 3: 9; Luke 1: 55, 73; 13: 16; 16: 30; John 8: 33 ff., 53 ff.; Acts 7: 2; 13: 26; Rom. 4: 1, 12 ff.; 9: 7; 11: 1; II Cor. 11: 22; Gal. 3: 16; Heb. 2: 16; also Jos. *Ant.* I. 7. 2.

[2] I, 14.

[3] Other passages referred to by S–B in this regard are Tanch ויחי end (58*b*); Gen. R. 99 (63*a*); Num. R. 13 (169*cd*); S.S.R. on 4: 7 (113*b*).

[4] E.g. Gaechter, *Matthäus*, p. 36.

[5] *Matthew*, pp. 2–3; according to this view, it is difficult to explain why Matthew gives the father of Judah as Jacob while in I Chron. 2: 1 it is 'Israel'.

[6] Cf. Alfred Loisy, *Les Évangiles Synoptiques* (2 vols. 1907), I, 320: 'La mention des frères de Juda s'explique par l'intention de signaler en bloc les patriarches des tribus israélites, héritières des promesses.'

emphasis that is strong among the Rabbis who speak of the gathering of the dispersed tribes in the Messianic age. We find also the emphasis on the land and people of Israel in the narrative of Matthew, in which the twelve apostles are sent to the 'lost sheep of the house of Israel',[1] and in which Jesus says that the apostles will 'sit on twelve thrones, judging the twelve tribes of Israel'.[2] In this emphasis on the wholeness of Israel, Matthew is close to the Chronicler[3] as well as to Rabbinic theology.

(*d*) We come now to that aspect of the genealogy which most clearly reveals its relationship with Rabbinic speculation on the ancestry of the Messiah, namely the four women. In the text of Matthew, they are introduced in the following ways:

(1) Ἰούδας δὲ ἐγέννησεν τὸν Φάρες καὶ τὸν Ζάρα [p[1], B: Ζαρε] ἐκ τῆς Θαμάρ (verse 3). It is possible that this reference to the brother and mother of Perez, which seems to be an extraneous element in the sparse style of the genealogy, can be explained on the assumption that the author had before him the text of I Chron. 2: 3–4 and intended merely to distinguish Judah's sons with Tamar from his sons with 'Bathshua the Canaanitess'. However, as the Rabbinic texts dealing with Tamar will demonstrate, it is much more probable that the reference to Tamar was drawn from a tradition which was aware of the stories in Gen. 38 concerning Tamar's harlotry and Judah's illicit relationship with her.

(2) Σαλμὼν δὲ ἐγέννησεν τὸν Βόες [Koine, Βοοζ] ἐκ τῆς Ῥαχάβ (verse 5). This statement cannot be explained on the basis of the OT since Rahab occurs only in the book of Joshua as the Canaanitess who protected the spies sent to Jericho by Joshua; the OT knows nothing of Rahab's connection with the tribe of Judah or her inclusion in the ancestry of David.

(3) Βόες δὲ ἐγέννησεν τὸν Ἰωβὴδ ἐκ τῆς Ῥούθ (verse 5). This datum is derived not from I Chronicles but from the OT book of Ruth, 4: 13–22, where Ruth, the Moabitess and proselyte, is reckoned as the great-grandmother of David.

(4) Δαυίδ δὲ ἐγέννησεν τὸν Σολομῶνα ἐκ τῆς τοῦ Οὐρίου (verse 6). Again the compiler departed from the text of Chronicles, where the mother of Solomon is designated by name without

[1] 10: 6; cf. 15: 24.
[2] 10: 23.
[3] See above, pp. 48 f., 52 ff.

the mention of her husband: לבת־שוע בת־עמיאל (I Chron. 3: 5). Hence the text of Matt. 1: 6 reflects the incident in II Sam. 11 of David's adultery with בת־שבע בת־אליעם אשת אוריה החתי (verse 3; in the LXX Βηρσαβεε θυγάτηρ Ελιαβ γυνὴ Ουριου τοῦ Χεταίου) and possibly alludes also to the non-Israelitic status of Uriah and thus also, according to the Rabbinic view, of Bathsheba.

But why are these women included in a genealogy of the Messiah? It has been pointed out that names of women are rare in Jewish genealogies, and that exceptions occur only in the case of irregularity of descent or where there is something noteworthy about the woman's name.[1] Most often women are mentioned in the OT genealogies when it was desired to distinguish among different groups (tribes, clans, families, individuals) who were traditionally traced to the same figure in the past. This distinction was accomplished by assigning the various groups to different wives or concubines.[2] But the selection of these particular four women seems highly anomalous in the genealogy of Jesus since two were harlots (Tamar and Rahab) and one an adulteress (Bathsheba). Moreover, it is highly probable that, at the time of the composition of Matthew, each of the four, in Jewish tradition, was considered to be of Gentile stock. The OT itself provides evidence of the Moabite ancestry of Ruth and the Canaanite ancestry of Rahab. As for the other two, indirect reference to the 'wife of Uriah' in Matt. 1: 6 probably serves as a reminder that Bathsheba's husband was a Hittite, hence that she herself was not a full Israelite from the later Rabbinic point of view. As for Tamar, the OT nowhere explicitly states her ancestry, although perhaps the

[1] Cf. S–B, I, 15.

[2] Among the more important examples in the OT are: Sons of Nahor born to his wife, Milcah, and his concubine, Reumah (Gen. 22: 20–4); sons of Abraham born to his wives, Sarah and Keturah, and his concubine, Hagar (Gen. 16: 15; 21: 1–5; 25: 1–6); sons of Jacob born from his two wives and two concubines (Gen. 35: 22*b*–26); sons of Judah from Bathshuah and Tamar (I Chron. 2: 3–4); sons of Caleb from Azubah and Ephrath (I Chron. 2: 18–20) and from his concubines (I Chron. 2: 46 ff., 48 ff.); daughters of Sheshan and grandsons from his daughter's marriage to his slave (I Chron. 2: 34–41). But women are mentioned also for other reasons: the wife of Aaron is named since she was a Judahite, daughter of Amminadab and sister of Nahshon, head of the tribe during the exodus (Exod. 6: 23; cf. Num. 1: 7; 7: 12; Matt. 1: 4; Luke 3: 32–3).

majority of commentators conclude that in Gen. 38 she is intended to be portrayed as a Canaanitess.[1] Appendix 4 contains a summary of speculation on the ancestry of Tamar in the later Jewish tradition in which she is known generally as 'a daughter of Aram'[2] and more specifically as the daughter of Noah's son, Shem, who is identified with Melchizedek. The latter description is most probably a means of alluding to the non-Abrahamitic, hence Gentile, descent of Tamar. Hints of polemic are not wanting in later Rabbinic sources in which Tamar's place in the ancestry of David seems to have been used to castigate his genealogical purity.

Thus we conclude that the compiler of the Matthean genealogy possibly drew on a tradition in which at least three of the women were considered morally assailable and all four to have been of Gentile ancestry—or at least not full Israelites. The question then arises regarding the purpose of their inclusion in the Matthean genealogy rather than more innocuous figures in the OT who occasioned no suspicion, such as the 'four ancestral mothers' mentioned several times in the Rabbinic literature, namely Sarah, Rebekah, Rachel, and Leah.[3] Modern scholars have provided several possible solutions to this problem which we may categorize roughly in the following ways:

(1) It has been suggested that the mention of the four women was intended to foreshadow the concern of Jesus in Matthew for sinners and Gentiles. This seems to have been the prevailing attitude of the Church fathers, among them Origen, Chrysostom, Jerome, and Ambrose.[4] Also included here are Luther,[5] Plummer,[6] and—tentatively suggesting a parallel between the

[1] Cf. S. Cohen, 'Tamar', *IDB*, IV, 515; C. A. Simpson, *Genesis*, *IB*, I, 757–8.

[2] Jub. 41: 1; T. Jud. 10: 1.

[3] S–B, I, 29–30, refer to Targ. Jer. II on Gen. 49: 25; Targ. Num. 23: 9; Targ. Dt. 33: 15; Siphre Dt. 33: 15, par. 353 (146*b*); bR. H. 11*a*; bNaz. 23*b*; Gen. R. 72 (46*d*); Gen. R. 58 (36*d*).

[4] Cited by Andrew D. Heffern, 'The Four Women in St Matthew's Genealogy of Christ', *JBL*, XXXI (1912), 68–81; Origen, 28th *Homily on Luke*; Jerome, *Matthew Commentary*, ed. Vallarsi, pp. 7–9; Ambrose on exposition of Luke 3.

[5] Cited by H. A. W. Meyer, *Critical and Exegetical Handbook to the Gospel of Matthew*, tr. P. Christie (rev. ed. 1890), p. 38.

[6] Alfred Plummer, *An Exegetical Commentary on the Gospel According to St Matthew* (2nd ed. 1910), pp. 2–3.

four 'foreign' women and Mary—Lohmeyer, who writes: 'Alle vier Frauen treten als Fremde, sei es nach Blut und Glauben oder nach ihrem Leben und Schicksale, in die Verheissung des Messias-Geschlechtes ein; wenn Mt vorausgesetzt hat, dass Maria aus dem fernen und verfemten Galiläa stammte (s. zu 2: 19–22), so wäre damit eine gewisse Analogie gegeben.'[1] The most convincing argument of this sort has been advanced by Heffern:[2] the author 'has selected all four on account of their heathen origin or associations, and ... means to utilize their incorporation into Israel and their direct connection with the Messianic hope in the solution of one of the most pressing practical problems of the Apostolic age—the admission of Gentiles into the Church'.[3] Other proponents of this general view (without advocating a specific *Sitz im Leben*) are D. M. Stanley,[4] J. Henschen,[4] T. H. Robinson,[5] H. Milton,[6] A. Durand,[7] J. R. Rice,[8] R. Glover,[8] and F. Rienecker.[9] But one might ask whether the emphasis on Jesus as the friend of sinners and Gentiles in Matthew is sufficient reason for the author to introduce blots into the genealogy of the Messiah. Could not this have been accomplished equally as clearly without opening the door to aspersions on the ancestry of Jesus? Yet the suggestion of Heffern does have the merit of finding a significance for the genealogy within the milieu of the author.

(2) Others have emphasized an intention akin to the first mentioned but in a somewhat broader fashion: the women are introduced to demonstrate that God can use even the humble and despised to accomplish his purpose, even though human sin often necessitates detours along the way. So S–B: 'Er [the evangelist] hat wohl auf das souveräne Walten der

[1] Ernst Lohmeyer, *Das Evangelium des Matthäus* (1956), p. 5.

[2] Pp. 77–8; a similar view is that of W. Grundmann, cited by Anton Vögtle, 'Die Genealogie Mt. 1: 2–16 und die matthäische Kindheitsgeschichte (Schlussteil)', *BZ*, IX (1965), 39 n. 148.

[3] Pp. 77–8.

[4] Cited by Vögtle, p. 39 n. 146.

[5] *The Gospel of Matthew* (Moffatt Commentary) (1951), p. 3.

[6] 'The Structure of the Prologue to St Matthew's Gospel', *JBL*, LXXXI (1962), 176.

[7] *Vangelo secondo San Matteo* (Verbum Salutis) (1955), p. 7; cited by Vögtle, p. 39 n. 150.

[8] Cf. Vögtle, p. 39 n. 150.

[9] *Das Evangelium des Matthäus* (1953), p. 15.

göttlichen Gnade hinweisen wollen, der alles, auch menschliche Eigenmächtigkeit und Sünde, dienen musste, um der Welt den Erlöser zu schenken.'[1] In general this view is represented also by B. Weiss,[2] Lagrange,[3] Allen,[4] Michaelis,[5] Dillersberger,[6] Lohmeyer,[7] Gaechter,[8] Filson,[9] G. Kittel,[10] and most recently by Anton Vögtle.[11] Again, our comment on the preceding group holds: there was sufficient opportunity to allude to human frailty and sin among the various links in the genealogical chain itself; one has only to think of Ahaz, Manasseh, and Amon in the biblical record.

A variation of this view is suggested by Renée Bloch, who, after an analysis of the Rabbinic tradition contained in the Targums, concludes:

> ...Il ne semble guère douteux que si l'évangéliste a fait une place à Tamar dans sa généalogie, c'est parce qu'il connaissait, par lui-même ou par les sources dont il s'était servi, la tradition juive qui, dans le prolongement de la tradition biblique, voyait en Tamar non seulement une ancêtre du Christ, mais une femme qui avait ardemment désiré cette grâce, cette participation à la bénédiction messianique.[12]

Doubtless this aspect played a role in the inclusion of Tamar, but, as we shall see, the Rabbinic tradition found some difficulty with Tamar's position in the Davidic ancestry and at times the references seem to reflect a polemical background. The inclusion of the four women demands a more explicit explanation.

[1] I, 15; cf. Tanch B וישב par. 13 (92*b*), S–B, I, 16.

[2] *Matthäus*, p. 31.

[3] *Matthieu*, p. 4.

[4] Willoughby C. Allen, *A Critical & Exegetical Commentary on the Gospel according to St Matthew* (ICC) (1907), p. 2.

[5] D. Wilhelm Michaelis, *Das Evangelium nach Matthäus* (2 vols. 1948), I, 46.

[6] Josef Dillersberger, *Matthäus* (6 vols. 1953), I, 56 f.

[7] *Matthäus*, pp. 5 f.: 'Wenn an allen diesen Frauen Gottes Walten über alles menschliche Verstehen und Urteilen wundersam ist, um wieviel mehr ist es bei der Mutter Jesu sichtbar! Das deutet der letzte Satz freilich mehr an, als dass er es sagt.'

[8] *Matthäus*, pp. 36–7.

[9] *A Commentary on the Gospel according to St Matthew* (Black's NT Commentaries) (1960), pp. 52–3.

[10] 'Θαμάρ, 'Ραχάβ, 'Ρούθ, ἡ τοῦ Οὐρίου', in *TWNT*, III, 1–3, esp. p. 1.

[11] *BZ*, IX (1965), 40–1.

[12] 'Juda engendra Pharès et Zara, de Thamar (Matth. 1: 3)', in *Mélanges Bibliques rédigés en l'honneur de André Robert* (n.d.), pp. 381–9.

(3) In this third group there is some variety but the common factor is that the four women are considered 'types of Mary', intended by the author to prepare the reader for the account of the virgin birth of Jesus from Mary. Emphasis is often placed on the 'unexpected and sudden intrusion' of the four women as an anticipation of the 'even more amazing' introduction of Mary in 1: 18 ff. This view is represented by H. J. Holtzmann (following Strauss, Gfrörer, and Hilgenfeld),[1] Loisy,[2] H. A. W. Meyer[3] (following Paulus, deWette, Ebrard, and Grotius), Klostermann,[4] Schlatter,[5] B. D. T. Smith,[6] Allen,[7] Michaelis,[8] M. Krämer,[9] Stendahl,[10] Jeremias,[11] and M. J. Moreton.[12] What distinguishes this view from the following is that this suggestion is made without any direct connection of Matthew's inclusion of the four women to Jewish calumnies on Mary. Loisy's comment may be noted:

Toutes ces femmes sont entrées par une voie extraordinaire ou irrégulière dans la lignée messianique, et l'on dirait qu'elles sont, pour l'évangéliste, comme des types de Marie, qui entre, elle aussi, par une voie miraculeuse, dans la même généalogie...C'est plutôt l'intrusion de Marie dans la généalogie qui a besoin d'être préparée. L'évangéliste a signalé toutes les femmes qui pouvaient y figurer. On conçoit qu'il ait négligé Athalie...Il ne paraît pas possible d'aller plus loin, en supposant, par exemple, que Matthieu aurait voulu répliquer aux calomnies des Juifs sur la naissance de Jésus...[13]

It is difficult, however, to explain the suitability of four women who were associated with immorality and Gentile ancestry to serve as parallels to the introduction of Mary in the genealogy of Jesus.

(4) Closely related to the third group, but more explicit, is

[1] *Die Synoptischen Evangelien* (1863), pp. 171–2; p. 172 n. 1.
[2] *Évangiles Synoptiques*, I, 320. [3] *Matthew*, p. 38.
[4] *Das Matthäusevangelium* (2nd ed. 1927), p. 2.
[5] *Der Evangelist Matthäus* (3rd ed. 1948), pp. 2–3.
[6] *The Gospel According to S. Matthew* (Cambridge Greek Testament) (1922), p. 76.
[7] *Matthew*, p. 2. [8] *Matthäus*, pp. 46 f.
[9] 'Die Menschwerdung Jesu Christi nach Matthäus', *Biblica*, XLV (1964), 47.
[10] 'Matthew' in *Peake's Commentary on the Bible* (1962), p. 771.
[11] *Jerusalem*, p. 327.
[12] 'The Genealogy of Jesus', *TU*, LXXXVII (1964), 223.
[13] *Évangiles Synoptiques*, I, 320–1, p. 320 n. 5.

the contention that Matthew, by including the four women, is consciously refuting or mitigating attacks on the legitimacy of Jesus' birth, pointing to blemishes in the biblical pedigree of David and the Davidic kings themselves. This view goes back to Grotius and was expressed in detail by T. Zahn, who writes:

Wenn Juden die ihnen aus christlichen Kreisen zugekommene Kunde, dass Jesus allerdings nicht der leibliche Sohn seines Vaters Joseph sei, ohne Grund und Beweis dahin verdrehen, dass er ein Bastard sei, und wenn sie daraufhin ohne weiteres bestreiten, dass der so schimpflich Geborene der verheissene Davidssohn sei, so sollten sie bedenken, dass an dem davidischen Hause, aus dem auch nach ihrer Hoffnung der Messias hervorgehen soll, Makel genug haften, welche nicht durch eine grundlose Verleumdung, sondern durch die auch ihnen heiligen Schriften bezeugt sind.[1]

This approach is represented also by Wetstein (1751),[2] J. Weiss,[3] McNeile,[4] Box,[5] V. Taylor,[6] R. Leany,[7] J. Schniewind,[8] C. G. Montefiore,[9] and F. W. Beare.[10] But it has obvious weaknesses: the 'refutation' is of such a nature as to encourage calumny; if there were blemishes in the four ancestresses of David, could not an opponent of Christian Messianic claims consider the case of Mary as a parallel to them? 'Das wäre eine bedenkliche Apologie der Jungfraugeburt.'[11] It is much more probable that such calumnies[12] were stimulated by the genealogy and the birth narratives themselves.[13] The conclusive argument

[1] *Matthäus*, p. 64; on the four women, see pp. 61–8; and *Introduction to the NT*, tr. from 3rd German ed. by M. W. Jacobus *et al.* (3 vols. 1909), II, 536–7.

[2] Cited by Meyer, *Matthew*, p. 52, and Heffern, *JBL*, XXXI (1912), 75.

[3] *Die Schriften des NT*, p. 234; cited by F. Spitta, 'Die Frauen in der Genealogie Jesu bei Matthaus', *ZWT*, LIV (1912), 1 ff.; and Heffern, p. 76.

[4] *Matthew*, p. 5.

[5] *Virgin Birth*, p. 14.

[6] *Virgin Birth*, pp. 89–90.

[7] 'The Birth Narratives in St Luke and St Matthew', *NTS*, VIII (1962), 165.

[8] *Das Evangelium nach Matthäus* (*Das Neue Testament Deutsch*) (1937), pp. 210–11 [10–11].

[9] *The Synoptic Gospels* (2nd ed., 2 vols. 1927), II, 4.

[10] *The Earliest Records of Jesus* (1962), p. 30.

[11] Klostermann, p. 2; cf. Loisy, *Évangiles Synoptiques*, I, 321.

[12] Rabbinic references to Jesus and his immediate ancestry are collected by S–B, I, 36–42; for an analysis, see Goldstein, *Jesus*, *passim*.

[13] Cf. Davies, *Setting*, pp. 65–6.

against this approach, however, is the fact that in the Jewish tradition, which we will now examine more closely, we find numerous evidences of the tendency to exonerate each of the women and to picture at least Rahab and Ruth as exemplars of conversion and faith.[1]

(1) *Tamar*. According to Jub. 41: 1 and T. Jud. 10: 1 she is a 'daughter of Aram', a datum that is made more specific in Rabbinic literature where she is said to be the daughter of Shem, Noah's son, who is identified with Melchizedek.[2] The tendency to exonerate Tamar appears early: she is favorably mentioned even in Ruth 4: 12 as mother of the prosperous house of Perez. In Jub. 41 and T. Jud. 10: 6 a large share of the responsibility for Tamar's act of harlotry is imputed to the Canaanite wife of Judah who refused to allow Shelah to marry Tamar according to the Levirate law. T. Jud. 12: 2 also refers to 'a law of the Amorites, that she who was about to marry should sit in fornication seven days by the gate'; hence Tamar's action was in accord with the customs of her people. While Tamar is wholly and conspicuously absent in the writings of Josephus, we find a remarkable development in Philo: on the basis of Gen. 38, Tamar is not only exonerated but made a type of virtue and even of chastity. Tamar was a widow, that is, widowed of passions and pleasures, who received divine impregnation, conceived virtue and bore noble actions.[3] The details of Tamar's reception are treated with elaborate allegorization: virtue sits at the cross-roads;[4] Judah, a mind bent on purchasing piety, gave pledges—fidelity, constancy, discipline;[5] finally, in *Virt.* 220–2,[6] Tamar is described as 'a woman from Syria Palestine who had been bred up in her own native city, which was devoted to the worship of many gods... But, when

[1] Although there have been other occasional suggestions made, none of them can be considered adequate: Fritzche (cited by Meyer, *Matthew*, p. 52) writes vaguely about Matthew's desire for 'exactness'; J. Schmidt (*Das Evangelium nach Matthäus* (2nd ed. 1952), pp. 31–2) is concerned simply with showing the OT or traditional basis for Matthew's text; Lagrange considers the allusion to Bathsheba to be due to her role in the throne succession at David's death (p. 4).

[2] See Appendix 4.

[3] *Quod Deus* 136 f. (Loeb).

[4] *Congr.* 124–6 (Loeb).

[5] *Fug.* 149–56; *Mut.* 134–6 (Loeb).

[6] Loeb, VIII; on Tamar in Philo, see the summary in the index of names in Loeb, X, 427–8.

she, emerging, as it were, out of profound darkness, was able to see a slight beam of truth', she 'exerted all her energies to arrive at piety; and living virtuously was exactly identical with living for the service of and in constant supplication to the one true God... But even though she was a foreigner still she was nevertheless a freeborn woman, and born also of freeborn parents of no insignificant importance...'[1] Thus, for Philo, Tamar is a Gentile and, although not a proselyte in the full sense, yet a model of spiritual illumination.

In the later Rabbinic sources[2] (third century and later), Tamar and Judah are exonerated on every hand and in a variety of ways. In Gen. R. 85 (787) Tamar's harlotry is led back to God's initiative:

R. Samuel b. Naḥmani [P, 3; third century] commenced thus [on Gen. 38: 1]: 'For I know the thoughts that I think toward you, saith the Lord' [Jer. 29: 11]. The tribal ancestors were engaged in selling Joseph, Jacob was taken up with his sackcloth and fasting, and Judah was busy taking a wife, while the Holy One, blessed be He, was creating the light of the Messiah...

Sometimes Judah is vindicated at the expense of Tamar:

'When Judah saw her,' etc. [Gen. 38: 15 f.]. R. Aḥa [*c.* 250–80] said: A man should become familiar with his wife's sister and with his female relations, so as not to fall into sin through any of them. From whom do you learn this? From Judah: 'When Judah saw her he thought her to be a harlot'. Why so? 'For she had covered her face'—while in her father's house. Another interpretation: 'When Judah saw her' he paid no attention to her. But since she covered her face he reasoned, If she were a harlot, would she actually cover her face! R. Johanan [d. 279] said: He wished to go on, but the Holy One, blessed be He, made the angel who is in charge of desire appear before him, and he said to him: 'Whither goest thou, Judah? Whence then are kings to arise, whence are redeemers to arise?' Thereupon, 'And he turned unto her'—in spite of himself and against his wish...[3]

With this one might compare bSotah 10*a* cited above, and the following from the Palestinian Talmud:

R. Hezekiah [*c.* 350] said in the name of R. Aha [*c.* 320]: R. Ḥiyya [the elder, *c.* 200] interpreted three passages favorably: Gen. 38: 14,

[1] Yonge's trans. III, 504–5.
[2] See S–B, I, 15–18.
[3] Gen. R. 85 (794–5).

'Tamar...sat at the entrance to *Enaim* [עינים].' Is this possible? Much more probably these words mean that she lifted up her eyes to the gate to which all eyes [עינים] look [viz. to God]. She spoke to Him: Lord of the world, may I not go away empty from this house.[1]

It is noteworthy that, according to the introduction to this anecdote, Gen. 38: 14 is one of three passages which R. Ḥiyya interpreted 'öffentlich zum Lobe' (or, according to the translation of M. Schwab, '... R. Hiya interprète les trois versets... dans le sens favorable (malgré leur apparence de blâme)'). In view of the common positive attitude toward Tamar among later Rabbis, this mention of a favorable interpretation of Gen. 38: 14 seems superfluous unless we see a hint of polemic here. It is possible that Tamar was not in all circles of earlier Judaism held up as a model of virtue and piety. Another hint in this direction is bSot. 10*b* (48–9):

'When she was found' [Gen. 38: 25]. The verb should have been 'brought forth!' R. Eleazar [*c.* 270] said: [The verb in the text implied] that after her proofs were found, Samuel came and removed them, and Gabriel came and restored them. That is what is written, 'For the chief musician, the silent dove [viz. Tamar] of them that are afar off. Of David, Michtam' [Ps. 56: 1].—R. Johanan [d. 279] said: At the time when her proofs were removed, she became like a silent dove. 'Of David', 'Michtam'—[That means] there issued from her David who was meek [*mach*] and perfect [*tam*] to all...

It cannot be merely accidental that Ps. 56, a psalm of personal lament, is related to Tamar, 'a dove', in its title (למנצח על־יונת רחקם לדוד מכתם). While the point of the above anecdote hinges on a double meaning of רחקם (the pledges given by Judah being *distant*; the descendant of Tamar, namely David, is in the *distant* future), it is entirely possible that the content of the psalm caused it to be applied to Tamar in the Rabbinic tradition. For in the psalm we read: 'Be gracious to me, O Lord, for men trample upon me; all day long foemen oppress me... All day long they seek to injure my cause; all their thoughts are against me for evil... '(verses 2, 6 [EV, verses 1, 5]). As such,

[1] pSotah 1: 4 (16*d*, 5*a*); par.: Gen. R. 85: 7 (794); Tanch B וישב par. 17 (93*b*).

this Rabbinic passage may point to the polemic role of Tamar in discussions among Jewish interpreters of Scripture.[1] Early criticism of Judah's act is also expressed in Tos. Ber. 4: 18 by the question, 'Does one [God] give a reward for sin?'[2] At any rate, Tamar is honored by the later Rabbis as the ancestress of kings and prophets: 'Ulla [*c.* 260] said: Tamar committed adultery, and Zimri also committed adultery. Tamar committed adultery and kings and prophets descended from her; Zimri committed adultery and through him many ten thousands of Israel fell.'[3]

(2) *Rahab*. Rahab is mentioned neither in the apocrypha, the pseudepigrapha, nor by Philo. In Josephus, however, she is presented in a favorable light as the keeper of an inn, not once being mentioned as a harlot.[4] In the NT she appears along with Abraham in Jas. 2: 25 (Ῥαὰβ ἡ πόρνη) as one who is justified by her works; and in Heb. 11: 31, with the same form of the Greek, she is mentioned as an example of faith along with several prominent OT figures. In later Christian literature, in what may be a reminiscence of the NT, we read that 'on account of her faith and hospitality, Rahab the harlot was saved...'.[5]

In the Rabbinic tradition concerning Rahab, we find various kinds of details but, unlike the fate of Tamar, there are few traces of polemic. The reason is not difficult to find: *in the entirety of the Rabbinic tradition there is no explicit connection of Rahab with the ancestry of David.*[6] We provide some of the earlier selections almost at random, as illustrating this tradition:

Rahab is throughout mentioned as a harlot, usually, as in Hebrews, James, and I Clement, 'Rahab the harlot':

The Rabbis taught [i.e. an old tradition]: There have been four women of surpassing beauty in the world—Sarah, Rahab, Abigail, and Esther...Our Rabbis taught: Rahab inspired lust by her name...[7]

[1] The LXX rendering of the title of this psalm (55, LXX) does not permit the Rabbinic interpretation.

[2] Cf. S–B, I, 18.

[3] bHor. 10*b* (74); see also bHor. 10*b* (48) (par. bMeg. 10*b* (57–8)) where Isaiah and David are descendants of Tamar.

[4] *Ant.* v. 9.

[5] I Clem. 12.

[6] But see below.

[7] bMeg. 15*a* (87), bar.

In spite of her harlotry she is praised as a proselyte[1] and as one who gave assistance to Israel during the conquest:

They say: Rahab was ten years old when Israel went out from Egypt. And during all the forty years that Israel was in the wilderness, she practised harlotry. At the end of her fiftieth year she became a proselyte, saying before the Holy One, blessed be He: 'I have sinned in three things, forgive me because of three things, because of the cord, the window, and the wall', as it is said: 'Then she let them down by a cord through the window; for her house was upon the side of the wall, and she dwelt upon the wall' [Josh. 2: 15].[2]

She was rewarded for her bravery by being saved with her family from the destruction of Jericho. This appears in a midrashic discussion of I Chron. 4: 21–3, in the context of which several Rabbis of the early and middle second century are named:

And what is the meaning of the words, 'And all the families also they brought out' [Josh. 6: 23, suggested by I Chron. 4: 21*b*, 'The families of the house of linen workers']? R. Simeon b. Yoḥai (*c.* A.D. 150] taught: that even if her family consisted of two hundred individuals, and they attached themselves to two hundred other families, all were delivered by her merit, since it does not say 'all her family', but 'all her families'.[3]

Later Rabbis interpreted I Chron. 4: 21*b* differently: R. Samuel b. Naḥmani (third century) applied it to David 'who busied himself with the curtain [of the Ark]'.[4] But the earliest extant Rabbinic tradition applied it to Rahab. According to a piece of midrashic exegesis that may be traced to the first century (the R. Eliezer mentioned is most probably Eleazar, T, 2, *c.* 80–120 A.D.), Rahab was rewarded by becoming the ancestress of several priestly prophets:

The same [i.e. because she drew near to God, God drew her near to himself] is true of Rahab the harlot. R. Eliezer [*c.* A.D. 80–120] says: '[The words, "of the house of Asheba" (I Chron. 4: 21)] refer to

[1] She is frequently mentioned, with Jethro, as an exemplary proselyte: cf. S.S.R. 1: 3, 3 (39); 1: 5, 2 (87); 4: 1, 2 (177); 6: 2, 3 (258); Num. R. 3: 2 (68); Eccl. R. 5: 11 (150–1); Pes. R. 9 (167*b*); pBer. 2: 8.

[2] Mekilta on Exod. 18: 1 (Amalek III; 24 ff.) (pp. 163–4, Lauterbach, III); par. bZeb. 116*b* (575).

[3] Ruth R. 2: 1 (23–4); par. pBer. 4: 1 (8*b*, 41) and Eccl. R. on 5: 6 (135).

[4] Ruth R. 2: 2 (25).

Rahab the harlot who was an innkeeper. Eight priests and eight prophets descended from her! They are: Jeremiah, Hilkiah, Seraiah, Machsaiah, Baruch, Meraiah, Hanamel, and Shallum.' R. Jehuda [b. Elai, *c.* 150] says: 'Also Hulda the prophetess was a descendant of Rahab.' Now if she, who came from a people of whom it is said [Deut. 20: 16]: 'Thou shalt not leave alive any soul,' because she drew near [to God], God drew her near [to himself], much more so with Israel...[1]

The latter two extracts, Ruth R. 2: 1 (23–4) and Sifre Num. 78, provide a clue by which we might gain a solution to a difficult problem: why Matthew alone among all Jewish or Christian sources of biblical and Talmudic times connects Rahab to the tribe of Judah and the ancestry of David. In the Midrashim she is represented as a proselyte and, especially in the later sources, as the wife of Joshua, who bore no sons, but only daughters, from whom descended the priests and prophets.[2] On what basis did Matthew include Rahab in the ancestry of David? A possible answer is suggested by the fact that, in these two sources, a passage from the Chronicler's genealogy of Judah is applied to Rahab by a play on words. Hence Rahab was at some point in the Jewish tradition considered a proselyte belonging to the tribe of Judah. This conclusion is supported by the observation that in the context of both passages Ruth, whose part in the Davidic ancestry of David is a constantly recurring theme, is dealt with in a similar fashion. Ruth and Boaz are 'the potters' of I Chron. 4: 23; Ruth lived to see Solomon since it says 'they dwelt there with the king for his work' (I Chron. 4: 23).[3] The Gentile descent of Rahab and Ruth is not disregarded, but in both sources they are praised as ancestresses of prominent OT figures and also as adhering to the tribe of Judah. That Rahab's descendants were priests does not necessarily contradict the tradition of her belonging to Judah since another tradition holds that her daughters married into the priesthood.[4] The date of this midrashic exegesis of I Chron. 4: 21–3 is relatively early;

[1] Mid. Sifre on Numbers, 78 (Levertoff, pp. 52–3); par. bMeg. 14*b* (85–6) and Ruth R. 2: 1 (25); cf. Num. R. 8: 9 (234).

[2] S–B, I, 23, refer to b.Meg. 14*b* (85–6) (Rab Naḥman, d. 320, and R. Judah, *c.* 150, are cited); Num. R. 8: 9 (234); and Eccl. R. on 8: 10 (223) (attributed to R. Abin).

[3] Ruth R. 2: 2 (26–7); the last datum is found also in Sifre (53).

[4] Num. R. 8: 9.

the application of I Chron. 4: 21 to Rahab is attributed in Ruth R. to R. Ḥama (mid second century), Rabbi (b. 135), and R. Judah b. Simon (*c.* 165–200?). In Sifre it is attributed to R. Eliezer (*c.* 80–120), thus even earlier than in Ruth R. We conclude that the compiler of the Matthean genealogy included Rahab in the ancestry of David on the basis of an old Rabbinic tradition according to which Rahab belonged, as a proselyte, to the tribe of Judah. Whether this tradition identified Rahab as the mother of Boaz, we cannot say.

(3) *Ruth.* Ruth, the model proselyte of the OT, continued to be praised in the later tradition. While she is neglected in the apocrypha and pseudepigrapha, Philo, and the Dead Sea Scrolls, her story is paraphrased by Josephus in a favorable way.[1] Yet even here there are hints of a tendency which became full-blown in the later Rabbinic tradition; she is praised as an ancestress of David but with some hesitancy concerning her Moabite ancestry.

I was therefore obliged to relate this history of Ruth, because I had a mind to demonstrate the power of God, who, without difficulty, can raise those that are of ordinary parentage to dignity and splendour, to which he advanced David, though he were born of such mean parents.[2]

As for the Rabbinic tradition on Ruth, we cite representative passages in a somewhat systematic, rather than chronological, fashion. Although the most important direct references are from the later Tannaitic and the Amoraic periods (second and third centuries), traces of the polemic situation of Ruth in the ancestry of David are found in relatively early Rabbinic sources.

Ruth is throughout 'the Moabitess', and as such is brought into connection with other passages dealing with Moab in the OT. She is the granddaughter of Eglon, king of Moab, who was the grandson of Balak:

Rab Judah [d. 299] said in the name of Rab [d. 247]: Let a man always engage in Torah and the performance of commandments even though his motive be ulterior because ulterior motive will ultimately lead to disinterested [study and performance]; for as a

[1] *Ant.* v. 9.
[2] *Ant.* v. 9. 4.

reward for the forty-two sacrifices which the wicked Balak offered [Num. 23] he gained the privilege of having Ruth descended from him; for R. Jose b. R. Ḥanana [*c.* 270] said: Ruth was the daughter of the son of Eglon [Judg. 3: 12] who was the son of the son of Balak the king of Moab.[1]

As an ancestor of Ruth, Eglon receives favorable mention:

R. Bibi [*c.* 250?] said in the name of R. Ruben [early 3rd century]: Ruth and Orpah were the daughters of Eglon...and it is written, 'And Ehud came unto him...and Ehud said: I have a message from God unto thee. And he arose out of his seat' [Judg. 3: 20]. The Holy One, blessed be He, said to him: 'Thou didst arise from thy throne in honour of Me. By thy life, I shall raise up from thee a descendant sitting upon the throne of the Lord.'[2]

Although Ruth, alone among the four women of Matthew's genealogy, is herself free from a taint of immorality (in the Rabbinic tradition), her Moabite ancestry recalled the incestuous relationship between Lot and his daughters, from whom Moab and Ammon were born:

'And Lot had flocks, and herds, and tents' [Gen. 13: 5]. R. Tobiah b. R. Isaac [*c.* 300] said: He had two tents, viz., Ruth the Moabitess and Naamah the Ammonitess. Similarly, it is written, 'Arise, take thy wife and thy two daughters that are found' [Gen. 19: 15]. R. Tobiah said: That means two 'finds', viz., Ruth and Naamah. R. Isaac [*c.* 300] commented, 'I have found David my servant' [Ps. 89: 21]: Where did I find him? In Sodom [i.e. the daughters of Lot were in Sodom].[3]

Since Ruth was the ancestress of David, and Naamah a wife of Solomon, Lot's daughters were considered ancestresses of the Messiah.

'Come, let us make our father drink wine...that we may preserve seed of our father' [Gen. 19: 22]. R. Tanḥuma [*c.* 380] said in Samuel's name [*c.* 260]: It is not written 'That we may preserve a child of our father', but 'That we may preserve *seed* of our father': viz., the seed that comes from a different source, which is the King Messiah.[4]

[1] bHor. 10*b* (75); cf. S–B, I, 24; par. bNaz. 23*b* (84–5).

[2] Ruth R. 2: 9 (31); par. Tanch B ויהי, par. 14 (110*b*).

[3] Gen. R. 50 (440).

[4] Gen. R. 51: 8 (447–8); cf. S–B, I, 26–7 on the phrase 'from a different source'.

But the Gentile ancestry of David through Ruth was not casually accepted on all sides. The ancient law of Deut. 23: 3 could thus be applied to David through Ruth and to the royal line through both Ruth and Naamah: 'No Ammonite or Moabite shall enter the assembly of the Lord, even to the tenth generation.' Indeed, of all four women in Matt. 1: 3–6, it is especially Ruth who seems to have been the subject of numerous polemical disputes on the ancestry of the Messiah. In their most extreme form these disputes are recorded as conversations with Doeg the Edomite and Ahitophel, who represent the anti-Davidic point of view:

'And the Lord said unto Noah: Come thou and all thy house into the ark' [Gen. 7: 1]. It is written, 'Thou destroyest them that speak falsehood' [Ps. 5: 7]: This refers to Doeg and Ahitophel...'the men of blood and deceit' [Ps. 5: 7].[1]

The specific charges against David by Doeg are contained in two haggadic passages:

(*a*) Another interpretation of 'Dead flies make the ointment of the perfume fetid and putrid' [Eccl. 10: 1]: it speaks of Doeg and Ahitophel. Yesterday they used vile language against David, saying, 'He comes from a disqualified family, for is he not descended from Ruth the Moabitess!' But today they utter words which reflect their sense of shame.[2]

(*b*) 'And when Saul saw David go forth against the Philistine, he said unto Abner, the captain of the host: Abner, whose son is this youth? And Abner said, as my soul liveth, O King, I cannot tell' [I Sam. 17: 55]...It is this that Saul meant, Whether he descended from Perez, or from Zerah. If he descended from Perez, he would be a king...If, however, he is descended from Zerah, he would only be an important man...Doeg the Edomite then said to him, 'Instead of inquiring whether he is fit to be king or not, inquire whether he is permitted to enter the assembly or not!' 'What is the reason?' 'Because he is descended from Ruth the Moabitess.' Said Abner to him, 'We learned: "An Ammonite", but not an Ammonitess; "A Moabite", but not a Moabitess... '.[3]

The fate of Doeg and Ahitophel in Jewish tradition is curious. In the Mishnah they are denied a lot in the world to come;[4]

[1] Gen. R. 32: 1 (249).
[2] Eccl. R. 10: 1 (261).
[3] bYeb. 76*b* (516–17); par. Ruth R. 4: 6 (55–6), where Doeg is referred to as a 'heretic'.
[4] mSan. 10: 2 (397); par. Mid. Ps. 5: 10 (90).

they are remembered as excelling in knowledge of Torah,[1] while Ahitophel is also adept at astrology. Both were chiefs of the Sanhedrin.[2] Although originally not enemies of David both were guilty of 'slander' against David;[3] consequently, they 'fell from their greatness and went down to Gehenna';[4] Doeg became leprous.[5] Such traditions are only partially based on the OT and would seem to be well suited for a picture of a 'heretical' party within Judaism which was opposed by the Rabbis. The opponents' knowledge of Scripture and their slanders of David would fit either the priestly Sadducees or possibly such groups as the Essenes or the later Karaites.[6]

Although the bulk of the explicitly polemical references to Doeg and Ahitophel is anonymous and probably late, the background is to be located in earlier discussion on the inclusion of Ammonites and Moabites within Israel. A decision on this problem is given in the Mishnah, indicating that this question was discussed by the Tannaim:

> 'An Ammonite or a Moabite' [Deut. 23: 3] is forbidden and forbidden for all time, but their women are permitted forthwith. An Egyptian or an Edomite [Deut. 23: 7] whether male or female is forbidden only for three generations. R. Simeon [b. Yohai, T, 4, *c.* 140–65] declares their women forthwith permitted...[7]

The basis for this decision lay in the fact that the text used the masculine form of the two nouns, Ammonite and Moabite, rather than the feminine. It is probably the same Simeon who is referred to in the following extract:

> The question is a matter of dispute between Tannaim: 'An Ammonite', but not an Ammonitess; 'a Moabite', but not a Moabitess. So R. Judah [b. Ilai, T, 4; *c.* 140–65]. R. Simeon, however, said: 'Because they did not meet you with bread and with water' [Deut. 23: 5]...Raba [d. 352] made the following exposition: What was meant by, 'Thou hast loosed my bonds!' [Ps. 116: 16]? David said

[1] bHag. 15*b*; Mid. Ps. 52: 4 (I, 479): 'R. Isaac [*c.* 300] said: Doeg was called the Edomite because he used to redden (*ma'adim*) with shame the faces of all who argued the law with him'; bSan. 106*b*; mAb. 6: 3 (459).

[2] Mid. Ps. 3: 4 (I, 57); 49: 2 (I, 465); 52: 3 (I, 478).

[3] Mid. Ps. 7: 7 (I, 108); 52 (I, 475–8); bZeb. 54*b*; Mid. Sam. 22.

[4] Mid. Ps. 49: 2 (I, 465).

[5] Mid. Ps. 52: 1 (I, 475).

[6] On Doeg and Ahitophel, see *JE*, *ad rem.*

[7] mYeb. 8: 3 (229).

o the Holy One, blessed be He, 'O Master of the world! Two bonds were fastened on me, and you loosed them: Ruth the Moabitess and Naamah the Ammonitess.'[1]

Ruth and Naamah are several times mentioned together, an indication of a possible polemical background:

(*a*) R. Eleazar [*c.* 270?] further stated: What is meant by the text, 'And in thee shall the families of the earth be blessed' [Gen. 12: 3]? The Holy One, blessed be He, said to Abraham, 'I have two goodly shoots to engraft on you: Ruth the Moabitess and Naamah the Ammonitess'.[2]

(*b*) [Ulla (*c.* 280) said:] The Holy One, blessed be He, said to him [Moses]: '...Two doves have I to bring from them [The Moabites and Ammonites]: Ruth the Moabitess and Naamah the Ammonitess.'[3]

References to 'the law of the Ammonites and Moabites' are even more frequent. According to R. Meir (*c.* 145, T, 3), when Mahlon and Chilon married Orpah and Ruth the 'new law' about Ammonites and Moabites had not yet been propounded;[4] it was in effect, however, by the time of David,[5] and even when Boaz married Ruth.[6] In Ruth R. 4: 1 (49–50), in a saying introduced by the phrase, 'the Rabbis say', Jesse vowed to 'slay or be slain' until he 'publicly' established the law, 'Ammonite but not Ammonitess, Moabite, but not Moabitess'.[7]

Finally, we cite a passage which, although relatively late, obviously reflects a polemical discussion about Davidic descent:

R. Abba b. Kahana [P, 3; third century] opened, 'Tremble and sin not' [Ps. 4: 5]. David said to the Holy One, blessed be He, 'How long will they rage [רגז, "tremble" or "rage"] against me and say, "Is he not of tainted descent? [לא פסול משפחה הוא]. Is he not a descendant of Ruth the Moabitess?" "Commune with your own heart upon your bed" [Ps. 4: 5]. Ye also, are ye not descended from

[1] bYeb. 77*a* (519); Tamar and Ruth are mentioned in this saying in Mid. Ps. 116: 9 (228).

[2] bYeb. 63*a* (420); S–B, I, 26.

[3] bB.K. 38*b* (216); S–B, I, 26.

[4] Ruth R. 2: 9 (30–1).

[5] Ruth R. 4: 6 (56).

[6] Ruth R. 7: 7 (85) and 7: 10 (86), both attributed to Samuel b. Nahman.

[7] Other passages referring to this 'law' are bKid. 75*a* (383); bNaz. 23*b* (83); Ruth R. 8: 1 (93); and Mid. Ps. 1: 2 (I, 4), where mYeb. 8: 3 is referred to.

two sisters?[1] Look upon your own genealogy [עיקרכם] "and be still" [Ps. 4: 5]. And Tamar who married your ancestor Judah—is it not a tainted descent? She was but a descendant of Shem the son of Noah.[2] Have you then an honourable descent [מה אתם ישלכם יוחסים]?'[3]

The references to 'tainted descent', 'your genealogy', Ruth, Tamar, and the two sisters are unmistakable. It is a kind of summary of a polemical tradition, without the assumption of which it would be difficult to account for the frequency of references to the 'law concerning Ammonites and Moabites' in the Rabbinic sources. As for the date of the polemic, it would be hazardous, on the basis of the extant sources, to assign it to the Maccabean period, as does Aptowitzer.[4] On the other hand, the Tannaitic references to the law of the Ammonites and Moabites and the note appended to Josephus' account of Ruth do allow the possibility that the question of the Moabite ancestry of David was acute in Judaism as early as the first century. This conclusion must be taken into account in our interpretation of the role of the four women in the Matthean genealogy.

(4) *The wife of Uriah*. The incidents recorded in II Samuel of David's dealings with Uriah and Bathsheba are not forgotten or overlooked in the later tradition. Josephus introduces the entire account as 'a very grievous sin',[5] but adds that David 'was without controversy a pious man, and guilty of no sin at all in his whole life, excepting those in the matter of Uriah'.[6] In T. Jud. the warnings against immorality may cast a forward glance at David: 'For even though a man may be a king and commit fornication, he is stripped of his kingship by becoming the slave of fornication, as I myself also suffered... And the angel of God showed me that for ever do women bear rule over king and beggar alike. And from the king they take away his glory, and from the valiant man his might, and from the beggar even that little which is the stay of his poverty.'[7] In chapter 17

[1] This is most often understood as a reference to Rachel and Leah (e.g. Rabinowitz, *Ruth R.* p. 92 n. 2; S–B, I, 24, and Wm. G. Braude, *The Midrash on Psalms* (2 vols. 1959), I, 72 n. 32; but there may also be a glance at the daughters of Lot.

[2] See Appendix 4.

[3] Ruth R. 8: 1 (92); par. Mid. Ps. 4: 9 (72).

[4] See above, pp. 131–6.

[5] *Ant.* VII. 7. 1.

[6] *Ant.* VII. 7. 3.

[7] T. Jud. 15: 2–6.

of T. Jud. there seems to be an allusion to Solomon: 'For even wise men among my sons shall [love of money and beautiful women] mar, and shall cause the kingdom of Judah to be diminished...'[1]

Perhaps the most striking reference to David's sin in the literature contemporaneous with the NT is in the so-called Damascus Document:

The builders of the wall who follow a precept [בוני החיץ אשר הלכו אחרי צו]—the precept is a preacher [מטיף], because it says, 'They will surely preach' [הטף יטיפון]—they will be caught in two nets: in fornication by taking two wives during their lifetime, whereas the foundation of the creation is, 'male and female he created them' [Gen. 1: 27]; and those who went into the ark, 'two by two they went into the ark' [Gen. 7: 9]. And concerning the prince [נשיא] it is written, 'He shall not multiply wives for himself' [Deut. 17: 17].

But David did not read the sealed book of the law which was in the ark; for it was not opened in Israel from the day of the death of Eleazar and Joshua and the elders who served the Ashtaroth, but was hidden and not disclosed until Zadok arose. The deeds of David were overlooked [יעלו, Charles: 'glorified'], except the blood of Uriah, and God left them to him.[2]

In this passage, which almost certainly antedates the composition of Matthew, there are several signs of a polemic which is directed against certain pivotal aspects of Rabbinic theology that are a part of its oldest tradition: (*a*) 'The builders of the wall who walk after law' (Charles), while being borrowed in part from Ezek. 13: 10 (בוני החיץ) is in all probability a derisive reference to the Rabbinic maxim, 'make a fence around the Law' (עשו סייג לתורה) which, in mAb. 1: 1, is attributed to the 'men of the Great Synagogue' who followed Ezra. The substitution of חיץ, 'to make a partition-wall', for סיג, 'to fence about', may imply 'that the Pharisees did not by this means so much protect the Law against profanation from without as create division among the ranks of the faithful within'.[3] (*b*) The reference to the Law as 'preacher' (מטיף, tr. by Lévi as 'bavardage'[4] (gossip, chatter)) may be a satirical allusion to

[1] 17: 3.

[2] CD 5: 1–5 (Charles, *A & P*, II, 7: 1–7); Burrows' trans., DSS, pp. 352–3.

[3] Charles, II, 819; he cites as par. Eph. 2: 17 and Phil. 3: 2.

[4] Cited by Charles, II, 810.

the oral law (תורה שבעל פה), adherence to which was a characteristic mark of the Pharisees as against the Sadducees. The oral law was to serve as the 'fence' or 'wall' around the written Law. (*c*) The substitution of צו, 'precept', for תורה, Torah, may itself be a result of the polemic intention—the oral law is not Torah but precept. (*d*) In the official Rabbinic view, the chain of oral tradition from Moses to Tannaitic times runs from Moses to Joshua to 'the elders' to 'the prophets' to 'the men of the Great Synagogue' (mAb. 1: 1). Hence the reference to 'the elders who served Ashtarath' (derived from Judg. 2: 13) is an attack on the basis of the oral law itself—it cannot be transmitted from Moses in an uncontaminated form since the second link from Moses consisted of idolaters.

Assuming the nature of CD 7 as a polemic against the Pharisees, what is the significance of the reference to David? In the mind of the writer, polygamy was an example of fornication, on the basis of the Pentateuch. Even David, according to the written Torah, would be guilty of polygamy, but since the Torah was hidden until Zadok (presumably during the reign of Solomon), only one sin of David is counted against him, namely the murder of Uriah; for that he is culpable. As Charles remarks, 'Our author clearly disapproves of the praise of David in I Kings 15: 5, which seems to have been in his thoughts'.[1] The significance of this passage for our purposes is that anti-Pharisaic sentiments are expressed in the context of a discussion of David's sin with Bathsheba. It must be admitted, however, that opposition to David is not yet full-blown in this passage. Yet it may be noteworthy that the Davidic ancestry of the 'Messiah of Israel' is not alluded to in the best-preserved documents at Qumran but is confined to a few fragments which may date from an early period of the community.[2]

The Rabbinic treatment of David's sin is by no means uniform. Among the examples of those who maintain David's guilt in a straightforward fashion is an old tradition traced to Shammai and earlier:

Now, when it was taught: If he says to his agent, 'Go forth and slay a soul', the latter is liable, and his sender exempt. Shammai the Elder [*c.* 30 B.C.] said on the authority of Haggai the Prophet [i.e. an

[1] II, 810, on 7: 7.

[2] See above, pp. 126 f.

ancient tradition]: His sender is liable, for it is said, 'Thou hast slain him with the sword of the children of Ammon' [II Sam. 12: 9, of David and Uriah].[1]

It is significant to note that Shammai's view is presented as an alternative to the official position. Later tradition revoked Shammai's argument: 'You cannot be punished for the sword of the children of Ammon, so will you not be punished for Uriah, the Hittite. What is the reason? He was a rebel against sovereignty, for he said to him [David], "and my lord Joab..." [II Sam. 11: 11].'[2] But our sources do not permit us to discover whether this attitude of Shammai's affected his view of the Messiah.

The recollection of David's guilt is, however, preserved by some of the later Rabbis:

(*a*) 'Deliver me from bloodguiltiness, O God' [Ps. 51: 16]. R. Joshua b. Levi [*c.* 250] said: 'Uriah the Hittite, thirty-seven in all' [II Sam. 23: 39]...R. Hanina b. Papa [*c.* 300] in the name of R. Hanina [*c.* 225] brought proof [for David's bloodguiltiness] from II Sam. 12: 9: 'Why have you despised the word of the Lord?...and have slain him with the sword of the Ammonites.' The Rabbis said: The words, 'and have slain him', show that he had slain many righteous men who were like his [Uriah].[3]

(*b*) R. Abbahu [*c.* 300] said: It is written: 'Answer me when I call, O God of my right! Thou hast given me room when I was in distress' [Ps. 4: 1]. David spoke before God: Lord of the world, in every need...Thou hast made breadth for me; I am in need because of Bathsheba, and Thou hast sent me Solomon.[4]

David's guilt is a frequent subject of discussion in the Midrash on Psalms. Usually a statement that the effects of David's sin are permanent is put on the lips of his opponents, while the Rabbis maintain his forgiveness:

(*a*) 'How great are they that say of my soul: "There is no help for him in God, ever"' [Ps. 3: 3]. R. Samuel [B, 1; *c.* 250] interpreted this verse as referring to Doeg and Ahitophel: 'great are they' in learning, 'that say'. What is it they say? 'Is it possible that a man who took the ewe lamb, murdered its shepherd, and caused the

1 bKid. 43*a* (214–15).
2 bKid. 43*a* (214–15).
3 Mid. Sam. 25: 2 (61*b*); tr. S–B, I, 29.
4 pTaan. 2: 10 (65*d*); tr. S–B, I, 29.

people of Israel to die by the sword, can make amends? No! "There is no help for him in God, ever."'[1]

(*b*) A further comment on the verse, 'Thou who hast set me at large when I was in distress' [Ps. 4: 1]. According to R. Johanan [d. 279] there were three matters that David was distressed about: the site of the house of God; the taking of Bathsheba; and Solomon's succession to the kingship. But the Holy One, blessed be He, set his mind at rest about them...

And David was distressed about his taking of Bathsheba, for men were speaking against him in Israel, and saying: 'Is it possible that he who took the ewe lamb, murdered its shepherd, and caused the people of Israel to die by the sword can ever have help from God?' But the Holy One, blessed be He, set his mind at rest, for Nathan said to David, 'The Lord also hath put away thy sin; Thou shalt not die' [II Sam. 12: 13].

About the third matter, Israel said: 'What does David think? That his kingship can be continued through Bathsheba's son?' But the Holy One, blessed be He, set David's mind at rest, for the word of the Lord came to David, saying: 'Behold, a son shall be born to thee, who shall be a man of rest...his name shall be Solomon' [I Chron. 22: 9]...[2]

Finally, we cite two passages; the first, summarizing the accusations against David, is anonymous but perhaps late; the second summarizes the attempts of early and middle second-century Rabbis to exonerate David.

(*a*) 'And Shimei went along the rib [צלע] of the hill' [II Sam. 16: 13*b*], the word 'rib' intimating that as Shimei went along, he recalled to David the incident of the rib [creation of Eve], of which David was to say 'I have been made ready for the rib' [כי־אני לצלע נכון] [Ps. 38: 18]. By this David meant to declare to the Holy One, blessed be He: Master of the universe! It is revealed and known to thee that Bath-sheba was held ready for me from the six days of Creation, yet she was given to me for sorrow: 'My sorrow is continually before me' [Ps. 38: 18]. And David was to instruct and point out to Solomon his son and say to him: 'Shimei...abused me with grievous [נמרצת] abuse in the day when I went to Mahanaim' [I Kings 2: 8*a*]. How is *NMRST* to be understood? As an acrostic [lit. 'notarikon']: The letter N stands for *no'ef*, 'Adulterer'; the letter M, for 'Moabite'; the letter R, for *roseah*, 'murderer'; the letter S for *sores*, 'persecutor'; and the letter T for *to'ebah*, 'abomination'.

[1] Mid. Ps. 3: 5 (57); cf. 4: 8 (71). [2] Mid. Ps. 4: 2 (60–1).

Shimei had previously said to David, 'Behold, thou art taken in thine own mischief' [II Sam. 16: 8]. What was he referring to?... According to R. Abba bar Kahana [*c.* 310], to Bath-sheba's canopied litter which David had along with him.[1]

(*b*) R. Samuel b. Naḥmani [*c.* 260] said in R. Jonathan's name [b. Eleazar, *c.* 220]: Whoever says that David sinned is merely erring, for it is said, 'And David behaved himself wisely in all his ways; and the Lord was with him' [I Sam. 18: 14]. It is possible that sin came to his hand, yet the Divine Presence was with him? Then how do I interpret, 'Wherefore hast thou despised the word of the Lord, to do that which is evil in thy sight?' [II Sam. 12: 9]? He wished to do [evil], but did not. Rab [d. 247] observed: Rabbi, who is descended from David, seeks to defend him, and expounds [the verse] in David's favour. [Thus:] the 'evil' here is unlike every other 'evil' elsewhere in the Torah. For of every other evil in the Torah it is written, 'and he did', whereas here it is written, 'to do'; [this means] that he desired to do, but did not. 'Thou hast smitten Uriah the Hittite with the sword' [II Sam. 12: 9]: thou shouldst have had him tried by the Sanhedrin, but didst not. 'And hast taken his wife to be thy wife'; thou hast marriage rights with her. For R. Samuel b. Naḥmani [*c.* 260] said in R. Jonathan's name [*c.* 220]: Everyone who went out in the wars of the house of David wrote a bill of divorcement for his wife...'And thou hast slain him with the sword of the children of Ammon' [II Sam. 12: 9]: just as thou art not punished for the sword of the Ammonites, so art thou not punished for Uriah the Hittite. What is the reason? He [Uriah] was rebellious against royal authority, saying to him, 'And my lord Joab, and the servants of my lord, are encamped in the open field [etc.]' [II Sam. 11: 11; he disobeyed David's order to go home].

Rab [d. 247] said, When you examine [the life of] David, you find nought but 'save only in the matter of Uriah the Hittite'.[2]

We conclude our survey of the treatment of the Bathsheba incident in Jewish tradition by suggesting that this matter was discussed in polemic fashion even in pre-Christian times, while the later Rabbinic tradition is divided between those who would exonerate David and those who maintain his guilt. The ascription of strongly anti-Davidic sentiments to Doeg, Ahitophel, and Shimei reveals clear traces of polemic.[3]

[1] Mid. Ps. 3: 3 (I, 53).

[2] bShab. 56*a* (259–60).

[3] Other passages reflecting the Bathsheba incident are Num. R. 11: 3 (420); Num. R. 10: 4 (532–3); Lev. R. 12: 5 (159–60); Gen. R. 32: 1 (249).

(5) *Summary: the role of the four women in Matt. 1: 3–6.* In spite of different approaches to the question, scholars have tended to agree in their assumption that the four women in Matt. 1: 3–6 share something in common. Some have found this common ground to be Gentile ancestry, although it is rarely seen that not only Rahab and Ruth, but also Tamar and 'the wife of Uriah', were most probably considered Gentiles by the compiler of the genealogy. Hence the women are thought to foreshadow Jesus' concern for Gentiles or to reflect the problem of universalism—inclusion of Gentiles—in the early church. Others find the common ground to be scandal in connection with immorality, although here again Ruth is felt to be an exception. (We have seen, however, that David's descent from Ruth recalled her descent from the incestuous relationship between Lot and his daughters.) Assuming immorality to be the common ground, one can consider the inclusion of the women to be intended to silence Jewish calumny against Jesus' birth or, in a more positive sense, to point to the boundless grace of God and his power to reconstitute human life.

What appears to me a more fruitful method, however, may yield different results. It is the method I have attempted to follow above, namely an examination of the fate of the four women in Jewish tradition. It is not a new approach, having been used already by Friedrich Spitta in 1912.[1] Spitta's conclusion, however, that the women are all vindicated and praised in the Jewish tradition, has been shown to be inadequate. The judgment of the Rabbis is by no means uniform;[2] Matthew, therefore, could not assume that the mention of these four women would be understood as a glorification of the Messianic pedigree. It is my contention that an adequate investigation should go one step further. The clue to the interpretation of the four women is to be found precisely in the fact that the Jewish tradition is divided with regard to the fate of the women. The common ground for the four is that they occupied an important place in later Jewish speculation and that this speculation was largely polemic in nature. Thus, in dealing separately with each, I have attempted to document this ambivalence and have pointed out that the women were subjects of controversy in the oldest post-biblical sources. Hence, those who consider the role

[1] *ZWT*, LIV (1912), 1–8. [2] Cf. Kittel in *TWNT*, III, 2.

of the women to be related to polemics are right, but not in tracing the polemic to Jewish calumnies against the idea of the virgin birth. *The polemic took place within Judaism itself.* A detailed analysis of this intra-Jewish controversy is, by the nature of the sources, obviously impossible. But a hypothesis can be suggested to account for the text of Matt. 1 that does justice to the bulk of the evidence. I do so tentatively, advancing the reconstruction as one of the possible solutions:

The roots of this polemic must be much older than most of the Rabbinic evidence we have adduced. This is suggested by the treatment of Tamar in the Testaments, Jubilees, and Philo; of Ruth in Josephus and the relative age of the idea of the 'law of the Ammonites and Moabites'; of the Bathsheba incident in CD and a saying attributed to Shammai; and especially by the early unofficial midrashim which preserve traces of a tradition that linked Rahab to the tribe of Judah, a phenomenon that is otherwise unique to Matthew, and which is contradicted by later Rabbinic sources.[1]

The polemic was concerned with the ancestry of the Messiah. Again, this emerges with clarity in all cases except that of Rahab, who is alone among the four women in that her share in the ancestry of David and her relationship to the tribe of Judah is not mentioned in the OT. Thus it was possible for partisans of the expectation of the Davidic Messiah to deny the validity of an earlier tradition which connected Rahab to Judah.

The attack on the ancestry of David can most naturally be explained as applying to the expectation of the Davidic Messiah. This is seen most sharply in the mention of David in CD 7, where the beliefs of the Pharisees are slighted, but also in the Rabbinic references to 'the law of the Ammonites and Moabites' and to Doeg and Ahitophel.

The only alternative to the idea of the Davidic Messiah at the time of the composition of Matthew was, as far as we know, the expectation of the Levitical Messiah. The latter expectation is strongly represented in Palestinian Jewish sources prior to

[1] Another indication of early date is the mention of Rahab and Ruth in sequence in a passage attributed to R. Eliezer (*c.* 80–100) (Sifre on Num. 78 (52–4)); cf. Pes. R. 9 (S–B, I, 20). In Ruth R. 2: 1–2 (23–7), Rahab, Ruth, and Bathsheba are considered in sequence; in Mid. Ps. 116: 9 (II, 228) Tamar and Ruth are brought together in an anonymous passage.

A.D. 70, especially in the Testaments and the Dead Sea Scrolls. After A.D. 70, however, the influence of the Sadducees and Essenes came to an abrupt end, and the categories applied to the Levitical Messiah came to be attributed, in the Talmud, to Elijah and also to the Messiah b. Joseph. I suggest, therefore, that opponents of the idea of the Davidic Messiah brought into the polemic an emphasis on the four women as blots in the Davidic ancestry. The partisans of the expectation of the Davidic Messiah—the Pharisaic element—were unable to deny the place of these women (with the exception of Rahab) in the ancestry of David and, consequently, could only put the most charitable construction on them as was possible. The controversy continued in later Judaism either as scribal reflection on the past polemic or as a result of more participation in Rabbinic schools by priests and Levites from those groups whose influence declined after A.D. 70.

Matthew's handling of the four women can best be explained by viewing his work in its proper setting. He wrote after A.D. 70 to Jewish or Jewish-Christian readers who were aware of the polemic on the ancestry of the Messiah which had been carried on within Judaism, a polemic in which the four women had already come to occupy a prominent place. It was apparent to our author that the Pharisaic element within Judaism would become predominant—perhaps he himself had belonged to their number. Thus, Matthew wrote to show that in every respect the Pharisaic expectation of the Messiah had been fulfilled in Jesus of Nazareth, who was the son of David and therefore a descendant of the four women. The four women, then, do serve an apologetic purpose, but not as this has been commonly understood. The Messianic categories which, according to our author, were fulfilled in Jesus were precisely those of that element within Judaism which was vindicated by the cruel historical events of A.D. 66–70, and the succeeding years. To counter this Christian claim that Jesus was the Davidic Messiah (a claim that came to be almost universally accepted by Christianity) the Rabbis could not criticize the genealogy, either in its structure or its details, which were dependent on biblical data and Pharisaic tradition as far as possible, but could only point to the irregularity in Jesus' birth and apply to him the scandal associated with an affair of a young Jewish maiden with a Roman soldier who lived at a time considerably prior to the birth of Jesus.[1]

(*e*) A special relation of several individuals in Matthew's list to the Messiah is spoken of in the Rabbinic tradition. S–B provide the details: Judah is specifically mentioned as an ancestor of the Messiah;[2] Perez is sometimes identified with the Messiah[3] or the Messiah is given the name Ben Perez.[4] Similarly, the Messiah could be called Ben Nahshon.[5] Among descendants of David, Jehoshaphat was expected by some to be the future Messiah,[6] although the expectation of Hezekiah is more frequently attested, even in a citation attributed to Johanan b. Zakkai at the destruction of Jerusalem in A.D. 70:

> R. Jacob b. Idi [*c.* 280] said in the name of R. Joshua b. Levi [*c.* 250]: When R. Johanan b. Zakkai [*c.* 80] escaped, he ordered: Remove the impurity and make ready a royal throne for Hezekiah, king of Judah![7]

These references demonstrate the common Rabbinic idea that the Davidic Messiah would be descended from the line of the kings of Judah, an idea which is adopted by Matthew.

(*f*) The 'unknown' names between Zerubbabel and Joseph. These names have in common a biblical basis, especially from the later parts of the OT, for example Chronicles, Ezra, Nehemiah, and Job: Ἀβιούδ (אביהוד) in the OT exclusively refers to the son of Aaron, although אביהוד in I Chron. 8: 3 is an unknown Benjaminite. The name does not occur in *Corpus Papyrorum Judaicarum*, although Ἀβδιοῦς seems to have been common in the Ptolemaic period.[8] Kuhn suggests that the second part of the name in its Semitic form אביהוד, namely הוד, goes back to the הודיה of I Chron. 3: 24 who is represented also in Luke 3: 26 (Ἰωδά).[9] Matthew's sequence, according to

[1] Cf. M. Goguel, *Jesus and the Origins of Christianity* (2 vols. 1960) (Fr. or. 1932), I, 74.

[2] References in S–B, I, 14.

[3] Aggad. Ber. 63, 3 (44*b*); S–B, I, 18.

[4] Gen. R. 12: 6 (91–2); Tanch Bereshith 4*a*; and Tanch B Bereshith 18 (6*b*).

[5] Num. R. 13: 12 (523); S–B, I, 14, 19–20.

[6] pSotah 9: 16; pA.Z. 3: 1; bBer. 28*b*; cited by S–B, I, 30.

[7] pSotah 9: 16; par., bBer. 28*b*; cf. bSan. 99*a* (669).

[8] *CPJ*, III, App. II, p. 167.

[9] G. Kuhn, 'Die Geschlechtsregister Jesu bei Lukas und Matthäus nach ihrer Herkunft untersucht', *ZNW*, XXII (1923), 212, 218–19.

this suggestion, is a summary of the Chronicler's data in chapter 3.

'Ελιακίμ (אליקים) in the OT is either an alias for Jehoiakim, or a prophet of the time of Nehemiah (12: 41) or master of the house of king Hezekiah to whom God promised to give the 'key of the house of David' (Isa. 22: 19–25). There is no occurrence in *CPJ*.

'Αζώρ (עזור) in Jer. 28 [35]: 1 is the father of Hananiah the prophet at the time of Zedekiah; no occurrence in *CPJ*.

Σαδώκ (צדוק), common priestly name throughout Jewish literature; no occurrence in *CPJ*.

'Αχίμ, not in LXX; but 'Αχείμ translates אחיאם (I Chron. 11: 35) and יכין (Gen. 46: 10; I Chron. 24: 16 [17]). No recurrence in *CPJ*.

'Ελιούδ, a transliteration of אליהוא (I Chron. 12: 20 [ms. A]); cf. 'Ελίου (I Chron. 26: 7) and 'Ελιοῦς (Job 32–6); no occurrence in *CPJ*. 'Ελεάζαρ is common as son of Aaron and father of Phinehas in the main line of priests; it is used of others also in Chronicles, Ezra, and Nehemiah. 'Ελεάζαρος seems to have been in common use among Egyptian Jews during the Ptolemaic and early Roman periods; there are five occurrences in *CPJ*.[1]

Μαθθάν occurs once explicitly in the OT in Jer. 38 [45]: 1 (מתן); it occurs also in B* for Μαθθανιαν, original name of Zedekiah (II Kings 24: 17). There is no occurrence of the name in *CPJ*.

'Ιακώβ—used only of the patriarch in the OT and NT; 'James' in the NT is 'Ιάκωβος. In *CPJ* it occurs frequently: 'Ιακοῦβις four times in documents from Ptolemaic times; 'Ιάκουβος nine times in the early Roman period; 'Ιάκοβος thrice in the middle Roman period; and 'Ιακώβ twice in the late Roman period.

The names in Matt. 1: 13–15, therefore, are found in the late writings of the OT while three of the ten were used among the Jews in Egypt during NT times. The evidence does not appear to allow a definitive conclusion regarding the currency of the names in Palestine at the time of the writing of Matthew's gospel. Neither can we isolate any general characteristic of the names, although several were priests in the OT text. In short, the names remain Jewish, but otherwise unknown.

[1] III, App. II, p. 175.

(*g*) The conflicts of detail betwen Matt. 1: 1–16 and the OT data. The essential difficulties are the following:

(1) The omission of three of the four kings between Ἰωράμ and Ἰωαθάμ (verse 8). The sequence of the six kings (omitting Athaliah the queen who does not officially continue the royal line) can be tabulated according to the orthography of the MT and LXX in the following way:

	II Kings[1]		II Chron.[2]		I Chron. 3: 11–12		
	MT	LXX	MT	LXX	MT	LXX	Matt. 1:8–9
1	יהורם	Ιωραμ	יהורם	Ιωραμ	יורם	Ιωραμ	Ἰωράμ
2	אחזיהו אחזיה	Οχοζιας	אחזיהו	Οχοζιας	אחזיהו	Οχοζια Οζεια Οζιας	
3	יהואש יואש	Ιωας	יאש יואש	Ιωας	יואש	Ιωας	
4	אמציהו	Αμμεσιας	אמציהו	Αμασιας	אמציהו	Αμασιας	
5	עזריה עזיה	Αζαριας Οζιας	עזיהו	Οζιας Οχοζιας(B)	עזריה	Αζαρια Οζιας	Ὀζίας
6	יותם	Ιωαθαμ	יותם	Ιωαθαμ	יותם	Ιωαθαμ	Ἰωαθάμ

We see that there is some confusion in the text concerning the second and fifth kings in our list, caused originally by the alternative Hebrew names for the fifth king, Azariah/Uzziah. The table shows that a confusion of the two kings can scarcely be due, in Matthew, to a misreading of the Hebrew text in any of the three OT sources. Despite the confusion of the Hebrew between Azariah and Uzziah both names begin with **עז־**, Ahaziah always with **אחז־**. The confusion must stem from the Greek. But Matthew's omission occurs in no other text; hence at some point in the compilation of the Matthean genealogy kings numbers 2 and 5 in our list were identified; or, more probably, in copying the sequence from a MS. in which king number 5 was written in some form of Οζιας or even Οχοζιας (thus almost identical with the Greek of king number 2), the scribe's eye passed from Ιωραμ to Uzziah (Οζιας), or from Ahaziah (Οζιας, Οχοζιας?) to Ιωαθαμ. The chart reveals that this is a

[1] II Kings 8: 16; 8: 25; 9: 29; 12: 1; 13: 1; 14: 1; 15: 1, 13; 15: 5, 7.
[2] II Chron. 21: 1; 22: 1, 2; 24: 1; 25: 1; 26: 1; 27: 1.

possibility in I Chron. 3: 11–12, although we have insufficient information on the variants for Uzziah in verse 12. At any rate the omission was necessary for the general structuring of the genealogy, since without the omission there would be seventeen, not fourteen, kings from Solomon through Jeconiah. Did the structuring of the genealogy necessitate and determine the omission? The textual confusion in the LXX at precisely the point of the Matthean omission argues to the contrary. Then we must assume that accident was turned into virtue—that after the accidental omission the scribe discovered a second pattern of fourteens which came to determine the structure of the genealogy (verse 17).[1]

(2) The variance between 'Ασάφ and Ασα in verses 7–8 probably does not reflect a confusion between the king (usually 'Ασάφ; אסף) and the temple-singer of David in I Chron. 25: 1 ff. ('Ασάφ; אסף), but is rather a difference in orthography, the longer form being a later transliteration.

(3) The original reading 'Αμώς rather than 'Αμών in verse 10 is not due to a glance at the prophet; the same differences appear in the Greek MSS. at II Kings 21: 19–25; II Chron. 33: 21–5, with most MSS. supporting 'Αμώς.

(4) Perhaps the most difficult problem in the Matthean genealogy is the position of 'Ιεχονίας in verses 11–12. In comparison with the OT data, Matthew is deceptively simple: 'Josiah begat Jeconiah and his brothers at the time of the deportation to Babylon; after the deportation (presumably in exile) Jeconiah begat Salathiel...' The data provided by the OT, however, are more complex; there the sequence of kings is:

Josiah	640–608 B.C.
Jehoahaz	608
Eliakim (Jehoakim)	608–597
Jehoiachin (Jeconiah)	597
Zedekiah	597–586

The genealogical relationships are:

Josiah

Jehoahaz | Jehoiakim = (Eliakim) | Zedekiah | Shallum

Jehoiakim = (Eliakim) → Jehoiachin = (Jeconiah)

[1] Cf. Lambertz, 'Die Toledoth', pp. 213 f.

The difficulty is increased by the fact that, in spite of Matt. 1: 11, no brothers of Jeconiah are mentioned in the OT.[1] Possibly, whether knowingly or by misreading of the OT data, the compiler of the Matthean genealogy confused יהויקים and יהויקין, since several brothers of the former are known in the OT. It is difficult to understand why the compiler of the genealogy would have intentionally committed the error since it leaves the third group with only thirteen names and thus breaks the scheme of verse 17. Moreover, it is not at all certain that the genealogy existed originally in Hebrew or Aramaic; as we have seen above, certain signs point to a Greek original. Various explanations of this confusion have been offered. Schlatter[2] contends that the author wrote the same name twice (verse 11 and verse 12) although he knew they were two different persons. This is supported by Lohmeyer's observation that in the LXX the same name, Ιωακιμ, is used throughout for Johoiakim and Jehoiachin.[3] Klostermann[4] suggests that only one person is intended, but is counted twice since he is the turning-point of the μετοικεσία. Perhaps the most cogent argument for the old theory of an unintentional error is Vögtle's:[5] The author of the genealogy (identical with the evangelist) wrote in verse 11, 'Josiah begat Jehoiakim and his brothers', but could not continue the scheme with '*After* the deportation Jehoiakim begat Jeconiah' because he knew that Jeconiah was born considerably *prior* to the exile. So he continued, 'Jeconiah begat Salathiel...' An early copyist of the genealogy (rather than a translator) was responsible for the error of replacing Jehoiakim in verse 11 with Jeconiah. One weakness of this explanation is the lack of any manuscript evidence for an alternative reading in verse 11.

Another influence may be at work here, however. Among the Amoraic Midrashim, there is much discussion of the divine decree of Jer. 22: 30 which cursed Jeconiah to childlessness: 'Thus says the Lord, "Write this man down as childless, a man

[1] On the confused position of Zedekiah in the OT, see above, pp. 46 f. The Rabbis resorted to the niceties of exegesis in order to explain the relationships of the last kings of Judah; see pSotah 8: 3 (22*c*, 39); pShek. 6: 1 (49*d*); bHor. 11*b* (84–5); bKer. 77*b*; cf. S–B, I, 32.

[2] *Matthäus*, p. 3.

[3] *Matthäus*, p. 3.

[4] *Matthäus*, p. 6.

[5] *BZ*, IX (1965), 42–5.

who shall not succeed in his days; for none of his offspring shall succeed in sitting on the throne of David and ruling again in Judah".' The Rabbis point out that in I Chron. 3: 17 the sons of Jeconiah are listed, among them Shealtiel. Thus Jer. 22: 30 had to be explained; in general the removal of the divine decree is said to have been effected by Jeremiah's repentance.[1] Another haggadah relates the story of how the wife of Nebuchadnezzar, Shemira'am (Semiramis), persuaded the king to allow Jeconiah the company of his wife.[2]

This emphasis and also the fact that the deportation of Jeconiah is mentioned in other contexts,[3] despite the relative insignificance of his reign in the OT text, may indicate that Matthew is here aware of a Rabbinic emphasis on Jeconiah and thus brings him into prominence in the genealogy as one of the pivots of his scheme. Any dogmatic conclusion, however, is precluded by the nature of the texts, including the late date of the relevant Rabbinic passages.

(5) The statement in Matt. 1: 12, Σαλαθιὴλ δὲ ἐγέννησεν τὸν Ζοροβαβέλ, is based on the LXX of I Chron. 3: 9: καὶ υἱοὶ Σαληθιηλ· Ζοροβαβελ καὶ Σεμεϊ; the Hebrew has ובנו פדיה זרבבל ושמעי. Although the datum of the LXX at this point is supported by the Hebrew of Haggai 1: 1; Ezra 3: 2, 8, we may regard this detail as another indication of the original Greek form of the genealogy.

(*h*) The allusion to Mary. It is customary to speak of the impossibility of reconciling the aim of a genealogy using the verb ἐγέννησεν with the 'Dogma der Theogonie'[4] which immediately follows the genealogy; thus it is commonly assumed that Matt. 1: 1–17 could not have been written by the author of 1: 18 f. As the text now stands, only one alternative reading is different *in essential meaning* from the Nestle text, namely that of the Sinaitic Syriac, which presumes the following Greek text: Ἰωσὴφ δέ, ᾧ ἐμνηστεύθη παρθένος Μαρία, ἐγέννησεν Ἰησοῦν

[1] Lev. R. 10: 5 (128); par. Lam. R. on 8: 6; Pesik. 162*b*; cited by S–B, I, 33–4. See also S.S.R. 7: 14. 1 (301); 8: 6. 2 (306); bSan. 37*b*.

[2] Lev. R. 19: 6 (248–9).

[3] S–B, I, 32–5, cite pShek. 6: 3 (50*a*, 45); Lev. R. 19 (248); bSan. 37*b*; Pesik. 163*b*.

[4] Lambertz, 'Die Toledoth', p. 215; also Hahn, *Christologische Hoheitstitel*, pp. 242 ff.

τ. λ. Χ.[1] If this reading be adopted as the original, it is difficult to ascribe it to the author of 1: 18 ff., but almost as difficult to explain how an editor could have used it from another source immediately before the account of Mary's conception. The best explanation for origin of the Sy^{syr} reading is still that of Burkitt:[2] it is derived from the reading of the Ferrar group, namely Ἰακὼβ δὲ ἐγέννησεν τὸν Ἰωσήφ, ᾧ μνηστευθεῖσα παρθένος Μαριὰμ ἐγέννησεν Ἰησοῦν τ. λ. Χ. The translator took ᾧ to refer to ἐγέννησεν as well as μνηστευθεῖσα whereas in the Greek the subject of ἐγέννησεν is Μαριάμ, similar to Luke 1: 13, ἡ γυνή σου Ἐλισάβετ γεννήσει υἱόν. The origin of such a discrepancy as exists in Syr^{s} can be attributed more easily to a translator than to an author who is using various materials for his own theological purpose.

A Rabbinic reader would perhaps find little difficulty in the Nestle text of Matt. 1: 16.[3] The verse shows that, for the author, Jesus is recognized as the son of Joseph through Joseph's marriage with Mary, and so also he is the 'son of David' in 1: 1. S–B refer to the custom recorded in mB.B. 8: 6 (378): 'If a man says, "This is my son", he may be believed', that is, he is accounted to him as heir without further ado.[4] Thus the verse forms at once a fitting culmination of the genealogy and an introduction to the following account of the conception of Mary.

Of course, it is one thing to assert the possibility of placing the genealogy in juxtaposition with the virgin birth story (this is after all a fact in chapter 1), and quite another to identify the reason for doing so. Two recent attempts may be noted: (1) W. D. Davies suggests that the two Matthean pericopes are related to the two versions of the creation story in Gen. 1–2.[5] Among other details, he finds hints of a parallel between the 'catalogic account of the stages of the process of creation which culminates in man' in the priestly creation account (Gen. 1) and the 'catalogic account of Jesus' ancestors culminating in

[1] For a discussion of the textual variants, see esp. F. C. Burkitt, *Evangelion da Mepharreshe*, 1904, II, 262–6; Zahn, *Introduction*, II, 565–7; McNeile, *Matthew*, pp. 4–5; *et al.*

[2] *Ev. da Meph.* II, 262–3.

[3] One might compare the remarks of S. Schechter on the opening section of Matthew's gospel in *Studies in Judaism* (1958) (2nd and 3rd series, or. 1908–24), pp. 56 f.

[4] S–B, I, 35.

[5] *Setting*, pp. 70 ff.

him' in the Matthean genealogy. Matt. 1: 18–25, by the same token, is a more concentrated treatment of the way in which Jesus came into being, corresponding to the second account of creation. The common motif in both Matthean pericopes is that of Jesus Christ as the New Creation. (2) H. Milton suggests that the juxtaposition of genealogy and birth story is deliberately intended 'to confront the reader with a paradox, in the ancient sense of a marvel or wonder... By this structuring of the two pericopes a paradoxical Christology is presented which denies any attempt to reduce Jesus to a mere inspired prophet, or to a pagan demigod, or to a phantom... '[1] This view involves the assumption that there is an anti-gnostic element in the birth narrative, as had been suggested by Bacon. (3) On pp. 224–8 below, I offer the tentative suggestion that the two pericopes are related by serving as midrashim on those two titles which Matthew could ascribe to Jesus at the moment of his birth, namely Son of David and Son of God. It is possible that the occasion for the juxtaposition of these midrashim was the observance of the two titles, Christ and Son of God, in the first verse of Mark.

(*i*) Summary. We have found indications of the author's use of the Greek OT rather than the Hebrew: the omission of the three kings cannot be explained from the Hebrew; and the Greek text of I Chron. 3: 19 names Shealtiel as father of Zerubbabel while the Hebrew has Pedaiah.[2] Similarly, the '*biblos geneseos*' of 1: 1 probably reflects an awareness of the LXX reading at Gen. 2: 4*a* and 5: 1. But the genealogy in its details shows awareness of developments within the Rabbinic tradition in centering the attention on Abraham and David, and especially in its allusions to the four women which can best

[1] *JBL*, LXXXI (1962), 177–8. On the anti-gnosticizing element in the birth narrative, see B. W. Bacon, *Studies in Matthew* (1930), pp. 148–50.

[2] This conclusion (that the genealogy betrays a use of the Greek OT) should be compared with the analysis of the language of OT citations in Matthew by Bacon, pp. 134–8, 470–7: the author (Bacon's 'redactor') was a converted Rabbi who preferred to use Greek, although he was also at home in Aramaic or, possibly, Hebrew; as a rule OT citations are from the Greek OT ('ninety per cent leave no doubt regarding their source as between Hebrew and Greek text' (p. 470)). Bacon relies on the analysis of Allen, *Matthew*, pp. lxi–lxii. On Stendahl's analysis of the OT citations, see below, pp. 214 ff.

be explained as being derived from scribal polemics. There need be no conflict or tension between the author's use of Greek and his knowledge of Rabbinic theology. It is well known that knowledge of Greek was common even among Aramaic-speaking peasants in Palestine, and especially among the upper and middle classes, including Palestinian Rabbis.[1] In the Mishnah there are references to the inscription of Greek letters on the baskets for Terumah;[2] similarly, the Greek language was considered by R. Simeon b. Gamaliel (*c.* 140) to be second only to Hebrew as a fitting language for the books of Scripture:

The Books [of Scripture] differ from phylacteries and *Mezuzahs* only in that the Books may be written in any language, while phylacteries and *Mezuzahs* may be written in the Assyrian writing only [i.e. in Hebrew with the 'square' characters]. Rabban Simeon b. Gamaliel says: The Books, too, they have only permitted to be written in Greek.[3]

The use of Greek is revealed in a negative way by the prohibition against its study in mSot. 9: 14 (305; anonymous):

During the war of Vespasian [A.D. 66–70] they forbade the crowns of the bridegrooms and the [wedding] drum. During the war of Titus [A.D. 70; variant, 'Quietus', governor of Judea in A.D. 117] they forbade the crowns of the brides and that a man should teach his son Greek. In the last war [of Bar Kokba, A.D. 132–5] they forbade the bride to go forth in a litter inside the city.

The Gemara on this Mishnah is more instructive and is here quoted in full:

'And that nobody should teach his son Greek.' Our Rabbis taught [i.e. an old source]: When the kings of the Hasmonean house fought one another, Hyrcanus was outside and Aristobulus within. Each day they used to let down *denarii* in a basket, and haul up for them [animals for] the continual offerings. An old man there [in Jerusalem] who was learned in Greek wisdom, spoke with them [the besiegers]

[1] Saul Liebermann, *Greek in Jewish Palestine* (1942), pp. 1, 15–18. That a sharp distinction cannot always be made between Rabbinic and Hellenistic Judaism is shown also by E. J. Bickermann, 'Symbolism in the Dura Synagogue: A Review Article', *HTR*, LVIII (1965), 127–51. W. D. Davies had previously presented forceful arguments for the same conclusion (*Paul*, pp. 4 ff.).

[2] mShek. 3: 2 (154–5); see also mMen. 6: 3 (499).

[3] mMeg. 1: 8 (202); cf. mGitt. 9: 6, 8 (320).

in Greek [so that the people in the city would not understand], saying, 'As long as they carry on the Temple-service they will never surrender to you'. On the morrow they let down *denarii* in a basket and hauled up a pig. When it reached half way up the wall, it stuck its claws [into the wall] and the land of Israel was shaken over a distance of four hundred parasangs. At that time they declared, 'Cursed be a man who rears pigs and cursed be a man who teaches his son Greek wisdom!' Concerning that year we learnt that it happened that the '*omer* had to be supplied from the gardens of Zarifim and the two loaves from the valley of En-Soker. But it is not so! For Rabbi [second century] said: Why use the Syrian language in the land of Israel? Either use the holy tongue or Greek! And R. Joseph said: Why use the Syrian language in Babylon? Either use the holy tongue or Persian!—The Greek language and Greek wisdom are distinct [the language is permitted but not the wisdom]. But is Greek philosophy forbidden? Behold, Rab Judah declared that Samuel said in the name of Rabban Simeon b. Gamaliel [I, *c*. A.D. 70; II, *c*. A.D. 140], What means that which is written, 'Mine eye affected my soul, because of all the daughters of my city'? [Lam. 3: 51]. There were a thousand pupils in my father's house; five hundred studied the Torah and five hundred studied Greek wisdom, and of these there remained only I here and the son of my father's brother in Assia! It was different with the household of Rabban Gamaliel [I, *c*. A.D. 40; II, *c*. A.D. 100) because they had close associations with the Government...They permitted the household of Rabban Gamaliel to study Greek wisdom because they had close associations with the Government.[1]

This tradition agrees with the previous citation of mMeg. 1: 8 in ascribing a fondness of Greek to Simeon b. Gamaliel. Liebermann considers bSot. 49*b* to be 'first-hand evidence that an academy of Greek wisdom existed in Jewish Palestine under the auspices of the Patriarch' at the turn of the second century A.D.[2]

Another indication of the knowledge of Greek among the Rabbis is pMeg. 1: 11 (71*c*):

Rabban Simeon b. Gamaliel [I, *c*. A.D. 70; II, *c*. A.D. 140] said: ...It was investigated and found that the Tora could not be perfectly translated except in Greek...R. Jeremiah [*c*. 300] in the name of R. Hiyya b. Abba [third century] said: Aquila the Proselyte presented his translation of the Tora before R. Eliezer [*c*. A.D. 80–

[1] bSot. 49*b* (268–70); par. Josephus, *Ant*. XIV. 2. 2.

[2] *Greek*, pp. 1, 20.

120] and R. Joshua [*c.* 80–120] and they praised him and said to him: 'Thou art fairer than the children of men' [Ps. 45: 3].[1]

Thus we have clear evidence that at the probable time of the composition of Matthew [*c.* A.D. 80–100] Greek was known and studied by Rabbis in the line of Hillel. It is necessary only to add to Liebermann's discussion that Paul and Josephus, both Pharisees, could write fluent and compelling Greek. This use of both Aramaic and Greek by Palestinian Rabbis was pointed out already by A. Schlatter.[2]

Thus the evidence from details of the text points toward an author converted from Judaism who addressed himself to those groups within Judaism (and Christianity) who shared the expectation of the Davidic Messiah to the exclusion of other concepts, chief of which was the hope for a priestly Messiah. The genealogy was written, after A.D. 70, to show that this expectation had been fulfilled, and that the Messianic age had been—or was about to be—inaugurated by the Davidic Messiah.

2. *Evidence from the structure of Matthew 1: 2–17*

We have seen that the details of Matt. 1: 1–17 reveal a close knowledge of both the OT and also current Rabbinic biblical interpretation. It is possible, moreover, that the close parallels between post-biblical structuring of history and the overall design of Matthew's genealogy can be fruitfully explored in an attempt to understand the thought-forms of both the readers and the author of the genealogy. That this structure in the Matthean genealogy is not due to mere chance should be obvious from the conclusion to the genealogy in verse 17: Πᾶσαι οὖν αἱ γενεαὶ ἀπὸ Ἀβραὰμ ἕως Δαυὶδ γενεαὶ δεκατέσσαρες, καὶ ἀπὸ Δαυὶδ ἕως τῆς μετοικεσίας Βαβυλῶνος γενεαὶ δεκατέσσαρες, καὶ ἀπὸ τῆς μετοικεσίας Βαβυλῶνος ἕως τοῦ Χριστοῦ γενεαὶ δεκατέσσαρες. The conjunction οὖν indicates that verse 17 has the function of showing the logical conclusion of the whole genealogy.

We have here a structuring of Israelitic history (beginning

[1] Liebermann, pp. 17–18.

[2] *Der Evangelist Matthäus, ad rem*; cited by Bacon, *Matthew*, pp. 496–7. (The same information is provided in Schlatter's later edition.)

with Abraham)[1] according to three groups of fourteen 'generations' (γενεαί) each, with four pivotal events marking the limits of the groups, namely Abraham, David 'the King', the deportation to Babylon, and Ἰησοῦς ὁ λεγόμενος Χριστός. Is this periodization of history a *de novo* creation of the author of the genealogy, or is it an adaptation of similar reconstructions of which he was aware? We turn to an examination of its possible background.

(*a*) It has been suggested that the background of this construction is to be found in the genealogical tradition of the OT which is dominated by the basic conception that God alone governs history and orders the generations to a final goal.[2] Vögtle alludes to the 'special conception, attested since the book of Daniel, that the sovereign will of God is manifested in a secret, established numerical periodization of world-events'. In this periodization the number seven and its multiples play an important role, for example in the seventy year-weeks of Dan. 9: 1–27 and the 'ten week apocalypse' of I Enoch 91, 93. Finally, Vögtle alludes to the tendency in the OT generally towards a *heilsgeschichtlich* interpretation of events and epochs, evidenced by 'the numerical scheme' of Gen. 5 and 11, and the multiples of seven in the genealogies of Chronicles.[3]

There is one close parallel to Matthew's structure in the OT which, to my knowledge, has not been pointed out. That is the genealogy of the High Priest in I Chron. 5: 27–41 (ET, 6: 1–15).[4] Here there is a list of twenty-three priests from Aaron up to the exile, the list being divided into two equal parts by the mention of the beginning of the cultus in Solomon's temple, and ending with a reference to the exile. Thus the number of members in the genealogical chain is symmetrical, and the list is divided into

[1] It was more common, even in Jewish sources, to include also the pre-Abrahamitic period in such arrangements of history into epochs.

[2] So, most recently, Vögtle, *BZ*, IX (1965), pp. 36–8; also Lagrange, *Matthieu*, pp. 2 f.; P. Benoit, *L'Évangile selon St Matthieu* (1950), p. 41; J. Schmid, *Matthäus*, pp. 33–4.

[3] Neither of these points is explained or developed by Vögtle. Actually, it is the number six and its double that are prominent in the tribal genealogies (see above, pp. 24 f.), while number seven is inconspicuous in genealogies apart from the Chronicler (possibly excepting Aaron and Moses being the seventh from Abraham, and Enoch the seventh from Adam).

[4] See above, pp. 45–8, esp. p. 47.

epochs by certain pivotal events, as in Matt. 1: 2–17. Such schematizations in the OT with the accompanying fondness for certain numbers and their multiples are important as forming the general background which made such reconstructions as the Matthean genealogy meaningful.

The Rabbinic tradition, also, shows an awareness of the significance of numbers of generations. Particularly relevant is an anonymous passage from Num. R. 7: 15 (on Num. 13: 14 (529, 530–1)):

'One golden disk of ten shekels' was to symbolize the ten generations from Perez to David...'One young bull' symbolizes Abraham who was the root of the genealogical tree...'Five rams, five male goats, and five male lambs a year old'—this makes a total of fifteen kings who succeeded each other from Rehoboam to Zedekiah, as kings the sons of kings, some of them absolutely righteous, others middling, and others absolutely wicked.

The same interest can be seen in a saying emanating from the third century A.D.:

'He hath remembered His covenant forever, the word which He commanded to the thousandth generation' [Ps. 105: 8]. R. Levi [P, 3; third century] said in the name of R. Samuel b. Naḥmani [P, 3; third century]: Nine hundred and seventy-four generations which were to have descended from the people of the generation that perished in the flood were wiped out with them. The Holy One, blessed be He, had intended that the Torah be given to the thousandth generation of mankind, but you can count only ten generations from Adam to Noah, ten from Noah to Abraham, and six from Abraham to Moses. Hence it is said, 'the word which He commanded to the thousandth generation', 'the word' being the Torah, of which it is said 'And God spoke all these words' [Exod. 20: 1].[1]

The Rabbinic tradition, like the OT, reveals patterns of thought within which the genealogy could have been written and understood. But can we find a more specific parallel to the 3×14 scheme?[2]

[1] Mid. Ps. 105: 3 (II, 181).

[2] Heer (*Die Stammbäume Jesu* (see n. 5, p. 143 above), pp. 113–15) mentions, but rejects, two further OT parallels: (1) In the Hebrew text of I Kings 8: 65 it is said that Solomon held a feast in celebration of the dedication of the temple 'seven days and seven days, fourteen days'. (2) It has been suggested that the forty-two names in Matthew are intended to

(*b*) According to a commonly accepted view, the figure fourteen was reached by gematria, that is, the sum of the numerical value of the letters in the name דוד ($4+6+4 = 14$), proving Jesus to be the 'thrice-Davidic Son of David'. This suggestion was first advanced by Gfrörer[1] and is accepted by G. Box,[2] J. Jeremias,[3] R. T. Hood,[4] A. W. Argyle,[5] B. H. Throckmorton,[6] J. M. Heer,[7] and others.[8] It will be noted that this use of gematria cannot be based on the Greek form of the name David[9] and, consequently, one must, on accepting the theory of gematria, assume either that the genealogy or its prototype was at some point written in Hebrew or Aramaic, or that a bilingual author was aware of the numerical value of the Hebrew/Aramaic name דוד and compiled the genealogy in Greek. But we have found embedded within the genealogy at several points a dependence on the Greek OT which strongly points away from an Aramaic or Hebrew original.[10] And on the second assumption it is difficult to see how the point of the gematria would be grasped by readers who did not know Aramaic or Hebrew, even though the theory of a Greek original does not necessarily preclude Jewish-Christian readers. Yet, as W. D. Davies points out,[11] gematria does occur in at least two

recall the forty-two years of wandering in the wilderness after the exodus. Origen and Jerome, representing the exegesis of the Alexandrian school, point out that the forty-two years of wanderings were ended by Joshua (who is, in the LXX, consistently Ἰησους), who led his people into the promised land. Although the view of Jesus as the new Joshua is found in the early fathers (see Justin, *Dial.* 113), this explanation is fanciful at best since in the NT Joshua is not a prominent figure, being mentioned only in Acts 7: 45 and Heb. 4: 8; moreover, there is no hint of any division of the forty-two years into three periods.

[1] Davies, *Setting*, p. 74.

[2] 'The Gospel Narratives of the Nativity and the Alleged Influences of Heathen Ideas', *ZNW*, VI (1905), 80 f.; *Virgin Birth, ad rem.*

[3] *Jerusalem*, p. 326.

[4] 'The Genealogies of Jesus', in *Early Christian Origins*, ed. A. Wikgren (1961), p. 10.

[5] *The Gospel According to Matthew* (1963), p. 24.

[6] 'Genealogy (Christ)', *IDB*, II, 365.

[7] *Die Stammbäume Jesu*, pp. 122–5.

[8] Cf. Vögtle, *BZ*, IX (1965), 36.

[9] The numerical value of the various Greek transliterations of the name would be: Δαβιδ, 21; Δαυειδ, 424; Δαυιδ, 419.

[10] See above, pp. 186 f.

[11] *Setting*, p. 75.

Greek documents, namely the NT Apocalypse and the Sibylline Oracles. In *Sib. Or.* I. 324 ff., the gematria involves the numerical value of *Greek* letters (also *Sib. Or.* V. 12, 14, 21, 24, 25, 28, 38, 40); in Rev. 13: 18, however, the gematria may be based on the *Hebrew* transliteration of the Greek, Νέρων Καῖσαρ.[1] If the latter hypothesis be accepted, we have a close parallel with the suggestion of gematria in Matt. 1: 1–17, since this, too, would involve a calculation based on the numerical value of a *Hebrew* name occurring in a *Greek* transliteration. It is difficult to set forth convincing arguments on either side of this question; perhaps it is best with Lagrange[2] to consider the possibility of gematria as a 'coincidence' that gave secondary support to the author's structuring of the genealogy, and to find the primary significance of the three fourteens elsewhere.

(*c*) Heer[3] raises the possibility that the clue to the lists in Matthew and Luke is to be found in the total number of members, namely forty-two in Matthew (according to verse 17, but not in the present text of verses 2–16) and seventy-two in the original text of Luke (while the present text includes seventy-seven, a reconstruction based on variant readings resulting in seventy-two names is commonly suggested). He refers to Bacher's discussion of the cabalistic speculation on the number of letters in the divine names in later Judaism,[4] in which the numbers 42 and 72 again are important. But, as Heer points out, it is extremely doubtful whether this speculation was at all current in the first century; much more probably, reflection led from the biblical tetragrammaton to a pre-Christian 'dodekagrammaton' to a name of forty-two letters and thence to the final seventy-two letters. The parallel has little to recommend it as relevant to the study of Matthew's genealogy.

(*d*) The origin of the Messianic value of the number fourteen in a survey of holy history is found in the 'Messiah Apocalypse' of II Baruch 53–74, where world history 'from creation to consummation' is divided into fourteen epochs symbolized as a vision of thirteen alternations between black and bright waters

1 Cf. Martin Rist, *Revelation*, IB, XII, 466 f.

2 *Matthieu*, p. 3.

3 *Die Stammbäume Jesu*, pp. 115–19.

4 *Die Agada der babylonischen Amoräer* (1878), pp. 17–19; Heer, p. 115.

followed by the Messianic age, symbolized by lightning.[1] The first twelve waters are considered to be historical events or persons, while the last two are the action of God: number thirteen is the apocalyptic tribulation; number fourteen the Messiah's appearance. The epochs according to this scheme are the following ('black waters' are the odd numbers; 'bright' the even):

1. The fall of Adam (56: 5).
2. Abraham and his descendants (57).
3. Slavery in Egypt (58).
4. Moses, Aaron, Miriam, Joshua, Caleb, the exodus (59).
5. The works of the Amorites during the time of the Judges (60).
6. David and Solomon; the temple (61).
7. Jeroboam; division of the kingdom (62).
8. Hezekiah (63).
9. Manasseh (64–5).
10. Josiah (66).
11. The exile (67).
12. The rebuilding of Zion (68).
13. The apocalyptic tribulations (69–71).
14. The Messianic age (72–4).

According to Charles, this apocalyptic section must have been written before A.D. 70 since Jerusalem is still standing;[2] hence it is contemporaneous with the author of Matthew and, as a structuring of pre-Messianic history, is an important parallel with the periodization of Israelitic history in the Matthean genealogy. But the differences between the two are clear: the apocalypse has *one* group of fourteen which is not formally governed by genealogical succession. Moreover, there is included here also the pre-Abrahamitic history of the OT, as is explicitly intended (56: 2). Perhaps the major difference is the peculiar arrangement of the apocalypse whereby OT history is seen as a continuous alternation between good and evil, 'deceit' and 'truth' (56: 2*b*), 'black waters' and 'bright waters'. But the significance of this reconstruction is that it testifies to the existence of a Jewish Messianic tradition contemporaneous with

[1] This parallel was noted by Leo Wohleb; cf. Heer, p. 120.

[2] *A & P*, II, 475; based on 68: 5, 6 (see Charles on 68: 6; p. 517).

Matthew in which the number fourteen has structural significance.[1]

(*e*) What Heer sets forth as the most convincing parallel to the structure of Matt. 1: 2–17 is a Rabbinic tradition on the three sacrifices of Balak and Balaam in Num. 23.[2] According to the word of Yahweh, Balaam three times commanded Balak, king of Moab, to build seven altars on which were offered seven bulls and seven rams. In the Talmud it is noted that the total number of offerings was forty-two and that these sacrifices made Balak worthy of becoming an ancestor of Ruth:

Rab Judah [d. 299] said in Rab's name [d. 247]: One should always occupy himself with Torah and good deeds, though it be not for their own sake, for out of good work misapplied in purpose there comes [the desire to do it] for its own sake. For as a reward for the forty-two sacrifices offered up by Balak, he was privileged that Ruth should be his descendant, [as] R. Jose b. Hana [*c.* 270] said: Ruth was the daughter of Eglon, the grandson of Balak, king of Moab.[3]

Here we have not only the total number forty-two, but also the components of three fourteens. Moreover, Balak's deed results in his becoming an ancestor of the Messiah. But the analogy is unconvincing because the Messianic aspect is not emphasized and this haggadic tradition is rather late.

(*f*) Another parallel drawn from apocalyptic sources[4] that has been supported by several scholars[5] is that of S–B, namely the 'Ten-week apocalypse' of I Enoch 93, 91.[6] The text of chapters 91 and 93 shows definite signs of transposition since the

[1] It is unconvincing when S–B, IV (Excursus 30, 'Vorzeichen und Berechnung der messianischen Zeit'), p. 987, classify this apocalypse as an example of the division of the world history into *twelve* periods; twelve waters are mentioned prior to the thirteenth of tribulation and the final Messianic age.

[2] Pp. 121–2.

[3] bSan. 105*b* (719); par. bHor. 10*b* (75); see also bSotah 47*a*.

[4] The suggestion of M. J. Moreton (*TU*, LXXXVII (1964), 223) that the number forty-two is intended to correspond to the forty-two months (three and one-half 'times') of Dan. 12: 7, and thus to announce the apocalyptic fulfillment in Jesus, does not take into account the fact that the Matthean genealogy places the emphasis on 3 × 14 rather than on the number 42.

[5] Esp. Karl Bornhäuser, *Geburts- und Kindheitsgeschichte*, pp. 16–20; criticisms of this par. in Lambertz, 'Die Toledoth', pp. 218 ff.; Jeremias, *Jerusalem*, p. 326 n. 138.

[6] S–B, I, 44–5.

first seven weeks are found in chapter 93 while the last three are in chapter 91. According to the reconstruction of S–B, there were, in the original text, three periods of pre-Abrahamitic history, and seven of Israelitic history, the characteristic mark of each week being:

1. Enoch.
2. The flood, Noah, and the Noachian commandments.
3. Abraham (placed at the end of the week).
4. The Mosaic Law.
5. The building of the temple.
6. Idolatry of the nation.
7. The destruction of the temple at the exile.
8. The return from exile.
9. The Period of the Sword and the building of the Messianic temple.
10. The Messianic age.

S–B assume from the reference to Enoch as 'born the seventh in the first week' (93: 3) that each week was composed of seven 'days' or generations. Thus the parallel with Matthew is drawn: from Isaac to Solomon (weeks 4–5) fourteen generations pass; from Solomon to the exile the same (weeks 6–7); and, after another fourteen generations (weeks 8–9), the Messianic age is inaugurated. Assuming the correctness of this reconstruction, one finds a rather close parallel with the list in Matthew and one which, in all probability, antedated the composition of Matthew: Israelitic history is structured with three fourteens from Isaac to the in-breaking of the Messianic age.

But there are several uncertainties here. It is not explicit in the text of I Enoch that each week was considered to encompass precisely seven generations; even assuming that it was, there is no emphasis on the number fourteen, as in Matthew. Again, the building of the temple under Solomon appears to be a pivotal event in the apocalypse, while the corresponding pivot in Matthew is David, 'the King', a significant variation. One other objection, raised by Vögtle,[1] that the apocalypse places Abraham at the end of the last week of world history rather than at the beginning of the first week of Israelitic history (as in Matthew), can be explained as an illustration of the general structure of the apocalypse in which each pivotal figure or event

[1] *BZ*, IX (1965), 35.

appears at the end of his respective week.[1] But, most importantly, it must be remembered that the reconstruction of the 'original' apocalypse by S-B can be called into question. The text, as it stands, is comprehensible when seen as allotting seven weeks to world history, including four weeks of Israelitic history, and three weeks to eschatological events, namely (*a*) the purification of Israel (eighth week, 91: 12–13), (*b*) the judgment of the nations by the Messiah (ninth week, 91: 14), and (*c*) the Messianic age in which the angels are judged (tenth week, 91: 15) followed by the eschaton in which 'there will be many weeks without number for ever and all shall be goodness and righteousness, and sin shall no more be mentioned for ever' (91: 17). Thus, as the text stands in Charles's edition, the timetable of the end is closely akin to general Jewish Messianic expectations.

As a parallel with Matt. 1, however, the apocalypse of weeks is highly significant, since it is a Messianic periodization of history which antedated Matthew. There is no good reason to suppose that a Christian author, acquainted with apocalyptic speculation, should have slavishly adopted any one system; the meaning of the periodization of Matt. 1 would be easily understood by those to whom such systems were no novelty.[2]

(*g*) An instructive parallel from a post-Christian source is an anonymous haggadic passage in Ex. R. 15: 26 (196–8; on Ex. 12: 2) in which the generations from Abraham to the exile are divided into two equal parts according to the pattern of the phases of the moon:[3]

[1] Thus there is no contradiction (assumed by Vögtle, *BZ*, IX (1965), 35) between the apocalypse and the coming of the Messiah in Matthew where Jesus is the last member of the third group, corresponding to the ninth world-week in Enoch, the Messianic age following.

[2] One will also find the tenfold division of history in *Sib. Or.* 4. 47–86 and in the Ethiopic text of 4 Ezra 14: 11 f.; cf. S–B, IV, 987–9. For suggestions on the relation of I Enoch 93, 91 to other Jewish apocalyptic expectations, see Chaim Kaplan, 'Some NT Problems in the Light of Rabbinics and the Pseudepigrapha: the Generation Schemes in Matt. 1: 1–17, Luke 3: 24 ff.', *Bibliotheca Sacra*, LXXXVII (1930), 465–71.

[3] Par.: Pes. Kah. 53*a*; Pes. R. 76*b*; Lekah Tob 1: 48–9; Zohar II: 144*b*, cited by Kaplan, p. 466, who notes that all these assume the thirty-day lunar month as a parallel with the thirty generations from Abraham to the destruction of the temple. This passage was adduced as a parallel by S–B, I, on Matt. 1: 17 and is the basic presupposition of the interpretation of the Matthean genealogy in K. Bornhäuser, *Geburts- und Kindheitsgeschichte*, pp. 6 ff. See also

Another interpretation of 'this month shall be unto you' [Exod. 12: 2]. It is written: 'In his days let the righteous flourish, and abundance of peace, till the moon be no more' [Ps. 72: 7]. Even before God brought Israel out of Egypt, He intimated to them that royalty would last for them only until the end of thirty generations, for it says: 'This month shall be unto you the beginning of months'; just as the month has thirty days, so shall your kingdom last until thirty generations. The moon begins to shine on the first of Nisan and goes on shining till the fifteenth day, when her disc becomes full; from the fifteenth to the thirtieth day, her light wanes, till on the thirtieth it is not seen at all. With Israel too, there were fifteen generations from Abraham to Solomon. Abraham began to shine, for it says: 'Who hath raised up one from the east, at whose steps victory attendeth' [Isa. 41: 2]. Isaac also shone, for it says: 'Light is sown for the righteous' [Ps. 97: 11]. Jacob added to this light, for it says: 'And the light of Israel shall be for a fire' [Isa. 10: 17], and after them came Judah, Perez, Hezron, Ram, Amminadab, Nahshon, Salmon, Boaz, Obed, Jesse, David. When Solomon appeared the moon's disc was full, for it says: 'And Solomon sat upon the throne of the Lord as king' [I Chron. 29: 23]. Is it then possible for man to sit on the throne of God, of which it says: 'His throne was a flame of fire' [Dan. 7: 9]?...God made six heavens and resides in the seventh, and of the throne of Solomon we read: 'There were six steps to the throne' [I Kings 10: 19], while he himself sat on the seventh—thus the disc of the moon was at its fullest. Henceforth the kings began to diminish in power. 'And Solomon's son was Rehoboam; Abijah his son, Asa his son, Jehoshaphat his son, Joram his son, Ahaziah his son, Joash his son, Amaziah his son, Azariah his son, Jothan his son, Ahaz his son, Hezekiah his son, Manasseh his son; Amon his son, Josiah his son...and the sons of Jehoiakim: Jeconiah his son, Zedekiah his son' [I Chron. 3: 10–16]. With Zedekiah, of whom it is written: 'Moreover he put out Zedekiah's eyes' [Jer. 29: 7], the light of the moon failed entirely. All those years, although Israel sinned, the patriarchs prayed for them and made peace between them and God, as it says: 'Let the mountains bear peace to the people' [Ps. 72: 3], and 'mountains' refers to the patriarchs, for it says: 'Hear, O ye mountains, the Lord's controversy' [Mic. 6: 2].

the discussion by W. D. Davies, *Setting*, pp. 72 n. 2, 76 f. According to A. Finkel, *The Pharisees and the Teacher of Nazareth*, p. 104 n. 1, this parallel was already recognized by N. Krochmal, *More Nebokhe Hazeman*, ed. Zunz (Lemberg, 1863), p. 48. Finkel accepts this parallel as the clue to the Matthean structure and so also, apparently, J. Mann, *The Bible as Read and Preached in the Old Synagogue* (Cincinnati, 1940), Hebrew section, p. 200 (cited by Finkel, p. 104).

Till when did the patriarchs pray for them? Till Zedekiah lost his sight and the temple was destroyed..., that is, till [nothing remained of] the thirty generations during which Israel enjoyed a kingdom. Who makes peace for Israel since then? The Lord; for it says: 'The Lord lift up his countenance upon thee, and give thee peace' [Num. 6: 26].

The notion underlying such expositions as this is that the moon is symbolic of the fortunes of the Jewish nation, an idea traced by Kaplan to Ps. 89, in which the perpetuity of the Davidic line is a central notion:

> Once for all I have sworn by my holiness;
>   I will not lie to David.
> His line shall endure forever,
>   his throne as long as the sun before me.
> Like the moon it shall be established for ever;
>   it shall stand firm while the skies endure.[1]

According to the midrash cited, Abraham marked the beginning of the waxing of the moon; the climax came not, as in Matthew, with David, but with Solomon, after whom the moon began to wane until its light was extinguished when Zedekiah was made blind by the Babylonians.[2] The basis of this calculation was the lunar month, which, according to ancient Jewish reckoning, probably alternated between twenty-nine and thirty days.[3]

One can understand the possibility of a connection between Ps. 89: 38 [37] and a periodization of the Davidic line: Like the moon, the fortunes of the house of David will wax and wane, yet endure forever. So it is possible that Matthew, writing to demonstrate the fulfillment of the Davidic covenant, summarized Jewish history according to the phases of the moon, David and the Messiah being symbolized by the full moon. But there is one obstacle to this parallel. There is no direct evidence

[1] Ps. 89: 36–8 [ET, 35–7].

[2] Note that in the citation from Ex. R. there are actually eighteen kings named, even though the author explicitly states that he has thirty generations, fifteen from Abraham to Solomon and fifteen from Rehoboam to the exile. Since Jehoiakim is omitted in the Rabbinic texts (Kaplan, p. 466 n. 3), it must be inferred that Josiah was considered to have closed the second group.

[3] The lunar year included 354 days in 12 months; cf. Schürer, *Geschichte* (5th ed.), I, 745–60, J. van Goudoever, *Biblical Calendars* (2nd ed. 1961), p. 4 *et passim*; based on I Enoch 78: 15–16.

for the conception of a *lunar month of twenty-eight days* in ancient Judaism,[1] as would be necessary for the validity of the parallel between Ex. R. and Matt. I. Therefore it is best to regard the Rabbinic passage as typical of a general thought-pattern of the day rather than as being related more directly to Matt. I.

(*h*) A. Schlatter[2] and J. H. Ropes[3] suggest that the Rabbinic background of the Matthean genealogy consists in the fact that three fourteens are actually three times the seventy weeks of years (490 years) of Daniel. Thus, for each generation exactly thirty-five years would be allotted ($14 \times 35 = 490$). S–B allude to the Rabbinic parallels.[4]

(*i*) Another parallel to the sevenfold division of Israelitic history in Matt. I: I–17 may be found in the eschatological Rabbinic speculations in which the duration of the present world is patterned after the week of creation, namely seven 'days' of one thousand years each, based on Ps. 90: 4, 'A thousand years in thy sight are but as yesterday when it is passed'.[5] According to the most common reckoning, the first two millennia are the Torah-less age; the third and fourth are the age of the Torah; the fifth and sixth the Messianic age; while the seventh is the world Sabbath and belongs to God. After this creation-Sabbath comes the עולם הבא, the age to come. The earliest source for this schematization is II Enoch (Slavonic Enoch, dated by Charles *c.* A.D. I–50) 33: I–2, where God shows Enoch the duration of this world:

And I appointed the eighth day also, that the eighth day should be the first-created after my work, and that the first seven revolve in the form of the seventh thousand, and that at the beginning of the

[1] In I Enoch 73: 5–7 the moon itself is divided into fourteen parts but the duration of its increase and decrease seems to alternate between fourteen and fifteen days (hence months of twenty-nine or thirty days); Kaplan points out (p. 467) that the Babylonians celebrated their Sabbath on the 7th, 14th, 21st, and 28th days of the month. One possible resolution of this difficulty is that Matthew assumes a solar year of the customary 364 days (as in I Enoch and Jubilees), but divided into equal months, namely thirteen months of twenty-eight days each.

[2] *Matthäus*, p. 7.

[3] *The Synoptic Gospels* (1934), pp. 46–7.

[4] IV, 996–1011.

[5] From II Pet. 3: 8 we can infer that this verse was considered meaningful in Christian apocalyptic expectation as well as Rabbinic.

eighth thousand there should be a time of not-counting, endless, with neither years nor months nor weeks nor days nor hours.[1]

This tradition is reflected in bSan. 97*a* (657):

R. Kattina [*c.* 270] said: six thousand years shall the world exist, and one [thousand, the seventh] it shall be desolate, as it is written, 'And the Lord *alone* shall be exalted in that day' [Isa. 2: 11]. Abaye [280–338] said: It will be desolate two [thousand], as it is said, 'After two days will he revive us: in the third day, he will raise us up, and we shall live in his sight' [Hos. 6: 2].[2]

It emerges explicitly in two parallel passages in the Talmud, both of which are attributed to 'the Tanna debe Eliyyahu', a midrash compiled by R. Anan b. Anina in the third century.[3] We cite the form found in bAZ 9*a* (43), to which is appended an elaboration of the chronology of the 'world-week'.

The Tanna debe Eliyyahu taught: the world is to exist six thousand years; the first two thousand are to be void; the next two thousand are the period of the Torah, and the following two thousand are the period of the Messiah. Through our many sins a number of these have already passed [and the Messiah is not yet].

From when are the two thousand years of the Torah to be reckoned? Shall we say from the Giving of the Torah at Sinai? In that case, you will find that there are not quite two thousand years from then till now [i.e. the year A.M. 4000], for if you compute the year [from Creation to the Giving of the Torah] you will find that they comprise two thousand and a part of the third thousand;[4] the period is, therefore, to be reckoned from the time when Abraham and Sarah 'had gotten souls in Haran' (Gen. 12: 5), for we have it as a tradition that Abraham was at that time fifty-two years old.[5] Now, to what does our Tanna encroach [on the other thousand]? Four hundred and forty-eight years! Calculate it and you will find that from the time when 'they had gotten souls in Haran' till the giving of the Torah there are just 448 years.[6]

[1] *A & P*, II, 451.

[2] Par. b. RH 31*a*, 20.

[3] Final redaction took place in the tenth century; cf. *JE*, art. 'Tanna debe Eliyyahu'. S–B translate the term 'der Schule des Elias'; cf., for example, IV, 991.

[4] Namely 2,448 years; see Appendix 2, part A.

[5] That is, twenty-three years before his migration from Haran to Canaan (Gen. 12: 4).

[6] Our calculations in part A of Appendix 2 result in a span between Abraham and the exodus that is five years higher than the Talmud: Abraham born A.M. 1948; migration, A.M. 2023 (Gen. 12: 4); 'got souls in

It may be argued that Matthew, in the genealogy, is presenting seven epochs of Jewish history in a fashion parallel to the already existing conception of a universal world-week patterned after the seven days of creation. There are six periods of 'days' followed by the Messianic age, the 'Sabbath rest for the people of God' (Heb. 4: 9), akin to the theology of the Epistle to the Hebrews, especially 3: 7—4: 11.[1] But again the parallel is not exact. Matthew emphasizes three groups of fourteen each, not six groups of seven; and pre-Israelitic history (contrary to the oldest trace of this Jewish tradition in II Enoch 33) is ignored.[2] But the general idea of six weeks of years (cf. Dan. 9: 2, 24) patterned after the week of creation may be Matthew's structural principle.[3]

(*j*) One further possible parallel remains to be discussed, namely the suggested similarity between Matthew's basic fourteen and the number of links in the Pharisaic 'chain of tradition' preserved in the Mishnah treatise, Aboth (PA),[4] and the Aboth of Rabbi Nathan (ARN).[5] The Aboth begins by describing how the oral law of Pharisaism was transmitted from Moses through his successors down to tannaitic times. Finkelstein suggests that in the original tradition which was incorporated into both the PA and the ARN, there were exactly fourteen links in the chain of tradition, and that the number fourteen was retained by Rabbi Judah the Patriarch I, the final redactor of the Mishnaic treatise, even though he dropped two of the links in the prior list and added two to the end.[6] This

Haran', A.M. 2000 (75 − 52 = 23; 2023 − 23 = 2000); exodus 2023 + 430 (Exod. 12: 40) = 2453; the Talmud here presupposed a 425-year span between Abraham's migration and the exodus; hence the exodus takes place in the year A.M. 2448.

[1] One could compare also the use of seven in the NT Apocalypse; A. Farrer (*The Rebirth of Images* (1949), pp. 37 ff. *et passim*) finds the seventh seven sabbatical in nature.

[2] For other traces of this traditional concept see S–B, IV, 989–93.

[3] Cf. J. C. Fenton, *The Gospel of St Matthew* (Pelican Gospel Commentaries) (1963), p. 41.

[4] mAboth 1–2 (446–61).

[5] Judah Goldin, tr., *The Fathers According to Rabbi Nathan*; references to ARN are from Goldin's translation.

[6] Louis Finkelstein, *Mabo le-Massektot Abot ve-Abot d'Rabbi Nathan* [Introduction to the Treatises Abot and Abot of Rabbi Nathan] (1950), pp. x–xi.

suggestion involves the highly complicated problem of the literary analysis of the text of PA as well as the two versions of ARN. In the best such analysis,[1] Finkelstein maintains that the second version of ARN (not translated by Goldin) preserves the 'original form of the collection' in which the chain of tradition runs as follows:

1. Moses
2. Joshua
3. The elders
4. The judges
5. The prophets
6. Haggai, Zechariah, Malachi
7. The men of the Great Synagogue
8. Simeon the Just
9. Antigonus of Socho
10. Jose b. Joezer and Jose b. Johanan
11. Joshua b. Perahya and Nittai of Arbel
12. Judah b. Tabbai and Simeon b. Shattah
13. Shemaiah and Abtalion
14. Shammai and Hillel

With this may be compared the chain which is found in the present form of the Mishnaic version and the later form of ARN:[2]

mAboth	ARN
1. Moses	1. Moses
2. Joshua	2. Joshua
3. The elders	3. The elders
4. The prophets	4. The judges
5. The men of the Great Synagogue	5. The prophets
6. Simeon the Just	6. Haggai, Zechariah, Malachi
7. Antigonus of Socho	7. The men of the Great Synagogue
8. Jose b. Joezer and Jose b. Johanan	8. Simeon the Just
9. Joshua b. Perahyah and Nittai the Arbelite	9. Antigonus of Socho

[1] 'Introductory Study to *Pirke Abot*', *JBL*, LVII (1938), 13–50.
[2] Danby, *Mishnah*, pp. 446–8; Goldin, *The Fathers*, *passim*.

10. Judah b. Tabbai and Simeon b. Shetah	10. Jose b. Joezer and Jose b. Johanan
11. Shemaiah and Abtalion	11. Joshua b. Perahya and Nittai of Arbel
12. Hillel and Shammai	12. Judah b. Tabbai and Simeon b. Shattah
13. Johanan b. Zakkai[1]	13. Shemaiah and Abtalion
	14. Hillel and Shammai
	15. Johanan b. Zakkai

According to Finkelstein, the later versions of this list reflect the debated question of 'the matter in which the tradition was being preserved since the time of Hillel and Shammai'.[2] This conflict involved, on the one hand, the scholars who were active in teaching, and, on the other, the descendants of Hillel who had held the presidency of the Pharisaic order. Thus R. Akiba, 'the redactor of the earliest form of the treatise of *Abot*', added after the sayings of Shammai and Hillel a statement which was intended to show that the chain of tradition continued not with the descendants of Hillel, but with the voluntary teachers of each generation.[3] This statement is found in the present text of PA in 2: 8—'R. Johanan b. Zakkai received [the Law] from Hillel and from Shammai.' But the later editor of the Mishnah, R. Judah, himself the seventh in descent from Hillel, desired to show that the chain included not R. Johanan b. Zakkai but rather the descendants of Hillel, and thus inserted the material dealing with Gamaliel and his son, Simeon (mAboth 1: 16–17). But, in so doing, he deleted two members of the chain which had been included in the earlier sequence, namely 'the judges' and 'Haggai, Zechariah, and Malachi', so that there would still be preserved precisely *fourteen* links. Regarding this phenomenon, Finkelstein writes:

The number, 'fourteen', is not accidental. It corresponds to the number of High Priests from Aaron to the establishment of Solomon's temple; the number of High Priests from the establishment of the temple until Jaddua, the last High Priest mentioned in Scripture. It is clear that a mystic significance attached to this number, in both

[1] On the problem whether the final editor of the Mishnah considered Gamaliel and his son, Simeon, to belong in this list before Johanan b. Zakkai see below.

[2] *JBL*, LVII (1938), pp. 24 ff.

[3] *Ibid.* pp. 25 f.

the Sadducean and Pharisaic traditions. Each group maintained that it was no accident that the number of links in the chain of what it considered the authoritative tradition, from Moses and Aaron until the time of Alexander the Great, was a multiple of the mystic number 'seven'. This may seem a weak argument for the authenticity of a tradition; but antiquity was apparently prepared to be impressed by it. So impressive indeed was this argument, that in the Gospel of Matthew, the early Christian apologist, directing his argument against the Pharisees (and also the Sadducees) adopted a similar claim for Jesus, and traced his genealogy back to Abraham in a series of three chains of fourteen links each (Matt. 1: 17).[1]

Davies adduces these remarks as a possible indication of Matthew's purpose:[2] assuming that the older form, represented by ARN, was composed during the scholarly activity at Jamnia in the first century as a set of credentials for the Pharisaic tradition, he suggests the possibility that Matthew's genealogy, also based on the number fourteen, would be understood by Pharisaic readers as a counterpart to the opening sections of Aboth, and may have been so intended by the author of Matthew. This is a highly interesting suggestion, especially in view of our hypothesis that the mention of the four women in the genealogy reflects Pharisaic (as opposed to Sadducean) tradition, and thus points towards a date after A.D. 70 for the genealogy. But there are the following problems which remain with this suggested parallel:

(1) If, as Dr Finkelstein suggests, R. Judah received a form of the Aboth which included the mention of R. Johanan b. Zakkai as the successor of Shammai and Hillel, why did he retain the mention of b. Zakkai while at the same time adding Gamaliel and Simeon, especially if his purpose was to show that the latter and not b. Zakkai were the legitimate heirs of the tradition from Hillel in the chain? Finkelstein answers that the reference to b. Zakkai was retained by Judah I 'out of loyalty to the received text, and also perhaps to satisfy the opposition'.[3]

(2) The inclusion of b. Zakkai in the present text of the Mishnah tractate does disrupt any possible emphasis on the number fourteen in the chain. Therefore we may conclude that, if there was a traditional emphasis on the number of links in the

[1] *Mabo*, pp. x–xi.
[2] *Setting*, pp. 302–4.
[3] *JBL*, LVII (1938), 27 n. 27.

chain, it was apparently not significant for the final editors of either PA or ARN. In the Mishnaic tractate there are thirteen links, the final one being R. Johanan b. Zakkai. Or, if one adds the mention of R. Gamaliel and his son, Simeon, in 1: 14–15, there are fifteen. Similarly, in the later form of ARN, reflected in Goldin's translation, there are fifteen links in the chain, which does not include Gamaliel and Simeon.

(3) Nowhere in the history of the tradition of the Aboth is there *explicit* evidence that special significance was attached to the number of links, while in the Matthean genealogy the opposite is true.[1]

(4) There are several other problems which prevent one from making dogmatic statements concerning this parallel, for example the use of the formula, '[Name] received from [name]'. Are the links in the chain limited to those with whom this formula occurs? Also, there is the difficulty in the succession following the Great Synagogue: should Simeon the Just be counted as a separate link or as part of the Great Synagogue? The phrase '...received from...' is missing with Simeon.

In a private communication on 11 May 1965, Dr Finkelstein re-emphasized his view that the chain in the earlier form of the Aboth, ARN, did not go beyond Hillel and Shammai, and that Gamaliel and his son, Simeon, were added to the list in order to bring it down to the time of the destruction of the temple, while two preceding links were dropped. Thus the number fourteen was retained. R. Johanan b. Zakkai, in his view, begins a new series of authorities reflecting the views of Akiba subsequent to the destruction of the temple and this influence is felt in the present form of both ARN and PA. Nonetheless, it remains noteworthy that, while Matthew explicitly draws attention to his three-fourteens scheme, this is not done in the Aboth. One can perhaps best suggest a similarity in purpose rather than in scheme between the Matthean genealogy and the line of succession in the Rabbis: they both trace the origin of their tradition from an ultimate human source, either Abraham, the bearer of promise, or Moses, the receiver of Torah. And this is carried down to their own day in a sequence which is intended

[1] However, Davies, in a private communication, has pointed out that R. T. Herford lists fourteen links in the succession of the house of Hillel (in *The Ethics of the Talmud*, 1962, p. 36).

to be unbroken. But I tend to see a different tone between the Matthean genealogy and the Rabbinic chain: While the Rabbinic chain shows how something given in the past has been transmitted down to the present, the genealogy in Matthew shows how the past historical process has reached a fulfillment in the coming of the Messiah. Matthew's system, in short, is a genealogy of the Messiah and seems designed to establish the predetermined character of his coming; this gives to the Matthean list an eschatological—perhaps even apocalyptic—overtone.

Overview: the eschatological significance of the fourteens

We have summarized several parallels that can be drawn between the Matthean genealogy and roughly contemporary Jewish sources. To recapitulate, these are:

1. The genealogical data in the OT.
2. Gematria on the name David.
3. Speculations on the number of letters in the divine names.
4. The fourteen epochs of world history in II Baruch 53–74.
5. The Talmudic speculation on the three sacrifices of Balak and Balaam in Num. 23.
6. The Ten-week apocalypse of I Enoch 93, 91.
7. The division of Jewish biblical history according to the phases of the moon in Ex. R. 15: 26.
8. The seventy weeks of years in Daniel.
9. Rabbinic speculation on the duration of the world according to the seven days of creation week.
10. The Pharisaic chain of tradition in Aboth.

The question of date removes from serious consideration the parallel adduced from the speculation on the number of letters in the divine names. The remaining parallels are in large part a product of reflection on the OT data, but they are also one step removed from the OT since they stand within a period in which Messianic speculation had reached some degree of structure. A glance at these parallels reveals the significant fact that they share Messianic or eschatological overtones. Numbers four, six, eight, and nine above are explicitly eschatological; items two, five, and seven take on eschatological significance when introduced into a genealogy of the Messiah. This latter statement also holds true for the one parallel which seems to be not explicitly eschatological, namely the chain of tradition that serves as the 'credentials' of Rabbinic Judaism. For even with regard to this parallel it must be admitted that, if the Matthean genealogy was intended to provide Jesus with credentials, they are the credentials of the Messiah, and the legitimizing can be considered as a demonstration of the divine ordering of history so that it leads up to the Messianic age as its *telos*. Thus any of the parallels to the structure of Matt. 1: 1–17 might indicate an eschatological purpose for the genealogy. Perhaps it is impossible to state with certainty or even with probability whether any one of the six was in the mind of the author; but neither is it necessary to do so. The evidence indicates that Matthew's reconstruction, with its emphatic verse 17, would be understood by a learned Jewish reader to have eschatological significance. History is in order; the time is fulfilled; the Messiah has come. The function of the genealogy—the note of fulfillment—explains the lack of a precise and exact parallel with contemporary sources: *the two genealogies of Jesus in the NT are the only extant Messianic genealogies* which are written to prove that the Messiah has come. The pseudepigraphal apocalypses, which are in many respects the closest parallels with Matt. 1: 2–17, direct the reader's attention to the future; so also the history of Rabbinic Messianic speculation is governed by hope for the future with the concomitant setting of dates and reckoning of epochs.[1] But Matthew looks not only to the future,[2] but also—even mainly—to the fulfillment that has taken place in the past. And he does so using categories derived from apocalyptic and Rabbinic Judaism. If we ask what credentials a Pharisaic Rabbi might give to the Messiah when he should arrive, the answer is Matt. 1: 1–17, with the necessary changes in personal names. The Matthean genealogy, we may therefore suggest, was written by a scribe acquainted with Pharisaic Judaism who believed that the Messiah had come.[3]

[1] Cf. Abba Hillel Silver, *A History of Messianic Speculation in Israel* (1927, 1959), pp. 3–35 *et passim*.

[2] The future aspects of Messianism in Matthew are connected with the concept of the Son of Man.

[3] Another possible indication of the apocalyptic theme of the genealogy is the theory of Stendahl that Matthew, in the genealogy, distinguishes between the birth of Jesus and his future designation as Messiah; see below, pp. 221 f.

3. *Summary and conclusion: the Midrashic character of the Matthean genealogy*

(*a*) Our analysis has touched several points of detail in the text of Matt. 1: 1–17 which reflect an acquaintance with early Rabbinic discussions, the most important of which is the mention of the four women. We noted traces of polemic in the Rabbinic tradition on the women and suggested that the Matthean genealogy included the women because they had come to occupy a traditional place in the ancestry of the Davidic Messiah, especially in discussions with those who maintained the expectation of a Levitical Messiah. On this assumption, the genealogy can be considered to have been written after A.D. 70 as an apology for the Christian faith directed toward the Pharisaic element in Judaism and perhaps Christianity as well. The genealogy is thus among the most thoroughly Rabbinic parts of the NT.

(*b*) If the parallels adduced in section 2 above are an indication of the way the structure of the genealogy would be understood, we are justified in assuming that the author was also acquainted with Palestinian apocalyptic speculation. That the same author was influenced by both Rabbinic thought and methods of apocalyptic should not be surprising since it is impossible to maintain a sharp separation between the two. Scribal methodology can be discovered in several of the pseudepigraphal apocalypses and there is a considerable amount of eschatological speculation in the Rabbinic sources, both early and late.[1] R. Johanan b. Zakkai, a contemporary of the author of Matthew, seems to have been especially interested in matters of eschatology.[2]

(*c*) Assuming the validity of the first two points, we may conclude that the genealogy is essentially Midrashic in character. It is an interpretation of the structure and goal of history, tied to the details of Scripture, yet incorporating extra-biblical information such as the inclusion of Rahab in the genealogy of David. Therefore the attempt must be made not merely to investigate the historical reliability of the information given in

[1] See W. D. Davies, 'Apocalyptic and Pharisaism', in *Christian Origins and Judaism* (1962), pp. 19–30.

[2] Cf. Bacon, *Matthew*, pp. 71 ff.

the genealogy, but also to penetrate into the process and sequence of thought of the author in order to understand his purpose and so to be able to appropriate his message.

(*d*) Finally, these conclusions lead to an important observation concerning the author himself. His accomplishment was no mere compilation of names for preaching or catechesis, but rather a unified conception, utilizing varied elements from his own time in a creative way. We thus agree fully with the conclusion of Vögtle:

> ...Die Genealogie Mt 1: 2–17 in der vorliegenden originellen, systematisierenden Gestalt ihrem Ursprung nach *eine einheitliche Konzeption* ist...Ein derart wohlüberlegtes und kunstvolles Gebilde muss von Haus aus ein Produkt der Feder sein, das—gewiss aus verfügbaren Quellen und Traditionen schöpfend—auf ein konkretes schriftstellerisches Vorhaben hinweist. Dieses wird immer noch am plausibelsten mit unserem Mt.-Ev. selbst identifiziert, das sich im besonderen um den Nachweis bemüht, dass Jesus der verheissene Messias Israels und der Völker ist.[1]

It is to an examination of the relationship between the genealogy and the Gospel of Matthew that we now turn.

C. THE RELATION BETWEEN THE MATTHEAN GENEALOGY AND THE GOSPEL OF MATTHEW

We have cited Vögtle's conclusion that the Matthean genealogy is the product of a unified conception rather than a reworking of a previously existing list and that this unified conception can best be attributed to the author, that is, final redactor, of the gospel.[2] This view is by no means universally accepted. Thus Bacon writes: 'Prefixed to the first narrative section [Matt. 3: 1 ff.] we find two loosely connected chapters relating the birth and infancy of Jesus from sources elsewhere unknown.'[3] In general, those who consider the genealogy to have its origin

[1] *BZ*, IX (1965), 48.

[2] G. H. Box (*ZNW*, VI (1905), 80–101) maintains that Matt. 1–2 are from a single hand and 'display unmistakable midrashic features'; others who hold to identity of authorship are Allen (*Matthew*, p. 2), Lagrange (*Matthieu*, p. 3), J. Schmidt (*Matthäus*, p. 39), and W. D. Davies (*Setting*, p. 62). The most detailed argument for the integrity of Matt. 1–2 within the first gospel is that of Taylor, *Virgin Birth*, pp. 92–104.

[3] *Matthew*, p. xiv, see also ch. XI.

from a different hand base their argument on the assumption that the Sy^s reading at 1: 16 is the original, an assumption that supposedly proves an incompatibility between the genealogy and the immediately following account of the virgin birth.[1] But, as we have suggested, the Sy^s is in all probability not the original reading and, even if it should be so considered, it is obvious that the redactor of the gospel in its present form found no insuperable contradiction between the two pericopes. The most convincing demonstration of the integrity of the genealogy within the gospel, however, is to be found in an examination of the implicit similarities between the genealogy and the gospel in matters of form, language, and theology. We enumerate the following:

1. *The tendency towards numerical structure*

The gospel of Matthew, more than any of the others, shows a tendency towards recurring patterns which are often arranged by numerical structure. Von Dobschutz pointed out[2] that Matthew's stereotyped style betrays itself in the repetition of phrases or incidents that are found once or not at all in the parallel accounts in Mark and Luke. Thus the phrase θεραπεύων πᾶσαν νόσον καὶ πᾶσαν μαλακίαν in Matt. 4: 23 is repeated almost verbatim in 9: 35 and 10: 1, in each case being an addition to the Markan or Lukan account. Matthew repeats a word or phrase in the following places:

(*a*) Matt. 10: 6; 15: 24—the saying about the lost sheep of Israel.
(*b*) Matt. 9: 13; 12: 7—the quotation of Hos. 6: 5.
(*c*) Matt. 19: 30 (Mark 10: 31); 20: 16—'the first shall be last'.
(*d*) Matt. 12: 39; 16: 4 (Mark 8: 38)—'evil and adulterous generation'.
(*e*) Matt. 5: 32; 19: 9—παρεκτὸς λόγου πορνείας or μὴ ἐπὶ πορνείᾳ.
(*f*) Matt. 13: 12; 25: 29—'to him who has will more be given'.

[1] So, for example, H. A. Sanders, 'The Genealogies of Jesus', *JBL*, XXXII (1913), 188; Lambertz, 'Die Toledoth', pp. 218 ff.; F. Hahn, *Christologische Hoheitstitel*, pp. 242 ff.; H. von Campenhausen, *The Virgin Birth in the Theology of the Ancient Church*, tr. Frank Clarke (1964; Germ. or. 1962), pp. 11 ff.; A. Meyer and W. Bauer in E. Hennecke and W. Schneemelcher, *New Testament Apocrypha*, tr. R. McL. Wilson (1963), pp. 418 ff.

[2] 'Matthäus als Rabbi und Katechet', *ZNW*, XXVII (1928), esp. pp. 338–42.

(*g*) Matt. 14: 14; 9: 36 (Mark 6: 34)—compassion on the crowds without a shepherd.
(*h*) Matt. 10: 17–22 (Mark 13: 9–13); 24: 9–14—warning of eschatological woes.
(*i*) Matt. 5: 33–7; 23: 16–22—the saying about oaths.
(*j*) Matt. 3: 7; 23: 33—the vituperation, 'brood of vipers', applied to the Pharisees by both John and Jesus.

In the following places von Dobschutz finds the doubling of whole pericopes:

(*a*) Matt. 9: 27–31; 20: 29–34 (Mark 10: 46–52)—healing of two blind men.
(*b*) Matt. 9: 32–4; 13: 22 ff. (Luke 11: 14)—healing of a blind demoniac.
(*c*) Matt. 3: 17; 17: 5—similar heavenly voice at the baptism and at the transfiguration.

Similarly, Matthew tends to use the formula ἐν ἐκείνῳ τῷ καιρῷ as a simple bridge between sections where Mark uses τότε or καί, as in Mark 11: 25; 12: 1; 14: 1. The expression ἐκεῖ ἔσται ὁ κλαυθμὸς καὶ ὁ βρυγμὸς τῶν ὀδόντων is used exactly in 8: 12; 13: 42 and 50; 22: 13; 24: 51 and 25: 30.[1] The frequency of the fulfillment formulas is another example of Matthew's tendency toward reduplication.[2]

It will be admitted that this predilection for repetition is not a clear parallel to the numerical structuring of the genealogy. But the author also has a fondness for arranging his material in threes. Allen[3] has compiled the most extensive list of such triads:

three temptations	4: 1–11
three illustrations of righteousness	6: 1–18
three miracles of healing	8: 1–15
three miracles of power	8: 23—9: 8
three miracles of restoration	9: 18–34

[1] Von Dobschutz, pp. 341 f.

[2] Matt. 1: 22; 2: 15, 23; 4: 14; 8: 17; 12: 17; 13: 35; 21: 4; 2: 17; 27: 9; 26: 54–6.

[3] P. lxv; a few supposed triads listed by Allen which are not obviously so are omitted in the list given here, namely three childhood incidents in chapter 2; three incidents prior to Jesus' public ministry, 3: 1—4: 11; three prohibitions in 6: 19—7: 6; three commands in 7: 7–20; three prophetical parables in 21: 28—22: 14; three incidents that vexed the Pharisees in 12: 1–24.

threefold 'fear not'	10: 26, 28, 31
threefold answer to the question about fasting	9: 14–17
three complaints of the Pharisees	9: 1–17
three 'is not worthy of me'	10: 37–8
three parables of sowing	13: 1–32
three sayings about 'little ones'	18: 6, 10, 14
three questions	22: 15–40
three parables of warning	24: 43—25: 30
three prayers at Gethsemane	26: 39–44
three denials of Peter	27: 17, 21–3
three petitions in the Lord's Prayer	6: 11–13
three aspirations in the Lord's Prayer	6: 9*b*–10

It has also been suggested[1] that the bulk of the Sermon on the Mount is also arranged in triadic form, patterned after the well-known triad of Jewish piety preserved in mAb. 1: 2 (446):

Simeon the Just was of the remnants of the Great Synagogue. He used to say: By three things is the world sustained; by the Law [תורה], by the [temple] service [עבודה], and by deeds of loving-kindness [גמילות חסדים].

A similar triad may be reflected in the Sermon on the Mount: 5: 17–48, the Torah of Jesus; 6: 1–16, the true worship; 6: 19—7: 12, true piety and obedience. Thus in its overall design and within each section (e.g. 6: 1–18; 6: 9*b*–10; 6: 11–13) there is an implicit triadic arrangement in the Sermon.[2]

G. Bornkamm, in his essay on 'End-Expectation and Church in Matthew',[3] draws special attention to the trio, 'judgment, mercy, and faith' in Matt. 23: 23 as a Matthean summary of the essentials of the law which, although thoroughly Jewish in tone, are 'not to be found literally in this formulation—either in the OT or in Judaism'.[4] It is possible to find triadic grouping elsewhere in smaller sections of the peculiarly Matthean material. For example, in 23: 8–10 the disciples are not to be called Rabbi (verse 8), father (verse 9) or Master (verse 10); each one expresses the same thought. Thus, the Matthean fondness for numerical arrangement, especially in triads, cannot be doubted.

[1] Davies, *Setting*, pp. 305–7. [2] Davies, pp. 307–8.

[3] In G. Bornkamm, G. Barth and H. J. Held, *Tradition and Interpretation in Matthew*, Eng. trans. by P. Scott (1963).

[4] P. 26.

An emphasis on the number seven in Matthew occurs in 12: 45 (seven demons); 15: 34 (seven loaves); 15: 37 (seven baskets); 18: 21–2 (sevenfold forgiveness); 22: 25 (seven brothers); and chapter 23 (seven woes).

Considered in the light of this tendency toward numerical structure, the arrangement of the genealogy into 3 × 14 or 3 × 7 × 2 seems entirely congruous. The evangelist draws attention to the form of the genealogy (1: 17) because it is a survey of pre-Messianic history intending to underscore the predetermined character of the coming of Jesus, the Messiah.[1]

2. *Language*

We have found hints in the genealogy that it was originally written in Greek and that the author made use of the Greek OT. We have now to raise the question regarding the character of the OT citations in the remainder of the gospel, since, if in the matter peculiar to Matthew there is a clear dependence on the Hebrew OT, it would be difficult to assume common authorship of the genealogy and the gospel. A thorough study of the OT citations in Matthew has been made by K. Stendahl in *The School of St Matthew and its Use of the OT*.[2] Proceeding from an analysis of the forms of names in the genealogy, Stendahl concludes that 'the genealogical tables in Matthew... belong to the LXX material, as do the other names of OT figures occurring in the gospel. In the cases in which the names in these two tables agree with Luke, with two exceptions they have the same transcription...'[3] We have reached the same conclusion concerning the genealogist's OT from a different starting-point, namely details of the text.[4] Significantly, Stendahl finds the same influence

[1] Attempts to find triadic grouping in chapters 1–2 are less successful. It may be that the three occurrences of 'Behold,...' are remnants of a collection of three stories: 1: 20, ἰδοὺ ἄγγελος κυρίου; 2: 1, ἰδοὺ μάγοι; 2: 13, ἰδοὺ ἄγγελος κυρίου (so P. J. Thomson, 'The Infancy Gospels of St Matthew and St Luke Compared', *TU*, LXXXVII, 218–19). But the organization in chapters 1–2 may be thematic rather than numerical. K. Stendahl, 'Quis et unde?', finds the clue to the structure of chapter 1 to consist in an emphasis on personal names and in chapter 2 on place names (in *Judentum, Urchristentum, Kirche*, ed. W. Eltester (1960), pp. 94–105.

[2] Acta Seminarii Neotestamentici Upsaliensis (1954).

[3] Pp. 135–6.

[4] Cf. Bacon, *Matthew*, p. 57.

of the LXX, especially the text of Codex Alexandrinus, in the body of the gospel. Where Matthew takes the quotation from Mark, he often assimilates it more closely to the LXX, sometimes lengthening it.[1] In the quotations common to Matthew and Luke there is a clear dependence on the LXX, with less Semitic influence than in the other categories.[2] As for the material peculiar to Matthew, Stendahl distinguishes between the quotations with the fulfillment formula and those without. Regarding the former he concludes:

Certain interpretations of Matthew's require the LXX's understanding of the text for the function of the OT text in the Matthean context. On the whole there is scarcely any tradition of translation or interpretation which does not emerge in Matthew's manner of understanding his quotations. This leads us to presume that Matthew wrote Greek and rendered the OT quotations along the lines of various traditions and methods of interpretation.[3]

In the OT citations peculiar to Matthew, but without the fulfillment formula (e.g. the genealogy and the other allusions in Matt. 1–2), Stendahl finds a LXX element:

Such observations further strengthen the impression of the LXX as Matthew's Bible and place the formula quotations in a special class. The dependence on the Hebrew text is hardly a consistent feature in Matthew's quotations. There are, however, slight traces of Semitic text in some Matthean quotations outside the formula quotations.[4]

The reference to 'slight traces of Semitic text in some Matthean quotations' shows that Matthew did not use the LXX as consistently as, say, Luke or Paul. Moreover, an analysis of the Greek style of the peculiarly Matthean material as compared with that which is paralleled in Mark and/or Luke yields significant results. Soltau[5] has pointed out that the Matthean editor

[1] P. 147 f. [2] P. 148.

[3] Pp. 126–7; the conclusion that the evangelist could choose from several traditions in citing OT passages is used by Stendahl as support for his suggestion that the Gospel of Matthew is the product of a Christian school similar to Rabbinic houses of study. The 'mixture' of Scripture quotations has also been assigned to diversity of sources; see Bacon, p. 57.

[4] P. 136; on the LXX influence in Matthew's quotations see also Allen, *Matthew*, pp. lxi f., and Bacon, pp. 470–7, 496–504.

[5] W. Soltau, 'Zur Entstehung des 1. Evangeliums', *ZNW*, 1 (1900), 219–48; summarized by Bacon, pp. 135, 157–60.

whose hand is traced in the birth narrative in 'supplements' to the Markan material and parallels with Luke, and in a group of Scripture fulfillments, manifests a more 'Jewish-Christian' point of view than does the 'main substance of the Gospel'. In particular, he finds Hebraisms in the Greek of this peculiarly Matthean material, and only in this material. The editor (whom we identify as the evangelist) inserted the 'supplement' on the suicide of Judas (Matt. 27: 3–10), referring to the casting of the pieces of silver (ἀργύρια, according to Soltau not good Greek) 'into the treasury', εἰς τὸν κορβανᾶν, which is not translated. Soltau finds eight other expressions peculiar to the supplements and the birth narrative which betray awkward Greek usage:[1]

(1) κατ' ὄναρ: according to Phot. (p. 149. 25) κατ' ὄναρ οὐ χρὴ λέγειν· βάρβαρόν γε παντελῶς· ἀλλὰ ὄναρ. The phrase occurs in Matt. 1: 20; 2: 12, 13, 19, 22; 27: 19, all peculiar to Matthew.

(2) ὀψὲ δὲ σαββάτων in 28: 1 'is a highly awkward construction made necessary by the correction of Mark 16: 1 to a different sense'.

(3) μετοικεσία is found nowhere but in Matt. 1: 11, 17; better Greek usage is μετοίκησις.

(4) δειγματίζω, in 1: 19 is a 'wholly unGreek expression'.[2]

(5) γινώσκω of sexual intercourse occurs in later Greek but in the NT only in Matt. 1: 25; Luke 1: 34; it is probably a reminisence of the LXX at Gen. 4: 1, 17; 19: 8, etc.

(6) ἀπὸ τότε, 'an unGreek form', follows in three places the Matthean material instead of the frequent τότε.

(7) γεννᾶν, γεννᾶσθαι appear (with one exception, Matt. 26: 24; cf. Mark 14: 21) only in the Matthean 'supplements', i.e. in chapters 1–2 and in Matt. 19: 12; the term is common in John, Paul, and Acts.

(8) ἄγγελος κυρίου in 1: 20, 24; 2: 13, 19; 28: 2 recalls the OT angel or messenger of Yahweh.[3]

Soltau contends that such peculiarities point to a Jewish-Christian revision of a 'proto-Matthew'. For our purpose it is necessary only to refer to the Hebraic character of Matthew's Greek, which has been aptly described by R. Simon as 'Grec de la

[1] Soltau, pp. 239–40 (Bacon, pp. 158–9).

[2] But W. Bauer, *Greek–English Lexicon*, tr. Arndt and Gingrich, *ad rem*, provides parallels to this usage in Hellenistic texts.

[3] Although 'angel of the Lord' appears to be a characteristic Matthean expression, similar phrases occur in Luke 1: 11; 2: 9; Acts 5: 19; Mark has always simply 'angel' (once, in 1: 2, an OT citation, 'my angel').

Synagogue'[1] and, on the basis of a minute analysis of the text, by Schlatter as standing in close relation to linguistic idiosyncrasies of the Babylonian Talmud.[2] The combined research of Schlatter, Bacon, and Stendahl leads to the conclusion that the gospel as a whole cannot be considered to be a translation from a Semitic original. Rather, 'the evangelist, Hellenist in speech though he be, is certainly deeply imbued both with the spirit and the mode of expression of the rabbis'.[3] This being so, we have an important criterion for assessing the relation between the genealogy and the gospel. In both can be traced the influence of the Greek OT; in both there is a definite Jewish element, particularly in the knowledge of Rabbinic theology.[4] The author/redactor can therefore be described as a convert from Judaism who was trained in Rabbinic thinking. Further description of the author must take into account the fact that Jewish sources speak most often about Greek being used in the school of Gamaliel the Patriarch,[5] a figure roughly contemporary with the commonly accepted date of Matthew, *c.* A.D. 80–120. Linguistically, the genealogy and the gospel are at one.[6]

3. *Theology*

Several details of the text of Matt. 1: 1–17 reflect theological views of the body of the gospel and therefore may serve as an indication of the integrity of the genealogy within the gospel. We mention the following:

(*a*) *A 'Son of David' Christology*. The opening verse of Matthew's gospel introduces the genealogy of Jesus and at the same time strikes a note that is repeated nine times in the gospel: Jesus is υἱὸς Δαυίδ. It is significant that, in all the NT, this phrase as a Messianic title is found only in Matthew and in two parallels

[1] Cf. Bacon, p. 497.

[2] Cited by Bacon, p. 497.

[3] Bacon, p. 497.

[4] It is perhaps significant that S–B have a whole volume of 1,055 pp. on Matthew alone while for the other three gospels plus Acts there is one volume of 867 pp.; cf. also the remarks of von Dobschutz, *ZNW*, XXVII (1928), 343–5.

[5] Liebermann, *Greek*, pp. 15–28, 'The Greek of the Rabbis'.

[6] The same approach to this problem along with similar conclusions will be found in Taylor, *Virgin Birth*, pp. 92 ff.

which occur in both Mark and Luke, namely Matt. 20: 30–1 (Mark 10: 47–8; Luke 18: 38–9; the healing of the blind men) and Matt. 22: 42, 45 (Mark 12: 35, 37; Luke 20: 41, 44; 'The Lord said to my lord...'). Matthew inserts the title into parallel material from Mark (cf. Matt. 15: 22 with Mark 7: 24–30; the Canaanite woman). An excellent example of this is the adulation of the crowd at the triumphal entry (Matt. 21: 9; Mark 11: 9–10; Luke 19: 38; John 12: 13). Matthew alone includes, after ὡσαννά, the words τῷ υἱῷ Δαυίδ. Moreover, the title is put into the mouth of several speakers: an angel (to Joseph, 1: 20); two blind men (9: 27 and 20: 30); 'all the people' (12: 23); a Canaanite woman (15: 22); crowds at the triumphal entry (21: 9); children in the temple (21: 15) and, somewhat enigmatically, it occurs in Jesus' polemic with the Pharisees (22: 42 ff.).

Perhaps for our purposes the most important of these occurrences is 1: 20: ἰδοὺ ἄγγελος κυρίου κατ' ὄναρ ἐφάνη αὐτῷ [Joseph] λέγων· Ἰωσὴφ υἱὸς Δαυίδ, μὴ φοβηθῇς παραλαβεῖν Μαρίαν τὴν γυναῖκά σου... The application of the title 'Son of David' to Joseph serves to connect the birth pericope to the genealogy: Jesus is Son of David because Joseph is Son of David. Thus the force of the genealogy is derived from the (legal) fatherhood of Joseph. Moreover, the recurrence of the title throughout the gospel, in the material peculiar to Matthew, strengthens our contention that the genealogy (and also the virgin birth pericope) is not the afterthought of some arbitrary editor, but rather an integral part of the gospel in its finished form, representing the theological outlook of the author. But this allusion has a further significance. It is here not contained in a plea for help (as in 9: 27; 15: 22; 20: 30–1), nor in the wonderings of the crowds (12: 23), nor yet in the premature adulation of Passion Week (21: 9, 15), but rather it is ascribed to the 'angel of the Lord', the messenger of Yahweh, and consequently was considered by the evangelist to be a fitting and apt Messianic title. Thus, of all four Gospels, it is Matthew who most clearly interprets the significance of Jesus along the lines of the Pharisaic conception of the Davidic Messiah.[1]

[1] On Son of David as a special Messianic title for Jesus in Matthew, see Georg Strecker, *Der Weg der Gerechtigkeit: Untersuchung zur Theologie des Matthäus* (1962), pp. 118–20; and esp. Hahn, *Christologische Hoheitstitel*,

(*b*) '*Son of Abraham.*' It is clear that this title does not have the importance of 'Son of David' in Matthew. It occurs only in 1: 1 and apart from the genealogy (1: 17) there are but three additional references to Abraham in Matthew: 3: 9; 8: 11; 22: 32, each of them being paralleled in Luke. It is Luke among the four gospels who places the most emphasis on Abraham as the father of the Jewish nation (cf., for example, 1: 55, 73; 13: 16; 16: 24–30; 19: 9), a concern which is carried on into Acts (cf. esp. 3: 25; 7: 2, 32; 13: 26), and shows a close relationship to Paul, especially in Romans (4: 1, 12; 11: 1) and Galatians (3: 7, 16, 29; cf. also II Cor. 11: 22). Nonetheless, the references in Matthew are significant: God is able to replace the leaders of Judaism as children of Abraham (3: 7–10); Gentiles will share in the eschatological banquet with the Hebrew patriarchs while 'the sons of the kingdom' will be judged (8: 10–12); Abraham, Isaac, and Jacob prefigure the resurrection of the just (22: 29–33). In each of these passages the eschatological theme is dominant. The great patriarchs who stand at the beginning of Jewish history will also have an important role at its completion. As Abraham in the genealogy begins the historical process that culminates in the dawn of the Messianic age, so in the gospel the end-times will be a recapitulation of the beginning.

(*c*) *Eschatology*. We have alluded to the eschatological import of the genealogy as a whole, its function as a structuring of Israelitic history with a culmination in the dawn of the Messianic age in Jesus. Indeed, it may be said that the distinctive mark of the genealogy is this periodization of history into epochs written from the perspective of fulfillment. But this theme is to be found implicit in the gospel as well. (1) Elijah, the prophet of the end-times, has already come in the person of John the Baptist.[1] Although the precise time of the in-breaking of the Messianic age in Matthew is difficult to assess, and whatever the meaning of the specific terms in Matt. 11: 12–13, it is clear that John occupies a pivotal position in the schematization of the end-events. With the coming of John (ἕως Ἰωάννου) there is

pp. 242–79; also James M. Gibbs, 'Purpose and Pattern in Matthew's Use of the Title "Son of David"', *NTS*, x (1963–4), 446–64.

[1] Matt. 17: 12–13; only in Matthew is the identification of Elijah and John made explicit; cf. also Matt. 11: 14 and par.

implied a change in the role of 'the law and the prophets' or a different relationship between them and the people. There is, however, also in this passage (and the Lukan parallel) an implicit separation of the time of John from the time of Jesus: ἀπὸ δὲ τῶν ἡμερῶν Ἰωάννου τοῦ βαπτιστοῦ ἕως ἄρτι...[1] Yet in the immediately following pericope John and Jesus belong to the same γενεά (11: 16 ff.). In 9: 14–17 we find a Matthean emphasis on the newness of Jesus and his ministry as compared with that of the Baptist: Matthew alone puts the question in the mouth of the disciples of John: 'Why do we and the Pharisees fast, but your disciples do not fast?'[2] Jesus' answer about the wedding guests and the bridegroom, the unshrunk cloth, and the new wine indicates that there is a certain newness in his ministry as compared with that of either John or the Pharisees. Thus John occupies a position at the beginning of the end-times, yet distinct from the time of Jesus. (2) The ministry of Jesus is clearly seen to be a decisive event of eschatological history: in his ministry there was something greater than Solomon or Jonah (12: 41–2) or even than the temple (12: 6). Jesus' baptism had 'fulfilled all righteousness' (3: 15) and in the beginning of his ministry the Messianic light had dawned (4: 16). The powers (αἱ δυνάμεις) of the Age to Come were already at work in Jesus (14: 2) and he was then properly the Son of David, Messiah, Son of God, and Son of Man. But there is nonetheless a distinction in Matthew between the dawn of the Messianic Age and the future Age to Come, a distinction made explicit in 12: 32: 'Whoever says a word against the Son of man will be forgiven; but whoever speaks against the Holy Spirit will not be forgiven, either in this age or in the age to come [ἐν τῷ μέλλοντι].' This distinction is not made in the parallels in Mark (3: 29) or Luke (12: 10). According to Matthew, the fulfillment of the revelation in Jesus will take place at 'the close of the age' (συντέλεια τοῦ αἰῶνος) when Jesus as the Son of Man will preside over the final judgment (13: 39, 40, 49; 24: 3). There is thus an interim between the earthly ministry of Jesus and the close of the age, during which the resurrected Jesus is, in some sense, with his disciples (28: 20). This, for Matthew, is

[1] Also, the time of Jesus' ministry, especially the Passion, is three times set apart from the future fulfillment by the phrase ἀπ' ἄρτι.

[2] Cf. Mark 2: 18; Luke 5: 33.

the period of the church, a period of short duration. It is probably this Matthean eschatology which gives meaning to the addition of the phrase, ἀπ' ἄρτι, to Matt. 23: 39 (οὐ μή με ἴδητε ἀπ' ἄρτι ἕως ἂν εἴπητε· εὐλογημένος ὁ ἐρχόμενος ἐν ὀνόματι κυρίου); to 26: 29 (the eschatological saying in the Eucharistic words); and to 26: 64 where, in answer to the high priest, Jesus says: πλὴν λέγω ὑμῖν, ἀπ' ἄρτι ὄψεσθε τὸν υἱὸν τοῦ ἀνθρώπου κ.τ.λ. The ἄρτι is the fulfillment of Jesus' earthly ministry, at which point Matthew's attention is drawn to the future culmination of the present age.[1] The form which Matthew gives to the passages dealing with the kingdom of God (kingdom of heaven) reveals the same ambivalence: it is to come in the future;[2] it is imminent;[3] yet it is in some respects also present.[4] Thus Matthew distinguishes in several ways between Jesus' ministry of teaching and healing and his future appearance as the universal judge, the Son of Man.[5]

By way of summary, we may suggest that Matthew discerned several pivots in the sequence of the end-events: the appearance of John; the ministry of Jesus; and the appearance of the Son of Man at the close of the age. In all probability he considered the intervals between these pivots as separate eschatological events;[6] thus the periodization of history that is seen in the genealogy is continued within the gospel itself.

There may be a more precise indication of this relation between the genealogy and the gospel in the matter of eschatology, namely the explanation offered by K. Stendahl for the

[1] Perhaps this also explains the cry of the demons in 8: 29: 'What have you to do with us, O Son of God? Have you come here to torment us before the time?' The action of Jesus is premature, according to the expectations of the demons; it is wrought proleptically, in anticipation of the final defeat of evil at the close of the age.

[2] Cf. 8: 11; 7: 21; 18: 1–4; 19: 23; 5: 3, 10, 19–20; 10: 19.

[3] Cf. 3: 2; 4: 17; 10: 7; 11: 12; 10: 23.

[4] Cf. 23: 13; 12: 28; 19: 24; 21: 31, 43.

[5] At this point the Matthean eschatology stands in direct opposition to that of Heb. 9: 26, the only other occurrence in the NT of the phrase συντέλεια τοῦ αἰῶνος, where Jesus in his ministry is considered to have marked the 'close of the age': νυνὶ δὲ ἅπαξ ἐπὶ συντελείᾳ τῶν αἰώνων εἰς ἀθέτησιν τῆς ἁμαρτίας διὰ τῆς θυσίας αὐτοῦ πεφανέρωται.

[6] G. Bornkamm ('End-Expectation and Church in Matthew', in Bornkamm, Barth, and Held, *Tradition and Interpretation*, p. 34) speaks of Matthew's 'division of salvation-history into epochs'.

apparent failure of Matthew to follow his numerical scheme in the third group, which has only thirteen names from Shealtiel to Jesus inclusively. Stendahl raises the possibility that Matthew counts the Messiah (Χριστός, 16) as the fourteenth member, while Jesus is the thirteenth. '"Christ" would then refer to Jesus in his risen state and/or at his Coming (parousia) at the end of time',[1] in the sense in which the futuristic eschatology of the early church could include a prayer that God would 'send the Christ appointed for you, Jesus, whom heaven must receive until the time for establishing all that God spoke by the mouth of his holy prophets from of old' (Acts 3: 20; cf. 2: 36). There is much that can be said for this hypothesis. Stendahl rightly points out that the expression Ἰησοῦς ὁ λεγόμενος Χριστός is used by Matthew in a distinctive way, as can be seen from the parallel expression applied to Peter in Matt. 4: 18 and 10: 2, Σίμωνα τὸν λεγόμενον Πέτρον. The significance of the statement becomes apparent if one relates it, as does Stendahl, to Matt. 16: 17–18, where Jesus establishes Simon as Peter; thus the change of name is connected with the establishing of Simon as the head of the church. Accordingly, ὁ λεγόμενος in 4: 18 and 10: 2 might indicate that Simon is there only proleptically designated Peter. In each of the three cases, the Matthean formulation is missing in the parallels.[2] If the case of Simon Peter be considered a parallel, then, according to Matt. 1: 16, Jesus may be proleptically Χριστός and we should expect that at some time subsequent to his birth Jesus would be 'named' or designated Christ.

Another point of support for Stendahl's hypothesis may be drawn from the summary statement in verse 17 of Matt. 1. There are fourteen generations ἀπὸ Ἀβραὰμ ἕως Δαυίδ, counting inclusively; however, ἀπὸ Δαυὶδ ἕως τῆς μετοικεσίας Βαβυλῶνος one must reckon from Solomon through Jeconiah inclusively. The final group, ἀπὸ τῆς μετοικεσίας Βαβυλῶνος,

[1] Krister Stendahl, 'Matthew', in *Peake's Commentary on the Bible* (1962), pp. 770–1. The contention that in the original form of the genealogy Mary was the thirteenth member of the third group (the daughter of Joseph), while Jesus was the fourteenth, need not be considered here (see Blair, *TU*, LXXXVII (1964), 149–54).

[2] This formulation has no real parallels in Mark (cf. 15: 7) or Luke (cf. 22: 1, 47); cf. also John 4: 25; 9: 11; 11: 16; 20: 2; Matt. 27: 17, 22.

must begin with Shealtiel (Μετὰ τὴν μετοικεσίαν Βαβυλῶνος) while its end is indicated not by the phrase ἐπὶ τοῦ Ἰησοῦ, but rather by ἐπὶ τοῦ Χριστοῦ. This may indicate that the genealogy ends not with the birth of Jesus, but with the full revelation of his status as the promised Messiah.

There may also be a relation between this interpretation of the purpose of the genealogy and the enigmatic saying inserted into the warnings to the disciples at the time of their mission: 'Do not think that I have come to bring peace on earth; I have not come to bring peace, but a sword' (10: 34). Luke, who has this saying in a decidedly apocalyptic context, substitutes διαμερισμόν for μάχαιραν (12: 51). Can one legitimately find in Matt. 10: 34 an allusion to the role of the sword in the apocalyptic literature?[1] The 'sword' would then refer to the divisions and persecutions encountered by the Christian community during the period of the church, that is, between the ministry of Jesus and the 'close of the age'. It would correspond to the Messianic woes, the allusions being made to the Messianic peace or the pre-Messianic sword.[2] Against this interpretation of Matt. 10: 34 it must be noted that in Matthew it is the persecution of the disciples and/or the early church which is considered (on this hypothesis) to be the operation of the Messianic sword, while, in the apocalypses, the sword was to be wielded by the Messiah to vindicate the righteous.

Stendahl's suggestion, however, is made tenuous by the fact that in Matt. 1: 1 there is no observable distinction between the two names, Ἰησοῦς Χριστός. Moreover, his interpretation of the phrase, Ἰησοῦς ὁ λεγόμενος Χριστός is seriously weakened by Matt. 27: 17, 22, where it is twice attributed to Pilate. It thus seems to be a characteristically Matthean expression[3] without any implications for a distinction of time or status. Thus, if the genealogist intended to draw such a distinction, it would have been made more explicit.

[1] Cf. I Enoch 90: 19, where the Messianic sword precedes the final judgment, the new Jerusalem, the new temple, and the Messiah. See also CD9: 10 ff. (Charles, *A & P*, II, 816–17), where the sword marks 'the period of the visitation'; II Baruch 27, where the 'sending of the sword' is part of the Messianic woes; and I Enoch 93, 91 (the apocalypse of weeks), where, again, the sword precedes the revelation of the Messiah.

[2] Cf. Hahn, *Christologische Hoheitstitel*, pp. 166–7; S–B, I, *ad rem.*

[3] Bornkamm in *Tradition and Interpretation*, p. 32.

(*d*) *The place of the genealogy within the Matthean Christological tradition.* In spite of its tentativeness, Stendahl's hypothesis does raise the question of the general significance of the concept of the Davidic Messiah in Matthew and its relation to the other titles. If the genealogy is, as we have maintained, an integral part of the gospel, written by the evangelist for his purposes, we should expect that it has a function within Matthean Christology as a whole, a function that can be isolated. The ascertaining of this function is limited, however, by the observation of Bornkamm that 'in only a few passages does Matthew's Gospel reveal any theological reflections on the relation of these titles of honour to each other'.[1] There are, however, indications of a special understanding of the various titles in Matthew. The title, Son of David, for example, seems to be limited to the earthly ministry of Jesus and has special reference to Jesus' acts of mercy.[2] In his exaltation, on the other hand, Jesus is called Lord, Son of God, and—proleptically—Son of Man. So it might appear that the genealogy, included by Matthew as a midrash on the title, Son of David, has little to do with the titles which are related to the exaltation of Jesus. But, actually, *the whole of chapter 1 seems to be a midrash on those two titles which, for Matthew, were applicable to Jesus at the moment of his birth, namely Son of David and Son of God.* The title, Lord, used in the honorific sense as in Paul, presupposes the Christian community; similarly, Jesus' role as Son of Man would not be fully perceived until the 'close of the age'. But, for Matthew, Jesus is by virtue of his birth both Son of David and Son of God. Significantly, it is precisely the same two titles which occupy an important position in the Christological statement at the beginning of Romans, a passage which is generally considered to reflect pre-Pauline and 'pre-theological'[3] sentiments: [τὸ εὐαγγέλιον θεοῦ] περὶ τοῦ υἱοῦ αὐτοῦ τοῦ γενομένου ἐκ σπέρματος Δαυὶδ κατὰ σάρκα, τοῦ

[1] Bornkamm, p. 32.

[2] Bornkamm, p. 33 and n. 1; see also Hahn, pp. 242–79, esp. pp. 276–8: 'Die besondere Ausgestaltung des Motivs der Davidssohnschaft zeigt sich zunächst in Erzählungen, die Jesus als den Helfer der Notleidenden und Kranken darstellen und den festgepragten Bittruf "Davidssohn, erbarme dich mein" enthalten' (p. 268).

[3] Cf. C. H. Dodd, *Romans* (Moffatt Commentaries) (1932), pp. 3 ff., also E. Schweizer in *Studies in Luke-Acts* (Nashville, New York, 1966); ed. L. E. Keck and J. L. Martyn, pp. 186 f.

ὁρισθέντος υἱοῦ θεοῦ ἐν δυνάμει κατὰ πνεῦμα ἁγιωσύνης ἐξ ἀναστάσεως νεκρῶν... The priority of the latter title is indicated by the double reference to υἱὸς θεοῦ; but that υἱὸς Δαυὶδ and υἱὸς θεοῦ are understood as complementary is equally clear from the contrast κατὰ σάρκα and κατὰ πνεῦμα ἁγιωσύνης. Thus far, there is an exact parallel with Matt. 1: 1–17 and 1: 18–25. But, in the (pre-)Pauline tradition, Jesus is designated (ὁρισθέντος) Son of God at his resurrection, indicating that this tradition was separate from the idea of the virgin birth.[1] On what basis, then, did Matthew find it congenial to apply midrashim on these titles to Jesus at the beginning of his gospel? The answer which we tentatively propose is this: *Matt. 1 may be patterned after the beginning of Mark's gospel, which the author of Matthew had before him.* The opening sentence of Mark reads simply: Ἀρχὴ τοῦ εὐαγγελίου τοῦ Ἰησοῦ Χριστοῦ υἱοῦ θεοῦ.[2] This is Matthean, no less than Markan, Christology, but with one essential difference: for Matthew Χριστοῦ denotes the Davidic Messiah. Hence the meaning of Ἰησοῦ Χριστοῦ is elaborated by υἱοῦ Δαυὶδ υἱοῦ Ἀβραάμ. This assumes that the heading of Matthew's gospel applied especially to the genealogy which immediately follows and which serves as a midrash on the titles, Son of David and Son of Abraham. The virgin birth pericope, 1: 18–25, might be considered as a midrash on the second half of the Markan title, υἱοῦ θεοῦ. Thus the two are mutually complementary and, for Matthew, neither would be complete in itself. That this juxtaposition of the two titles is a special concern of Matthew can be seen from his handling of the gospel tradition. In Mark, Peter's confession consists in the simple σὺ εἶ ὁ Χριστός (8: 29); in Luke, τὸν Χριστὸν τοῦ θεοῦ (9: 20); but in Matthew the two

[1] The designation of Jesus as Son of God subsequent to his ministry corresponds to the Matthean view of Jesus as the essentially proleptic Son of Man.

[2] Although relegated to the apparatus in Nestle's 24th edition, υἱοῦ θεοῦ is represented by S[a], B, D, L, W, the Vulgate and some of the old Latin MSS., s[pe], sa bo, geo[2], arm (3 MSS.), Iren., and Aug.; the omission of the phrase is supported by S*, Koredethai, 28, sy[hier], geo[1], arm, Iren, Or.; modern printed editions are divided on the matter: the phrase is included by B. Weiss; also by von Soden who considers its omission equally attested; it is omitted by Westcott and Hort, who relegate it to the margin; it is included in the RSV.

titles are again placed in juxtaposition: σὺ εἶ ὁ Χριστὸς ὁ υἱὸς τοῦ θεοῦ τοῦ ζῶντος (16: 16). The same phenomenon is to be noted in the transmission of the high priest's question at the trial of Jesus, although here the Markan form is closer to Matthew: σὺ εἶ ὁ Χριστὸς ὁ υἱὸς τοῦ εὐλογητοῦ (Mark 14: 61); Luke 22: 67 has simply, εἰ σὺ εἶ ὁ Χριστὸς, εἰπὸν ἡμῖν. Matt. 26: 63 has εἰ σὺ εἶ ὁ Χριστὸς, ὁ υἱὸς τοῦ θεοῦ.[1] This complementary relation of the two titles also determined the form of the stories of healing and miracle in Matthew, in which the two titles figure prominently. Apart from the amorphous use of κύριος[2] and one occurrence of the title Son of Man taken from Mark,[3] Matthew tends to see the recognition of Jesus as Son of David as being related directly to acts of healing (9: 27; 15: 22; 20: 30); indeed, the act of healing a blind and dumb demoniac led 'all the people' to question whether Jesus was actually the Son of David (12: 22–3). Thus it seems clear that the healing ministry of Jesus was interpreted by Matthew as the proper work of the Jewish Messiah and that the most appropriate titles to designate this sphere of Jesus' activity were 'Son of David' and 'Christos'. If this is demonstrable, then the healing miracles of Jesus in the Synoptics (at least in Matthew) are remote from the Hellenistic concept of the θεῖος ἀνήρ. Now, the striking fact that there is no known OT or Jewish source which specifically refers to healing activity in the work of the Jewish Messiah has often been adduced as evidence that Matthew has applied to Jesus the characteristics of the θεῖος ἀνήρ.[4] What seems more probable to me, however, is that the author of Matthew made no distinction between expectations in the OT of a 'new age' without a Messiah on the one hand, and hopes for a period with the Messiah on the other. Thus, for example, such passages as Isa. 35: 5–7 could be interpreted as a promise of the Messiah which was fulfilled in the ministry of Jesus.[5] As for the other title, the demons recognized Jesus as Son of God and the episode of Jesus walking on the water drew a similar response from the

[1] Cf. the observation of von Dobschutz on Matthew's repetition of expressions, above, pp. 211 ff.

[2] Cf. Matt. 8: 2, 8, 25; 14: 30; 15: 22 ff.; 20: 31.

[3] Matt. 9: 6 (Mark 2: 1–12).

[4] Cf. R. Bultmann, *The History of the Synoptic Tradition*, tr. J. Marsh (1963), pp. 241, 424.

[5] Also Isa. 29: 18 ff.; 61: 1 ff.; Mal. 3: 20 (4: 2).

disciples: ἀληθῶς θεοῦ υἱὸς εἶ (14: 33). The designation of Jesus as Son of God is thus seen as denoting his sharing in the power and authority of God the Father (11: 25–30); the numinous quality of the baptism and transfiguration accounts serve the same purpose. In short, for Matthew, Jesus fulfilled the promises of the OT and the hopes of Judaism as the Davidic Messiah, but as Son of God the category of Messiah is heightened and to some extent universalized (28: 18–20).[1]

This extension or heightening of the idea of the Davidic Messiah also must be taken into account in the interpretation of the saying on David's son (22: 41–6), a datum derived from previous tradition (Mark 12: 35–7; Luke 20: 41–4). Matthew has made subtle changes from the Markan form: the discussion takes place not as the instruction of Jesus to 'the scribes' (Mark 12: 35) but, more specifically, as a conversation of Jesus with the Pharisees; the question is not 'How do the scribes say that the Messiah is David's son?' but rather τί ὑμῖν δοκεῖ περὶ τοῦ Χριστοῦ; τίνος υἱός ἐστιν;—Matthew's formulation of the question, if our exegesis of the genealogy be correct, presupposes an alternative, Son of David or Son of Aaron. The Pharisees answer in accordance with their almost unanimous view: Son of David. Jesus then asks how, if the Messiah is to be David's son, David could call him Lord (Ps. 110 [109]: 1). The view that the intention of the pericope is to reject the idea of the Davidic descent of Jesus (so Wrede on Mark)[2] must be denied, as Bornkamm[3] and Hahn[4] rightly contend. The positive sense in which Matthew uses the title Son of David is decisive on this point. Behind the irony of the passage—which may derive ultimately from Jesus—there is in Matthew an implicit heightening of the Pharisaic concept of the Davidic Messiah: the Son of David is at once David's Lord. Hence, Hahn's designation of this pericope as an example of a 'zweistufenchristologie'[5] is especially fitting; but we may question his view that the double-faceted character of the pericope consists in its relation between the Son

[1] Cf. Th. De Kruijf, *Der Sohn des lebendigen Gottes* (1962), *ad rem.*

[2] Cf. Hahn, *Christologische Hoheitstitel*, p. 259 n. 3; H. Köster follows Wrede on this point ('Die synoptische Überlieferung bei den apostolischen Vätern', *TU*, LXV (1957), pp. 145 f.).

[3] 'End-expectation...' in *Tradition and Interpretation*, p. 33.

[4] Pp. 259 ff.

[5] Pp. 260–8.

of David and 'der Kyriostitel auf den Erhöhten'.[1] In accordance with Matthew's connection of the titles Son of David and Son of God in two pivotal sections of his gospel (16: 16; 26: 63), we may suggest that the Matthean form of the pericope is determined by the conviction that Jesus, the Son of David, is also Son of God, and therefore also David's Lord.

One further problem for our hypothesis that Matt. 1 is a midrash on Mark 1:1 remains, namely that it depends in part on assuming a close relationship, if not identity, between the terms υἱὸς Δαυίδ and Χριστός in Matthew, since, according to our hypothesis, Matthew wrote his genealogy as a midrash on Mark 1: 1, where υἱὸς Δαυίδ is not mentioned. We suggest that ὁ Χριστός in Matthew is indeed often closely related to υἱὸς Δαυίδ, especially in Matt. 1: 1, Ἰησοῦς Χριστοῦ υἱοῦ Δαυίδ but also in Matthew's narrative where the healing ministry of Jesus to the blind, lame, deaf, lepers and poor is described as τὰ ἔργα τοῦ Χριστοῦ (11: 2) and thus close to the concept of the Son of David as denoting Jesus' ministry of healing in Matthew. Similarly, in Matt. 2: 4–6 the reference to ὁ Χριστός is intended to represent the general Jewish view of the provenance of the Messiah: he is to be born in Bethlehem, that is, he is to be υἱὸς Δαυίδ. As for the remaining occurrences of the title in Matthew, little light can be shed on the Matthean understanding of the term from the references to 'false Christs' in 24: 5, 23, which are drawn from other sources (cf. Mark 13: 21) nor yet from the use of the term at the trial of Jesus (26: 68) or by Pilate (27: 17, 22). In 23: 10 the title Χριστός is set in opposition to 'Rabbi', 'father', and 'master'—all titles apparently drawn from contemporary Judaism. So also ὁ Χριστός may be here understood in the categories of Rabbinic Judaism. In any case, Matthew assumes that ὁ Χριστός is at once Son of David and Son of God, and the importance of these two titles in the Gospel of Matthew is shown by the fact that this gospel begins with a midrash on each.[2]

[1] P. 261; we are inclined to attribute to Matthew a less lofty view of the *Kyrios* title than Bornkamm (pp. 41–3), who refers to it as a 'göttlicher Hoheitsnamen'.

[2] Although the title, 'Son of God', does not actually occur in Matt. 1: 18–25, I am assuming that the very *raison d'être* of the pericope is to serve as a confirmation of the title—almost in an etiological fashion. The account answers the question: 'How is Jesus the Son of God?' in a way that avoids adoptionism.

CHAPTER 6

THE GENEALOGY OF JESUS IN LUKE

When we turn to the Lukan genealogy of Jesus it is apparent that the situation is somewhat different from that of Matthew. Here, apart from verse 23, there is a simple list of names proceeding in linear form with no additional notes or elaboration. Luke offers no hint as to his special interest in recording the list, and therefore it is impossible to be dogmatic in the attempt to consider the purpose of the genealogy within the framework of Lukan theology, even if we could be sure what 'Lukan theology' really is. Moreover, in such an attempt we are immediately confronted with the form-critical question—is this list a Lukan construction, or was it shaped in some prior tradition which Luke has incorporated? And, if the latter is true, then to what extent can we expect to find here a congruity with Luke's purpose in writing the history of Jesus and the earliest church? While Schlatter's dictum that genealogies are 'in der Sache und der Form heimisches jüdisches Erbe'[1] is obviously true, yet it cannot be assumed that the lists as we have them in Matthew and Luke were taken over without modification or redaction from the Palestinian Jewish-Christian church.[2] There are two indications which seem to support this view: (1) Repetition of names in the list after David, some of which appear to be anachronisms, possibly suggesting that this list had its own history. Among these repetitions are: variations of Mattathias (five times), Jesus (twice), Joseph (three times), Simeon (Semein), Levi (twice), and Melchi (twice). The question of anachronism enters the picture here in light of the history of the usage of Jewish personal names. Jeremias points out that the use of the names of the twelve patriarchs of Israel as personal names cannot be traced to pre-exilic times; thus, 'when Luke, in the early period of the kings, names in succession Joseph, Judah, Simeon, and Levi as the sixth to ninth descendants of David, it is an anachronism which proves the pre-exilic section

[1] *Matthäus*, p. 2, cited by Hahn, *Christologische Hoheitstitel*, p. 242.
[2] Cf. Hahn, pp. 242 ff.

of the genealogy to be historically worthless'.[1] Material since published in the *Corpus Papyrorum Judaicarum* has tended to confirm the view that these names, together with the name Jesus (Joshua), were not commonly used among the Jews until the Ptolemaic and especially the Roman periods. It appears that there was a steady increase in the use of Hebrew biblical names from the Ptolemaic to the Roman periods, including the names Joseph and Jesus.[2] Thus, the Lukan list most probably does not derive from an actual genealogy of Joseph or Mary, but should be considered in light of the generally midrashic use of this *Gattung* in Judaism. This means that it is legitimate to inquire into the purposes for which it was constructed and for its inclusion in this gospel. (2) The genealogy is incorporated into a framework similar to that of Mark, that is, between the account of Jesus' baptism and his temptation. This is to say that Luke was not led to include the genealogy at this point merely because of a sequence found in his sources. Moreover, the break in the 'Markan' sequence at this crucial point would seem to suggest that Luke had some specific purpose in mind for the genealogy as well as for its position.

But what, from a form-critical point of view, can one make of the ὡς ἐνομίζετο in verse 23? Almost universally, this phrase is taken as a parenthesis, an editorial comment by Luke which is an indication of his awareness of the difficulty of tracing Jesus' descent from Joseph while at the same time holding to the tradition of the virgin birth.[3] Yet nowhere else in Luke 3–24 is there any hint of the idea of the virgin birth. Rather, as we shall see, Luke's use of the Son of God title seems to be at variance with the tradition of 1:26–38. Perhaps the ὡς ἐνομίζετο is best taken as an indication of Luke's uncertainty concerning the historical value of the list, or his realization that the genealogical

[1] Jeremias, *Jerusalem*, pp. 330–1, notes that the first occurrences of the names Joseph, Judah, and Simeon as personal names among the Israelites or Jews are to be found in Ezra, Nehemiah, and I Chronicles, while the name Levi occurs as a personal name first among the Maccabees and in NT times.

[2] *CPJ*, esp. 1, 83–4.

[3] Other views, that this phrase indicates that Luke was recording a tradition different from Matthew which he knew to be incorrect, or that the parenthesis includes also the mention of Joseph, are inept efforts at harmonization of Matthew and Luke at this point.

descent of Jesus was already a matter of polemics. In any case, verse 23 in its present form is Lukan, and a strong indication that the genealogy—perhaps in somewhat different form—originated at a time prior to Luke. But, by the same token, this Lukan phrase also points to the probability that the hand of Luke was operative also in other parts of the genealogy. At least it is almost certain that, whatever the purpose of Luke in including this pedigree, the list has some function within Lukan theology.

What is this function? Two methods of approach have been frequently attempted.

(1) The apocalyptic interpretation. The fact that the genealogy contains seventy-seven names has often intrigued scholars. Once again, it is Bornhäuser who has developed the apocalyptic interpretation on the basis of this figure most confidently.[1] The seventy-seven names are seen as eleven world-weeks, at the end of which the Messianic week begins. Thus a parallel is drawn with those apocalyptic reconstructions of history which are based on a division of world history into twelve parts. Thus, for instance, in the Latin and Arabic text of IV Ezra 14: 10 ff., history is divided into twelve parts, the last of which is apparently the Messianic age:

> For the age has lost its youth, and the times begin to grow old. For the age is divided into twelve parts, and nine of its parts have already passed, as well as half of the tenth part; so two of its parts remain, besides half of the tenth part. Now therefore, set your house in order...

The allusion to II Baruch 53–74 cannot be made here, however, since, as we have seen above, the apocalyptic periodization there is not based on the number twelve but rather fourteen.[2] The supposed parallel in Apoc. Abraham 29 is even more dubious. Nonetheless, the apocalyptic significance of Luke's genealogy is accepted by C. Kaplan,[3] K. H. Rengstorf,[4] E. Klostermann,[5] and F. Hahn.[6] The major weakness in this approach is the

[1] *Geburts- und Kindheitsgeschichte*, pp. 20–2.

[2] Above, pp. 194 f.

[3] *Bibliotheca Sacra*, LXXXVII (1930), 465–71.

[4] *Das Evangelium nach Lukas* (NTD, I. 2) (1937), pp. 49–50.

[5] *Das Lukasevangelium* (HNT), 2nd ed. 1929, p. 57.

[6] *Christologische Hoheitstitel*, p. 243.

doubtful condition of the text of Luke's genealogy, which does not permit us to know how many members there were in the list when incorporated into Luke's gospel: B, N, U, and other MSS. testify to seventy-two names. Most importantly, Irenaeus explicitly mentions seventy-two names in the Lukan genealogy, apparently alluding to the Jewish tradition that there were seventy or seventy-two nations in the world, a supposition derived by the Rabbis from Gen. 10:[1]

Wherefore Luke points out that the pedigree which traces the generation of our Lord back to Adam contains seventy-two generations, connecting the end with the beginning, and implying that it is He who has summed up in Himself all nations dispersed from Adam downwards, and all languages and generations of men, together with Adam himself.[2]

To complicate matters, the sy^{sin} has seventy-three names, Africanus omits Matthat and Levi in verse 24,[3] while the Western text has the list of Matt. 1 in reverse, but including the kings omitted by Matthew and adding the pre-Abrahamitic list from Genesis. Thus the genealogy when incorporated or written by Luke may have had only seventy-two names, and consequently the parallel with the twelvefold periodizations of history in the above-mentioned apocalypses is seriously weakened.[4] Again, if Luke had intended a symbolic apocalyptic meaning, one would expect a note similar to that in Matt. 1:17 which underlines the epochs and preserves the scheme in the Matthean list in spite of textual errors.[5] Finally, there is the theological question which must be raised. Several recent scholars have followed Conzelmann's analysis of the general conception of eschatological fulfillment in the theology of Luke.[6] According to Conzelmann, in Luke the realization of

[1] Cf. Moore, *Judaism*, I, 226, 278; 43 n. 2.

[2] *Adv. haer.* III. 22. 3.

[3] In Eus. *H.E.* I. 7. 5.

[4] On textual problems in the genealogy, see Kuhn, *ZNW*, XXII (1923), 206–8; also Jeremias, *Jerusalem*, p. 327, and Heer, *Die Stammbäume Jesu, ad rem.* Schlatter contends (*Matthäus*, p. 218) that τοῦ 'Αδμὶν τοῦ 'Αρνί are doubles, both representing Ram, and that τοῦ Μελεὰ τοῦ Μεννά were originally one name.

[5] Jeremias, *Jerusalem*, p. 327.

[6] *The Theology of St Luke*, tr. G. Buswell (from *Die Mitte der Zeit*, 1954), 1960, *passim.*

the apocalyptic fulfillment in the parousia is separated from the time of Jesus' ministry by the period of the church, a period of indeterminate length. Also, in interpreting the significance of Jesus' ministry, Luke excludes apocalyptic categories. The 'coming' of the end-events belongs to the future and is separated by a long interval from its proleptic manifestation in the ministry of Jesus. In short, according to Conzelmann, while Luke has not abrogated the traditional primitive Christian eschatology, he has placed the emphasis on the role of Christianity in history, and has begun to consider the ministry of Jesus as that of a historical figure. While the details of Conzelmann's treatment of Luke have been subjected to criticism,[1] his general evaluation of Lukan eschatology has been widely accepted.[2] If Conzelmann is generally right in his analysis of Luke's handling of primitive Christian eschatology, then the genealogy would have no primary apocalyptic significance for Luke. It should be noted also that Luke, in contrast to Matthew, leads the genealogy from Jesus *backwards* to Adam (or God), a procedure which is not well suited to convey the idea of Jesus as the *telos* of the historical process. In all apocalyptic reconstructions of history, the movement is from the past to the future fulfillment. We may therefore conclude that the eschatological interpretation of the purpose of the Lukan genealogy remains highly doubtful.

(2) Christ as the second Adam. It is customary also to main-

[1] See especially W. C. Robinson, *Der Weg des Herrn: Studien zur Geschichte und Eschatologie im Lukas-Evangelium; ein Gespräch mit H. Conzelmann* (1964), H. Flender, *St Luke: Theologian of Redemptive History*, tr. R. H. and I. Fuller (1967), who questions Conzelmann's interpretation of Lukan eschatology. E. Rasco (*Gregorianum*, XLVI (1965), 286–319) contends that Luke has not eliminated or historicized eschatology and that Conzelmann does not recognize the importance of OT tradition in Luke's theology. See also the reviews of Robert W. Funk in *JBR*, XXX (1962), 299–301; O. Piper in *Th. Tod.* XIX (1962), 146 ff.; D. Nineham in *Ch.Q.R.* CLXIII (1962), 498 ff.; *JBL*, LXXVI (1957), 319–22; H. J. Cadbury in *JBL*, LXXX (1961), 304 f.; *Verbum Domini*, XXXII (1955), 117 ff.

[2] C. K. Barrett, *Luke the Historian in Recent Study* (1961), pp. 40–6, 66. Also W. C. van Unnik, E. Käsemann, E. Grasser, S. Schulz, and Ulrich Wilckens (see van Unnik, 'Luke-Acts, A Storm Center in Contemporary Scholarship', in *Studies in Luke-Acts, Essays in Honor of Paul Schubert*, ed. L. E. Keck and J. L. Martyn (1966), pp. 15–32; U. Wilckens, 'Interpreting Luke-Acts in a Period of Existentialist Theology', *ibid.* p. 65).

tain that Luke has in mind a typological relationship of Jesus to Adam since he leads the genealogy back not to Abraham, as in Matthew, but to Adam, son of God.[1] This, it is said, has the function of illustrating Luke's general concern to portray the universal character of Jesus' ministry. Jeremias finds additional significance in this respect from the position of the genealogy immediately before the account of Jesus' temptation, which, he suggests, has the theme of showing how Jesus, like Adam, is tempted by Satan.[2] He refers to midrashic accounts in the Apocalypse of Moses (cf. chapter 24) and the Books of Adam and Eve in which it is said that Adam was honored by the beasts in Paradise, and there enjoyed angels' food.[3] So in the account of the temptation, after being tempted, Christ is with the wild beasts and is ministered to by the angels. 'He thus ushers in the paradisial state of the last days when there will be peace between man and beast...Jesus reopens the Paradise closed to the first man. This typology Adam/Christ perhaps underlies the tracing of the genealogy of Jesus back to Adam in Luke 3:38... The fact that the temptation story follows immediately in Luke 4: 1 ff. seems to support this; it may well be that as a follower of Paul Luke knew the Pauline typology Adam/Christ.'[4]

This approach has the merit of attempting to discover the significance of Luke's sequence in chapter 3, a sequence which apparently breaks the order of events derived from his source. Also the attempt to find a correlation between the mention of Adam, the father of all humanity, and the universal mission of Jesus in Luke is consistent with the well-known Lukan motif of Christianity as a world religion, offering salvation both to Samaritan and Jew, tax-collector and priest, women and men, a motif which can be traced throughout Luke/Acts. But the Christ/Adam typology hypothesis fails to take into account several objections: (1) The Pauline motif of Christ as second Adam is nowhere explicitly to be found in Luke/Acts. Can we

[1] Cf., for example, Wm. Manson, *The Gospel of Luke* (Moffatt NT Commentaries) (1930), p. 35; F. W. Beare, *Earliest Records*, p. 42; Hahn, *Christologische Hoheitstitel*, p. 243; A. Schlatter, *Das Evangelium des Lukas* (2nd ed., 1960), pp. 218–19.

[2] 'Adam', *TDNT*, I, 141 ff.

[3] Cf. Charles, *A & P*, II, 134 (*Vita Adae*, iv); Apoc. Mos. 24.

[4] *TDNT*, I, 141.

imagine, therefore, that we are to see in the genealogy a veiled allusion to such a distinctive idea, which Luke elsewhere ignores? (2) Jeremias' allusions to midrashic literature in which Adam was honored by the beasts in paradise and ate food of the angels do not apply to the form of the temptation account in Luke, which omits the Markan reference to wild beasts and the angels' ministrations (Mark 1: 13). If the temptation accounts do preserve a reflection of this midrash, it would apply only to Mark, and partially to Matthew, who retains mention of the angels (Matt. 4: 11). (3) The genealogy in fact does not end with Adam but with the phrase Ἀδὰμ τοῦ θεοῦ. Thus, if Luke intends a typological significance between the beginning and the end of the list, it would seem more appropriate to find it in the designation of Jesus as son of God.

A. JESUS AS SON OF GOD

Luke has inserted the genealogy of Jesus between two pericopes which have parallels in Mark. Can any significance be derived from this? The answer to this problem depends on the view of the first two chapters in Luke, since, if the genealogy were incorporated into this gospel before the first two chapters were added, then the present location of the genealogy would be the only natural place for its introduction. In 3: 1–3 Luke sets the beginning of the Baptist's ministry in relation to secular history and to geography. This leads directly to the account of the Baptist's ministry, to which Luke appends, somewhat breaking the order of Mark, a reference to John's imprisonment. The latter reference perhaps accounts for the curious lack of mention of John's actual baptizing of Jesus in verses 21–2; yet the baptism pericope follows the account of John in a way similar to that both of Mark and Matthew. On the assumption, then, that the gospel at one point began at 3: 1, this would be the first place where the author could introduce the genealogy without overly disrupting the flow of the narrative. (However, it still does disrupt the sequence to some extent, since 4: 1 would read most naturally immediately after 3: 22, to which it refers.)

But can we give credence to the assumption that the genealogy was incorporated at a time when the gospel began at 3: 1? This assumption was most forcefully propounded by the supporters of the 'Proto-Luke' hypothesis, according to which the material in Luke 1–2 was not placed at the beginning of this gospel until its final redaction. Streeter notes the 'curious position of the genealogy' and remarks: 'If this had been inserted by the last editor of the Gospel, we should have expected to find it, like the genealogy in Matthew, somewhere in chapters 1 or 2 in connection with the account of the Birth and Infancy. If, however, it was originally inserted in a book which only began with Luke 3: 1, its position is explained; for it occurs immediately after the *first* mention of the name Jesus.'[1] Streeter also supported his contention that the gospel at one time began with 3: 1 by the observation that this reads like the opening of a book, although this might be countered by suggesting that Luke's chronological and geographical references in 3: 1 ff. serve the important purpose of establishing the beginning of Jesus' ministry, and thus could not have occurred in chapters 1–2. The whole question of the relation of chapters 1–2 to chapters 3–24 is one around which there has grown a good deal of discussion to which I cannot now add, but refer to the summary of Kümmel: The hypothesis of a translation of chapters 1–2 as a whole from the Hebrew is hardly tenable in view of recent linguistic studies and 'the probability is that Luke revised at least three diverse traditions, which already in part had attained a certain linguistic firmness, and placed them before his representation of Jesus' public activity. If the slight linguistic variations in Luke 1, 2 in comparison with Luke 3–24 demand an explanation at all, they presumably can be traced back to the fact that the early history was written later than the remainder of the Gospel.'[2] There does now seem to be a tendency to emphasize the congruity of chapters 1–2 with chapters 3–24,[3]

[1] B. H. Streeter, *The Four Gospels* (4th ed. 1930), p. 209. Conzelmann raises the objection that this theory would require that Markan passages are built around the already existing genealogy, while actually the genealogy 'is carefully incorporated into a Marcan context' (*Theology of St Luke*, p. 22 n. 1). Streeter, however, argued convincingly (to my thinking) that the context into which the genealogy was placed was a mixture of Q and L, and not necessarily Markan (ch. 8).

[2] W. G. Kümmel, *Introduction to the NT* (Feine–Behm–Kümmel), tr. A. J. Mattill (1966), p. 96.

[3] H. H. Oliver, 'The Lucan Birth Stories and the Purpose of Luke–Acts', *NTS*, x (1963–4), 202–6, maintains, against Conzelmann, that the theo-

but such studies can demonstrate only that the hand of the editor of chapters 3–24 can be traced also in chapters 1–2; they cannot show that the first two chapters were an integral part of the gospel of Luke from the beginning; that is, they do not destroy the 'Proto-Luke' hypothesis.[1]

In view of the present situation, therefore, one cannot be dogmatic in drawing conclusions from the placement of the genealogy between the baptism pericope and that of the temptation. Yet, even accepting the conclusion of Kümmel, one should note the possibility that the final editor of the gospel as it has come down to us did have the opportunity of removing the genealogy from its position when the first two chapters were added. But the most compelling argument for finding significance in the position of the genealogy is the fact that the motif of Jesus as Son of God is found in both the baptism pericope and also the genealogy. There is nothing in the genealogy to suggest that its function is solely to emphasize the Davidic descent of Jesus, as is commonly assumed; moreover, there is nothing in the Gospel of Luke as a whole to suggest that the title, son of David, was especially important for Luke. But the fact that the Lukan genealogy runs *backwards* from Jesus to God is significant since there is no known parallel in the OT or in Rabbinic texts for a genealogy to begin with or to culminate with the naming of God.[2] Thus it is not impossible that Luke saw in the genealogy one way of understanding the ascription of the Son of God title to Jesus: Jesus is Son of God not through the categories of pre-existence or physical (or metaphysical) relationship between Father and Son, but through the line of OT patriarchs and post-biblical historical figures. In this way, Luke historicizes the

logical motifs of the first two chapters of Luke are similar to those in chs. 3–24; W. B. Tatum, 'The Epoch of Israel: Luke I–II and the Theological Plan of Luke–Acts', *NTS*, XIII (1967), 184–95, suggests that slight differences of motifs in chs. 1–2 from 3–24 can be explained as due to their position in Luke's periodization scheme, chapters 1–2 representing the 'epoch of Israel'. Also P. S. Minear, 'Luke's Use of the Birth Stories', in *Studies in Luke-Acts*, ed. Keck and Martyn, pp. 111–30, reviews again the linguistic peculiarities shared by the first two chapters with the body of the Gospel.

[1] The most important studies of the relation of chapters 1–2 to chapters 3–24 are listed by Kümmel, including those of Winter, Laurentin, Dibelius, Benoit.

[2] Gen. 5 is not a real exception even though it is a source used by Luke, since this is a ספר תולדות אדם.

title, emphasizing the continuity of the Son with the OT and with Judaism. The Lukan genealogy would therefore be a prime example of Luke's consciousness of the continuity of history in the midst of seeming discontinuity. Just as the church is, on the one hand, the successor of Israel but also, on the other hand, stands in the same line of redemptive history as does Judaism, so also Jesus inaugurates a new epoch and yet derives significance, in part, from the fact that he stands in historical continuity with the redemptive history of the OT and of Judaism.[1] As far as its position is concerned, therefore, the genealogy can be considered an attempt to clarify the meaning of the divine voice at Jesus' baptism, 'Thou art my beloved Son; with thee I am well pleased' (verse 22).

But how can this interpretation of Luke's use of the Son of God title be reconciled with the virgin birth tradition found in chapters 1–2? The answer is simply that the tradition of the miraculous birth of Jesus in 1: 26–37 (though not in 2: 1–10) is not taken into account in chapters 3–24 at all. Rather, in the body of the gospel, the Son of God title seems to be almost identical with 'Messiah'. Thus, in 4: 41, Jesus prevents the demons from designating him as the Son of God 'because they knew that he was the Christ'. And similarly, in the transfiguration account Jesus is addressed as God's Son, his chosen (9: 35), while in 23: 35 the Messiah is called 'the Chosen'. While this may be due especially to Luke's failure clearly to distinguish the distinctive meanings of specific Christological titles in the tradition coming down to him, Conzelmann seems correct when he describes Luke's conception of the title, Son of God, as connected with a subordinationism that reveals itself in a complete lack of the idea of pre-existence. 'We know from the absence of the idea of pre-existence that there is no idea of a physical divine nature in the title of "son". Luke does not think in such categories at all.'[2]

[1] A similar interpretation of the position of the genealogy was already noted by J. C. K. von Hofmann: Jesus in verse 22 was pronounced God's Son and this is made clear by the genealogy, which shows in what sense he is derived from God (cited by R. C. H. Lenski, *The Interpretation of St Luke's Gospel* (reprinted 1946), p. 220). The position of the genealogy and its relation to the baptism pericope was noticed by Eusebius; cf. *Quaestiones Evangelicae ad Stephanum*, III (Migne, *Patrologia Graec.* XXII, 896).

[2] *Theology of St Luke*, pp. 173–4.

In summary, it seems best to conclude that the situation of the Lukan genealogy was determined not merely by necessity, or by the order of Luke's sources, but also by the desire to link together two pericopes which deal with the title, Son of God. The baptism pericope, because of its brevity and basic similarity with the Markan parallel, does not provide any certain clues as to the manner of Luke's conception of the Son title. If we could be certain that the Western reading of verse 22*b* ('You are my son, today I have begotten you') were original, then we would have a clear indication that the traditions in the birth stories are basically pre-Lukan. As it is, the Lukan account of the baptism is not striking. Jesus' baptism is mentioned as one detail among the baptism of 'all the people' (verse 21) and, in view of the close relationship in the body of the gospel between the title 'Messiah' and 'son of God', it is not improbable that Luke sees the baptism as the beginning of Jesus' Messianic consciousness. If, indeed, the two titles are almost synonymous in the gospel of Luke, then the function of the genealogy as an elaboration of the Son title is explicable, since the roots of the Messiah are to be found in the historical past of his people, especially in his descent from David.

This interpretation of the genealogy, however, leads directly to the question of its provenance. If Jesus is shown to be Son of God by virtue of his descent from Adam, the son of God *par excellence*, does this not constitute a close parallel with the Hellenistic and Roman attempts to prove the 'divinity' of heroes and emperors by tracing their pedigree to a god?[1] Although Luke may have been aware that such a genealogy would have a special significance to his readers among the Gentiles,[2] the answer must clearly be in the negative, since the evidence points to a Jewish provenance of the genealogy, at least in part, as I shall point out from the second motif discernible in Luke's genealogy.

[1] See examples above, pp. 112–14; also Hood, in *Early Christian Origins*, pp. 3–5.

[2] Cf. Hood, p. 13.

B. JESUS AS PROPHET

Perhaps the most surprising aspect of the Lukan genealogy is its rejection of the royal line of Judah. Rather than enumerating the royal succession from David to the exile, as does Matthew, Luke proceeds from David to his third son born in Jerusalem, Nathan (II Sam. 5: 14; I Chron. 3: 5; 14: 4), and from him through a series of unknown names up to Shealtiel and Zerubbabel and thence, again through a series of unknown names, to Joseph. This deviation from the kings of Judah is highly significant since the genealogy not only rejects the royal line, but also fails to incorporate any OT genealogical data between Nathan and Zerubbabel. Yet, as we have seen, the history of the usage of Jewish personal names scarcely permits the conclusion that Luke here has access to an actual genealogy of Joseph.

It is entirely possible that Luke's tendency to avoid any political overtones in his presentation of Christianity that might worsen the church–state relationship[1] lies behind his rejection of the royal line: Jesus is the Davidic Messiah, but not through the OT royalty, and therefore his Messiahship is not to be considered as opposed to the legally ordained rulers of the state. Yet, while this may be a subsidiary influence for Luke's deviation from Matthew at this point, it does not explain his decision to trace the ancestry of Jesus through Nathan, a relatively insignificant son of David.

An explanation of Luke's series of names must take into account the beginning of the deviation from the royal line, namely Nathan, son of David. Of special importance in this regard are the references to Nathan in the Jewish and also the Christian traditions. We cite four passages:[2]

(*a*) In Zech. 12: 10–14 there is a description of the mourning of Jerusalem 'when they look on him whom they have pierced'. Verse 12 reads:

וספדה הארץ משפחות משפחות לבד
משפחת בית־דויד לבד ונשיהם לבד
משפחת בית־נתן לבד ונשיהם לבד
משפחת בית־לוי לבד ונשיהם לבד
משפחת השמעי לבד ונשיהם לבד

[1] On Luke as political apologist, see Conzelmann, *Theology of St Luke*, pp. 138–44.

[2] See also Appendix 5, pp. 273 ff.

The land shall mourn, each family by itself; the family of the house of David by itself, and their wives by themselves; the family of the house of Nathan by itself, and their wives by themselves; the family of the house of Levi by itself, and their wives by themselves; the family of the Shimeites by itself, and their wives by themselves.

It is significant that Luke has incorporated each of these four names into his pre-exilic section. There is in this verse, however, no statement about the relationship of Nathan to David; it appears rather that each of the persons mentioned is considered as the father of a leading family or clan at the time of the oracle.

In the Targum on Zechariah, we find a surprising development: in one manuscript, Codex Reuchlinianus, the Nathan of Zech. 12: 12 is identified with both the son of David and the prophet Nathan of II Sam. 7.[1] The reading at Zech. 12: 12 is:[2]

ויספדון דיירי ארצא זרעיין זרעיין גבריהון
להוד ונשיהון להוד זרעית שלמה מלכא דבית דוד
להוד גבריהון להוד ונשיהון להוד זרעית בית נתן
נבייא בר דוד גבריהון להוד ונשיהוד להוד

We have here in juxtaposition 'the descendants of King Solomon of the house of David' and 'the descendants of the house of Nathan the prophet, son of David...' Immediately following, in verse 13, we read of 'the descendants of the house of Levi' and 'the descendants of the house of Mardokai, son of Jair, son of Shimei...' In the edition of Sperber,[3] however, the reading of Codex Reuchlinianus is relegated to the margin and the pertinent passage reads:

זרעית בית דויד גוברהון להוד ונשינון להוד
זרעית בית נתן גוברהון להוד ונשיהון להוד
זרעית בית לוי גוברהון להוד ונשיהון להוד
זרעית בית שמעי להוד ונשיהון להוד

[1] This was first noted by Eb. Nestle in 'Salomo und Nathan in Mt 1 und Lc 3', *ZNW*, VIII (1907), 72, where the parallel with Luke is drawn; but Nestle was apparently not aware of the confusion of the Targum text at this point.

[2] Text from Paulus de Lagarde, *Prophetae Chaldaicae* (1872), p. 484.

[3] Alexander Sperber, *The Latter Prophets According to Targum Jonathan* (vol. 3 of *The Bible in Aramaic*) (Leiden: E. J. Brill, 1962), pp. 495–6; Sperber utilizes a number of MSS. and printed editions.

In view of the confusion in the textual tradition it would be hazardous—on the basis of the Targum alone—to suggest even an approximate date for this identification of David's son Nathan with the prophet, especially since the edition of Sperber, which lacks the identification, is much closer to the Hebrew OT. But other sources which reflect the same identification prove that it was relatively early:

(*b*) Angelo Mai in *Bibliotheca nova Patrum*, IV, 231, 273, gives the text of a portion of Africanus' *Letter to Aristides* which immediately precedes the beginning of the letter in Eusebius (*H.E.* I. 7). The subject-matter is the same as that of the portion of the letter in Eusebius, that is, the NT genealogies of Jesus. We note also a similarity of style and the acuteness of argument which argue for its integrity within Africanus' letter. The translation which follows is from *The Ante-Nicene Fathers*.[1]

Some indeed incorrectly allege that this discrepant enumeration and mixing of names both of priestly men, as they think, and royal, was made properly, in order that Christ might be shown rightfully to be both Priest and King; as if any one disbelieved this, or had any other hope than this, that Christ is the High Priest of his Father, who presents our prayers to Him, and a supramundane King, who rules by the Spirit those whom He has delivered, a co-operator in the government of all things. And this is announced to us not by the catalogue of the tribes, nor by the mixing of the registered generations, but by the patriarchs and prophets. Let us not, therefore, descend to such religious trifling as to establish the kingship and priesthood of Christ by the interchanges of names. For the priestly tribe of Levi, too, was allied with the kingly tribe of Judah through the circumstance that Aaron married Elizabeth the sister of Naason [Exod. 6: 23], and that Eleazar again married the daughter of Phatiel [Exod. 6: 25], and begat children. The evangelists, therefore, would thus have spoken falsely, affirming what was not truth, but a fictitious commendation. And for this reason the one traced the pedigree of Jacob the father of Joseph from David through Solomon; the other traced that of Heli also, though in a different way, the father of Joseph, from Nathan the son of David. And they ought not indeed to have been ignorant that both orders of the ancestors enumerated are the generation of David, the royal tribe of Judah. For if Nathan was a prophet, so also was Solomon, and so was the father of both of them; and there were prophets belonging to many

[1] Vol. VI, p. 125.

of the tribes, but priests belonging to none of the tribes, save the Levites only. To no purpose, then, is this fabrication of theirs...For if the generations are different, and trace no genuine seed to Joseph, and if all has been stated only with the view of establishing the position of Him who was to be born—to confirm the truth, namely that He who was to be would be king and priest, there being at the same time no proof given, but the dignity of the words being brought down to a feeble hymn—it is evident that no praise accrues to God from that...Therefore, that we may expose the ignorance also of him who speaks thus, and prevent any one from stumbling at this folly, I shall set forth the true history of these matters.

In this passage there is an anticipation of the quotation in Eusebius: Jacob (Matt. 1: 15 f.) and Heli (Luke 3: 23) are both fathers of Joseph, though in different ways, that is, one the actual father and the other the legal. The passage is concerned with refuting the argument, apparently adduced by some in order to explain the divergence of the two genealogies, that one (probably Luke's) was intended to demonstrate Jesus' priestly office, the other his royal.[1] Then, unexpectedly, the author refers to Nathan, maintaining that his function as prophet has nothing to do with priesthood. Again we may suppose that in some circles Nathan was considered a prophet (in this passage probably a priestly prophet), even though the basis for this identification cannot be determined. What is significant for our purpose, however, is that the author of this passage treats the identification of Nathan, son of David, as the prophet as something that may be assumed, even though he emphasizes that this prophetic role of Nathan has nothing to do with a priestly genealogy. At any rate, if this passage can be ascribed to Africanus, we are enabled to date the identification of Nathan as the prophet to the second century.

(*c*) Our third datum is found in Eusebius' *Questiones Evangelicae ad Stephanum*, III. 2:[2]

Διαφόρων γὰρ παρὰ Ἰουδαίοις ὑπολήψεων περὶ τοῦ Χριστοῦ κεκρατημένων, καὶ πάντων μὲν συμφώνως ἐπὶ τὸν Δαβὶδ ἀναγόντων, διὰ τὰς πρὸς τὸν Δαβὶδ τοῦ θεοῦ ἐπαγγελίας, ἤδη δὲ τῶν μὲν ἀπὸ

[1] See below, pp. 273 ff., for a presentation of the view against which Africanus argues.

[2] Migne, *Patrologia Graec.* XXII, 895; this passage is referred to by G. Kuhn, *ZNW*, XXII (1923), 206–28.

Δαβὶδ καὶ Σολομῶνος καὶ τοῦ βασιλικοῦ γένους πειθομένων ἔσεσθαι τὸν Χριστόν, τῶν δὲ ταύτην μὲν φευγόντων τὴν δόξαν, διὰ τὸ πλείστην ἐμφέρεσθαι τῶν βεβασιλευκότων κατηγορίαν, διά τε τὸ ἐκκήρυκτον ὑπὸ τοῦ προφήτου Ἰερεμίου γεγονέναι τὸν Ἰεχονίαν, καὶ διὰ τὸ εἰρῆσθαι μὴ ἀναστήσεσθαι ἐξ αὐτοῦ σπέρμα καθήμενον ἐπὶ θρόνου Δαβίδ, διὰ δὲ οὖν ταῦτα, ἑτέραν ὁδευόντων, καὶ ἀπὸ μὲν Δαβὶδ ὁμολογούντων, οὐ μὴν διὰ Σολομῶνος, ἀλλὰ διὰ Νάθαν, ὃς ἦν τοῦ Δαβὶδ παῖς (φασὶ δὲ τὸν Νάθαν καὶ προφητεῦσαι κατὰ τὰ ἐν ταῖς βασιλείαις φερόμενα), ἀπό τε τοῦ Νάθαν διαδόχων προελεύσεσθαι τὸν Χριστὸν διαβεβαιουμένων, καὶ τόν γε Ἰωσὴφ ἐκεῖθέν ποθεν γενεαλογούντων, σφόδρα ἀναγκαίως ὁ Λουκᾶς τὴν τούτων ἀνιστορῶν δόξαν, ἀλλ' οὐ τὴν αὐτοῦ, προσέθηκε τῇ κατ' αὐτὸν ἱστορίᾳ τὸ 'ὡς ἐνομίζετο', τῷ Ματθαίῳ παραχωρήσας μὴ τό, ὡς ἐνομίζετο, ἱστορεῖν, ἀλλ' ὡς εἶχεν ἀληθείας τὰ τῆς γενέσεως· αὕτη μὲν οὖν ἡ πρώτη ἀπόδοσις.

For differing opinions concerning the Messiah prevail among the Jews, though all agree in leading [the pedigree] up to David, because of the promises of God to David. But yet some are persuaded that the Messiah will come from David and Solomon and the royal line while others eschew this opinion because serious accusation was levelled against the kings and because Jeconiah was denounced by the prophet Jeremiah and because it was said that no seed from him [Jeconiah] should arise to sit on the throne of David. For these reasons, therefore, they go another way, agreeing [with the descent] from David; not, however, through Solomon but rather through Nathan, who was a child (παῖς) of David (they say that Nathan also prophesied, according to what is said in the books of Kings). They are certain that the Messiah would come forth from the successors of Nathan and trace the ancestry of Joseph from that point. Therefore, Luke, necessarily taking account of their opinion—though it was not his own—added to his account the ὡς ἐνομίζετο. In doing this he allowed Matthew to relate [the matter], not on the basis of supposition but as having the truth in the matters of the genealogy. This, then, is the first reply [to Stephanus].[1]

Eusebius here accounts for the differences between the two genealogies by supposing that Luke merely recorded the opinion held by some, though not by himself, that the curse of God on Jeconiah in Jer. 22: 24–30 made it impossible for the Messiah to descend from the royal line of the kings of Judah. Consequently, they affirmed that the Messiah would spring from Nathan, who was the head of a non-royal line of Davidic

[1] My translation.

descent. As we have seen,[1] the curse on Jeconiah was a subject of discussion among the Rabbis. What is significant for our purpose is that here again Nathan is mentioned in a prophetic role, and that this characterization is attributed to those who maintained the position of Nathan in the Messianic pedigree. Whether Eusebius attributes this opinion to Jews or Christians is not clear, in spite of the opening phrases. Of course, only Christians would include Joseph in a Messianic genealogy. In any case, the reference to the prophetic role of Nathan is introduced as a more or less traditional point of view in some circles.

(*d*) We have next to mention a later development of these ideas contained in an unofficial haggadic work, the Apocalypse of Zerubbabel.[2] Here the Messiah son of David is named Menahem ben Ammiel; he was born at the time of David but remains hidden until his revelation at the end.[3] His birth at the time of David is further explained by the assertion that his mother was Hephzibah, 'the wife of Nathan the prophet',[4] a statement without basis in the OT. But, since this is the Davidic Messiah, the Ammiel mentioned must be the father of Bathsheba (II Chron. 3: 5) and the following relationships are thus assumed in this apocalypse:

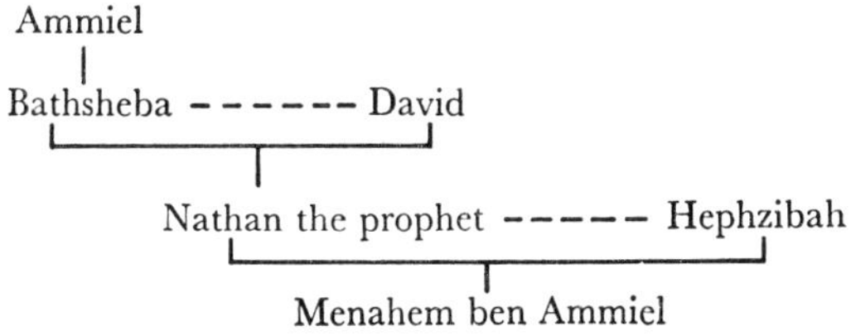

Once again, the identification of David's son Nathan with the prophet of the same name is not labored or supported by argument but rather assumed.[5]

[1] See above, pp. 183 f.

[2] Text and French translation by Lévi, *RÉJ*, LXVIII (1914), 135–57; the document is dated by Lévi *c.* A.D. 629–36; on this paragraph, see above, pp. 135 f.

[3] Lévi, p. 148.

[4] Lévi, p. 151; cf. pp. 150, 157.

[5] Other information on the prophet Nathan's relationships to David is provided by Ps. Jerome: *Quaestiones Hebraicae in II Regum et in II Paralip.*, in Migne, *Patrologia Lat.* XXIII, 1329–1402. In I Chron. 20: 7, the author identifies Nathan the prophet with Jonathan, David's nephew, who slew a

In the light of this evidence it seems clear that there was a Jewish tradition—definitely a minority view—that not only identified David's son with the prophet, but also held that the Messiah would descend from this non-royal line. How can this development be explained? Aptowitzer[1] fits these data into his overall hypothesis that most of the Jewish speculation on the descent of the Messiah is to be traced to polemics between the Hasmoneans and their opponents during the reign of the later Maccabees. He ascribes the origin of the emphasis on Nathan to Hasmonean (priestly) accusations of taints in the royal line because of the Ammonite ancestry of Rehoboam through his mother, Naamah the Ammonitess, wife of Solomon. The anti-Hasmoneans, according to Aptowitzer, attempted to evade this charge by explaining that the Messiah would descend not from Solomon but rather from Nathan. Aptowitzer suggests that this polemic is reflected in the Lukan genealogy.

But there are obvious weaknesses in this explanation. Apart from the difficulty of dating the Nathan tradition to so early a time (in view of the somewhat esoteric nature of this tradition it is not an impossible assumption), it is doubtful whether the charge against Naamah the Ammonitess was sufficient to account for the rejection of the royal line in the Messianic pedigree. As we have seen, the Mishnah already records the 'law of the Ammonites and Moabites' which exempted the women of those two peoples from the prohibition of Deut. 23: 3; and later tradition specifically related this 'law' to Ruth and Naamah. But, also, the introduction of Nathan into the pedigree would not answer the accusations made, according to Aptowitzer's hypothesis, by the Hasmoneans against Tamar, Ruth, and Bathsheba, who would necessarily be included in any genealogy of a Messiah ben David.

While any reconstruction of the rise of the Nathan tradition is made problematical by the paucity of evidence, it must proceed from what evidence there is. The earliest datum, Zech. 12: 12, indicates that there was in late OT times an important clan

Philistine giant. This may represent a later attempt to harmonize the Jewish tradition of the identification of the prophet with David's son, Nathan, with the official royal Messianism.

[1] *Parteipolitik*, pp. 113–16 and notes. Aptowitzer refers only to the Targum, Luke's genealogy, and the Apocalypse of Zerubbabel.

in Judah that traced its descent from Nathan. Whether this Nathan is understood by the biblical writer to be either the son of David or the prophet cannot be determined; but the possibility of an identification of the Nathan of Zech. 12: 12 with both of these biblical figures is obvious. That this was actually accomplished is indicated by the sources adduced above, especially the Targum of Jonathan. Yet Luke 3: 31 is the earliest extant source for the inclusion of Nathan in the genealogy of the Messiah. We suggest that at this point the witness of Eusebius, noted above, be given its due weight, namely that the origin of the position of Nathan in the Lukan genealogy is to be found in a difference of opinion within Jewish discussion of the ancestry of the Messiah. The Targum on Zech. 12: 12 and the later development in the Apocalypse of Zerubbabel serve to confirm this statement of Eusebius and to suggest that his further contention that Luke's genealogy shows an awareness of the Nathan tradition may in fact be accurate. His further suggestion that the origin of the Nathan tradition was due in part to the curse of God on Jeconiah also deserves scholarly respect, especially in view of the Rabbinic concern over Jer. 22: 24–30 and their attempts to mitigate the effects of this curse.[1] In any event, there is no explanation of the Lukan rejection of the royal line that can better account for the evidence, namely the position of Nathan in the Jewish and Christian traditions subsequent to Luke.

If we accept as a working hypothesis the conclusion that Luke's genealogy reflects, in part, an esoteric haggadic tradition within Judaism, a further question is raised concerning the extent to which the genealogy was a pre-Lukan compilation; on this question there is room for various opinions ranging from, on the one hand, ascribing the entire genealogy (apart from the mention of Joseph and Jesus) to a pre-Lukan Jewish or Christian list to, on the other hand, considering the list as the work of Luke, who incorporated into it the Nathan tradition derived from Judaism. For our purpose, however, the one important question is whether Luke was aware of the Jewish identification of the Davidic Nathan with the prophet of the same name. The

[1] Of course, Eusebius' belief that Luke's genealogy represents only this Jewish tradition and not his own view is due to the desire to explain the discrepancies between the two NT genealogies and cannot be taken seriously.

only possibility of answering this question lies in a consideration of the Lukan emphasis on the role of prophecy in the ministry of Jesus and in the mission of the church.

That this emphasis on the prophetic function is an especially important characteristic of Luke-Acts is seen in a variety of ways.[1]

(1) There is throughout the Lukan corpus an appeal to *the prophets of the OT as witnesses to the validity of the ministry of Jesus*; these prophets are distinguished from Jesus as the new prophet by the phrase προφήτης τῶν ἀρχαίων (9: 8, 19—a phrase incorporated by Luke into the Markan source; cf. Luke 1: 70; Acts 3: 21). There are several references to the OT prophets in general (Acts 3: 18, 24; 7: 42; 10: 43; 13: 40; 15: 15; 26: 27; Luke 18: 31; 24: 25, 27, 44), who are twice designated by the same phrase as 'holy' (Luke 1: 70; Acts 3: 21). Mentioned explicitly are Isaiah (Luke 3: 4; 4: 17; Acts 8: 28; 28: 25; cf. 7: 48), Joel (Acts 2: 16), Samuel (Acts 3: 28; 13: 20, 27), Moses (Luke 24: 27; Acts 3: 22), Elijah (Luke 1: 17; 4: 25–6; 9: 8, 19, 30 ff., 54), Elisha (Luke 4: 27), and also, significantly, David as a prophet (Acts 2: 30). In Luke's version of the reference to the apocalyptic banquet (cf. Matthew 8: 11), there are in the kingdom of God not only Abraham, Isaac, and Jacob, but also 'all the prophets' (13: 28). Thus, the greatness of the age of the historical Israel is considered by Luke to have centered in the role of the prophets who anticipated the coming Christ (Luke 10: 24).

(2) Luke considers also *the ministry of Jesus in a large part to be a prophetic ministry*. Already in the birth narratives—which in this respect are in full accord with the body of Luke-Acts[2]—the coming of John and Jesus as prophetic figures (cf. Luke 1: 76) is the substance of prophetic utterance attributed to angels (1: 13–17, 30–6), to Mary (1: 46–55), to Zechariah (1: 67–79), to Simeon (2: 29–35), and to Anna (2: 36–8). Of utmost significance in Luke-Acts is the view that Jesus himself was a prophet. Luke records and heightens the effect of passages in his sources

[1] Cf. G. W. H. Lampe, 'The Holy Spirit in the Writings of St Luke', in *Studies in the Gospels: Essays in Memory of R. H. Lightfoot*, ed. D. E. Nineham (1955), esp. pp. 173 ff.

[2] Cf. Oliver, *NTS*, x (1963–4), 202–26; W. B. Tatum, *NTS*, xiii (1967), 184–95.

which present Jesus as prophet: the saying, 'No prophet is acceptable in his own country' (4: 24; Mark 6: 4; Matthew 13: 57) is placed within the reaction to the first appearance of Jesus in his ministry. Prophecy had been fulfilled (4: 21), an indication that the true prophet had appeared, as is shown by the reference to Elijah and Elisha in this context (4: 25–7). Also recorded from his sources are the views of some of the people that Jesus was an OT prophet *redivivus*; but the special wording of this popular opinion by Luke, namely προφήτης τις τῶν ἀρχαίων, which occurs twice (Luke 9: 8; cf. Mark 6: 15; and Luke 9: 19; cf. Mark 8: 28; Matt. 16: 14), indicates that this view was wrong only in so far as Jesus was considered to be one of the OT prophets, but was correct in attributing to him the prophetic role.[1] That Luke considers the prophetic designation to be legitimately applied to Jesus is certain from a consideration of his peculiar (special) material. The reference to the raising of the widow's son at Nain (7: 11–17), which bears a close relationship to the story of Elijah raising the widow's son (I Kings 17),[2] is clear in its significance:

> Fear seized them all; and they glorified God, saying, 'A great prophet has arisen among us!' and 'God has visited his people!'

The reaction of the people is presented in a positive light; that is, it is Luke's own response. In this respect the title 'prophet' is used in a way similar to that of the 'Son of David' in Matthew. A similar judgment must be passed on the saying of Simon the Pharisee in response to the washing of Jesus' feet by a 'sinner': 'If this man were a prophet, he would have known who and what sort of woman this is who is touching him, for she is a sinner' (Luke 7: 39). The view of Luke is thus far implicit: Jesus was indeed a prophet. But this Lukan view also emerges explicitly in two passages of central importance. In 13: 33, the climax of a passion prediction which immediately precedes the lament over Jerusalem, Jesus says: 'I must go my way today and tomorrow and the day following; for it cannot be that a

[1] This is an important point of detail which argues against the thesis of P. Dabeck ('Siehe, es erscheinen Moses und Elias', *Biblica*, XXIII (1942), 175–89, esp. pp. 180–9) that Luke presents Jesus as the new Elijah. Dabeck's creative study, however, does underline the prophetic element in Luke.

[2] Cf. Dabeck, p. 181.

prophet should perish away from Jerusalem.' Here the passion is viewed as a fulfillment of the role of the prophet and should be considered in the light of the Lukan emphasis on the killing of the OT prophets by 'the fathers' of the Jews (Luke 11:47–51). In Acts 7:52 the parallel between the death of the prophets and the death of 'the Righteous One' is explicitly drawn. In the Emmaus incident the essentially Lukan view of Jesus' ministry appears again: 'Jesus of Nazareth, who was a prophet mighty in word and deed before God and all the people' (Luke 24:19). The correction of the disciples' view of Jesus' ministry is not a repudiation of the prophetic role as such, but rather a demonstration that Jesus as prophet had to endure the passion and death predicted of him by the OT prophets (verses 25–7). Similarly, in Acts there occur the only two explicit references in the NT to the well-known words of Deut. 18:15: 'The Lord your God will raise up for you a prophet like me from among your brethren.' In Acts 3:12–26, Peter's speech in the temple, Luke gives a summary of 'the verbal proclamation of the gospel to Israel...',[1] maintaining that 'the things which God foretold by the mouth of all the prophets, that his Christ should suffer, he thus fulfilled' (verse 18). As one example of this prophetic foretelling, Luke adduces Deut. 18:15 in verse 22: Jesus is the 'prophet like Moses', which Lampe rightly describes as 'a thought which plays a prominent part in Luke's Christology'.[2] The other occurrence is in the speech of Stephen, Acts 7:37.

In a recent study,[3] C. F. D. Moule suggests that Luke maintains 'a subtle but precise distinction between men's recognition of Jesus during his ministry as one of the prophets, and the express claim of the post-resurrection church...that he is the fulfilment of the Deuteronomic expectation—the Moses-prophet'. Moule emphasizes the fact that Luke does not allude to Deut. 18:15 until after the resurrection, and that those allusions prove that Luke considered Jesus to be not merely a prophet, but *the* eschatological prophet. But it is doubtful that such a distinction can be drawn. There is nothing in the body of the Gospel of Luke to suggest that the author considered the

[1] G. W. H. Lampe, 'Acts', in *Peake's Commentary*, p. 890.

[2] In *Peake's*, p. 891.

[3] 'The Christology of Acts', in *Studies in Luke-Acts*, ed. Keck and Martyn, esp. pp. 161–3.

prophetic designation unworthy or inappropriate for Jesus. It is not enough to say that most of the occurrences of the prophetic designation of Jesus are placed on the lips of those who are not yet full believers, since Jesus' self-designation as a prophet, especially in Luke 13: 33 (a passage without parallel in the other gospels), is too striking to explain away. The response of the people to Jesus as a prophet is acceptable to the author, but he would emphasize the uniqueness of Jesus' prophetic role in the sense that he is the fulfillment of the expectations of the previous prophets. I would agree with the position of Lampe: 'Jesus [in Luke-Acts] stands in the succession of prophets who were persecuted and martyred by the Jews of Jerusalem; like them, therefore, he must meet his death in the capital...Jesus thus stands at the climax of the prophetic tradition, heralded by the last and greatest of the prophets of the old order. He is himself marked out from the latter as one greater than they...'[1] The evidence of both Luke and Acts, therefore, allows us to conclude that Luke interprets Jesus' ministry as the ministry of a prophet, but a prophet who stands in a pivotal position in sacred history.[2]

(3) Thirdly, Luke also views *the church as a continuation of the prophetic ministry* which, as in the epoch of the OT and in Jesus' ministry, is inextricably connected with the work of the Spirit. At Pentecost, the prophecy of Joel is fulfilled: 'Your sons and daughters will prophesy...On my menservants and maidservants in those days I will pour out my Spirit; and they shall prophesy' (Acts 2: 17–18). The work of Christian prophets is underscored throughout the book of Acts (cf. 11: 27; 13: 1; 15: 32; 19: 6; 21: 10). Thus, for Luke, the whole of redemptive history in its three epochs (OT, Jesus' ministry, the church) is the history of prophecy under the guidance of the Spirit of God.

When the genealogy is seen in the light of this strong emphasis on prophecy, the Jewish identification of David's son, Nathan, with the prophet takes on added significance. Luke obviously had some reason to choose to lead the genealogy of Jesus from

[1] In *Studies in the Gospels*, ed. Nineham, p. 173.

[2] I see little justification for the distinction drawn by W. B. Tatum (*NTS*, XIII (1967), pp. 190 ff.) between 'the prophetic Spirit', operative in the birth narratives (Luke 1–2) and 'the messianic Spirit', operative after the beginning of Jesus' ministry.

David through Nathan rather than through the royalty of Judah. The explanation which best accounts for the evidence is that Luke was aware of the Jewish tradition which identified the two Nathans of II Samuel and constructed (or edited) his genealogy in accordance with his view of the importance of prophecy in the OT and also in the ministry of Jesus. In such a way, the Davidic descent of Christ was maintained while there would arise no occasion from the genealogy to consider Jesus a royal–political Messiah.

SUMMARY

Our study has attempted to relate the Lukan genealogy to two characteristic Christological titles of the Gospel, namely Son of God and prophet. The importance of the former title in the genealogy is suggested by the immediately preceding baptism pericope which culminates in the divine proclamation of Jesus' sonship. The genealogy, however, historicizes the title by tracing the sonship of Jesus through a succession of figures from the OT and Judaism back to God, emphasizing at once the Lukan concern for the continuity of the history of salvation and also the culmination of that history in the new beginning in Jesus. Hence, there is an external similarity between the Lukan genealogy and those Graeco-Roman pedigrees which attempted to connect an emperor or member of the nobility with a traditional mythical god or hero. But that this similarity is merely external is proved by the awareness of esoteric Jewish haggadah which is deeply embedded within the genealogy in the Nathan tradition. Luke's rejection of the royal line in favor of David's son, Nathan, also suggests the importance for his Christology of the motif of the prophet as applied to Jesus since it is highly probable that Luke was aware of the identification in certain Jewish circles of David's son Nathan with the prophet of the same name. This interpretation of the deviation of the Lukan genealogy from Matt. 1: 1–17 is supported also by the strong emphasis within the Gospel and also Acts on the role of prophecy in the OT, in Jesus' ministry, and in the mission of the church.

CHAPTER 7

SUMMARY AND CONCLUSION

Our survey of genealogical interest in the Bible and in late Judaism is now finished. A great number of specific texts and traditions have necessarily been examined; this, in itself, is a warning against overly facile generalizations. Yet, throughout, one observation is suggested which should be given its due significance: the biblical genealogies are closely attached to their contexts and to the narrative in which they occur in regard to language, structure, and theology. In the priestly narrative of the Pentateuch the genealogical system is linked with the theology implicit in the narrative. Here we find the priestly concern for order and purpose in history—even in the pre-history of Israel. This concern emerges in the genealogical organization of the various Israelitic traditions of primeval history, in discerning the genealogical relationships among the various Semitic tribes and peoples, and also in the division of history into well-ordered epochs by chronological speculation attached to the genealogies. Moreover, in the Priestly Toledoth book we are able to discern an interest in the cultus, the foundation of which by Aaron is the culmination of the divine purpose in all history anterior to the exodus. The Chronicler is a prime example of our conclusion: contrary to the common assumption of separate authorship for genealogies and narrative in I, II Chronicles, our study has shown that each of the major theological motifs and tendencies discernible in the narrative is reflected in the genealogical data. In Ezra-Nehemiah, which stands in a close relationship to Rabbinic genealogical interest, the genealogical data are so closely woven into the fabric of the books as a whole that it becomes difficult to determine precisely the boundaries between genealogy and narrative.

Our survey of the genealogical interest in later Judaism (chapter 4) was intended to prepare the way for a discussion of the NT genealogies of Jesus. We found that the strong genealogical interest in later Judaism did not result in generally available family pedigrees, especially among the laity. Since the society of the Jewish nation was based on a genealogical division of the people, reliance in the ascertaining of genealogical purity was placed on both oral tradition and midrashic exegesis of the OT, by which individuals might be linked to prominent biblical names, thus assuring genealogical legitimacy. Along with the concern for genealogical purity there was in later Judaism considerable discussion of the ancestry of the Messiah (or Messiahs). This, too, was largely carried on by midrashic exegesis. These facts must be taken into account in a study of the genealogies of Jesus.

As for the NT, the two genealogies of Jesus are examples of the tendency towards the historification of traditional motifs in the gospel tradition. This means that the NT genealogies do not come from the earliest strata of the gospel tradition, as can be shown from the relation of the titles Son of God and Son of David in Rom. 1: 3–4 and Matt. 1, respectively. Moreover, the contradictions between Matt. 1 and Luke 3 make impossible the belief that both genealogies are the result of accurate genealogical records; and the use of the genealogical *Gattung* in Judaism renders it highly improbable that either list preserves the family records of Joseph. Both of the lists fall into the category of Midrash, which has a homiletical and hortatory function, and thus may be considered part and parcel of the tendency towards historification of 'non-historical' materials.[1] But, in spite of the relative lateness of the genealogies in the gospel tradition, it is clear that they do not arise out of the Hellenistic church.

In Matthew this midrashic quality emerges most clearly. The genealogy has become a means of structuring history which finds its closest parallels in similar schemes that appear in the apocalyptic literature. This structure serves to communicate the author's deep sense of eschatological fulfillment: all prior history was ordered to lead up to the culminating event in Jesus of Nazareth. This is entirely consonant with the common description of Matthew as 'the most apocalyptic of the Gospels'. In point of detail, however, the author reveals a knowledge of the Rabbinic haggadic tradition. Especially, his inclusion of the four OT women in the genealogy, each of whom played an

[1] Terms from E. Käsemann, 'The Problem of the Historical Jesus', section 3, in *Essays on NT Themes*, tr. W. J. Montague (1964), pp. 24–9.

important and often polemical role in Rabbinic sources, was intended to demonstrate more certainly and clearly the conviction that the main Rabbinic Messianic expectation—a Messiah ben David—had been fulfilled in Jesus. In other points of detail as well, the author touches points of discussion among the Rabbis. All of this is congruous with, and leads to, the conclusion that the author of the genealogy addressed himself to a group acquainted with Rabbinic theology. Whether they were converts to Christianity or still members of a Jewish community has not been determined, although the author's use of the Greek OT may indicate that the readers belonged to a group associated with Gamaliel the Patriarch (see above, pp. 181 ff., 186–9).

As for the relation of the genealogy to Matthean Christology, we have suggested that it is one example of the author's emphasis on the title Son of David. Indeed, the whole of Matt. 1 appears to be a midrash on the two titles derived from Mark 1 : 1, that is, Christ (for Matthew, carrying the meaning 'Son of David'; 1: 1–17) and Son of God (Matt. 1: 18–25). It is precisely the same two titles that are underscored in the earliest Christological tradition (e.g. Rom. 1: 1 ff.). Thus we have an explanation for the relation of Matt. 1 : 1–17 to 1 : 18–25 as well as for the relation of the genealogy to the body of Matthew's Gospel. Linguistically, structurally, and theologically, the genealogy and the Gospel are at one.

Similarly, Lukan theology finds an echo in the genealogy of Luke 3: 23–38. Luke, by tracing Jesus' ancestry back to God through OT and Jewish personalities, historicizes the title 'Son of God' (with which the genealogy is connected to the immediately preceding account of Jesus' baptism), avoiding metaphysical and adoptionistic connotations. At the same time, the genealogy serves as an example of Luke's idea of the history of salvation as the continuity of the work and word of God. One other peculiarity of the Lukan genealogy betrays a knowledge of a somewhat esoteric Jewish haggadah: Luke's rejection of the royal line in favor of Nathan, son of David, is most probably a reflection of a Jewish tradition that identified this Nathan with the prophet. Assuming such a background of the title, the emphasis throughout the Gospel and Acts on the role of prophecy in the OT, in Jesus' ministry, and in the history of the church lends strong support for the integrity of the genealogy within the Gospel of Luke.

Finally, we again refer to the adaptability of the genealogical form to widely varied literary purposes. When compared with the primitive interest in genealogies in the ancient Semitic world (reflected to some extent in the J-strand), which was the product of strong tribal feelings, the priestly genealogies of the OT and those of later Judaism and the NT reveal a marked transition to literary functions. The genealogical form was made to serve the interpretation of history and, as such, illumines the author's view of historical relationships more than the actual course of historical events itself. This is certainly true of the NT genealogies, which reflect the tradition of Jesus' Davidic descent but which are not actual family pedigrees. Rather, they reveal the hand of the author and can therefore be considered apologetic attempts to express more fully the Christian conviction that Jesus is the fulfillment of the hope of Israel. Here, too, Lefèvre's remark holds true: 'The genealogy was a work of art.'

APPENDIXES

BIBLIOGRAPHY

INDEX

APPENDIX I

METHODOLOGY IN THE STUDY OF OLD TESTAMENT CHRONOLOGY

It would seem necessary to emphasize the basic difference in methodology followed in my section on OT chronology (pp. 28–36) from that of much recent scholarship. As a competent example of the latter, the article on 'Chronology of the OT' by S. J. de Vries in the *Interpreter's Dictionary of the Bible* may be mentioned. The following remarks apply *mutatis mutandis* also to the comprehensive, and in many ways excellent, work of Jack Finegan, *Handbook of Biblical Chronology* (1964). Included in this handbook are data taken from most of the relevant non-biblical sources (there are 119 tables of figures), including early Christian chronographers. Yet the underlying attempt here, as in the article mentioned, is to correlate the biblical data with the non-biblical in order to arrive at dates for the various biblical events that have a high degree of historical probability. Throughout, the *religionsgeschichtliche* method is used to set Israelite history into the framework of world history; hence the concern for absolute dating. But neither of the studies takes into account the possibility of the reflection of speculative interest in the biblical information. It is this concern for absolute dating that explains the surprising lack of any consideration of the chronology of the Hebrew text of Gen. 5 and 11 in the *Handbook*. De Vries, however, does allude to Gen. 5 and 11:

There have been three distinct ways of understanding this genealogy. The first interpretation is that of Ussher, which takes the list to indicate successive generations from father to son; the second interpretation is the same except that it assumes that many links have dropped out of the genealogy, as in the case of Kainan (retained by the LXX in Gen. 11: 13);[1] the third is to understand the names as dynasties or peoples instead of as individuals. With the

[1] The absence of Kenan in the MT and Samaritan Pentateuch is usually considered to represent earlier tradition than the LXX and Jubilees, where it occurs.

latter two methods no estimate of the age of the world can be obtained[!].[1]

While it is admitted that 'the conventional and schematic structure of this list of patriarchs should be apparent',[2] De Vries does not draw any conclusions regarding the nature of the information from this observation. In a later section of the study we read:

When they come to the period of the Divided Monarchy, students of biblical chronology are at first sight delighted with the wealth of data available to them...

Nonetheless, various scholars who have worked with these data have found the chronology of this period almost beyond solution. They have discovered, to their dismay, that many of the...details seem to contradict one another. E.g. the total of years for Judah does not agree with the total for Israel; besides, the totals of either kingdom do not seem to fit the synchronisms. But worst of all is that the chronologies which many have attempted to construct from the biblical data fail to agree with historical information now available from a considerable variety of Assyrian and Babylonian documents.[3]

But what if the biblical data as we have them cannot bear the weight of this methodology? I have tried to point out in chapter I above that the chronological data found in the pre-exilic history of Israel are explicitly artificial and speculative in character. It would not be crucial for my methodology to be shown that my particular reconstruction of the scheme is faulty. The essential point is that the biblical chronological data have been pressed into the function of highlighting certain pivotal events in Israel's heritage and probably also of leading to an *annus magnus* or *annus mirabilis* at the close of the epoch. The marks of manipulation in the several lists have been mentioned above, and further details are noted in the articles cited in the text. If we are able to trace the present condition of the biblical dating to a revision during the Maccabean period, we would simply have adduced an illustration of the dividing of history into epochs which is characteristic also of the Rabbis in connection with Messianic speculation.[4] In any case, the 'conventional and schematic structure' of the entire biblical chronology must be

[1] *IDB*, p. 581. [2] P. 581. [3] P. 584.

[4] S–B, IV, Exkurs 30, pp. 986–1015, 'Vorzeichen und Berechnung der Tage des Messias'.

taken into account as a possible explanation for the dismay felt by 'various scholars who have worked with these data [and] have found the chronology...almost beyond solution'. Is the solution perhaps to be found using a *redaktionsgeschichtliche* methodology?[1]

[1] The approach followed in this study is that suggested also by Gerhard von Rad, *Genesis*, p. 67: in Gen. 5 'interest is immediately attracted, of course, to the numbers. It is quite probable that the number of years given in ch. 5 has some mysterious proportional relation to other dates in the Biblical sacred history (construction of the Tabernacle? conquest? building of the Temple?); but a satisfactory key to the theological meaning of that assumed system has not yet been found. It is to be supposed that the numbers in the table of Semites (ch. 11: 10 ff.) are harmonized with those from our list into a system. If one adds the time spans of both lists and reckons to them the dates of chapters 21: 5; 25: 26; 47: 9; and Exod. 12: 40, the result is the year 2666 for the exodus from Egypt. That would be two-thirds of a world era of four thousand years...One must reckon with the possibility that...the various texts [MT, LXX, Sam. Pent.] were thoroughly corrected with reference to one another...'

APPENDIX 2

THE CHRONOLOGY OF THE PRIESTLY NARRATIVE[1] IN TABULAR FORM

A. ACCORDING TO THE MASORETIC TEXT

Name	First-born	Remainder	Total	Birth[2]	Death[2]	Source
Adam	130	800	930	0	930	Gen. 5
Seth	105	807	912	130	1042	Gen. 5
Enosh	90	815	905	235	1140	Gen. 5
Kenan	70	840	910	325	1235	Gen. 5
Mahalalel	65	830	895	395	1290	Gen. 5
Jared	162	800	962	460	1422	Gen. 5
Enoch	65	300	365	622	987	Gen. 5
Methuselah	187	782	969	687	1656	Gen. 5
Lamech	182	595	777	874	1651	Gen. 5
Noah	500	450	950	1056	2006	Gen. 5: 32; 9: 29
Noah to flood	—	—	600	—	—	—
Year of flood	—	—	—	—	1656	Gen. 7: 6, 11
Shem	100 (102?)[3]	500	600	1556	2156	Gen. 11
Arpachshad	35	403	438	1656	2094	Gen. 11
Shelah	30	403	433	1691	2124	Gen. 11
Eber	34	430	464	1721	2185	Gen. 11
Peleg	30	209	239	1755	1994	Gen. 11
Reu	32	207	239	1785	2024	Gen. 11
Serug	30	200	230	1817	2047	Gen. 11
Nahor	29	119	148	1847	1995	Gen. 11
Terah	70	135	205	1876	2081	Gen. 11: 26, 32
Abraham	100	75	175	1946	2121	Gen. 21: 5; 25: 7
age at migration		—	75	—	2021	Gen. 12: 4
Isaac	60	120	180	2046	2226	Gen. 25: 26; 35: 28
Jacob	130[4]	17	147	2236[4]	2253	Gen. 47: 9, 28
Joseph	—	—	110	2196?	2306?	Gen. 37: 2; 41: 46, 47, 54; 45: 6; 47: 9, 28; 50: 22, 26
Israel in Egypt:			430	Exodus:	2666	Exod. 12: 40
Exodus to Solomon's temple:			480		3146	I Kings 6: 1
Thence to start of second temple:			480		3626	I, II Kings; Ezra 3: 8[5]
538 B.C. to 164 B.C.			374		4000	

[1] See the bibliographical references on p. 36 n. 1, above. [2] *Anno Mundi.*

[3] According to Gen. 5: 32; 7: 6, Shem was 100 years old at the beginning of the flood, yet according to Gen. 11: 10*b* Shem begat Arpachshad two years after the flood; hence two years may have to be added to the figures for birth and death A.M. from Shem and on.

[4] The year Jacob moved to Egypt.

[5] For details on this figure, cf. E. L. Curtis, 'Chronology of the OT', *HDB*, I, 401–3.

B. ACCORDING TO THE SAMARITAN PENTATEUCH

Name	First-born	Remainder	Total	Birth A.M.	Death A.M.
Adam	130	800	930	0	930
Seth	105	807	912	130	1042
Enosh	90	815	905	235	1140
Kenan	70	840	910	325	1235
Mahalalel	65	830	895	395	1290
Jared	62	785	847	460	1307
Enoch	65	300	365	522	887
Methuselah	67	653	720	587	1307
Lamech	53	600	653	654	1307
Noah	500	450	950	707	1657
Noah to flood:			600	year of flood:	1307
Shem	100	500	600	1207	1807
Arpachshad	135	303	438	1307	1745
Shelah	130	303	433	1442	1875
Eber	134	270	404	1572	1976
Peleg	130	109	239	1706	1945
Reu	132	107	239	1836	2075
Serug	130	100	230	1968	2198
Nahor	79	69	148	2098	2246
Terah	70	75	145	2177	2322
Abraham	100	75	175	2247	2422
age at migration:			75		2322
Isaac	60	120	180	2347	2527
Jacob	130	17	147	2407	2654

Duration of the 'dwelling of the sons of Israel and their fathers...in the *land of Canaan and* [*sic*] the land of Egypt' (Exod. 12: 40): 430

Year of exodus (reckoning from the migration of Abraham): 2752

C. ACCORDING TO THE SEPTUAGINT

Name	First-born	Remainder	Total	Birth A.M.	Death A.M.
Adam	230	700	930	0	930
Seth	205	707	912	230	1142
Enosh	190	715	905	435	1340
Kenan	170	740	910	625	1535
Mahalalel	165	730	895	795	1690
Jared	162	800	962	960	1922
Enoch	165	200	365	1122	1487
Methuselah	167[1]	802[2]	969	1287	2256
Lamech	188	565	753	1454	2207
Noah	500	450	950	1642	2592
Noah to flood:			600		2242
Shem	100	500	600	2142	2742
Arpachshad	135	430	565	2242	2807
Kenan	130	330	460	2377	2837
Shelah	130	330	460	2507	2967
Eber	134	370	504	2637	3141
Peleg	130	209	339	2771	3110
Reu	132	207	339	2901	3240
Serug	130	200	330	3033	3363
Nahor	79	129	208	3163	3371
Terah	70	—[3]	—[3]	3242	—[3]
Abraham	100	75	175	3312	3487
age at migration			75		3387
Isaac	60	120	180	3412	3592
Jacob	130[4]	17	147	3602[4]	3619
Joseph			110		

Duration of the 'dwelling of the sons of Israel which they sojourned in the land of Egypt *and in the land of Canaan*' (Exod. 12: 40): 430 years.[5]

Year of exodus (reckoning from migration of Abraham): 3817

Exodus to the beginning of Solomon's temple: 440 years 4257

[1] MSS. A, pm, have 187.

[2] MSS. A, pm, have 782; these are most probably corrections from the MT, made in order to avoid the awkward situation of placing the death of Methuselah after the flood.

[3] The addition of ἐν Χαρραν in the LXX of Gen. 11: 32 makes impossible the reckoning of the total age of Terah.

[4] The year Jacob moved to Egypt.

[5] MS. B reads '435 years'.

D. ACCORDING TO THE BOOK OF JUBILEES

Name	Birth A.M.	Name	Birth A.M.
Adam	0	Shelah	1432
Seth	130	Eber	1503
Enosh	235	Peleg	1567
Kenan	325	Reu	1589
Mahalalel	395	Serug	1687
Jared	461	Nahor	1744
Enoch	522	Terah	1806
Methuselah	587	Abraham	1876
Lamech	652	Isaac	1982
Noah	707	Jacob	2041
Shem	1207	Joseph	2132
Flood	1308	Moses	2330
Arpachshad	—	Exodus	2410
Kenan	1375	Conquest	2450

E. ACCORDING TO JOSEPHUS

Name	First-born	Remainder	Total	Birth A.M.	Death A.M.	Source
Adam	230	700	930	0	930	*Ant.* I. 2. 3; 3. 4
Seth	205	707	912	230	1142	*Ant.* I. 3. 4
Enosh	190	715	905	435	1340	*Ant.* I. 3. 4
Cainan	170	740	910	625	1535	*Ant.* I. 3. 4
Mahalalel	165	730	895	795	1690	*Ant.* I. 3. 4
Jared	162	800	962	960	1922	*Ant.* I. 3. 4
Enoch	165	200	365	1122	1487	*Ant.* I. 3. 4
Methuselah	187	782	969	1287	2256	*Ant.* I. 3. 4
Lamech	182	595	777	1474	2251	*Ant.* I. 3. 4
Noah	—	—	—	1656	2606	*Ant.* I. 3. 9
Flood	—	—	—	—	2656	*Ant.* I. 3. 3
Abraham	—	—	—	2946	—	*Ant.* I. 6. 5

(On dating Isaac, Jacob, and Joseph, see *Ant.* I. 12. 2; I. 17. 1; I. 22. 1; II. 8. 1; II. 8. 2; II. 9. 1; II. 15. 2.)

Exodus: 'Four hundred and thirty years after our forefather Abraham came into Canaan, but two hundred and fifteen years only after Jacob removed into Egypt. It was the eightieth year of the age of Moses, and of that of Aaron three more...' (*Ant.* II. 15. 2).

Two conflicting chronologies preserved by Josephus may be listed thus:

(1) *Ant.* VIII. 3. 1

Adam	0 (A.M.)
Flood	1662
Migration of Abraham	2082
Exodus	2510
Building of the Temple	2102

(2) *Ant.* X. 8. 4–5

Adam	0
Flood	1556
Exodus	2451
Building of the Temple	3043
Destruction of the Temple	3513

(To this last date may be added the 411 years of *Ant.* XII. 7. 6 which would place the re-dedication of the temple by the Maccabees in the year 3924 A.M.)

APPENDIX 3

THE ANCESTRY OF ELIJAH IN LATER JEWISH SOURCES

As a comparison with Jewish speculation on the ancestry of the Messiah and as an example of Rabbinic genealogical exegesis, it may be helpful to allude to the frequent discussions in the Rabbinic writings on the ancestry of the Messiah.[1] There are three mutually exclusive views on this matter: Elijah is a descendant either of Gad, of Benjamin, or of Levi. Since the debate on ancestry hinges on rather fanciful exegetical feats one might conclude that these discussions were little more than light-hearted haggadoth. S–B, however, contend that behind each ancestral derivation lies a different conception of the role of Elijah in the end-times:[2] *Elijah from the tribe of Gad* is considered to be the one who himself prepares the way for God and who delivers Israel;[3] in short, he is here either an eschatological figure with no connection with a Messiah, or he is himself the Messiah. He is to 'overthrow the foundations of the heathen' and will 'troop upon their heel'.[4] *Elijah from the tribe of Benjamin*, however, is the forerunner of the Messiah,[5] a position similar to

[1] Rabbinic sources on Elijah are cited in S–B, VIII, 764–98: 'Der Prophet Elias nach seiner Entrückung aus dem Diesseits'; also R. B. Y. Scott, 'The Expectation of Elijah', *Can. Jour. Theol.* III (1926), 490–502; Georg Molin, 'Elijahu: der Prophet und sein Weiterleben in den Hoffnungen des Judentums und der Christenheit', *Judaica*, VIII (1952), 65–92, esp. pp. 82–4. A popular, though comprehensive, collection of Jewish traditions on Elijah in English is that of Samuel Michael Segal, *Elijah: A Study in Jewish Folklore* (1935). Aptowitzer, *Parteipolitik*, pp. 95–104 (and notes), attempts to account for the origins of the Elijah speculations in the Maccabean power struggles. See also M. Friedmann, introduction to *Seder Elijahu* (Vienna, 1902), pp. 2–44, cited by Klausner, *Messianic Idea*, p. 451 n. 2: 'Everything in Jewish literature pertaining to Elijah has been diligently and expertly collected by M. Friedmann...' See also Jeremias in *TDNT*, II, 928–41.

[2] IV, 782.

[3] Gen. R. 99 (985 f.); 71 (659 f.); Targ. Jer. II on Gen. 30: 11.

[4] Gen. R. 99: 11 (985 f.); cf. also Gen. R. 71: 9 (659 f.).

[5] Cf. Seder Elij. Rab. 18.

that occupied by the Messiah ben Joseph (or Ephraim),[1] and identical with the concept of Elijah in the NT. (But this function of Elijah in the end-times is not emphasized in the pseudepigrapha or even in the Rabbis. It is possible that, in reaction to Christian claims that John the Baptist was Elijah *redivivus*,[2] the Rabbis allowed the figure of the Messiah b. Joseph to supplant the role of Elijah as forerunner of the Messiah, Elijah becoming more and more the idealization of the perfect scribe-priest who would settle all Rabbinic disputes at his appearance.) Finally, according to S–B, *Elijah from the tribe of Levi*[3] is the high priest of the Messianic age. The idea of an eschatological high priest is reflected as early as the Testaments of the Twelve Patriarchs, esp. T. Levi 18 and T. Jud. 21. The Rabbis traced Elijah to the tribe of Levi by applying Mal. 3: 23 [EV, 4: 5]; 3: 1, and 2: 4 f. to Elijah.[4] Hence Elijah (3: 23) is the messenger (3: 1) who is also the messenger of the covenant of life and peace with Levi (2: 4, 5, 7). But in Num. 25: 11–13 it is with Phinehas ben Eleazar that God establishes a 'covenant of peace' which is to be the 'covenant of a perpetual priesthood'. The natural deduction was made, namely that the Elijah who is to come is Phinehas b. Eleazar b. Aaron. According to S–B, this identification of Phinehas with Elijah is to be found in the most varied circles of Jewish scholarship, and especially in the later Rabbinic writings, as the best answer to the question regarding who would serve as high priest in the Messianic age.[5] S–B refer to a passage in the Mid. Ps.: 'The Psalm [43: 3] says, "O send out thy light and thy truth". The light refers to the prophet Elijah who is a descendant of the house of Aaron. Truth refers to the Messiah

[1] The implication of S–B that the idea of the Messiah b. Joseph antedates the concept of Elijah as forerunner of the Messiah is highly problematical. The earliest explicit source for the Messiah b. Joseph is bSuk. 52*a*, a passage probably post-Hadrianic; see above, p. 130 n. 1.

[2] Cf. Justin, *Dial.* 49; Matt. 11: 14; 17: 12 (Mark 9: 11–13); cf. Matt. 16: 14 (Mark 8: 28; 6: 15; Luke 9: 19, 8); contrast John 1: 21.

[3] Gen. R. 71 (659 f.); Seder Elij. Ra. 18; Elijah is called 'high priest' in Pseudo-Jon. on Deut. 30: 4, Targ. on Lam. 4: 22; also Pesikta Rab. 4; Mid. Ps. on 43: 1 ff. (445).

[4] S–B attribute this development among the Rabbis to a reaction against the Christian view of Jesus in the Epistle to the Hebrews in which the functions of Messianic high priest and Messianic king are combined. But there is no direct evidence to support this claim.

[5] S–B, IV, 790.

of the house of David.'[1] Actually, S–B are much too dogmatic in their conclusions on the prevalence of this identification of Elijah with Phinehas. The clearest sources for this identification are: Targ. Jer. I on Exod. 6: 18; Yalk. Sim. on Num. 25: 11; Pirke d. R. Eliezar 29, end: 'He called the name of Phinehas by the name of Elijah...' S–B actually mitigate their broad conclusion by the admission that 'der frühste ausdrückliche Hinweis auf den priesterlichen Stand des Elias dürfte aus der Zeit um 135 n. Chr. stammen'.[2] This may even be too early, since it is based on a saying attributed to Akiba in the late Mid. Mishle 9: 2.

As for the function of the Messianic priest, Elijah–Phinehas, S–B find no limitation to a sacerdotal role: rather the emphasis is placed on Elijah as restorer of Israel and its institutions.[3] This 'restoration' includes the straightening out of questions of family purity;[4] deciding various questions that were unresolved by the scribes;[5] bringing peace;[6] bringing genuine repentance to Israel;[7] restoring from the first temple the vessel of manna, the water of purification, and the cup with the oil of anointing;[8] and the ingathering of the Israel of the dispersion.

Such, with some elaboration and evaluation added here, is the contention of S–B. Some additional qualification must be made. That these three views of the ancestry of Elijah did not always represent three distinct conceptions of his function in the end-times is indicated by the confused and variegated character of the sources. Thus, for example, Justin has Trypho, representing the Jewish point of view, say: 'But Christ [Messiah]—if he has indeed been born, and exists anywhere—is unknown, and does not even know himself, and has no power until Elias come to anoint him, and make him manifest to all.'[9] Here the view of Elijah as forerunner and announcer of the Messiah (according to S–B the function of the Benjaminite Elijah) is

[1] On 43: 1 ff. (445).

[2] IV, 791.

[3] Cf. Mark 9: 12, par.; Ben Sir. 48: 10*b*; S–B, IV, 790.

[4] mEd. 8: 7 (436–7).

[5] mEd. 8: 7; bBek. 33*b*; bShab. 108*a* (523); Num. R. 3; bMen. 45*a*; also mShek. 2:5 (154); mB. Metz. 1: 8 (348); 2: 8 (350); 3: 4, 5 (351); see also Davies, *Setting*, pp. 159–60.

[6] mEd. 8: 7.

[7] Pirke d. R. Eliezer 43, 60*a* (ed. Friedlander, p. 344).

[8] Mek. on Ex. 16: 33; cf. II Macc. 2: 4–8.

[9] *Dial*. 8.

combined with a distinctly priestly role, the anointing of the royal Messiah.[1] Moreover, the passages which are assigned to the function of Elijah as the Messianic priest by S–B (see previous page) are by no means explicit in linking Elijah to the tribe of Levi. Thus, in the numerous passages which depict Elijah as the one who would settle matters of dispute among the Rabbis,[2] there is no clear connection of Elijah to Levi. Indeed, one might say that the discussions of the ancestry of Elijah were carried on more or less independently of the discussion of his function in the end-times.

[1] Significantly, the idea of the royal Messiah being anointed occurs in no other sources through Talmudic times; the only other known source for this idea is found in a ninth-century Karaite manuscript.

[2] For passages adduced by S–B, see above, p. 268 n. 5. Other passages adduced by L. Ginzberg (*Eine unbekannte jüdische Sekte* (New York, 1922), pp. 303 ff., cited by Davies, *Setting*, p. 159) are: bBer. 35*b* (222–3); bPes. 13*a* (57–8); bPes. 70*b* (360–1); bHag. 25*a* (157); bYeb. 35*b* (221); bYeb. 41*a* (270); bYeb. 102*a* (700); bGit. 42*b* (183); ARN; bTaan. 22*a* (109–10); pBer. 1*c*. Among the subjects of the Rabbinic disputes that are to be settled by Elijah in these passages are: blessings over meals, the burning of the *Terumah* at Passover, the abrogation of the Passover *Hagigah* on the Sabbath, betrothals, *halitzah*, legitimacy of descent, confusion in matters of borrowing money, and—especially—questions of genealogical purity in specific instances. Davies, *Setting*, p. 160, suggests that the implication of this function of Elijah is that Elijah will 'give the true interpretation of the Law'.

APPENDIX 4

THE ANCESTRY OF TAMAR IN LATER JEWISH TRADITION

There is frequent speculation on the ancestry of Tamar in the later Jewish tradition. In the pseudepigrapha Tamar is twice referred to as 'a daughter of Aram',[1] and thus more closely related to the Hebrew than Bathshua, the Canaanite wife of Judah.[2] The Rabbis provide more information: Tamar was the daughter of Noah's son, Shem, the father of Aram (Gen. 10: 22):

Ephraim Mikshaah, a disciple of R. Meir [S–B; *c.* A.D. 150], said in the latter's name: Tamar was the daughter of Shem, for it it written: 'And the daughter of any priest, if she profane herself by playing the harlot...she shall be burned with fire' [Lev. 21: 9]; consequently, 'And Judah said: bring her forth, and let her be burned' [Gen. 38: 24].[3]

Shem is the direct father of Tamar, just as Jacob is of Judah:

When Scripture states, 'Which wise men have told from their fathers, and have not hid it' [Job. 15: 18] it alludes to Judah who confessed and said: 'She is more righteous than I' [Gen. 38: 26] and did not conceal it from Jacob or from Shem.[4]

That Shem was a priest is seen in another tradition, also traced to the middle of the second century A.D.:

R. Johanan [d. A.D. 279] observed in the name of R. Eliezer [*c.* A.D. 140–65], the son of R. Jose the Galilean [*c.* A.D. 120–40]: When Noah left the ark a lion struck and maimed him so that he was unfitted to offer sacrifices, and Shem his son offered them in his stead.[5]

[1] Jub. 41: 1; T. Jud. 10: 1.
[2] T. Jud. 10: 6.
[3] Gen. R. 85: 11 (796).
[4] Num. R. 13: 4 (508), anonymous.
[5] Lev. R. 20: 1 (250); cf. the later tradition in bMak. 23*b* (168): 'R. Eliezer [*c.* 270] said: the Holy Spirit manifested itself in three places: at the tribunal of Shem, at the tribunal of Samuel of Ramah, and at the tribunal of Solomon...'

And how is Shem a priest? A haggadic tradition dating from approximately the same time, knowledge of which is to be assumed in the passages just cited, supplies the answer: Shem is identified with Melchizedek:

It was taught at the school of R. Ishmael [hence, *c.* A.D. 140–65]: The Holy One, blessed be He, sought to make Shem the progenitor of the priesthood; for it says: 'And Melchizedek king of Salem...was a priest of God' [Gen. 14: 18].[1]

It is significant that in this passage it is not the identification of Shem with Melchizedek that is being proved—this again is treated as common knowledge—but that Shem was intended to be the beginning of the priesthood.[2] Hence, in order of development we have the following progression: (1) Shem is Melchizedek; (2) Shem was a priest; (3) Shem was the father of Tamar. The diversity of sources datable to the middle of the second century and the tacit assumption of points one and two make it entirely possible that such discussion of the ancestry of Tamar was current at the time of the composition of Matthew. If this is so, what is the significance of positing Shem-Melchizedek as the father of Tamar? It is probably a way of alluding to the non-Abrahamitic, hence Gentile, descent of Tamar, since Shem was but a distant ancestor of Abraham. This pejorative sense of designating Shem as father of Tamar can be seen in later passages reflecting polemical discussions: one of these is attributed to R. Abba b. Kahana (third century) in which David defends himself from slanders against his ancestry by asking his accusers: '...And Tamar who married your ancestor Judah—is it not a tainted descent? She was but a descendant of Shem the son of Noah. Have you then an honourable descent?'[3] In another passage there is a reference to 'the entrance of our father Abraham' and a view of Tamar as a proselyte:

'She sat in the gate of Enaim [עינים]' [Gen. 38: 14]. R. Alexander [*c.* 280] said: It teaches that she went and sat at the entrance of our

[1] Lev. R. 25: 6 (319).

[2] Cf. an anonymous tradition in Num. R. 4: 8 (102): 'There is proof that Shem offered sacrifices; since it says: "And Melchizedek, king of Salem, brought forth bread and wine; and he was priest of God the Most High" [Gen. 14: 18].' Here again the identification of the two figures is presumed.

[3] Ruth R. 8: 1 (92).

father Abraham, to see which place all eyes [עינים] look...R. Samuel b. Nahmani [*c.* 260] said:...When [Judah] solicited her, he asked her, 'Art thou perhaps a Gentile?' She replied, 'I am a proselyte.' 'Art thou perhaps a married woman?' She replied, 'I am unmarried.' 'Perhaps thy father has accepted on thy behalf betrothals?' She replied, 'I am an orphan.' 'Perhaps thou art unclean?' She replied, 'I am clean.'[1]

Both sayings, of Alexander and of Samuel, deal with the ancestry of Tamar. The first is an allusion to Tamar's longing to be Abrahamitic; the second appears to put the later objections to Tamar's inclusion in the genealogy of David and the Messiah into the mouth of Judah, namely the objections that, while presenting herself as a harlot, she was a Gentile, married, betrothed, or unclean. Moreover, it is significant that none of the data in Tamar's responses necessarily contradicts the older tradition of Shem–Melchizedek as her father, even though the tendency to absolve Judah of guilt is obvious. Tamar, according to her own statements, is a proselyte (hence of Gentile origin); unmarried (in reality, a widow); unbetrothed;[2] an orphan (according to the chronology of the MT, Shem died in A.M. 2156 while Jacob and Esau were born in A.M. 2106).[3] Thus it would be possible for the Rabbis to consider Tamar at once as the daughter of Shem and yet a contemporary of Judah and his sons; but the death of Shem, according to this view, would occur soon after the birth of Tamar, possibly giving rise to the idea that she was an orphan from an early age. In any case the conversation between Judah and Tamar can best be understood as an attempt to absolve Judah of guilt in this affair; his reluctance and insistence on knowing Tamar's background are emphasized. It is possible that the conversation reflects two sides of a polemic, Judah's questions those who castigated this spot in the ancestry of the Davidic Messiah, and Tamar's answers representing the partisans of the Messiah b. David.

[1] bSotah 10 (47).

[2] Contrast T. Jud. 13: 4: καὶ εἰς Θαμὰρ τὴν νυμφευθεῖσαν τοῖς υἱοῖς μου (text, M. deJonge).

[3] See Appendix 2.

APPENDIX 5

A NEGLECTED MANUSCRIPT BEARING ON THE GENEALOGIES OF JESUS[1]

In the manuscript of the Didache edited and published by P. Bryennios (Constantinople: S. I. Boytira, 1883, pp. 148 ff.) there is an anonymous fragment of a passage dealing with early Christian interpretation of the genealogies of Jesus. The point of view represented here seems to be similar to that which is opposed by Africanus, as indicated below, and apparently reflects divergent opinions on the ancestry of the Messiah both in Christian and Jewish speculation. The pertinent text reads:

Ἰωσὴφ ὁ ἀνὴρ Μαρίας, ἐξ ἧς ἐγεννήθη ὁ Χριστός, ἐκ λευϊτικῆς φυλῆς κατάγεται, ὡς ὑπέδειξαν οἱ θεῖοι εὐαγγελισταί. Ἀλλ' ὁ μὲν Ματθαῖος ἐκ Δαβὶδ διὰ Σολομῶντός τε καὶ Νάθαν υἱοὶ Δαβίδ. Παρεσιώπησαν δὲ οἱ εὐαγγελισταὶ τῆς ἁγίας παρθένου τὴν γέννησιν, ἐπειδὴ οὐκ ἦν ἔθος Ἑβραίοις οὐδὲ τῇ θείᾳ Γραφῇ γενεαλογεῖσθαι γυναῖκας, νόμος δὲ ἦν μὴ μνηστεύεσθαι φυλὴν ἐξ ἑτέρας φυλῆς. Ὁ γοῦν Ἰωσὴφ δαυϊτικοῦ καταγόμενος φύλου, πρὸς μνηστείαν τὴν ἁγίαν παρθένον ἠγάγετο, ἐκ τοῦ αὐτοῦ γένους οὖσαν· δείξαντες δὲ τὸ τοῦ Ἰωσὴφ γένος ἠρκέσθησαν. Ἦν δὲ νόμος ἀγόνου ἀνδρὸς τελευτῶντος, τὸν τούτου ἀδελφὸν ἄγεσθαι πρὸς γάμον τὴν γαμετήν, καὶ ἐγείρειν σπέρμα τῷ τελευτήσαντι· τὸ γοῦν τικτόμενον κατὰ φύσιν μὲν ἦν τοῦ δευτέρου ἤτοι τοῦ γεγεννηκότος, κατὰ νόμον δὲ τοῦ τελευτήσαντος. Ἐκ τῆς σειρᾶς τοίνυν τοῦ Νάθαν, τοῦ υἱοῦ Δαβίδ, Λευὶ ἐγέννησεν τὸν Μελχί· ἐκ δὲ τῆς σειρᾶς Σολομῶντος Ματθὰν ἐγέννησεν τὸν Ἰακώβ· τελευτήσαντος δὲ τοῦ Ματθάν, Μελχὶ ὁ υἱὸς Λευί, ὁ ἐκ τῆς φυλῆς τοῦ Νάθαν, ἔγημεν τὴν μητέρα τοῦ Ἰακώβ, καὶ ἐγέννησεν ἐξ αὐτῆς τὸν Ἡλί. Ἐγένοντο οὖν ἀδελφοὶ ὁμομήτριοι, Ἰακὼβ καὶ Ἡλί· ὁ μὲν Ἰακὼβ ἐκ φυλῆς Σολομῶντος, ὁ δὲ Ἡλὶ ἐκ φυλῆς Νάθαν. Ἐτελεύτησεν οὖν Ἡλὶ ἐκ τῆς φυλῆς τοῦ Νάθαν ἄπαις, καὶ ἔλαβεν Ἰακὼβ ὁ ἀδελφὸς αὐτοῦ τὴν γυναῖκα αὐτοῦ, καὶ ἐγέννησεν τὸν Ἰωσήφ, καὶ ἀνέστησεν σπέρμα τῷ ἀδελφῷ. Ὁ τοίνυν Ἰωσήφ, φύσει μέν ἐστιν υἱὸς τοῦ Ἰακὼβ τοῦ ἀπὸ Σολομῶντος καταγομένου, νόμῳ δὲ Ἡλὶ τοῦ ἐκ Νάθαν.

[1] This document was kindly brought to my attention by Professor Robert A. Kraft of the University of Pennsylvania.

This document bears a close relationship to Julius Africanus' Letter to Aristides in two different respects: On the one hand, it presents an identical system of Levirate marriages to explain the discrepancies between the two NT genealogies (see above, p. 141). On the other hand, the author affirms that Joseph descended 'from a Levitical tribe', even though it is pointed out that both genealogies trace the line of descent back to David. Apparently it is assumed from the occurrence of the name Λευί (Luke 3: 24, 29) that the ancestry in the Lukan list was mingled with men of priestly descent, thus legally providing Levitical descent for Joseph. This appears to represent the position against which Africanus argues in that portion of his letter which immediately precedes the section quoted by Eusebius (cited above, p. 242). Africanus refers to the 'discrepant enumeration and mixing of names both of priestly men, as they think, and royal...' and to 'the catalogue of the tribes [and]...the mixing of the registered generations' in the attempt to 'establish the kingship and priesthood of Christ by the interchanges of names...' Africanus then maintains that both the Matthean and Lukan genealogies affirm the Davidic, hence, Judahite, ancestry of Joseph. Such a close relationship, both positive and negative, between J. Africanus and the anonymous manuscript would seem to suggest an early date for the latter—probably earlier than Africanus, since he argues against an already existing point of view.

One other aspect of this fragment should be noted, namely its reference to the 'customs of the Hebrews' and the provisions of 'the divine Scripture'. The former phrase undoubtedly is an allusion to such Rabbinic genealogical interest as is described above (pp. 87–115). The latter term, τῇ θείᾳ Γραφῇ, denotes the OT in distinction from οἱ θεῖοι εὐαγγελισταί (these terms, also, suggest a date prior to the completion of the Christian canon). Three regulations are traced to the OT or to the Rabbis: (1) women are not genealogized; (2) marriage is confined to members of the same 'tribe'; (3) the law of Levirate marriage. The last custom is, of course, well known. The second statement is unparalleled in any biblical or Jewish source known to me; the Rabbis are in general agreement that marriage between full Israelites is legal without regard to tribal origin (above, pp. 88–95). The only similar statement in Jewish sources would seem to be Philo's assertion that the High Priest could marry only within the same γένος (*On Monarchy*, II. 11); this statement is, however, contradicted by the Rabbis.[1] The first rule applies only *mutatis mutandis*, since there are several examples of women mentioned in OT genealogies (above, pp. 153–4, esp. p. 153 n. 2). This inexact knowledge of Rabbinic tradition suggests a specifically Christian derivation of the argument presented.

[1] See also V. Aptowitzer, 'Spuren des Matriarchats im jüdischen Schrifttum', *HUCA*, IV (1927), 207–40.

BIBLIOGRAPHY

I. DICTIONARIES, ENCYCLOPEDIAS, AND SOURCE BOOKS

The Ante-Nicene Christian Library, ed. A. Roberts and J. Donaldson. 10 vols. New York, 1902–13.

The Apocrypha and Pseudepigrapha of the Old Testament, ed. R. H. Charles. 2 vols. Oxford, 1913 (reprinted 1963).

The Babylonian Talmud, Eng. trans. ed. by I. Epstein. London, 1935.

Baur, W. *A Greek–English Lexicon of the NT*, Eng. trans. ed. by Arndt and Gingrich. Chicago, 1957.

Brown, Driver, Briggs. *A Hebrew and English Lexicon of the OT*. Oxford, 1907.

Dictionary of the Bible, ed. J. Hastings. 5 vols. New York, 1898.

Dictionnaire de la Bible, 3rd ed. Paris, various dates.

Dictionnaire de la Bible—Supplément v, ed. L. Pirot. Paris, 1957.

The Fathers According to Rabbi Nathan, Eng. trans. by J. Goldin. New Haven, 1955.

Hastings' Dictionary of the Bible. 5 vols. Edinburgh, 1900.

Hastings' Dictionary of the Bible, rev. by F. C. Grant and H. H. Rowley. New York, 1963.

Hatch, E. and Redpath, H. A. *A Concordance to the Septuagint and Other Greek Versions of the OT*. Oxford, 1897–1907.

The Iliad of Homer, tr. R. Lattimore. Chicago, 1951.

The Interpreter's Bible. 12 vols. Nashville and New York, 1951–.

The Interpreter's Dictionary of the Bible. 4 vols. Nashville and New York, 1962.

Jacoby, F., ed. *Fragmente der griechischen Historiker*. Berlin, 1923.

Jastrow, M. *Dictionary of the Targumim, the Talmud Babli and Yerushalmi and the Midrashic Literature*. 2 vols. New York, 1903 (reprinted 1950).

The Jewish Encyclopedia, ed. Isidore Singer. 12 vols. New York, 1901.

Koehler, L. and Baumgartner, W. *Lexicon in Veteris Testamentie....* Leiden, 1958.

Lagarde, Paulus de. *Prophetae Chaldaicae*. Lipsiae, 1872.

The Latter Prophets According to Targum Jonathan (vol. 3 of *The Bible in Aramaic*), ed. A. Sperber. Leiden, 1962.

Liddell and Scott. *Greek–English Lexicon*. Abridged from the 7th ed. 2 vols. New York, 1895.

The Loeb Classical Library. Cambridge, Mass., various dates.

Mekilta, Eng. trans. and Heb. text ed. by J. Z. Lauterbach. Philadelphia, 1933–5.

The Midrash on Psalms, Eng. trans. by W. G. Braude. 2 vols. New Haven, 1959.

Midrash Rabbah, Eng. trans. ed. by H. Freedmann and M. Simon. 9 vols. London, 1939.

Midrash Sifre on Numbers, Eng. trans. by P. Levertoff. London, 1926.

The Mishnah, Eng. trans. and notes by H. Danby. Oxford, 1933.

Patrologie cursus completus...Ecclesiae Latinae, ed. J. P. Migne. 222 vols. Paris, various dates.

Der Pentateuch der Samaritaner, ed. A. F. von Gall. Giessen, 1918.

Pirkê de Rabbi Eliezer, Eng. trans. by G. Friedlander. New York, 1916.

Septuaginta, ed. A. Rahlfs. 2 vols. Stuttgart, n.d.

Strack, H. L. and Billerbeck, P. *Kommentar zum Neuen Testament aus Talmud und Midrasch*. 6 vols. München, 1922–9.

Talmud Yerushalmi, Le Talmud de Jérusalem, French trans. by M. Schwab. N.p., 1871–90.

The Targum of Isaiah, ed. and tr. J. F. Stenning. Oxford, 1949.

Targum Onkelos, ed. A. Berliner. Berlin, 1884.

Testamenta XII Patriarcharum, ed. M. de Jonge, Leiden, 1964.

Theologisches Wörterbuch zum Neuen Testament, ed. G. Kittel and G. Friedrich. 7 vols. Stuttgart, 1933–64 (Eng. trans. of vols. I–III by G. W. Bromiley; Grand Rapids, Mich., 1964–6).

The Tosephta, ed. M. S. Zuckermandel. Pasewalk, 1880.

The Vocabulary of the Greek Testament, J. H. Moulton and G. Milligan. New York, 1914–29.

The Works of Flavius Josephus, Eng. trans. by W. Whiston. Edinburgh, n.d.

II. BOOKS REFERRED TO IN PART I

Batten, Loring W. *A Critical and Exegetical Commentary on the Books of Ezra and Nehemiah* (ICC). New York, 1913.

Bennett, W. H. *The Books of Chronicles* (Expositor's Bible). London, 1894.

Benzinger, I. *Die Bücher der Chronik*. Tübingen and Leipzig, 1901.

Bury, J. B. *The Ancient Greek Historians*. New York, 1909.

Cassuto, U. *A Commentary on the Book of Genesis*, Eng. trans. by G. Abrahams. 2 vols. Jerusalem, 1961–4.

Cook, S. A. *The Old Testament: a Reinterpretation*. Cambridge, 1936.

Curtis, E. L. and Madsen, A. A. *A Critical and Exegetical Commentary on the Books of Chronicles* (ICC). New York, 1910.

Davies, W. D. *Paul and Rabbinic Judaism*, 2nd ed. London, 1955.

Delaporte, L. J. *Chronographie de Mar Élie bar Sinaya*. Paris, 1910.

Dentan, Robert C., ed. *The Idea of History in the Ancient Near East*. New Haven, 1955.

Doughty, Charles M. *Travels in Arabia Deserta.* New York, n.d.
Driver, S. R. *The Book of Genesis*, 9th ed. London, 1913.
Eliade, Mircea. *Cosmos and History: The Myth of the Eternal Return*, Eng. trans. by W. R. Trask. New York, 1959.
Elmslie, W. A. L. *The Books of Chronicles* (Cambridge Bible), 2nd ed. Cambridge, 1916.
Chronicles (IB, III). New York and Nashville, 1952.
Eltester, W., ed. *Judentum, Urchristentum, Kirche.* Berlin, 1960.
Finegan, Jack. *Handbook of Biblical Chronology.* Princeton, N.J., 1964.
Frankfort, H., Wilson, J. A., Jacobsen, T. and Irwin, W. A. *The Intellectual Adventure of Ancient Man.* Chicago, 1946.
Goldziher, Ignaz. *Muhammedanische Studien.* Halle, 1889–90.
Mythology Among the Hebrews, Eng. trans. by R. Martineu. London, 1877.
Groningen, B. A. van. *In the Grip of the Past* [Philosophia Antiqua, 7]. Leiden, 1953.
Gunkel, H. *Genesis* (Göttinger Handkommentar), 5th ed. Göttingen, 1922.
Hooke, S. H. *Middle Eastern Mythology.* Baltimore, 1963.
Jacob, B. *Das erste Buch der Tora.* Berlin, 1934.
Jacobsen, Thorkild. *The Sumerian King List.* Chicago, 1939.
Jeremias, Joachim. *Jerusalem zur Zeit Jesu*, 3rd ed. Göttingen, 1962. Eng. trans. in preparation.
Kuhl, Curt. *The Old Testament: Its Origins and Composition*, Eng. trans. by C. T. M. Herriott. Richmond, 1961 [German or. 1953].
Linton, Olof. *Synopsis Historiae Universalis* (Festskrift udgivet af Københavns Universitet). København, 1957.
Littmann, Enno. *Safaitic Inscriptions* (Publications of the Princeton University Archeological Expeditions to Syria in 1904–5 and 1909, Division IV, 'Semitic Inscriptions', section C). Leiden, 1943.
M'Lennan, J. F. *Studies in Ancient History.* London, 1896.
Meyer, Eduard. *Die Israeliten und ihre Nachbarstämme.* Halle, 1906.
Moore, George Foot. *Judaism in the First Centuries of the Christian Era.* 3 vols. Cambridge, Mass., 1927.
Mowinckel, Sigmund. *The Two Sources of the Predeuteronomic History (JE) in Gen. 1–11.* Oslo, 1937.
Noth, Martin. *Das System der zwölf Stämme Israels* (Beiträge zur Wissenschaft vom Alten und Neuen Testament IV, 1). Stuttgart, 1930.
Überlieferungsgeschichte des Pentateuch. Stuttgart, 1948.
Überlieferungsgeschichtliche Studien, 2nd ed. Tübingen, 1957.

Peake's Commentary on the Bible, rev. ed. by M. Black and H. H. Rowley. New York, 1962.

Pritchard, James, ed. *Ancient Near Eastern Texts*. Princeton, 1955.

Proksch, Otto. *Die Genesis*, 3rd ed. Leipzig, 1924.

Rad, Gerhard von. *Genesis*, Eng. trans. by J. H. Marks. Philadelphia, 1961.

Das Geschichtsbild des Chronistischen Werkes (Beiträge zur Wissenschaft vom Alten und Neuen Testament). Stuttgart, 1930.

Die Priesterschrift im Hexateuch (Beiträge zur Wissenschaft vom Alten und Neuen Testament). Stuttgart, 1934.

Rehm, Martin. *Die Bücher der Chronik* (Das Alte Testament). Würzburg, 1949.

Rothstein, J. *Die Genealogie des Königs Jojachin und seiner Nachkommen*. Berlin, 1902.

Rothstein, J. and Hänel, J. *Das erste Buch der Chronik*. Leipzig, 1927.

Rudolph, Wilhelm. *Chronikbücher* (HAT). Tübingen, 1955.

Ryckmans, G. *Inscriptiones Safaiticae* (Corpus Inscriptionum Semiticarum, Pars Quinta, 'Inscriptiones Saracenicae', Sectio Prima). Parisiis, 1950.

Sachau, C. Edward. *The Chronology of Ancient Nations*. London, 1879.

Schnabel, Paul. *Berossos und die Babylonisch-Hellenistische Literatur*. Leipzig und Berlin, 1923.

Simpson, C. A. *The Book of Genesis* (IB). New York and Nashville, 1952.

Skinner, John. *A Critical and Exegetical Commentary on Genesis* (ICC). Rev. ed. New York, 1925.

Slotki, I. W. *Chronicles*. London, 1952.

Smith, Sidney. *Early History of Assyria*. London, 1928.

Smith, William Robertson. *Kinship and Marriage in Early Arabia*, new ed. London, 1903.

The Religion of the Semites, 3rd ed. London, 1927.

Vaux, Roland de. *Ancient Israel: Its Life and Institutions*, Eng. trans. by J. McHugh. London, 1961.

Welch, Adam C. *Post-Exilic Judaism*. Edinburgh and London, 1935.

The Work of the Chronicler. London, 1939.

Wellhausen, Julius. *Prolegomena to the History of Ancient Israel*, Eng. trans. by Menzies and Black. New York, 1957 [German or. 1883].

Skizzen und Vorarbeiten [Reste Arabischen Heidentums]. Berlin, 1887.

Wiseman, D. J. *The Alalakh Tablets*. London, 1953.

Yadin, Yigael. *The Scroll of the War of the Sons of Light Against the Sons of Darkness*, Eng. trans. by Batya and Chaim Rabim. Oxford, 1962.

III. ARTICLES REFERRED TO IN PART I

Albright, W. F. *JBL*, LVII (1938), 230–1; LVIII (1939), 91–103 [reviews of S. Mowinckel, *Two Sources*...].

Auerbach, E. 'Die Herkunft der Sadokien', *ZAW*, XLIX (1931), 327–8.

Black, M. 'The "Son of Man" in the Old Biblical Literature', *ET*, LX (1948), 13 ff.

Bork, F. 'Zur Chronologie der biblischen Urgeschichte', *ZAW*, XLVII (1929), 206–22.

Bousset, D. W. 'Das Chronologische System der biblischen Geschichtsbücher', *ZAW*, XX (1900), 136–47.

Brunet, A.-M. 'Le Chroniste et ses Sources', *RB*, LX (1953), 481–508; LXI (1954), 349–86.

'La théologie du Chroniste: théocratie et messianisme', in *Sacra Pagina*, ed. J. Coppens, pp. 384–97. Gembloux, 1959.

Budde, K. 'Ella Toledoth', *ZAW*, XXXIV (1914), 241–53; XXXVI (1916), 1–7.

Burrows, M. 'Ancient Israel', in *The Idea of History in the Ancient Near East*, ed. R. C. Dentan, pp. 125 ff. New Haven, 1955.

Ehrenzweig, A. 'Kain und Lamech', *ZAW*, XXXV (1915), 1–11.

Freedman, D. H. 'The Chronicler's Purpose', *CBQ*, XXIII (1961), 436–42.

'OT Chronology', in *The Bible and the Ancient Near East*, ed. G. E. Wright. Garden City, 1961.

Hauret, C. 'Réflexions pessimistes et optimistes sur Gen. 4: 17–24', in *Sacra Pagina*, ed. J. Coppens, pp. 358–65. Gembloux, 1959.

Jacoby, F. 'Über die Entwicklung der griechischen Historiographie', *Klio*, IX (1909), 80–123.

Jepsen, A. 'Zur Chronologie des Priesterkodex', *ZAW*, XLVII (1929), 251–5.

Lefèvre, A. 'Note d'Exégèse sur les Généalogies des Qehatites', *RSR*, XXXVII (1950), 287–92.

Luther, B. 'Die israelitischen Stämme', *ZAW*, XXI (1901), 1–76.

Mendenhall, G. E. 'The Census Lists of Numbers 1 and 26', *JBL*, LXXVII (1958), 52–66.

Mühling, G. J. 'Neue Untersuchung über die Genealogien der Chronik I. 1–9 und deren Verhältniss zum Zweck dieser Bücher', *Theologische Quartalschrift*, LXVI (1884), 403–50.

Murtonen, A. 'On the Chronology of the OT', *Studia Theologica*, VIII (1955), 133–7.

Noordtzij, A. 'Les intentions du Chroniste', *RB*, XLIX (1940), 161–8.

North, R. 'Theology of the Chronicler', *JBL*, LXXXII (1963), 369–81.

Noth, M. 'Eine siedlungsgeographische Liste in I Chr. 2 und 4', *Zeitschrift des Deutschen Palästina-Vereins*, LV (1962), 97–124.

Obermann, J. 'Early Islam', in *The Idea of History in the Ancient Near East*, ed. R. C. Dentan, pp. 244–92. New Haven, 1955.

Philippson, P. 'Genealogie als mythische Form: Studien zur Theologie des Hesiod', *Symbolae Osloensis*, Fasc. Suppl. VII (1936).

Podechard, A. 'Le premier Chapitre des Paralipomènes', *RB*, XIII (1916), 363–86.

Poebel, A. 'The Assyrian King List from Khorsabad', *JNES*, I (1942), 247–306, 460–92; II (1943), 56–90.

Richardson, H. N. 'The Historical Reliability of Chronicles', *JBR*, XXVI (1958), 9–12.

Richter, Georg. 'Zu den Geschlechts-Registern I Chronik 2–9', *ZAW*, XLIX (1939), 260–70.

Rowley, H. H. 'Nehemiah's Mission and its Background', *BJRL*, XXXVII (1954–5), 528–61.

Ryckmans, G. 'A Propos des Noms de Parenté en Safaïtique', *RB*, LX (1953), 524–5.

'Les Noms de Parenté en Safaïtique', *RB*, LVIII (1951), 377–92.

Simons, J. 'The Table of Nations (Gen. 10): Its General Structure and Meaning', *OTS*, X (1954), 168 ff.

Smith, Sidney. 'A Preliminary Account of the Tablets from Atchana', *Antiquaries Journal*, XIX (1939), 38–48.

Speiser, E. A. 'The Wife–Sister Motif in the Patriarchal Narratives', in *Biblical and Other Studies*, ed. by A. Altmann, pp. 28 ff. Cambridge, Mass. 1963.

Stinespring, W. F. 'Eschatology in Chronicles', *JBL*, LXXX (1961), 209–19.

Vries, S. J. de. 'Chronology of the Old Testament', *IDB*, I, 580–99.

Waterman, Leroy. 'Some Repercussions from Late Levitical Genealogical Accretions in P and the Chronicler', *AJSLL*, LVIII (1941), 49–56.

Wiesenberg, Ernest. 'The Jubilee of Jubilees', *RQ*, III (1961), 3–40.

IV. BOOKS REFERRED TO IN PART II

Allen, W. C. *A Critical and Exegetical Commentary on the Gospel According to St Matthew* (ICC). New York, 1907.

Aptowitzer, V. *Parteipolitik der Hasmonäerzeit im Rabbinischen und Pseudoepigraphischen Schrifttum*. Vienna, 1927.

Argyle, A. W. *The Gospel According to Matthew*. New York and London, 1963.

Bacher, W. *Die Agada der babylonischen Amoräer*. Strassburg, 1878.

Bacon, B. W. *Studies in Matthew*. New York, 1930.
Barrett, C. K. *Luke the Historian in Recent Study*. London, 1961.
Beare, F. W. *The Earliest Records of Jesus*. Oxford, 1962.
Bengel, J. A. *Gnomon of the New Testament*, Eng. trans. by C. T. Lewis and M. R. Vincent. Philadelphia, 1860 (German or. 1762).
Benoit, P. *L'Évangile selon St Matthieu*. Paris, 1950.
Black, M. *The Dead Sea Scrolls and Christian Doctrine*. London, 1966.
Bock, E. *Kindheit und Jugend Jesu* (Beiträge zur Geistesgeschichte der Menschheit). Stuttgart, 1956.
Bornhäuser, K. *Die Geburts- und Kindheitsgeschichte Jesu*. Gütersloh, 1930.
Bornkamm, G., Barth, G. and Held, H. J. *Tradition and Interpretation in Matthew*, Eng. trans. by P. Scott. London, 1963.
Box, G. H. *The Virgin Birth of Jesus*. London, 1916.
Bruce, F. F. *Biblical Exegesis in the Qumran Texts*. Philadelphia, 1960.
Bultmann, R. *The History of the Synoptic Tradition*, Eng. trans. by J. Marsh. Oxford, 1963.
Burkitt, F. C. *Evangelion da Mepharreshe*. 2 vols. Cambridge, 1904.
Burrows, M. *The Dead Sea Scrolls*. New York, 1955.
More Light on the Dead Sea Scrolls. New York, 1958.
Campenhausen, H. von. *The Virgin Birth in the Theology of the Ancient Church*, Eng. trans. by F. Clarke. Naperville, Ill., 1964.
Conzelmann, H. *The Theology of St Luke*, Eng. trans. by G. Buswell. New York, 1960.
Cross, F. M. *The Ancient Library of Qumran and Modern Biblical Studies*. Garden City, N.Y., 1958.
Cullmann, O. *The Christology of the NT*, Eng. trans. by S. C. Guthrie and C. Hall, 2nd ed. London, 1963.
Dalman, G. *Jesus Christ in the Talmud, Midrash, Zohar, and the Liturgy of the Synagogue*, Eng. trans. by A. W. Streane. Cambridge, 1893.
Davies, W. D. *Paul and Rabbinic Judaism*, 2nd ed. London, 1955.
The Setting of the Sermon on the Mount. Cambridge, 1964.
De Jonge, M. *The Testaments of the Twelve Patriarchs: a Study of their Text, Composition and Origin*. Manchester, 1953.
Dibelius, M. *Jungfrauensohn und Krippenkind* [1932] in *Botschaft und Geschichte*, I (1953), 1–78.
Dillersberger, J. *Matthäus*. 6 vols. Salzburg, 1953.
Dodd, C. H. *Romans* (Moffatt Commentaries). New York, 1932.
Driver, G. R. *The Judaean Scrolls*. Oxford, 1965.
Drummond, J. *The Jewish Messiah*. London, 1877.
Farrer, A. *The Rebirth of Images*. N.p., 1949.
Fenton, J. C. *The Gospel of St Matthew* (Pelican Gospel Commentaries). Harmondsworth, 1963.

Filson, F. *A Commentary on the Gospel According to St Matthew* (Black's NT Commentaries). London, 1960.

Finkel, A. *The Pharisees and the Teacher of Nazareth* (Arbeiten zur Geschichte des Spätjudentums and Urchristentums). Leiden, 1964.

Finkelstein, L. *Mabo le-Massektot Abot ve-Abot d'Rabbi Nathan* (Introduction to the Treatises Abot and Abot of Rabbi Nathan). New York, 1950.

Flender, H. *St Luke: Theologian of Redemptive History*, Eng. trans. by R. H. and I. Fuller. London and Philadelphia, 1967.

Gaechter, P. *Das Matthäus-Evangelium.* Innsbruck, 1963.

Godet, F. *A Commentary on the Gospel of St Luke*, 2nd ed., Eng. trans. by E. W. Shalders and M. D. Cusin. New York, 1881.

Goguel, M. *Jesus and the Origins of Christianity.* 2 vols. New York, 1960.

Goldstein, M. *Jesus in the Jewish Tradition.* New York, 1950.

Goudoever, J. van. *Biblical Calendars*, 2nd ed. Leiden, 1961.

Hahn, F. *Christologische Hoheitstitel*, 2nd ed. Göttingen, 1964.

Heer, J. M. *Die Stammbäume Jesu nach Matthäus und Lukas* (Biblische Studien xv (1910), 1–224). Freiburg, 1910.

Hennecke, E. and Schneemelcher, W. *New Testament Apocrypha*, Vol. 1, Eng. trans. ed. R. McL. Wilson. Philadelphia, 1963.

Herford, R. T. *The Ethics of the Talmud: Sayings of the Fathers.* New York, 1962 [orig. 1945].

Christianity in Talmud and Midrash. London, 1903.

Hervey, Arthur. *The Genealogies of Our Lord and Saviour Jesus Christ.* Cambridge and London, 1853.

Holtzmann, H. J. *Die Synoptischen Evangelien.* Leipzig, 1863.

Jeremias, J. *Jerusalem zur Zeit Jesu*, 3rd ed. Göttingen, 1962.

Keck, L. E. and Martyn, J. L., eds. *Studies in Luke-Acts* (Essays in Honor of P. Schubert). Nashville and New York, 1966.

Klausner, J. *The Messianic Idea in Israel*, Eng. trans. by W. F. Stinespring. New York, 1955.

Klostermann, E. *Das Lukasevangelium* (HNT), 2nd ed. Tübingen, 1929.

Das Matthäusevangelium, 2nd ed. Tübingen, 1927.

Kümmel, W. G. *Introduction to the NT* [Feine–Behm–Kümmel], Eng. trans. by A. J. Mattill. New York and Nashville, 1966.

Lagrange, M.-J. *Évangile selon Saint Matthieu*, 4th ed. Paris, 1927.

Laurentin, R. *Structure et Théologie de Luc I–II* (Études Bibliques). Paris, 1957.

Leaney, A. R. C. *The Rule of Qumran and its Meaning.* Philadelphia, 1966.

Liebermann, S. *Greek in Jewish Palestine.* New York, 1942.

Lohmeyer, E. *Das Evangelium des Matthäus.* Göttingen, 1956.

Loisy, A. *Les Évangiles Synoptiques*. 2 vols. Près Montier-en-Der, 1907.
McNeile, A. H. *The Gospel According to St Matthew*. London, 1915.
Manson, Wm. *The Gospel of Luke* (Moffatt NT Commentaries). New York, 1930.
Massaux, E., *et al. La Venue du Messie: Messianisme et Eschatologie*. N.p., 1962.
Meyer, H. A. W. *Critical and Exegetical Handbook to the Gospel of Matthew*, rev. ed. tr. P. Christie. Edinburgh, 1890.
Michaelis, D. W. *Das Evangelium nach Matthäus*. 2 vols. Zürich, 1948.
Milik, J. T. *Ten Years of Discovery in the Wilderness of Judea*. Naperville, Ill., 1959.
Montefiore, C. G. *The Synoptic Gospels*, 2nd ed. 2 vols. London, 1927.
Montefiore, C. G. and Loewe, H. *A Rabbinic Anthology*. London, 1938.
Moulton, J. H. *A Grammar of NT Greek*, 3rd ed. 3 vols. Edinburgh, 1908.
Odeberg, H. *3 Enoch*. Cambridge, 1928.
Plummer, A. *An Exegetical Commentary on the Gospel According to St Matthew*, 2nd ed. London, 1910.
Rabinson, M. *Le Messianisme dans le Talmud et les Midraschim*. Paris, 1907.
Rengstorf, K. H. *Das Evangelium nach Lukas* (NTD, I. 2). Göttingen, 1937.
Jebamot: Text, Übersetzung und Erklärung (Die Mischna, III. 1). Giessen, 1929.
Rienecker, F. *Das Evangelium des Matthäus*. Wuppertal, 1953.
Ringgren, H. *The Messiah in the OT*. Chicago, 1956.
Rist, Martin. *Revelation* (IB). New York and Nashville, 1952.
Robinson, T. H. *The Gospel of Matthew* (Moffatt Commentaries). New York, 1951.
Robinson, William C. *Der Weg des Herrn: Studien zur Geschichte und Eschatologie im Lukas-Evangelium; ein Gespräch mit H. Conzelmann*. Hamburg, 1964.
Ropes, J. H. *The Synoptic Gospels*. Cambridge, Mass., 1934.
Russell, D. S. *The Method and Message of Jewish Apocalyptic*. London, 1964.
Schechter, S. *Studies in Judaism*. New York, 1958 [2nd and 3rd series, or. 1908–24].
Schlatter, A. *Der Evangelist Matthäus*, 3rd ed. Stuttgart, 1948.
Schmidt, J. *Das Evangelium nach Matthäus*, 2nd ed. Regensburg, 1952.
Schniewind, Julius. *Das Evangelium nach Markus und das Evangelium nach Matthäus* (NTD). Göttingen, 1937.
Schürer, E. *Geschichte des jüdischen Volkes im Zeitalter Jesu Christi*, 5th ed., 3 vols. and index. Leipzig, 1920. (ET from second and rev. ed.; Edinburgh, 1885–96.)

Segal, R. Samuel Michael. *Elijah: A Study in Jewish Folklore.* New York, 1935.

Silver, Abba Hillel. *A History of Messianic Speculation in Israel.* Boston, 1959 (1st ed. 1927).

Smith, B. D. T. *The Gospel According to St Matthew* (Cambridge Greek Testament). Cambridge, 1922.

Stendahl, Kirster. 'Matthew', in *Peake's Commentary*, rev. ed. (see above).

The School of St Matthew and its Use of the Old Testament (Acta Seminarii Neotestamentici Upsaliensis). Uppsala, 1954.

ed. *The Scrolls and the New Testament.* New York, 1957.

Strack, H. L. *Introduction to the Talmud and Midrash*, Eng. trans., n. n. New York, 1931 (tr. from the 5th German ed., 1920).

Jesus: Die Häretiker und die Christen nach den ältesten jüdischen Angaben. Leipzig, 1910.

Strecker, G. *Der Weg der Gerechtigkeit: Untersuchung zur Theologie des Matthäus.* Göttingen, 1962.

Streeter, B. H. *The Four Gospels*, 4th ed. London, 1930.

Taylor, V. *The Historical Evidence for the Virgin Birth.* Oxford, 1920.

Tcherikover, V. A. and Fuks, A. *Corpus Papyrorum Judaicarum.* 3 vols. Cambridge, Mass., 1957–64.

Vezin, A. *Das Evangelium Jesu Christi.* Freiburg, 1938.

Volz, P. *Die Eschatologie der jüdischen Gemeinde im neutestamentlichen Zeitalter*, 2nd ed. Tübingen, 1934.

Weiss, B. *Das Matthäus-Evangelium.* Göttingen, 1890.

Woude, A. S. van der. *Die messianischen Vorstellungen der Gemeinde von Qumran.* Assen, 1957.

Young, R. *Christology of the Targums.* Edinburgh, n.d.

Zahn, T. *Das Evangelium des Matthäus*, 2nd ed. Leipzig, 1903.

Introduction to the NT, tr. from the 3rd German ed. by M. W. Jacobus *et al.* Edinburgh, 1909.

V. ARTICLES REFERRED TO IN PART II

Allegro, J. M. 'Further Messianic References in Qumran Literature', *JBL*, LXXV (1956), 174 ff.

Aptowitzer, V. 'Spuren des Matriarchats im Jüdischen Schrifttum', *HUCA*, IV (1927), 207–40.

Beasley-Murray, G. R. 'The Two Messiahs in the Testaments of the Twelve Patriarchs', *JTS*, XLVIII (1947), 1–12.

Bickermann, E. J. 'La Chaîne de la Tradition Pharisienne', *RB*, LIX (1952), 44–54.

'Symbolism in the Dura Synagogue: A Review Article', *HTR*, LVIII (1965), 127–51.

Black, M. 'The Judaean Scrolls' [review article], *NTS*, XIII (1966), 81–9.

Blair, H. A. 'Mt. 1: 16 and the Matthean Genealogy', *TU*, LXXXVII (1964), 149–54.

Bloch, Renée. 'Juda engendra Pharès et Zara, de Thamar (Matth. 1: 3)', in *Mélanges Bibliques rédigés en l'honneur de André Robert*, pp. 381–9. N.p., Blond and Gay, n.d.

'Midrash', in *Dictionnaire de la Bible—Suppl.* v (1957), 1263–82.

Bourke, M. M. 'The Literary Genius of Matthew 1–2', *CBQ*, XXII (1960), 160–75.

Box, G. H. 'The Gospel Narratives of the Nativity and the Alleged Influences of Heathen Ideas', *ZNW*, VI (1905), 80–101.

Brown, R. E. 'J. Starcky's Theory of Qumran Messianic Development', *CBQ*, XXVIII (1966), 51–7.

Dabeck, P. 'Siehe, es erscheinen Moses und Elias', *Biblica*, XXIII (1942), 175–89.

Davies, W. D. 'Apocalyptic and Pharisaism', in *Christian Origins and Judaism*, pp. 19–30. Philadelphia, 1962.

De Jonge, M. 'Christian Influences in the Testaments of the Twelve Patriarchs', *Nov. Test.* IV (1960), 182–235.

Dobschutz, E. von. 'Matthäus als Rabbi und Katechet', *ZNW*, XXVII (1928), 338–48.

Finkelstein, L. 'Introductory Study to *Pirke Abot*', *JBL*, LVII (1938), 13–50.

Friedrich, G. 'Messianische Hohepriestererwartung in den Synoptikern', *ZTK*, LIII (1956), 268–75.

Gibbs, J. M. 'Purpose and Pattern in Matthew's Use of the Title "Son of David"', *NTS*, X (1963–4), 446–64.

Ginzberg, L. 'Eine unbekannte jüdische Sekte', *MGWJ*, LVIII (1914), 395–429.

Gnilka, J., 'Die Erwartung des messianischen Hohenpriesters in den Schriften von Qumran und im Neuen Testament', *RQ*, II (1960), 395–426.

Grégoire, F. 'Le Messie chez Philon d'Alexandrie', *ETL*, XII (1935), 28–50.

Heffern, A. D. 'The Four Women in St Matthew's Genealogy of Christ', *JBL*, XXXI (1912), 69–81.

Higgins, A. J. B. 'The Priestly Messiah', *NTS*, XIII (1967), 211–39.

Holzmeister, U. 'Genealogia S. Lucae (Lk. 3: 23–38)', *Verbum Domini*, XXIII (1943), 9–18.

Hood, R. T. 'The Genealogies of Jesus', in *Early Christian Origins*, ed. A. Wikgren, pp. 1–13. Chicago, 1961.

Jeremias, J. 'Adam', *TDNT*, I, 139 ff.

Kaplan, C. 'Some NT Problems in the Light of the Rabbinics and the Pseudepigrapha, the Generation Schemes in Mt. 1: 1–17, Lk. 3: 24 ff.', *Bibliotheca Sacra*, LXXXVII (1930), 465–71.

Käsemann, E. 'The Problem of the Historical Jesus', section 3, in *Essays on NT Themes*, tr. W. J. Montague, 1964, pp. 24–9.

Kittel, G. 'Die γενεαλογίαι der Pastoralbriefe', *ZNW*, XX (1921), 49–69.

Köster, H. 'Die synoptische Überlieferung bei den apostolischen Vätern', *TU*, LXV (1957), 145 ff.

Krämer, M. 'Die Menschwerdung Jesu Christi nach Matthäus', *Biblica*, XLV (1964), 47 ff.

Kuhn, G. 'Die Geschlechtsregister Jesu bei Lukas und Matthäus, nach ihrer Herkunft untersucht', *ZNW*, XXII (1923), 206–28.

Lambertz, Maximilian. 'Die Toledoth im Mt. 1: 1–17 und Lc. 3: 23*b* ff.', in *Festschrift Franz Dornseiff*, ed. H. Kusch, pp. 211–25. Leipzig, 1953.

Lampe, G. W. H. 'The Holy Spirit in the Writings of St Luke', in *Studies in the Gospels: Essays in Memory of R. H. Lightfoot*, ed. D. E. Nineham. Oxford, 1955, pp. 173 ff.

Leaney, R. 'The Birth Narratives in St Luke and St Matthew', *NTS*, VIII (1962), 158–66.

Lévi, Israel. 'L'Apocalypse de Zorobabel et le Roi de Perse Siroès', *RÉJ*, LXVIII (1914), 129–60.

Liver, J. 'The Doctrine of the Two Messiahs in Sectarian Literature of the Second Commonwealth', *HTR*, LII (1959), 149–85.

'The Problem of the Davidic Family after the Biblical Period', *Tarbiz*, XXVI (1957), 229–54, i–iii.

Marmorstein, A. (Reviews of V. Aptowitzer, *Parteipolitik*...), *MGWJ*, LXXIII (1929), 244–50, 478–87.

Milton, H. 'The Structure of the Prologue to St Matthew's Gospel', *JBL*, LXXXI (1962), 176 ff.

Molin, Georg. 'Elijahu: der Prophet und sein Weiterleben in den Hoffnungen des Judentums und der Christenheit', *Judaica*, VIII (1952), pp. 65–92.

Moreton, M. J. 'The Genealogy of Jesus', *TU*, LXXXVII (1964), 223 ff.

Nestle, Eberhard. 'Salomo und Nathan in Mt 1 und Lc 3', *ZNW*, VIII (1907), 72.

Oliver, H. H. 'The Lucan Birth Stories and the Purpose of Luke–Acts', *NTS*, X (1963–4), 202–26.

Priest, John. 'Ben Sira 45: 25 in the Light of the Qumran Literature', *RQ*, V (1964), 111–18.

Ramlot, L. 'Les généalogies bibliques. Un genre littéraire oriental', *Bible et Vie Chrétienne*, LX (1964), 35–70.

Sanders, H. A. 'The Genealogies of Jesus', *JBL*, XXXII (1913), 184–93.

Schubert, Kurt. 'Zwei Messiasse aus dem Regelbuch von Chirbet Qumran', *Judaica*, XI (1955), 216–35.

Scott, R. B. Y. 'The Expectation of Elijah', *Canadian Journ. Theol.* III (1926), 490–502.

Silbermann, I. 'The Two Messiahs of the Manual of Discipline', *VT*, V (1955), 77–82.

Smith, Morton. 'What is Implied by the Variety of Messianic Figures?', *JBL*, LXXVIII (1959), 66–72.

Soltau, W. 'Zur Entstehung des I. Evangeliums', *ZNW*, I (1900), 219–48.

Spitta, F. 'Die Frauen in der Genealogie Jesu bei Matthäus', *ZWT*, LIV (1912), 1–8.

Starcky, J. 'Les quatre étapes du messianisme à Qumrân', *RB*, LXX (1963), 481–505.

Stendahl, K. 'Quis et unde?', in *Judentum, Urchristentum, Kirche*, ed. W. Eltester, pp. 94–105. Berlin, 1960.

Tatum, W. B. 'The Epoch of Israel: Luke i–ii and the Theological Plan of Luke–Acts', *NTS*, XIII (1967), 184–95.

Thompson, P. J. 'The Infancy Gospels of St Matthew and St Luke Compared', *TU*, LXXXVII (1964), 218–19.

Throckmorton, B. H. 'Genealogy (Christ)', *IDB*, II, 365–6.

Torrey, C. C. 'The Messiah Son of Ephraim', *JBL*, LXVI (1947), 253–77.

Vögtle, A. 'Die Genealogie Mt. 1: 2–16 und die Matthäische Kindheitsgeschichte', *BZ*, VIII (1964), 45–58, 239–62; IX (1965), 32–49.

Wieder, N. 'The Doctrine of the Two Messiahs Among the Karaites', *JJS*, VI (1955), 14–23.

Windisch, H. 'Zur Rahabgeschichte', *ZAW*, XXXVI–XXXVII (1916–18), 188–98.

INDEX OF PASSAGES CITED

A. THE OLD TESTAMENT

Genesis
1–2 185
1–11 4
1: 1 21
1: 26 f. 18
1: 27 f. 16, 16 n. 5, 171
2: 4*a* 14 n. 1, 15, 15 n. 4, 21, 146, 149, 186
2: 4*b*–3: 24 8 n. 2
3 10
3: 17–19 18
4–5 9
4: 1 216
4: 1–16 8 n. 2, 9 n. 2
4: 17 216
4: 17–22 4, 7, 8, 11
4: 17–24 10 n. 1, 29
4: 18 271 n. 2
4: 25 149
4: 25–6 4 n. 1, 8, 10
4: 26*b* 8 n. 2
5 8, 17, 22, 27, 28, 29, 30, 31, 31 n. 4, 33, 33 n. 1, 78, 190, 237, 237 n. 2, 259, 261 n. 1, 262
5: 1*a* 16, 16 n. 5
5: 1 15 n. 4, 21, 146, 149, 186
5: 1–6 18
5: 1*b* 18
5: 1*b*–2 16 n. 5
5: 3–4 29
5: 6–8 17
5: 10 21
5: 22–4 18
5: 23 29 n. 4
5: 28*b*–29 4 n. 1
5: 29 10
5: 32 13 n. 2, 262, 262 n. 3
6: 9–10 21, 22, 25 n. 2
7: 1 167
7: 6 262, 262 n. 3
7: 9 171
8: 1 102 n. 4
8: 19 20 n. 2
9: 18–19 4 n. 1
9: 19 77 n. 1
9: 29 262
10 5, 5 n. 2, 13 n. 2, 77, 126, 139, 232
10: 1 25 n. 2
10: 1*b* 19
10: 2–4 20, 22
10: 5*a* 19
10: 6–7 20, 22
10: 7 5, 6
10: 7*b* 6 n. 1
10: 8 19
10: 8–14 4 n. 1
10: 8–19 19
10: 11 5, 6 n. 2
10: 13 19
10: 15 19
10: 20 20, 22
10: 21 19
10: 22 5, 6 n. 2, 16, 22, 270
10: 22–3 20, 22
10: 24–30 4 n. 1, 19
10: 25 f. 5, 6 n. 3, 19
10: 28 6 n. 1
10: 31 20, 24
10: 32 20, 24, 25 n. 4
11 26, 27, 31 n. 4, 33, 78, 190, 259, 262
11: 10 16, 22
11: 10 ff. 261 n. 1
11: 10–26 18, 28, 33 n. 1
11: 10–27 22
11: 10*b* 262 n. 3
11: 11 262
11: 13 25 n. 2, 259
11: 21 22
11: 24 32 n. 7
11: 26 19, 25 n. 5, 262
11: 27 16, 19, 25 n. 5
11: 27–32 13 n. 2
11: 31 ff. 24 n. 1
11: 32 262, 264 n. 3
12: 1 150
12: 2 150
12: 3 169
12: 4 34 n. 1, 201 n. 6, 262
12: 5 201
13: 5 166
14: 18 271

Genesis (*cont.*)
15: 12–16 33 n. 2
15: 13 34 n. 2
15: 13–16 32 n. 3
15: 18–19 11 n. 1
16: 15 163 n. 2
18: 7 150
19: 8 216
19: 15 166
19: 22 166
19: 36–8 4 n. 2, 77
21: 1–5 153 n. 2
21: 5 261 n. 1, 262
22: 20–4 5, 13 n. 2, 14, 24 n. 3, 77, 153 n. 2
23: 4 33 n. 2
24 21 n. 1
24: 10 4 n. 1
24: 38 20 n. 2
25: 1–6 5, 6, 14, 77, 153 n. 2
25: 2 6 n. 3, 24 n. 3
25: 2 f. 5
25: 3 5, 5 n. 2, 6 n. 1, 6 n. 2
25: 7 262
25: 12 19, 20, 20 n. 3, 24 n. 2, 25
25: 12–16 16, 24 n. 3, 77
25: 12–17 22
25: 13 15 n. 3
25: 16 20
25: 19 19, 24 n. 2
25: 19–20 16, 22
25: 26 261 n. 1, 262
26: 34 16 n. 3
28: 9 16 n. 3
29–30 26 n. 3
29: 31–2 21 n. 1
30: 1–3 4 n. 1
30: 6 4 n. 1
30: 11 266 n. 3
30: 12 95
30: 17–20 4 n. 1
30: 21 4 n. 1
31: 53 4 n. 1
35: 22*b*–26 21, 21 n. 1, 26 n. 3, 153 n. 2
35: 28 262
36 77
36: 1–6 16 n. 4
36: 2 16 n. 4
36: 4 19
36: 9 25
36: 9 ff. 20
36: 9*b* 20 n. 3
36: 9–14 22, 25
36: 9–43 16
36: 11 5 n. 2, 6 n. 6
36: 12 19
36: 14 19
36: 15 5 n. 2
36: 20 24 n. 3
36: 22 95
37: 1–2 16, 21
37: 2 146 n. 2, 262
38 152, 154, 159
38: 1 160
38: 14 161, 271
38: 15 f. 160
38: 24 270
38: 25 161
38: 26 270
41: 46 262
41: 47 262
41: 54 262
45: 6 262
46 44, 50, 51, 80
46: 8–27 21, 21 n. 1, 26 n. 3
46: 10 180
47: 9 33 n. 2, 261 n. 1, 262
47: 28 33 n. 2, 262
49: 1–28*a* 21 n. 1
49: 10 126
49: 13 109
49: 25 154 n. 3
49: 28 151
50: 22 262
50: 26 262

Exodus
1: 1–5 21 n. 1
2: 18 9 n. 2
2: 22 54 n. 6
6: 14 89 n. 1
6: 14–25 20, 22
6: 16 20
6: 16–19 22
6: 16–25 25
6: 18 268
6: 19 15 n. 3, 20
6: 23 72 n. 2, 242, 153 n. 2
6: 24 72 n. 1
6: 25 20, 242
12: 2 197, 198
12: 40 32, 34, 202, 261 n. 1, 262, 263, 264
16: 33 268 n. 8
18: 1 163 n. 2

Exodus (*cont.*)
18: 1–12 9 n. 2
18: 3–4 54 n. 6
19: 3 27 n. 1
20: 1 191

Leviticus
21–2 96
21: 9 270
21: 14 100 n. 1
22: 13 ff. 96 n. 6
25: 23 57

Numbers
1: 2 64 n. 4
1: 3 63 n. 10
1: 3*b*–4 62 n. 7
1: 5–15 20 n. 4
1: 7 72 n. 2, 153 n. 2
1: 18 14
1: 20–40 17
1: 20–42 14 n. 2, 15 n. 3, 21 n. 1
2: 1–31 21 n. 1
3: 1 20 n. 3, 27
3: 1–3 16, 20, 20 n. 4, 22, 25
3: 5–13 71 n. 2
3: 18 59 n. 3
4: 3 42
5: 22 27 n. 1
6: 26 199
7: 2 62 n. 5
7: 12 153 n. 2
7: 12–78 21 n. 1
7: 15 ff. 150
8: 14 71 n. 2
8: 24 42 n. 1
10: 14–27 21 n. 1
10: 29 9 n. 2
13: 1–16 21 n. 1
13: 6 6 n. 7
13: 14 191
15: 30 95, 95 n. 3
17: 17 62 n. 10, 131
23 166, 207
24: 17 121
24: 21–2 9 n. 2, 11
25: 11 268
25: 11–13 267
25: 15 63 n. 1
26 44, 50, 51, 52, 63, 65, 67, 68, 80
26: 5–51 37 n. 1
26: 5–57 21 n. 1
26: 12–14 56
26: 29 ff. 51
26: 36 51
31: 25 ff. 62 n. 6
32: 12 70 n. 3
32: 13 6 n. 6
32: 28 ff. 62 n. 7
34: 19 6 n. 7
36: 1 ff. 62 n. 8

Deuteronomy
5: 9 3 n. 3
10: 8–9 71 n. 2
17: 17 171
18: 15 250
20: 16 164
23 4 n.
23: 2 147
23: 3 3 n. 3, 134, 168, 246
23: 4 3 n. 3
23: 5 168
23: 7 168
23: 9 3 n. 3
30: 4 267 n. 3
33: 7 131 n. 2

Joshua
2: 15 163
6: 23 163
7: 1 53
7: 24–6 53
14: 1 62 n. 9
15: 1 20 n. 2
15: 13 70 n. 3
15: 17 6 n. 6
15: 56–7 11 n. 1, 12 n. 2
19: 1–9 56
19: 2–8 58 n. 5
19: 10–13 109
19: 51 62 n. 9
21: 1–42 58 n. 5
21: 10 ff. 62 n. 9
22: 13 ff. 62 n. 8
24: 2 13 n. 2

Judges
1: 13 6 n. 6
1: 16 11 n. 1
1: 16–17 12 n. 2
1: 31 109
2: 13 172
3: 12 166
3: 20 166
4: 11 9 n. 2, 11, 11 n. 1

Judges (*cont.*)
7 70 n. 1
9: 43 f. 63 n. 7
18: 30 54 n. 6

Ruth
4: 12 159
4: 13–22 152
4: 18–22 16, 19, 78, 150

I Samuel
1: 1 3 n. 1, 7 n. 1, 80
2: 35 120 n. 5
9: 1 80
11: 8 63
11: 11 63 n. 7
13: 15 ff. 63 n. 11
13: 17 f. 63 n. 7
14: 3 40
14: 17 63 n. 11
15: 6 11 n. 1
17: 12 132 n. 3
17: 25 67
17: 55 167
18: 4 175
22: 7 67
22: 9 40
22: 20 40
26: 19 57
27: 10 11 n. 1, 70 n. 3
30: 14 70 n. 3
30: 29 11 n. 1, 12, 70 n. 3

II Samuel
3: 4 93
5: 14 59 n. 3, 135 n. 3, 240
5: 14–16 45 n. 2
7 241
7: 11–14 127
7: 11–16 116
8: 17 40, 40 n. 2
11 153
11: 11 173, 175
12: 9 173, 175
12: 13 174
15: 4–5 63 n. 11
15: 36 40 n. 4
16: 8 134, 175
16: 13*b* 174
18: 1–2 63 n. 7, 63 n. 11
20: 1 3 n. 1, 80
23: 39 173
24 63

I Kings
2: 8*a* 134, 174
4: 1–4 41 n. 1
4: 2 40 n. 4, 41
4: 31 70 n. 1
6: 1 32 n. 4, 35 n. 2, 41 n. 1, 262
7: 1 35 n. 2
8 35 n. 2
8: 20*b*–21 54 n. 2
8: 51 54 n. 2
8: 53 54 n. 2
8: 65 191 n. 2
10: 19 198
14: 21 135 n. 1
14: 31 135 n. 1
15: 5 172
17 249
17: 9 109
20: 15 63 n. 11
20: 26 63 n. 11

II Kings
5: 17 57
8: 16 181 n. 1
8: 25 181 n. 1
9: 10 132 n. 3
9: 29 181 n. 1
12: 1 181 n. 1
13 181 n. 1
13: 1 181 n. 1
14: 1 181 n. 1
14: 25 109
15: 1 181 n. 1
15: 5 181 n. 1
15: 7 181 n. 1
21: 1 136 n. 2
21: 19–25 182
24: 17 47 n. 1, 180
25: 18 40 n. 3

I Chronicles
1–8 52
1–9 44, 46, 51, 76, 86, 87 n. 1
1: 1 10
1: 29 14 n. 2
2–8 60, 61, 63, 64, 67, 78
2–9 55
2: 1 151, 151 n. 5
2: 3–4 152, 153 n. 2
2: 9 7 n. 1
2: 18–20 153 n. 2
2: 18 ff. 7 n. 1

I Chronicles (*cont.*)
2: 19 132 n. 3
2: 32 39 n. 2
2: 34–41 153 n. 2
2: 46 ff. 153 n. 2
2: 48 ff. 153 n. 2
2: 55 9 n. 2, 11 n. 1, 153 n. 2
3: 5 59, 135 n. 3, 153, 240
3: 8 46, 47
3: 9 184
3: 10–16 198
3: 11–12 182
3: 15 47 n. 1
3: 15–16 47
3: 16 46
3: 17 184
3: 19 186
3: 24 179
4–8 99 n. 2
4: 21 165
4: 21–3 163, 164
4: 34–7 67
4: 41 62 n. 3
5: 7 14 n. 2
5: 22 46
5: 23–6 68 n. 2
5: 27–41 36 n. 3, 38, 39, 44, 46, 78, 190
5: 36*b* 41
5: 41 43 n. 2
6: 1–15 44, 78
6: 7–15 7 n. 1
6: 17 59
6: 35–8 39
7 68 n. 2
7: 1–5 64
7: 6 46 n. 1
7: 6–11 64
7: 9 14 n. 2
7: 13 46 n. 1
7: 14–19 51
7: 20–9 51
7: 30–40 64
8 51
8: 3 179
8: 38 86
9 38, 46
9: 2 38
9: 2–34 37
9: 10 119 n. 1
9: 11 38, 39, 40 n. 3
9: 44 86
11 68 n. 2
11: 35 180
12: 20 180
12: 32–4 45
12: 40 45
14: 4 135 n. 3, 240
20: 7 245 n. 5
22: 9 174
23: 3 42
23: 24 41, 42
23: 27 41, 42
24: 16 180
25: 1 ff. 182
26: 7 180
29: 23 198

II Chronicles
1: 22 219
3: 5 136, 245
12: 13 135 n. 1
21: 1 181
22: 1 181
22: 2 181
24: 1 181
25: 1 181
26: 1 181
27: 1 181
28: 7 38 n. 2
30: 10 45
30: 11 38 n. 2, 45
30: 18 38 n. 2, 45
31: 17 41, 42
33: 21–5 182
34: 9 38 n. 2
36: 10 47

Ezra
2 43, 89
2: 1 60 n. 1
2: 1–63 42 n. 2
2: 1–70 147 n. 2
2: 2 69 n. 4
2: 2–63 89
2: 61–3 96
2: 62–3 43 n. 1
2: 70 60 n. 1
3: 2 40, 69 n. 4, 184
3: 8 42, 184, 262
3: 10 42 n. 4
4: 3 42 n. 4
5: 2 69 n. 4
5: 11 42 n. 4
6: 16 42 n. 4
7: 1–5 38, 39, 71
7: 15 39

Ezra (*cont.*)
9–10 44, 97
9: 1–10: 4 91 n. 5
9: 2 43 n. 6, 80
9: 8 43 n. 6
9: 11 43 n. 6
10: 10 43 n. 6
10: 18–22 90 n. 1
10: 18–24 97
10: 23–4 90 n. 1
10: 25–43 90 n. 1

Nehemiah
1: 6 42 n. 4
2: 10 42 n. 4
7 43, 89
7: 5 38, 147
7: 6 60 n. 1
7: 6–65 89
7: 61 ff. 42 n. 3
7: 63–5 96
7: 64 71 n. 2
7: 64–5 43 n. 1
8: 9 111
9: 2 43 n. 6
9: 8 149
10: 34 43 n. 5
11 38
11: 3–4*a* 38
11: 3–24 37
11: 3 ff. 38 n. 1
11: 4 69 n. 3
11: 10 119 n. 1
11: 11 38, 39, 40 n. 3
11: 12*b* 38
12: 4 3
12: 10 39 n. 1, 43 n. 2
12: 12–23 43
12: 16 3
12: 22 43 n. 3
12: 23 39 n. 2, 43 n. 4
12: 26 69 n. 5
12: 41 180
12: 44–13: 3 75
13: 1 ff. 4 n.
13: 1–3 43 n. 6, 44 n. 1
13: 23–31 97 n. 1

Esther
2: 5 102

Job
1: 17 63 n. 7
6: 19 5 n. 2
15: 18 270
32–6 180

Psalms
3: 3 173
4: 1 173, 174
4: 4 133
4: 5 169, 170
5: 7 167
38: 18 133, 174
43: 3 267
45: 3 189
50: 20 95
56: 1 161
72: 3 198
72: 7 198
80: 2 131 n. 2
80: 3 131 n. 2
87: 3 88
87: 6 89 n. 1
89: 21 150, 166
89: 36–8 199, 199 n. 1
97: 11 198
105: 8 191
110: 1 227
110: 4 129, 132
116: 16 135, 168
132: 8–11 54 n. 2

Proverbs
10: 30 57

Ecclesiastes
7: 19 150
10: 1 167

Isaiah
2: 11 201
10: 17 198
11: 1 117 n. 2
11: 1–4 127
11: 10 117 n. 2
21: 13 f. 5 n. 2
22: 19–25 180
29: 18 ff. 226 n. 5
41: 2 198
45: 1 32 n. 6, 116 n. 2
61: 1 ff. 226 n. 5

Jeremiah
2: 26 120 n. 5
4: 9 120 n. 5

Jeremiah (*cont.*)
8: 1 — 120 n. 5
13: 13 — 120 n. 5
21: 11–14 — 117 n. 3
22: 1–5 — 117 n. 3
22: 24–30 — 117 n. 3, 142, 244, 247
22: 30 — 183, 184, 244
25: 23 — 5 n. 2
28: 1 — 180
29: 7 — 198
29: 11 — 160
33: 17–22 — 120 n. 5
35 — 9 n. 2
38: 1 — 180
52: 24 — 40 n. 3

Lamentations
3: 51 — 188
4: 22 — 267 n. 3
5: 11 — 92

Ezekiel
13: 10 — 171
25: 18 — 5 n. 2
27: 20 — 5 n. 2
27: 22 — 5 n. 2
28: 25 — 57
38: 13 — 5 n. 2
44–6 — 120 n. 5
44: 9 — 91 n. 5
44: 15–31 — 96 n. 6

Daniel
7 — 116
7: 9 — 198
9: 1–27 — 190
9: 2 — 202
9: 24 — 202

Hosea
1: 2 — 57
2: 23 — 57
3: 5 — 117 n. 1

Amos
6: 5 — 117 n. 1
9: 11 — 117 n. 1, 127
9: 15 — 57

Micah
5: 4 — 150
6: 2 — 198

Zephaniah
1: 1 — 3, 80

Haggai
1: 1 — 39 n. 1, 43 n. 2, 120 n. 5, 184
6: 2 — 201
6: 5 — 211

Zechariah
1: 1 — 3 n. 1, 80
2: 3 — 129
2: 16 — 57
4: 14 — 116 n. 2, 120 n. 5, 129
12: 1–13: 9 — 59
12: 7 — 59 n. 3
12: 10–14 — 240
12: 12 — 59 n. 3, 135, 241, 246, 247

Malachi
2: 4 f. — 267
3: 1 — 267
3: 20 — 226 n. 5
3: 23 — 267
4: 2 — 226 n. 5

B. THE APOCRYPHA AND PSEUDEPIGRAPHA OF THE OLD TESTAMENT

IV Ezra
10: 45 f. — 35 n. 5, 36 n. 4
12: 32 — 119
14: 10 ff. — 231
14: 11 f. — 197 n. 2

Tobit
1: 1–2 — 102

Judith
8: 1 — 102
9: 2 — 102

Ben Sira
44: 16 — 18 n. 1
45: 6–7, 13 — 118 n. 2
45: 24–5 — 118 n. 3
47: 11 — 118 n. 1

Ben Sira (*cont.*)
47: 22 117
48: 10*b* 268 n. 3
50: 1 ff. 118 n. 2

I Maccabees
2: 1 119 n. 1
2: 1 ff. 132 n. 1
2: 51–60 151
2: 54–7 118

II Maccabees
2: 4–8 268 n. 8

Jubilees
passim 36 n. 4
4: 17 ff. 18 n. 1
41: 1 154 n. 2, 159, 270 n. 1
50: 4 35 n. 1
50: 9 34 n. 3

I Enoch
73: 5–7 200 n. 1
78: 15–16 199 n. 3
90: 19 223 n. 1
93, 91 36 n. 4, 190, 195, 197 n. 2, 207 n. 1, 223 n. 1

II Enoch
33: 1–2 200

Testaments of the XII Patriarchs
Reuben
6: 5–12 121
6: 7, 11 122 n. 7
6: 8 122 n. 4
6: 8, 10 122 n. 6
Simeon
7 132 n. 2
7: 1–2 122 n. 6
7: 1 f. 121
7: 2 122 nn. 4, 5

Levi
2: 11 132 n. 2
8: 11–12 122 n. 6
8: 14 121 n. 2
18 267
18: 1 ff. 122 n. 3

Judah
1: 6 122 n. 1
10: 1 154 n. 2, 159, 270 n. 1
10: 6 159, 270 n. 2
12: 2 159
13: 4 272 n. 2
15: 2 122 n. 1
15: 2–6 170 n. 7
17: 3 171
17: 5–6 122 n. 1
21 267
21: 1–2 122 nn. 1, 7
21: 4 122 n. 2
22: 2–3 122 n. 5
22: 3 122 n. 1
24: 1–2 122 n. 4
24: 5–6 122 n. 5
25: 1–2 122 n. 7

Issachar
5: 7 122 nn. 3, 6

Dan
4: 7 122 n. 6
5: 4, 10 122 n. 3
5: 10 132 n. 2

Gad
8: 1 122 nn. 3, 6, 132 n. 2

Naphtali
5: 3–4 122 n. 7
5: 31 122 n. 3
8: 2–3 122 n. 6

Joseph
19 132 n. 2
19: 11 122 nn. 3, 6

Assumption of Moses
passim 36 n. 4
1: 1 f. 35 n. 1

II Baruch
27 223 n. 1
53–74 193, 207, 231

Psalms of Solomon
17: 4 119
21 119
36 119

Apoc. Abraham
29 231

Sibylline Oracles
I. 324 ff. 193
IV. 47–86 197 n. 2
V. 12 193
14 193
21 193
24 193
25 193
28 193
38 193
40 193

C. THE DEAD SEA SCROLLS

Damascus Document (CD)
passim 132 n. 2
5: 1–5 170 n. 2
7 172, 177
9: 10 ff. 223 n. 1
12: 23 126
14: 18 126
17: 1 ff. 104 n. 4
19: 10 126

IQS
4: 1–28 128
9: 10 f. 123, 124, 126
9: 11 125

War Scroll (IQM)
passim 63 n. 4, 68

IQSa
2: 18 ff. 125
11–22 125

4Q Patr. Bl.
passim 126 n. 3

4Q Flor.
passim 127 n. 1

D. THE NEW TESTAMENT

Matthew
1 146, 148, 150, 200, 254, 255
1–2 112 n. 1, 210 n. 2
1: 1 146, 147, 149, 219, 223, 228
1: 1–16 146, 181
1: 1–17 41, 103, 119 n. 5, 140, 142, 144 n. 1, 189, 193, 197 n. 2, 200, 208, 209, 217, 225, 252, 255
1: 1–18 f. 184, 185
1: 2–17 191, 195, 208, 210
1: 3 256 n. 12
1: 3–6 176
1: 4 153 n. 2
1: 6 153
1: 11 183, 217
1: 12 184
1: 13–15 180
1: 15 f. 243
1: 16 144 n. 3, 185, 222
1: 17 197 n. 3, 205, 217, 219, 222, 232
1: 18–25 186, 225, 228 n. 2, 255
1: 19 217
1: 20 216, 217, 218
1: 22 212 n. 2
1: 24 216
1: 25 217
1: 30 119 n. 5
2: 4–6 228
2: 12 216
2: 13 216, 217
2: 15 212 n. 2
2: 17 212 n. 2
2: 19 216, 217
2: 22 216
2: 23 212 n. 2
3: 1 ff. 210
3: 2 221 n. 3
3: 7 212
3: 7–10 219
3: 9 151 n. 1, 219
3: 15 220
3: 17 212
4: 1–11 212
4: 11 235
4: 14 212 n. 2
4: 16 220
4: 17 221 n. 3

Matthew (*cont.*)
4: 18 222
4: 23 211
5: 3 221 n. 2
5: 10 221 n. 2
5: 19–20 221 n. 2
5: 32 211
5: 33–7 212
6: 1–18 212
6: 9*b*–13 211
7: 21 221 n. 2
8: 1–15 212
8: 2 226 n. 2
8: 8 226 n. 2
8: 10–12 219
8: 11 219, 221 n. 2, 248
8: 17 212 n. 2
8: 23 212
8: 25 226 n. 2
8: 29 221 n. 1, 225
9: 1–17 213
9: 6 226 n. 3
9: 8 212
9: 13 211
9: 14–17 213, 220
9: 18–34 212
9: 20 225
9: 27 119 n. 6, 218, 226
9: 27–31 212
9: 32–4 212
9: 35 211
9: 36 212
10: 1 211
10: 2 222
10: 6 211
10: 7 221 n. 3
10: 17–22 212
10: 19 221 n. 2
10: 23 221 n. 3
10: 26 213
10: 28 213
10: 31 213
10: 34 223
10: 37–8 213
11: 2 228
11: 12 221 n. 3
11: 12–13 219
11: 14 219 n. 1, 267 n. 2
11: 16 ff. 220
11: 25–30 227
12: 6 220
12:7 211, 212 n. 2
12: 22–3 226
12: 23 119 n. 6, 218
12: 28 221 n. 4
12: 32 220
12: 39 211
12: 41–2 220
12: 45 214
13: 1–32 213
13: 12 211
13: 22 ff. 212
13: 35 212 n. 2
13: 39 220
13: 40 220
13: 49 220
13: 57 249
14: 2 220
14: 14 212
14: 30 226 n. 2
14: 33 227
15: 22 119 n. 6, 218, 226
15: 22 ff. 226 n. 2
15: 24 211
15: 34 214
15: 37 214
16: 4 211
16: 14 267 n. 2
16: 16 226, 228
16: 17–18 222
17: 5 212
17: 12 267 n. 2
17: 12–13 219 n. 1
18: 1–4 221 n. 1
18: 6 213
18: 10 213
18: 14 213
18: 21–2 214
19: 9 211
19: 12 216
19: 23 221 n. 2
19: 24 221 n. 4
20: 16 211
20: 29–34 212
20: 30 218, 226
20: 30–1 218
20: 31 226 n. 2
21: 4 212 n. 2
21: 8 119 n. 6
21: 9 218
21: 15 119 n. 6, 218
21: 31 221 n. 4
21: 43 221 n. 4
22: 15–40 213
22: 25 214
22: 29–33 219

Matthew (*cont.*)
22: 32 219
22: 41–6 227
22: 42 218
22: 42 ff. 218
22: 45 218
23 214
23: 10 228
23: 13 221 n. 4
23: 16–22 212
23: 23 211
23: 33 212
23: 39 221
24: 3 220
24: 5 228
24: 9–14 212
24: 23 228
24: 43–25: 30 213
25: 29 211
26: 24 217
26: 29 221
26: 39–44 213
26: 54–6 212 n. 2
26: 63 226, 228
26: 68 228
27: 3–10 216
27: 9 212 n. 2
27: 17 222 n. 2, 223, 228
27: 19 216
27: 21–3 211
27: 22 222 n. 2, 223, 228
28: 1 216
28: 2 217
28: 18–20 227
28: 20 220

Mark
1: 1 228, 255
1: 13 235
2: 1–12 226 n. 3
2: 18 220 n. 2
6: 4 249
6: 14 249
6: 15 249, 267 n. 2
6: 34 212
7: 24–30 218
8: 12 212
8: 28 249, 267 n. 2
8: 38 211
9 267 n. 2
9: 12 107 n. 5, 268 n. 3
10: 31 211
10: 46–52 212
10: 47 f. 119 n. 6
10: 47–8 218
11–13 267 n. 2
11: 9–10 218
11: 10 119 n. 6
11: 25 212
12: 1 212
12: 35 218
12: 35–7 227
12: 37 218
13: 9–13 212
13: 21 228
13: 42 212
14: 1 212
14: 21 216
14: 61 226
15: 7 222 n. 2
16: 1 216

Luke
1 143 n. 10
1–2 236, 237, 251
1: 11 216 n. 3
1: 13–17 248
1: 17 248
1: 23 229, 230, 231
1: 26–37 238
1: 26–38 230
1: 27 119 n. 5
1: 30–6 248
1: 32 119 n. 5
1: 34 216
1: 46–55 248
1: 55 151 n. 1, 219
1: 67–79 248
1: 70 248
1: 73 151 n. 1, 219
1: 76 248
2: 4 119 n. 5
2: 9 216 n. 3
2: 29–35 248
2: 36–8 248
2: 36 102
3 234
3–24 230, 236, 237, 238
3: 1 236
3: 1–3 235
3: 4 248
3: 21–2 235
3: 22 235
3: 23 143
3: 23*b* ff. 144 n. 1, 243
3: 23–38 103, 119 n. 5, 140, 254, 255

Luke (*cont.*)
3: 24 274
3: 24 ff. 197 n. 2
3: 26 179
3: 29 274
3: 31 247
3: 32–3 153 n. 2
3: 38 10, 234
4: 1 235
4: 1 ff. 234
4: 7 248
4: 21 249
4: 22 143
4: 24 249
4: 25–6 248, 249
4: 27 248
4: 41 238
5: 33 220 n. 2
7: 11–17 249
7: 39 249
9: 8 248, 249, 267 n. 2
9: 19 248, 249, 267 n. 2
9: 30 ff. 248
9: 35 238
10: 24 248
11: 14 212
11: 47–51 250
12: 10 220
12: 51 223
13: 16 151 n. 1, 219
13: 28 248
13: 33 249, 250
16: 24–30 219
16: 30 151 n. 1
18: 31 248
18: 38–9 218
19: 9 219
19: 38 218
20: 41 218
20: 41–4 227
22: 1 222 n. 2
22: 47 222 n. 2
22: 67 226
23: 35 238
24: 19 250
24: 25 248
24: 27 248
24: 44 248

John
1: 21 267 n. 2
1: 45 143 n. 10
4: 25 222 n. 2
6: 42 143, 143 n. 10
8: 33 ff. 151 n. 1
8: 53 ff. 151 n. 1
9: 11 222 n. 2
11: 16 222 n. 2
12: 13 218
20: 2 222 n. 2

Acts
2: 16 248
2: 17–18 251
2: 25–31 119 n. 5
2: 30 248
2: 36 222
3: 12–26 248
3: 18 248
3: 20 222
3: 21 248
3: 22 248
3: 24 248
3: 25 219
3: 28 248
5: 19 216 n. 3
7: 2 151 n. 1, 219
7: 6 34 n. 2
7: 32 219
7: 37 250
7: 42 248
7: 45 192 n.
7: 48 248
8: 28 248
10: 43 248
11: 27 251
13: 20 248
13: 23 119 n. 5
13: 26 151 n. 1
13: 27 248
13: 34–7 119 n. 5
13: 40 248
15: 15 248
15: 16 119 n. 5
15: 32 251
19: 6 251
21: 10 251
26: 27 248
28: 25 248

Romans
1: 1 ff. 255
1: 3 119 n. 5
1: 3–4 254
4: 1 151 n. 1, 219
4: 12 219

Romans (*cont.*)
4: 12 ff. 151 n. 1
9: 7 151 n. 1
11: 1 151 n. 1, 219

II Corinthians
11: 22 151 n. 1

Galatians
3: 7 34 n. 2
3: 16 151 n. 1, 219
3: 17 34 n. 2
3: 29 34 n. 2

Ephesians
2: 17 171 n. 3

II Timothy
2: 8 119 n. 5

Philippians
3: 2 171 n. 3
3: 4 102

Hebrews
2: 16 151 n. 1
3: 7–4: 11 202
4: 8 192 n.
4: 9 202
7: 14 119 n. 4
9: 26 221 n. 5
11: 5 18 n. 1
11: 31 162

Jude
7: 16 63 n. 7
14 18 n. 1

Revelation
3: 7 119 n. 5
5: 5 119 n. 5
13: 18 193
22: 16 119 n. 5

E. RABBINIC SOURCES

1. *The Mishnah*

Bikkurim
1: 5 97 n. 4

Shekalim
2: 5 268 n. 5
3: 2 187 n. 2

Taanith
par. 1 134 n. 4
4: 5 102

Megillah
1: 8 187 n. 3

Yebamoth
2: 4 92 n. 4
4: 13 103, 105 n. 3, 147
5: 2 97 n. 4
6: 2 92 n. 4
6: 4 98
7–8 96 n. 7
8: 3 134 n. 2, 168 n. 7, 169 n. 7
9 97 n. 4

Ketuboth
2: 7–8 99 n. 3
2: 9 92 n. 5

Sotah
4: 1 97 n. 4
8: 3 97 n. 4
9: 14 187

Gittin
9: 6, 8 187 n. 3

Kiddushin
4: 1 90 n. 2, 91, 92
4: 1–7 97 n. 4
4: 3–7 92 n. 4
4: 4 91 n. 8, 98 n. 1, 101
4: 5 91 n. 7, 92 n. 1, 98 n. 1, 101

Baba Metzia
1: 8 268 n. 5
2: 8 268 n. 5
3: 4, 5 268 n. 5

Baba Bathra
8: 6 185

Sanhedrin
4: 5 94 n. 5
10: 2 167 n. 4

Eduyoth
8: 7 — 88 n. 2; 107 nn. 4, 6, 129 n. 2, 268 nn. 4, 5, 6

Aboth (Pirke Aboth)
1: 1 — 171, 172
1: 2 — 213
1: 16–17 — 204
1–2 — 202 n. 4
6: 3 — 168 n. 1

Horayoth
3: 8 — 91, 94 n. 1

Menahoth
6: 3 — 187 n. 2

Bekhoroth
7 — 97 n. 3

2. *The Babylonian Talmud*

Berakoth
1*c* — 269 n. 2
27*b* — 92 n. 2
28*b* — 179 nn. 6, 7
35*b* — 269 n. 2
41*b* — 132 n. 3

Shabbath
55*b* — 132 n. 3
56*a* — 175 n. 2
108*a* — 268 n. 5

Pesahim
passim — 87 nn. 1, 2
13*a* — 269 n. 2
62*b* — 86 nn. 3, 4
70*b* — 269 n. 2

Yoma
71*b* — 94 n. 4, 132 n. 3

Sukkah
6*a* — 132 n. 3
52*a* — 130 n. 1
52*b* — 129

Rosh ha-Shanah
11*a* — 154 n. 3
20 — 201 n. 2
31*a* — 201 n. 2

Taanith
17*a* — 132 n. 3
22*a* — 269 n. 2

Megillah
10*b* — 162 n. 3
14*b* — 164 nn. 1, 2
15*a* — 162 n. 7

Hagigah
15*b* — 168 n. 1
25*a* — 269 n. 2

Yebamoth
35*b* — 269 n. 2
37*a* — 90
41*a* — 269 n. 2
49*a* — 147 n. 3
54*b* — 168 n. 3
63*a* — 135, 169 n. 2
76*b* — 167 n. 3
76*b*–77*a* — 134 n. 2
77*a* — 135 n. 2, 169 n. 1
85*a* — 90
102*a* — 269 n. 2

Ketuboth
5*a* — 91 n. 5
62*b* — 93 n. 1, 104

Nazir
23*b* — 154 n. 3, 166 n. 1, 169 n. 7

Sotah
10 — 272 n. 1
10*b* — 161
11*b* — 132 n. 3
43*a* — 134 nn. 4, 7
47*a* — 195 n. 3
49*b* — 188

Gittin
42*b* — 269 n. 2

Kiddushin
2*b* — 132 n. 3
4 — 106 n. 2
43*a* — 173 nn. 1, 2
66*a* — 92 n. 5, 134 n. 3
70*a* — 107 n. 6
70*b* — 87 n. 3, 91 n. 6
71*a* — 88 n. 2, 107 nn. 3, 4, 109
71*b* — 92 n. 5

Kiddushin (*cont.*)
72*a* 89 n. 2
75*a* 90, 169 n. 7
76*a* 101 n. 1
76*b* 102 n. 1
79*a* 101 n. 1

Baba Kamma
38*b* 169 n. 3

Baba Bathra
17*a* 132 n. 3
109*b* 134 n. 4
110*a* 134 n. 7

Sanhedrin
22*b* 132 n. 3
37*b* 184 nn. 1, 3
52*b* 150
82*b* 134 n. 4
97*a* 120 n. 1, 201
98*a* 120 n. 1
99*a* 179 n. 7
99*b* 95 n. 3
105*b* 195 n. 3
106*b* 168 n. 1

Makkoth
3: 1 97 n. 4
23*b* 270 n. 5

Shebuoth
18*b* 132 n. 3

Abodah Zarah
5*a* 120 n. 1
9*a* 201

Horayoth
10*b* 162 n. 3, 166 n. 1, 195 n. 3
11*b* 183 n. 1
13*a* 94 n. 1, 130 n. 3

Menahoth
45*a* 268 n. 5
53*a* 95 n. 1

Bekhoroth
33*b* 268 n. 5

Kerithoth
13*b* 132 n. 3
77*b* 183 n. 1

3. *The Palestinian Talmud*

Berakoth
2: 8 163 n. 1
4 163 n. 1

Kilaim
9: 4 102 n. 4

Shekalim
6: 1 183 n. 1
6: 3 184 n. 3

Taanith
passim 111 n. 1
2: 10 173 n. 4
4: 2 105, 110, 148
4: 3 147

Megillah
1: 11 188

Yebamoth
4: 15 147 n. 3
8: 3, 9 134 n. 2

Ketuboth
12: 3 102 n. 4

Sotah
1: 4 161 n. 1
8: 3 183 n. 1
9: 16 179 nn. 6, 7

Abodah Zarah
3: 1 179 n. 6

4. *The Midrashim*

Genesis Rabbah
12: 6 179 n. 4
32: 1 167 n. 1
33: 3 102 n. 4
36: 13 134 n. 7
39: 4 150
39: 10 150 n. 1
43 129 n. 6
50 166 n. 3
51: 8 166 n. 4
58 154 n. 3
71 109, 266 n. 3, 267 n. 3
71: 5 130 n. 4, 135 n. 7
71: 9 266 n. 4
72 154 n. 3
85 160 n. 3

Genesis Rabbah (*cont.*)
85: 7 161 n. 1
85: 11 270 n. 3
98 148
98: 8 105, 110, 111 n. 1
98: 11 110 n. 1
99 151 n. 3, 266 n. 3
99: 11 266 n. 4

Exodus Rabbah
1: 17 132 n. 3
7, end 134 n. 4
15: 26 197, 207

Leviticus Rabbah
1: 3 110 n. 4
10: 5 184 n. 1
12: 5 175 n. 3
19 184 n. 1
19: 6 184 n. 2
20: 1 270 n. 5
25: 6 271 n. 1
33: 4 134 n. 4

Numbers Rabbah
3 268 n. 5
3: 2 163 n. 1
4: 8 271 n. 2
7: 15 191
8: 9 164 nn. 1, 2, 4
9: 7 88 n. 1, 91 n. 7, 97 n. 4, 98 n. 2
10: 4 175 n. 3
11: 3 175 n. 3
12: 4 87 nn. 3, 4, 88 n. 1, 96 n. 6
13 151 n. 3
13: 4 270 n. 4
13: 12 179 n. 5
13: 14 150 n. 2
14: 1 131 n. 2
18: 16 130
21: 2 134 n. 4

Ruth Rabbah
2: 1 110, 163 n. 3, 164
2: 1–2 177 n. 1
2: 2 163 n. 4, 164 n. 3
2: 9 166 n. 2, 169 n. 4
4: 1 134 n. 2, 169
4: 6 167 n. 3, 169 n. 5
7: 7 169 n. 6
7: 10 169 n. 6
8: 1 133, 169 n. 7, 170 n. 2, 271 n. 3

Ecclesiastes Rabbah
5: 6 163 n. 3
5: 11 163 n. 1
8: 10 164 n. 2
10: 1 167 n. 2

Song of Songs Rabbah
1: 3 163 n. 1
1: 5, 2 163 n. 1
2: 13 129 n. 5
4: 1, 2 163 n. 1
4: 7 151 n. 3
6: 2, 3 163 n. 1
7: 14. 1 184 n. 1
8: 6. 2 184 n. 1

Lamentations Rabbah
1: 16 130
8: 6 184 n. 1

Midrash Psalms
1: 2 169 n. 7
3: 3 134 n. 1, 175 n. 1
3: 4 168 n. 2
3: 5 174 n. 1
4: 2 174 n. 2
4: 9 170 n. 3
5: 10 167 n. 4
7: 5 133 n. 1
7: 7 168 n. 3
43: 1 ff. 267 n. 3, 268 n. 1
43: 3 267
49: 2 168 nn. 2, 4
52 168 n. 3
52: 1 168 n. 5
52: 3 168 n. 2
52: 4 168 n. 1
87: 6 89 n. 1
105: 3 191 n. 1
116: 9 169 n. 1, 177 n. 1

Midrash Samuel
22 168 n. 3
25: 2 173 n. 3

Pesikta Rabbati
4 267 n. 3
9 163 n. 1, 177 n. 1
15: 75*a* 129 n. 5
35, end 135 n. 6
76*b* 197 n. 3

5. *Other Rabbinic Writings*

Aboth of Rabbi Nathan
passim 202, 203, 205, 206

Mekilta
on Exod. 16: 33 268n. 8
on Exod. 18: 1 163 n. 2

Tosefta Berakoth
4: 18 162
5: 14 92 n. 2

Tosefta Rosh ha-Shanah
4: 1 91 n. 2

Tosefta Megillah
2: 7 91

Tosefta Horayoth
2: 9 130 n. 3

Sifra on Leviticus
18 130

Sifre on Numbers
passim 164 n. 3
15: 30 95 n. 3
par. 78 132 n. 3, 164, 177 n. 1
par. 131 134 n. 4
par. 157 134 n. 7

Sifre on Deuteronomy
33: 15, par. 353 154 n. 3

Pesikta Rabbah
51*a* 129 n. 5
115*b* 134 nn. 4, 6
162*b* 184 n. 1
163*b* 184 n. 3

Pirke d. R. Eliezer
29, end 268
33 109 n. 4
43 268 n. 7
60*a* 268 n. 7

Tanhuma
4*a* 179 n. 4
42*b* 150 n. 1

Tanhuma B.
13 156 n. 1
14 166 n. 2
17 151, 161 n. 1
18 179 n. 4

Targum on Numbers
23: 9 154 n. 3

Targum on Deuteronomy
33: 15 154 n. 3

Targum on Lamentations
4: 22 267 n. 3

Targum on Zechariah
12: 12 241, 247

Targum of Jonathan
on Ex. 6: 25 134 n. 5

Shemoneh Esreh
Bene. 15 and 14 120

F. CLASSICAL, HELLENISTIC, AND NON-CANONICAL CHRISTIAN WRITINGS

Polybius 112
Theophrastus 113
Juvenal, *Satire* I 113
Persius 114
Suetonius 114
Homer 65 n. 2
Josephus
Antiquities
I. I. 2 114 n. 5
I. 3. 4 30 n. 4
I. 3. 6 30
I. 3. 9 31 n. 4
I. 6. 5 34 n. 5
I. 7. 2 151 n. 1
I. 12. 2 265
I. 17. 1 265
I. 22. 1 265
II. 8. 1 265
II. 8. 2 265
II. 9. 1 265
II. 15. 2 34 nn. 4, 5, 265
III. 2. 4 132 n. 3

Josephus (*cont.*)
III. 12. 2 92 n. 5, 96 n. 4, 97 n. 2
V. 9 162 n. 4, 165 n. 1
V. 9. 4 133 n. 2, 165 n. 2
VII. 7. 1 170 n. 5
VII. 7. 3 170 n. 6
VIII. 3. 1 34 nn. 4, 5, 35 n. 4, 265
IX. 14. 3 108 n. 1
X. 8. 4–5 34 nn. 4, 5, 265
XI. 8. 5 40 n. 5
XI. 8. 6 101 n. 2, 108 n. 1
XII. 5 108 n. 2
XII. 10. 5 92 n. 5
XIII. 10. 5 134 n. 3
XIII. 14. 5 92 n. 5
XIV. 2. 2 188 n. 1

Contra Apion, I. 7 92 n. 5, 100 n. 5
Vita, 1 96 n. 1, 100 n. 5, 108 n. 2

Philo
On Monarchy
II. 8–11 96 n. 4
II. 11 96 n. 2, 275
Congr. 124–6 159 n. 4
Quod Deus 136 f. 159 n. 3
Fug. 149–56 159 n. 5
Mut. 134–6 159 n. 5
Virt. 220–2 159

I Clement 12 162 n. 5

Justin
passim 120 n. 3
Dialog. 8 268 n. 9
Dialog. 49, 129 n. 2, 135 n. 5, 267 n. 2
Dialog. 113 192

Origen
28th Homily on Luke 154 n. 4

Eusebius
Hist Eccl.
I. 6. 31 141 n. 1
I. 7 141 n. 1, 242
I. 7. 5 232 n. 3
I. 7. 13 87
I. 7. 13–15 103 n. 1
I. 7. 14 103 n. 3
I. 7. 15 104 n. 1
Quaes. Evang. ad Steph.
III. 2 243

Ambrose on Luke 3 154 n. 4

Jerome 154 n. 4

Tertullian 144

INDEX OF AUTHORS

Albright, W., 4 n. 1, 10 n. 2
Allegro, J., 126 n. 3
Allen, W., 151, 156, 157, 186 n. 2, 210 n. 2, 212, 215 n. 4
Aptowitzer, V., 107 n. 6, 128 n. 2, 129 n. 3, 130 nn. 1, 2, 131, 132 nn. 2, 3, 134 nn. 4, 6, 136, 137, 138, 246 n. 1, 266 n. 1, 275 n. 1
Argyle, A., 192
Auerbach, E., 40 n. 1

Bacher, 193
Bacon, B., 186 n. 1, 189 n. 2, 209 n. 2, 210, 214 n. 4, 217
Barr, J., 138 n. 2
Barrett, C., 233 n. 2
Batten, L., 37 n. 2
Bauer, W., 211 n. 2, 216 n. 2
Beare, F., 158, 234 n. 1
Beasley-Murray, 128 n. 2
Bengel, J. 143
Benoit, P., 190 n. 2, 237 n. 1
Bezold, C., 103 n. 2
Bickermann, E., 187 n. 1
Black, M., 18 n. 1, 125, 128 n. 2
Blair, H. 144 n. 3
Bloch, R., 112 n. 1, 156
Bock, E., 144
Bork, F., 24 n. 1, 36 n. 1
Bornhäuser, K., 142, 195 n. 5, 197 n. 3, 231
Bornkamm, G., 213, 221 n. 6, 223 n. 3, 224, 227 n. 3, 228 n. 1
Bosse, A., 36 n. 1
Bourke, M., 112 n. 1
Bousset, D., 33 n. 1, 36 n. 1
Box, G., 145, 158, 192, 210 n. 2
Braude, W., 170 n. 1
Brown, R., 128 n. 2
Bruce, F., 128 n. 2
Brunet, A.-M., 49 n. 3, 50 n. 2, 54 nn. 1, 2, 56 n. 2, 60 n. 3, 68 n. 1, 70 nn. 1, 2, 75 n. 4
Budde, K., 16 n. 1, 24 n. 1, 25 n. 1
Bultmann, R., 226 n. 4
Burkitt, F., 185 n. 1
Burrows, M., 75 n. 5, 124 n. 5, 125 n. 2, 126 n. 3, 127 nn. 1, 2, 171 n. 2
Bury, J., 19 nn. 2, 3
Buswell, G., 232 n. 6

Cadbury, H., 233 n. 1
Cassuto, U., 8 n. 1, 36 n. 1
Charles, R., 123, 171 nn. 2, 3, 4, 172, 194 n. 2, 200, 223 n. 1, 234 n. 3
Clark, F., 211 n. 1
Cohen, S., 154 n. 1
Conzelman, H., 232, 233, 238, 240 n. 1
Cook, S., 57
Cross, F., 123 n. 1
Cullmann, O., 128 n. 2
Curtis, E., 32 n. 5, 36 n. 1, 37 n. 2, 38 n. 4, 42 n. 4, 44 n. 2, 50 n. 2, 61 n. 1, 70 n. 2, 262 n. 5
Cusin, M., 143 n. 3

Dabeck, P., 249 nn. 1, 2
Danby, H., 90 n. 2, 96 n. 7, 98 nn. 3, 4, 5, 99 n. 1, 203 n. 2
Davies, W. D., 57 n. 5, 88 n. 2, 94 nn. 2, 5, 107 n. 6, 128 n. 2, 131 n. 3, 145, 148 nn. 2, 3, 4, 158 n. 13, 185, 187 n. 1, 192, 198 n. 3, 205, 209 n. 1, 210 n. 2, 268 n. 5, 269 n. 2
de Jonge, M., 121 n. 1, 122, 272 n. 2
De Kruijf, T., 227 n. 1
Delaporte, L., 36 n. 1
Derenbourg, J., 105 n. 3
de Vaux, R., 6 n. 5, 7 n. 1, 38 n. 3, 40 n. 2, 47, 59 n. 2, 71 n. 3
de Vries, S., 259
Dibelius, M., 237 n. 1
Dillersberger, J., 156
Dodd, C., 224 n. 3
Doughty, C., 12 n 5
Driver, G. R., 125, 126 n. 2, 127, 128 n. 2
Drummond, J., 120 n. 1
Durand, A., 155

Ehrenzweig, A., 12 n. 4
Eliade, M., 30 nn. 2, 3, 31 n. 4
Elmslie, W., 47 n. 4

Farrer, A., 202 n. 1
Fenton, J., 202 n. 3
Filson, F., 156

Finegan, J., 259
Finkel, A., 92 n. 2, 198 n. 3
Finkelstein, L., 202 n. 6, 203, 204, 205, 206
Flender, H., 233 n. 1
Freedman, D., 75 nn. 1, 6, 106 n. 2
Friedmann, M., 266 n. 1
Friedrich, G., 120 n. 5, 128 n. 2, 129 n. 3
Fuks, A., 143
Funk, R., 233 n. 1

Gaechter, P., 142, 151 n. 4, 156
Gfrörer, 192
Gibbs, J., 218 n. 1
Ginzberg, L., 124, 129 nn. 3, 4, 130, 169 n. 2
Glover, R., 155
Gnilka, J., 128 n. 2
Godet, F., 143
Goguel, M., 179 n. 1
Goldstein, M., 105 n. 3, 147 nn. 5, 6, 158 n. 12
Goldziher, I., 7 n. 4
Grant, F., 142 n. 4
Grasser, E., 233 n. 2
Grelot, P., 128 n. 2
Grundman, W., 155 n. 2
Gunkel, H., 8 n. 2

Hahn, F., 128 n. 2, 185 n. 4, 211 n. 1, 218 n. 1, 223 n. 2, 224 n. 2, 227 n. 2, 229 n. 2, 231, 234 n. 1
Hauret, C., 10 n. 1, 12 n. 2
Heer, J., 143, 191 n. 2, 192, 193, 194 n. 1, 195, 232 n. 4
Heffern, A., 154 n. 4, 155, 158
Henschen, J., 155
Herford, R. T., 206 n. 1
Herriott, C., 26 n. 4
Hervey, A., 142
Hicks, L., 25 n. 3
Higgins, A., 123 nn. 1, 2, 3, 124, 125, 127
Hogg, H., 51 n. 5
Holtzmann, H., 157
Hood, R., 192, 239 nn. 1, 2
Hooke, S., 8 n. 1, 10 n. 2, 11 n. 2, 29 n. 3
Hyatt, J., 3 n. 2

Jacob, B., 8 nn. 1, 2, 20 n. 1
Jacobsen, T., 10 n. 2, 29 n. 2, 31 n. 2
Jacoby, F., 19 n. 2
Jenni, E., 115 n. 1
Jepsen, A., 33 n. 1, 36 n. 1
Jeremias, J., 43 n. 7, 87 n. 1, 89 n. 3, 91 n. 3, 92 nn. 1, 3, 93 n. 2, 96 n. 3, 100 n. 5, 102 nn. 2, 4, 5, 103, 105 n. 2, 111 nn. 1, 3, 157, 192, 195 n. 5, 230 n. 1, 232 nn. 4, 5, 235, 266 n. 1
Johnson, R., 7 n. 1

Kaplan, C., 197 n. 3, 199 n. 2, 231
Käsemann, E., 233 n. 2, 254 n. 1
Kittel, G., 87 n. 1, 95 n. 2, 105 n. 3, 109 n. 2, 110, 111, 156, 176 n. 2
Klausner, 116 n. 1, 118 n. 3, 120 n. 1
Klostermann, E., 157, 158 n. 11, 183, 231
Kohler, K., 124
Köster, H., 227 n. 2
Kraft, R., 141 n. 2, 273 n. 1
Kramer, M., 157
Krochmal, N., 198 n. 3
Kuenen, A., 33 n. 1
Kuhl, C., 26 n. 4, 30 n. 1, 32 n. 7
Kuhn, G., 125 n. 6, 128 n. 2, 137 n. 3, 179 n. 9, 232 n. 4, 243 n. 2
Kümmel, W., 236, 237 n. 1

Lagrange, M.-J., 143 n. 1, 156, 159 n. 1, 190 n. 2, 193
Lambertz, M., 144 n. 1, 182 n. 1, 195 n. 5, 211 n. 1
Lampe, G., 248 n. 1
Landes, G., 12 n. 5
Laurentin, 237 n. 1
Leaney, A., 128 n. 2
Leany, R., 158
Lefèvre, A., 72 n. 2, 82 n. 1
Lenski, R., 238 n. 1
Levertoff, P., 132 n. 3, 164 n. 1
Lévi, I., 105 n. 2, 111 n. 2, 135 n. 8, 136 nn. 1, 3, 245 nn. 2, 3, 4
Lewis, C., 143
Liebermann, S., 187 n. 1, 188, 189 n. 1, 217 n. 5
Linton, O., 13 n. 4, 19 n. 1, 33 n. 2, 34 n. 5, 35 n. 3, 36 n. 1
Littmann, E., 61 nn. 3, 4, 5, 62 nn. 1, 2, 3
Liver, J., 93 n. 2, 108 n. 3, 126 n. 2, 128 n. 2, 130 n. 3, 131 n. 3
Loewe, H., 129 n. 4
Lohmeyer, E., 155 n. 1, 156, 183
Loisy, A., 151 n. 6, 157, 158 n. 11
Luther, B., 20 n. 2

Madsen, A., 37 n. 2, 38 n. 4, 42 n. 4, 44 n. 2, 50 n. 2, 61 n. 1, 70 n. 2
Mai, A., 242
Mann, J., 198 n. 3
Manson, W., 234 n. 1
Marmorstein, A., 131 n. 3, 137 nn. 1, 2, 4
Marquart, J., 51 n. 5
McNeile, A., 148, 158, 185 n. 1
Mendenhall, G., 63 n. 7, 64 n. 1, 67
Merz, 36 n. 1
Meyer, A., 211 n. 1
Meyer, E., 5 n. 3, 11 n. 3, 28 n. 3, 42 n. 4
Meyer, H., 154 n. 5, 157, 159 n. 1
Michaelis, D., 156, 157
Milik, J., 126 n. 1
Milton, H., 155, 186
Minear, P., 237
Molin, G., 266 n. 1
Montefiore, C., 129 n. 4, 158
Moore, G., 77 n. 3, 232 n. 1
Moreton, M., 157, 195 n. 4
Moule, C., 250
Mowinckel, S., 4 n. 1, 8 nn. 1, 2, 10 n. 2, 12 n. 4
Murtonen, A., 36 n. 4

Nestle, E., 241 n. 1
Nineham, D., 233 n. 1, 251 n. 1
Noordtzij, A., 75 n. 3
North, R., 53 n. 2, 54 nn. 3, 4
Noth, M., 10 n. 4, 16 n. 6, 21 n. 4, 26 n. 1, 37 n. 1, 38 n. 1, 50 nn. 3, 4, 53 n. 1, 58 n. 4, 71 n. 3

Obermann, J., 6 n. 5, 7 n. 4
Odeberg, H., 18 n. 1, 129 n. 5, 130 n. 1
Oliver, H., 236 n. 3, 248 n. 2
Oppert, 29 n. 6

Philippson, P., 19 n. 2
Philonenko, M., 123 n. 1
Piper, O., 233 n. 1
Plummer, A., 154 n. 6
Podechard, E., 74 n. 2
Priest, J., 118 n. 3
Pritchard, J., 10 n. 2
Proksch, O., 17 n. 1

Rabinowitz, 170 n. 1
Rasco, E., 233 n. 1
Rengstorf, K., 147 n. 6, 231
Rice, J., 155
Rienecker, F., 155
Rist, M., 193 n. 1
Robinson, T., 155
Robinson, W., 233 n. 1
Ropes, J., 200
Rothstein, 46 n. 2
Rowley, H., 69 n. 5
Rudolph, W., 38 n. 1, 41 n. 3, 46 nn. 1, 2, 50 n. 2, 53 n. 2, 55 nn. 5, 6, 57 n. 1, 60 n. 2, 61 n. 2, 75 n. 2
Russell, D., 128 n. 2
Ryckmans, G., 61 n. 3

Sanders, H., 211 n. 1
Sanders, J., 19 n. 4
Schechter, S., 185 n. 3
Schlatter, A., 157, 183, 189, 200, 217, 229, 232 n. 4, 234 n. 1
Schmidt, J., 159 n. 1, 190 n. 2, 210 n. 2
Schnabel, P., 28 n. 6, 29 n. 1, 31 n. 4
Schniewind, J., 158
Schubert, K., 128 n. 2
Schulz, S., 233 n. 2
Schürer, E., 96 n. 3, 100 n. 5, 199 n. 3
Schweizer, E., 224 n. 3
Scott, R., 266 n. 1
Segal, S., 266 n. 1
Shalders, E., 143 n. 3
Silbermann, H., 128 n. 2
Silver, A., 208 n. 1
Simons, J., 5 n. 1, 20 n. 1
Simpson, C., 8 n. 2, 12 n. 1, 21 n. 2, 154 n. 1
Skinner, J., 5 n. 3, 8 n. 1, 18 n. 2, 21 n. 4, 24 n. 4, 29 nn. 4, 5, 6, 36 n. 1
Smith, B., 157
Smith, M., 128 n. 2
Smith, S., 10 n. 2, 31 n. 3, 66 n. 3, 67 nn. 1, 3
Smith, W., 6 nn. 4, 5, 7 n. 2, 28 n. 6
Soltau, W., 215 n. 5, 216
Speiser, E., 73
Sperber, A., 241 n. 3
Spitta, F., 158 n. 3
Stanley, D., 155
Starcky, J., 126 n. 2, 128 n. 2
Stauffer, E., 105 n. 3
Steiner, R., 144
Stendahl, K., 157, 186 n. 2, 208 n. 3, 214, 215, 217, 221, 222, 224
Stinespring, W., 76 n. 1
Strack, H. L. and Billerbeck, P., 147, 150, 151, 153 n. 1, 154 n. 3, 155,

Strack, H. L. and Billerbeck, P. (*cont.*) 156 n. 1, 158 n. 12, 160 n. 2, 162 n. 2, 164 n. 2, 166 nn. 1, 3, 177 n. 1, 179 nn., 184 nn. 1, 3, 185, 195 nn. 1, 6, 196, 197, 201 n. 1, 217 n. 4, 266–9, 270.
Strecker, G., 218 n. 1
Streeter, B., 236

Tatum, W., 237, 248 n. 2, 251 n. 2
Taylor, V., 142, 158, 210 n. 2, 217 n. 6
Tcherikover, V., 143
Throckmorton, B., 192
Torrey, C., 130 n. 1

Van der Woude, A., 123 n. 1, 128 n. 2
Van Goudoever, J., 199 n. 3
Van Groningen, 19 n. 2
Van Unnik, W., 233 n. 2
Vezin, A., 143
Vincent, M., 143 n. 2
Vögtle, A., 155 nn. 2, 4, 7, 8, 156, 183, 190, 196, 210
von Campenhausen, H., 211 n. 1
von Dobschutz, 211, 212, 217 n. 4 226 n. 1
von Hofmann, J., 238 n. 1
von Rad, G., 10 n. 4, 11 n. 3, 15 n. 4, 16, 17 nn. 1, 2, 18 n. 4, 20, 20 n. 4, 46 n. 2, 261 n. 1

Weiss, B., 143, 156, 225 n. 2
Weiss, J., 158
Welch, A., 46 n. 3, 47, 59 n. 2
Wellhausen, J., 12 n. 5, 27, 32 nn. 2, 3, 40 n. 4, 41 n. 3, 45 n. 4, 49 n. 5, 52 n. 1, 69 n. 2
Wetstein, 158
Wieder, N., 128
Wiesenberg, E., 35 n. 1
Wilckens, U., 233 n. 2
Wiseman, D., 66 n. 3, 67 n. 2
Wohleb, L., 194 n. 1
Wrede, W., 227 n. 2

Yadin, Y., 68 n. 2
Young, R., 129 n. 3, 131 n. 2

Zahn, T., 142, 158, 185 n. 1
Zuckermandel, M., 91 n. 2